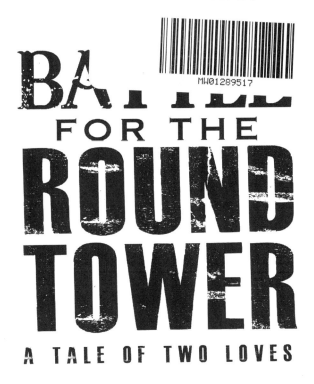

BATTLE
FOR THE
ROUND TOWER

A TALE OF TWO LOVES

PRESTON GILLHAM

PUBLICATION™

PERSPECTIVES ON
BATTLE FOR THE ROUND TOWER

Brilliantly readable! I see the characters, the scenes, everything! OMG it gives me gooseflesh.

—Nicole, a sister

Wow, Pres. This is huge. It is amazing. And more important, hopeful.

—Cathy, a marketing executive

You are an artist communicating God through what He has written on your heart.

—Victor, a sage

You have effectively communicated, capturing the burden while communicating His unfailing and unconditional love.

—Catherine, a mentor to women survivors of abuse

I loved the redirection I felt regarding solitude, worship, relying on the Holy Spirit, trusting, and knowing my identity in Christ.

—Laura, teacher

Congruent and clear. As in The Screw Tape Letters, *you provide a fresh look at spiritual warfare. Anyone of any faith level can grasp the important parts.*

—Randy, a social worker

As a woman, I especially appreciated the juxtaposition of the rugged masculinity with the sensitive vulnerability of Hank.

—Tricia, development officer

Rich. Rewarding. This manuscript represents a great work. The writing skill and turns of phrase are excellent.

—Lamar, a veteran

You develop scenes so well, bringing life to the surroundings. I love the way you do this.

—Elise, a volunteer

My heart responded at a deep and important level. There are many places I put the book down and went to Him, His Word, and His Life for a time of contemplation.

—Heather, a wife and mom

I like Hank tremendously. He is so normal, with a great sense of humor and real courage under fire. And, I LOVE Celia! The affection between her and Hank is heart-warming.

—Sandy, a guide and coach

I felt like I was there. When I "got into" the book, I would read over 100 pages in a sitting.

—Ty, a lawyer

I enjoyed reading. You are a good story teller.

—Anthony, a contractor

BATTLE
FOR THE
ROUND
TOWER

A TALE OF TWO LOVES

PRESTON GILLHAM

PUBLICATION™

Battle for the Round Tower is based on the historical record, but the work as a whole is a work of fiction. This is not a literal work and should not be treated as such. The dialogue and characterization reflect the author's interpretation. *Battle for the Round Tower* is a survey of life, spirituality, and ministry. It is not intended to be definitive nor is it intended to be a parsing of theology.

Published in the United States of America by
Bonefish Publication
2020 Wilshire Blvd
Fort Worth, TX 76110

For information regarding special discounts on bulk purchases please contact Bonefish Publication at: info@BonefishPublication.com.

For further information about *Battle for the Round Tower*, other works by the author, his blog, or to contact the author about speaking engagements or his coaching and consulting practice, please visit:

www.PrestonGillham.com

Library of Congress Control Number: 2013919114

ISBN: 978-1-4953231-6-4

10 9 8 7 6 5 4 3 2 1

ADDITIONAL BOOKS AND RESOURCES
from
Preston Gillham

No Mercy
Grace in Ungracious Places
Things Only Men Know
Life and Leadership, a blog at PrestonGillham.com
Conferences, coaching, mentoring, strategic thinking, transition, and
personal development
visit:
www.PrestonGillham.com

ADDITIONAL INFORMATION
about
Preston Gillham

visit:
www.PrestonGillham.com/about

DEDICATION

To those who believe,
    And walk in the light.
To those who aspire,
    To not walk in darkness.
To those who are called,
    And do not shrink.

CONTENTS

Encomium

ἀποθώμεθα οὖν τὰ ἔργα τοῦ σκότους,
ἐνδυσώμεθα δὲ τὰ ὅπλα τοῦ φωτός.

—Παῦλος ἀπόστολος

So then let us cast off the works of darkness
And put on the armor of light.

—Paul, an apostle

BEFORE YOU BEGIN...

If you have not read the first book in this series, No Mercy—*or if it has been a while—then let's set the stage for the pages that follow...*

In *No Mercy,* Henry "Hank" Henderson is caught between the spiritually powerful forces of the High King and his enemy, Zophos. Sweeping battles between light and dark, spirit and flesh ensue. Knights, dragons, compatriots, and accomplices align around Hank in spiritual conflict.

No Mercy is an adventure story. But it is more! It is an exploration of the enmity between flesh and spirit. Through the window of Hank's life, *No Mercy* examines whether this war is winnable. If so, at what cost? By what means? Rendering what outcome?

Battle for the Round Tower continues Hank's story. It showcases what life requires of a man equipped to engage a spiritual enemy, commissioned to fight for the Kingdom, and sent to rescue hearts compromised as his once was.

In Hank we have the opportunity to consider spiritual resource—to grapple with life in the light while walking in the midst of darkness. What must he do to maintain? Live? Keep his perspective? To wrestle doubt into submission? To conquer?

In the fictional character of Hank there is a portrait of what is true. I encourage you to ask your Father in heaven to guide you and speak to you as you read.

While this is a novel, the back story is the historical record—tested, proven, and authentic. Note the cairns of biblical reference as you read even though they are not traditionally labeled.

Now.

Be confident! Be encouraged! Enjoy, and thank you for reading.

Preston Gillham

Fort Worth, Texas

PROLOGUE

"The Sunrise from on high shall visit us, to shine upon those who sit in darkness."

—Luke the Apostle

Once upon a time, there was a land where light conquered darkness,

but men did not comprehend.

They were entrenched in darkness.

The light pursued men

farther into their darkness,

where there was insurrection.

The light dawned on men,

but men clung to darkness, preferring it over light,

as seemed best to them.

But the light still shined,

and some men—courageous souls—walked in the light,

warriors whom darkness could not overcome.

CHAPTER 1

January, Fort Worth, Texas, USA

Beads of sweat dribbled down Hank's forehead. They massed with other droplets, gathered momentum, and collected in his eyebrows as he attempted to pack his bag.

He wasn't hot.

Three days ago—four days before departing for his much-anticipated, winter camping trip with his Brother, Vassar—Hank's back muscles went into spasm. It wasn't the first time, nor would it be the last he figured, but it was a bad episode.

He was in pain.

Spasm was a constant for Hank, but he prevailed—most days. He lived with determination and thumbed his nose at the menace of every step, each bend, and all activity.

Ignoring pain was part of his swagger.

Somewhere along the way, Hank heard Johnny Cash sing, "I Won't Back Down." It had become his theme song. "Stand me up at the gates of hell," the "man in black" sang. And he determined to swagger. Tried to ignore.

But not today's pain.

This was different. This was sixteen-pills-per-day pain.

But I won't back down, Hank vowed. Again.

These episodes were always inconvenient, but never quite as inconvenient as now. Hank gritted his teeth and pursed his lips. *Montana in the winter is not for the weak.*

He thought about that for a moment.

I'll do well to sit on the plane, let alone sleep on the ground in a sleeping bag. All these months of preparation! Poof!

Hank moved woodenly as he packed. *I wonder why God doesn't fix this?* The thought marinated, a familiar distrust. *I believe God is good.* He checked himself on that conviction.

I just don't believe He's good to me. Doesn't add up.

Doubt was a hidden cancer. Stampeding like a bull in a china shop. After bouts against pain, Hank swept his shattered belief into a dustpan.

During Hank and Vassar's previous adventure to Montana—a summer, fly fishing trip—Hank's Heavenly Father met Hank's doubts about Him head on. That was just over two years ago. But as monumental experiences are prone to do, the sharp edge dulled with his raucous use upon life.

I've got to get packed, he thought, quarantining doubt.

Hank wiped his forehead on the sleeve of his pajama top.

January, SW Montana, USA

"Hello once again from the flight deck, ladies and gentlemen. Captain Simpson here. We're approximately seventy-five miles south-southwest of the Bozeman airport. We'll make our approach to Gallatin Field from the south today. I expect there will be a few bumps as we make our descent, so please be certain your seatbelts are securely fastened.

"The weather in Bozeman is clear with north winds at twenty, gusting to thirty miles per hour. Air Traffic Control reports blowing snow and a temperature of seven degrees Fahrenheit, minus fourteen Celsius. Thanks again for flying with us. We'll be landing shortly. Flight attendants, please prepare for landing."

Vassar and Hank flew often and were using frequent flyer miles for this trip. The cabin was occupied by a sparse assortment of college students returning early from Christmas break, a few skiers headed to Big Sky, and miscellaneous locals. Who else could possibly have any reason to be in Montana in the dead of winter?

It was a whim that hatched the crazy idea of winter camping. The two brothers had talked over and over about a reprise of their earlier fly fishing trip on Malden Creek, but life shifted and demanded they stay close to their daily grinds throughout the fishing season. Vassar suggested in passing that they ought to go in the winter. The silly notion caught in their dreams and became reality.

The flight was arduous for Hank, but he moved around the cabin, stood three hours by the toilets, dodging the coming-and-going flight attendants, and eventually getting used to the smell of latrine disinfectant. His back was sore and funky feeling, but the spasms had abated overnight. That was unexpected. Still, his muscles felt like jelly. He had already swallowed twelve pills. He rushed the third dose.

With the Captain's announcement, he moved gingerly up the aisle, making certain to maintain good posture and tight abs. He took his seat across from Vassar and buckled his seat belt. Then, he jerked it tight to secure his sacrum against the hard seatback. He glanced at his Brother and smiled. Vassar's brow furrowed.

Vassar and Hank collected their duffels from the baggage carousel, zipped up their coats, and made their way outside to meet the rental car bus. An array of idling ranch trucks, shuttles, and cars, their exhausts rising smoky behind them before quickly blowing away in the gusty wind, waited curbside. The two brothers hunched their shoulders, crossed their arms, and turned their backs to the north as they stood unprotected in the median between the first and second lanes of the airport road.

It was a fifteen-minute ride to the remote, car-rental lot. The shuttle bus was warm, a welcome relief from the piercing cold, but the ride wasn't long enough to overcome the ache that settled into Hank's irritable back and hip. The nagging was exacerbated by the inactivity and cold. Counting the delay on the tarmac, it had been four hours and fifteen minutes from Dallas-Fort Worth to Salt Lake and another hour and thirty-five minutes from Salt Lake to Bozeman. The stiffness in his hip joined the unhappiness in his back and settled in earnest while he stood on the naked concrete in Salt Lake waiting to board the commuter plane.

Since they didn't plan to use their rental car for much beyond transportation into Bozeman, Vassar and Hank had reserved a compact car online. With drama, the rental agent informed Vassar that they had no more compact cars. But not to worry, "I will upgrade you to the next model," she stated, clicking on her keyboard and smiling as she had been trained. Her magnanimity occurred twice more until the brothers found themselves seated in a brand new Escalade 4X4 for the price of a compact automobile. As they sat investigating the plethora of buttons, Hank was first to discover the Cadillac was equipped with seat warmers. His exclamation of delight was followed by Vassar's. Both sat waiting, anticipating, eyeing the lighted images on the dash of radiating seats.

The brothers turned into their motel parking lot about dusk, checked in, and unloaded their bags. Hank sat down on his bed, dialed the outfitter's number, and put the phone on speaker so Vassar could hear. It was a short conversation confirming directions and the time they would meet in the morning. Hank tapped "End" to conclude the call and stared at his Brother.

They still had a number of questions about this trip, especially the timing. But they were equally certain they were where they were supposed to be—wanted to be. Nevertheless, Hank's eyes asked his Older Brother if he was still certain of what they were about to attempt. Vassar nodded once and pursed his lips.

Taking the recommendation of the girl at the front desk, Vassar and Hank parked in back of the Treasure State Steakhouse and went around to the entrance. The fluorescent "Ope" sign flickered, the "n" having lost the day. Entering through the glass doors, they stepped onto hardwood floors covered with peanut husks. George Strait sang from speakers in the ceiling, "Does Fort Worth Ever Cross Your Mind?" The irony wasn't lost on either of them as they followed their hostess through the maze of tables occupied by men wearing cowboy hats and ladies in boots and jeans.

They settled into a booth away from the door. Vassar ordered the T-bone, Hank the Rib-Eye. Both liked their steak medium rare, accompanied by a baked potato dressed with butter and sour cream. It was a treat to eat like this—and a courtesy, a tip of the hat to Montana. It wouldn't be right to be in a state so similar in disposition to Texas and order chicken.

Vassar and Hank returned to their motel room, kicked off their boots, poured themselves two fingers apiece of the eighteen-year-old Scotch they purchased on their way into town, and sat down to review their plans. Working backward from their arranged meeting time with the outfitter of 8:30 AM, they decided to set their alarm for 6:30. All that was left to do before bedtime was pack their packs.

They mostly worked in silence, with precise efficiency, as they sorted the gear laid out on their beds. Each sipped his Scotch and humored the other with periodic quips about their sanity for heading into the Absaroka Wilderness mid-winter. Both harbored doubts, but like all good men, they attributed the feeling to anticipation, adrenalin, and nervous jitters. Since these attributions failed to fully assuage their tensions, they joked and cajoled in deference to the ominous emotion.

Another pair of socks. An extra pair of long underwear. An additional pair of regular underwear and undershirt, both synthetic blends. One extra mid-weight top for insurance. An emergency kit, a head lamp, extra batteries for the GPS, two sources of fire, a sheath knife, in addition to the pocket knife each carried (gifts to them from their Father), and a face mask in the event serious cold settled on them. Vassar carried the ultra-light stove, Hank the freeze-dried food assortment. They were responsible for their own water.

Hank hadn't told Vassar about his back spasms. He wanted to do his part and carry his load.

Both packed a bivy, or bivouac sack, for sleeping protection in lieu of a tent. At camp, they would place their down sleeping bag and sleeping pad inside their bivy sack and be protected from the worst Mother Nature could unleash, but without the bulk of packing a tent. After packing these belongings, they lashed their crampons and ice axes to the packs, made certain each fastener was secure, and called the process done. Everything left over would either be worn in the morning or left with their outfitter, Mr. Korhonen.

They turned out all but the bathroom light. Vassar sat on his bed and put his pillows behind his back. Hank turned a chair from the round table to face the bed. In the low light, finishing their Scotch, the brothers wordlessly contemplated tomorrow.

Aarne Korhonen, a second-generation Finlander whose Father immigrated first to Minnesota then to Montana ninety-one years ago, was happy to have the mid-winter work. While the sun had yet to rise, over breakfast Aarne mused about the job with incomplete sentences to his wife, Nelma.

Like her husband, Nelma was from hearty stock and sparing with her words. "That it is, Aarne. Odd indeed." She moved across the kitchen to fetch the coffee pot.

"Just can't figure. These boys...," he said to her, and left the remainder of the sentence unspoken. "Two snow machines, and only want us to drop them off."

"Where would that be?" she asked.

"Malden. It's closed now, you know. Must be fifteen miles from where the plow stops. Just past Victor's place, down south from Livingston. Last winter they didn't plow far enough. Blocked Vic's drive. He complained, he did. Went to the city himself. But it was the mailman not being able to deliver the mail that got the county out with their front loader."

"You're starting from Victor's then, are you?"

"That's right, Mother. He and Mattie are gone to Helena."

"Their daughter's there," Nelma offered. "You can park then without bothering them."

"That's right." Aarne tipped his cup and swallowed the rest of his coffee. "What do you figure, Mother?"

"Well, Aarne. Do you want the work or don't you? Just tell me now."

He didn't answer. She didn't expect him to. After forty-two years of marriage, complete sentences and answers were unnecessary. "Guess I'll be finishing already." Aarne placed his napkin beside his plate, his heavy hands taking special care—almost reverential—and scooted away from the table. It was Nelma's signal. She turned. He bent down and kissed her on the cheekbone as she placed her hand on the small of his back, the wool overalls scratchy under her fingers. He patted her shoulder as gently as he had handled the napkin and stepped to the door leading to the mud room. "Robert, from down at the school, is going to help me. You remember him."

"Robert's wife plays Bunko with Ida on Tuesday," Nelma said.

"She does, does she?" He had no idea what that information had to do with him. *Part of Nelma's way*, he thought, reaching for his checkered bomber hat as Nelma's words slipped quietly away. "Those boys want us to take them in, but not out, Mother. Don't know." Aarne pulled on his mittens. "I'll be off now." He pulled the back door closed, eased down the steps, and trudged across the crusty snow as Nelma watched her man from the window.

He double-checked the tie downs anchoring the two snow sleds to his trailer and made certain the lights were plugged in to the wiring harness. Aarne did this because he was Finnish, not because it needed doing. He unplugged the electrical cord keeping his engine block warm, coiled the cord out of his way, and started his pickup truck. The dash lights glowed green on his face. He adjusted the heater fan and listened to the news for a moment as the truck's engine growled against the cold. It was eleven below zero; normal for this time of year.

Aarne was seven minutes early, but Robert was waiting in front of his garage door when Aarne arrived. The truck door creaked as Robert opened the cab. "Morning, Aarne."

"Robert. Nice morning, it is."

"Yes, Aarne. A nice morning."

"Coffee?" It was a pleasant question. Aarne knew the answer.

"That'll be fine," Robert said.

Aarne parked across four parallel spaces to allow for his rig. He and Robert walked across the Quick Stop parking lot, stamped their boots before entering, and went inside. They slid into a booth with a Formica-top table worn white in the middle.

Ten blocks away, Vassar and Hank each sipped his third cup of coffee after a breakfast of eggs, bacon, hash browns, and biscuits. Vassar checked email while Hank stared into the awakening dawn, lost in reminiscence.

It had been 29 months since he and Vassar fly fished on Malden Creek. That many months since he was guided by Vassar into a secret meeting with their Father, a meeting that changed his perception of his Father, altered his life's course, and brought him back to Southwestern Montana. The preceding months had afforded him time to solidify his ability to trust his Father, time to distance himself from the circumstances that nearly overwhelmed him two years ago, and time to wrap his mind and heart around his Father's perspective about him rather than his own estimated self-worth. It was a perspective he treasured but that had taken a severe beating the last three days, what with the spasms and all. He felt bad about doubting, but he'd discussed matters with God during the flight to Bozeman. His back was achy and his soul inflamed, but at least his free fall had been arrested.

As he sipped his coffee and stared, Hank felt the form of his pocket knife through his wool pants. The gift from his Father was his constant accessory and most-prized possession.

Eight months ago, in a rush to get to the airport for a business trip, Hank habitually put the knife in his jeans pocket. He forgot all about it until the alarm sounded passing through security at DFW. There was no use explaining the importance of the knife to TSA as there is no provision for either understanding or allowance in their job description. Hank knew his options: Render the knife to the agent, knowing it would be destroyed; check it through as checked baggage, and risk it being lost; mail it home via the same folks who failed to deliver his certified letter the previous week; or take it back to the car and hope he made it back in time to catch his flight. He missed his flight.

In his mind, he envisioned the waterfall on Malden Creek that he and Vassar passed behind on their previous visit. *I wonder what it looks like in the winter?*

He and Vassar had talked numerous times about whether they could pass behind the falls as they had done in the summer. They knew there would be ice, thus the crampons and ice axes. If they couldn't pass behind the waterfall, could they still make the time transition into the medieval world they'd entered two years ago?

After much speculation, the only way to know was to go see.

His Father had told him he needed time to let the lessons of their first adventure settle from his head to his heart—to his outlook, and to his disposition. Hank knew this process had happened to some extent, but to what extent he couldn't be certain until he was tested. The test of the spasms did not bode well, but Hank ignored the indicator. It was too stark.

He didn't relish the intensity he recalled from his first passage into the other world—the "spiritual world," as Vassar termed it—but he knew it was the place he was destined to live. His Father had said so, and he had reiterated it on numerous occasions over the last 29 months.

Most of his Father's opinions occurred to Hank as thoughts, but he had learned to be careful who he told about these thoughts. After his previous trip to Malden Creek, he had enthusiastically talked about his tale and the experiences that shaped him. And right away he realized, *Not everyone—the majority of folks, in fact—believes my story.*

But Hank knew in his soul, or perhaps in his heart, someplace deep and profound, *My experiences in the other time dimension were real, and they were true. I just lack adequate words to describe my life there.*

Here, in this time dimension, he was the CEO of a media marketing firm. There, in the spiritual realm, he was a warrior. Here, he labored to believe his spiritual conviction mattered one iota. There, his spiritual identity defined him, gave his life meaning, and underscored his reason for being. Both here and there, he labored to trust—trust anyone, but especially his Father.

Hank shifted positions, crossing his legs the other way while resting on the other hip. He sipped his coffee and let the earthy aroma fill his nostrils.

Trust was the intersection between the two dimensions—temporal and spiritual. Passing through that intersection, Hank encountered the battle over his beliefs.

I'm a man living in two worlds, he thought, *the earthly and the spiritual. Most of my life, I have assumed the world I can see, touch, taste, feel, and hear is the real world. But try as I might, the tactile world lacks the depth to which my soul longs to delve. I desire more.*

Part man, part spirit—Hank wasn't certain which he was more of, but from his previous adventure with Vassar, Hank was progressively concluding the spiritual world actually governed his physical world, not the other way around. For all the physical trappings of success Hank had acquired, and the consequential demands those trappings required of his mind and time, there was a leanness in his soul—until two-and-a-half years ago when Vassar enticed him to venture behind the waterfall into the spiritual world of Gnarled Wood.

Life on the physical side of Malden Creek—this side—had its allure and objective ease. *All it demands is that I keep my daily allotment of plates spinning—while managing periodic mania like these spasms. No problem,* he thought sarcastically. *In exchange, I'm recognized as an approved contributor to the cycle of life—and I've got the paperwork to show for it. It's demanding, but no more so than anyone else's life. Each day, I get out of bed. I conduct myself to the best of my ability, and conclude the day by crawling back into bed. Coffee at the start, Scotch at the conclusion, sleep in between, and repeat...for as long as sustainable.* His face caught the first rays of light breaking dawn.

But life on the other side of Malden? That's a different proposition. Entirely.

In the spiritual world, Hank's soul came alive while his temporal humanity was pinched between the spiritual realm in which his Father lived and the spiritual aspirations under which his Father's enemy, Zophos, operated. His Father reigned over the Kingdom of Light. Zophos ruled the darkness. *I languish in between, a Prince of light, afflicted with a propensity to walk in darkness. I aspire to the light with all the desire my heart can muster, but when I think about my experiences, I'm astounded at my compulsion to deny my family identity and adopt hypocritical pity as though I am an orphan.* Hank shook his head.

When he sat and thought about it, the dichotomy of the two worlds was clear and the dynamic conflict of flesh versus spirit compelled his heart to scream allegiance to his Father. *But when conflict, or pain, becomes my experience....? That tension inevitably takes me to the intersection of trust/distrust. It's a simple intersection of two ways: mine and Father's. Upon whose resources will I depend? Mine or His?*

On this side of Malden, I've explored my own way. Hank tilted his head right, acknowledging. *During my earlier trip to the other side of Malden, I explored Father's way.* He nodded slightly—to himself and for his own benefit.

Hank knew the friction between the two ways wasn't as straightforward as it seemed. *On the contrary! It's confusing. Confusing as hell!* In fact, having polled any number of warriors, Hank had discovered the one, common denominator of combat is confusion.

Looking back, Hank could see the mercy of his Father during his previous trip. Knowing how confusing the battle can be, his Father required the combatants to disclose themselves visibly to Hank. *That was helpful, to say the least,* Hank noted to himself. *Especially now that both Jester and Magician wage their battles invisibly upon the field of my soul.*

Jester, the agent of Zophos and the Dark Army, assaulted Hank— 98% of the time, anyway—in accordance with Hank's habitual behaviors, thoughts, and feelings. Even in Gnarled Wood, Hank noted that most of Jester's attacks correlated with the habitual patterns under which he operated in the "normal" world. *Circumstance is Jester's platform, the place from which he strikes,* Hank thought. *Case in point, this doggone pain.*

Magician, representative of the Kingdom of Light and of Hank's Father, the King, counseled him based upon his Father's heart, teachings, and love. He was a constant advocate to Hank of his Father's redemption. Over and over, Magician reminded Hank that he once lived in darkness, but through his Father's intervention, he now lived in the light. *Magician uses circumstance to his advantage as well, but not like Jester. Magician prefers the advantage of my new heart, bequeathed to me by Father, the King. That's a big deal.*

Both Jester and Magician spoke to Hank in his thoughts, and most of the time, their thoughts to him were voiced with first-person pronouns—I, me, my, mine, and so forth.

In effect then, my battle to trust Father is waged by three combatants—Jester, Magician, and me—and all three of us sound exactly the same, like me, Henry H. "Hank" Henderson!

Yep! I'm a man caught in between two spiritual generals, each with his army poised in martial array, each fighting over the same piece of ground: my soul. And I worry about my back hurting. Hank huffed lightly through his nostrils, resolving to alter his focus.

The King of Light, my Father, claims to already possess my heart and desires now to align my soul with this reality—His reality. This was his rationale for instructing Vassar to bring me to Gnarled Wood the first time, and I presume, this time as well. Not a bad plan, Hank surmised, sitting and sipping.

Jester asserts largely upon circumstantial evidence that the King isn't telling me the truth. In fact, he is emphatic! Father isn't good, even though he claims to be. Worse yet, he makes a pretty good case that the King is actually duplicitous and capricious—selfish, deceitful, and whimsical. All one has to do to realize this, Jester asserts, is look around. Or in my case, simply face the reality of my spasms, resultant disappointment, and absent Father who one would think would care enough to heal this infirmity. Hank nodded again, acknowledging Jester's strong point. *No doubt about it: Jester's commentary on circumstance does indeed paint a compelling argument that the King is less than good.* Hank shifted positions, the discomfort in his hip serving as an exclamation point that this line of reasoning could not be ignored.

As Hank sipped coffee and stared through the window into the dawning cold of Bozeman, he rationally dismissed Jester's deceptions. *But it's easy—sitting here,* he thought. *I know better than to underestimate my nemesis. When the battle gets rolling, the pressures mount. When there are casualties*—he had been wounded grievously—*and when the voices speaking to me escalate their rhetoric, that experience is confusing. Warfare is brutal.*

I know spiritual battle rages on this side of Malden Creek, just as it does on the other side. But the spinning plates and noise of life drowns out the sound of spiritual conflict. This is why—one reason, why—I want to return to Malden Creek. In my heart, I desire the rigor of Father's life rather than the inanity of mine. This won't be an easy trip though, weather notwithstanding. But, I am compelled to make the journey—and I won't back down!

"Would you believe they disregarded that entire contract?!" Vassar's indignant tone snapped Hank back to the table. "Listen to this, little Brother."

Hank was patient as Vassar scrolled back up through the email to find his place. "Here it is. Okay, listen to this: While we appreciate your recommendations, and thank you for the obvious work you invested in our project, we prefer the position we have formulated. The Board believes its collective wisdom is more attuned to market conditions than is reflected in your proposal. We sincerely thank you and wish you all the best…blah, blah, blah."

"Huh!" Hank exclaimed, not because he understood the email, but in response to his Brother's bother.

"I didn't give them a recommendation! And I didn't give them a proposal either! I intended for them to take action! They don't understand what's at stake here."

"Maybe they do," Hank offered, "but have decided to go their own way."

Vassar looked at Hank for several seconds, his eyes squinting progressively as Hank's perspective settled on him. "Just like that?"

"Well, you know. It wouldn't be the first time your instructions were disregarded."

"Yeah, I know," Vassar conceded. "But these people agreed with me. They told me they would listen, take my guidance to heart."

"I'm sorry, Vassar."

He looked at his phone for a moment, pushed the button to lock the screen, and set the device on the table. "Thanks, Hank. I just wanted to tell someone. I know you understand."

"I don't know if I understand or not, but I'm grateful you told me. It's no good hauling stuff like that around by yourself."

"Well. Enough of that," Vassar said. "You ready to get rolling?"

Both visited the Men's Room before making their way to the Escalade. With Vassar at the wheel, Hank navigated to the Quick Stop. They pulled in behind Aarne's rig and parked after scanning the parking lot. "That's got to be it," Hank observed. It was the only blue truck towing a trailer loaded with two snowmobiles.

The four men met in the parking lot. Their greeting was brief, just long enough to confirm the plan.

Aarne and Robert followed Vassar and Hank to drop off the rental car. Although it wasn't necessary, Aarne and Robert both got out of the truck to help transfer the brothers' belongings. Since it was a remote, drop-off location, Vassar put the keys in the console of the rental car along with his signed paperwork, locked the doors, and climbed into Aarne's truck.

They covered the twenty-five miles to the outskirts of Livingston uneventfully, took the Park Street/Highway 89 exit, and headed south. Even though they had driven this highway before, everything looked foreign to the brothers given the passage of time and the snow. "I don't remember much of this," Vassar said.

"Much? I don't remember any," Hank countered.

The brothers did most of the talking, coaxing what they could from Aarne and Robert. How cold does it get? How much snow do you normally receive? How long have you had these snowmobiles? How fast will they run?

Aarne turned his rig into Victor's driveway, drove slowly toward the barn, turned around, and drove back toward the gate. Robert and Aarne were efficient enough at releasing the tie-downs that Vassar and Hank were no help, although they did assist in tugging the machines backward off the trailer.

Aarne handed Vassar and Hank snowmobile suits and helmets. The brothers wore their packs and strapped their snow shoes to the cargo rack on the front of Aarne's machine. Hank rode behind Robert, Vassar behind Aarne. Less than ten minutes after getting out of the truck, Vassar and Hank were enjoying a new experience: snowmobiling!

The riders turned right out of Vic's driveway. Aarne led the way slowly until he assessed the pile of snow at the end of the county road. Once he picked his path, Aarne applied the gas and the snow sled powered up the embankment and dropped over the top into softer snow. Aarne fed the engine more fuel and the powerful machine jumped, snow showering over the windscreen. With Robert not far behind and following his track, Aarne plunged ahead.

They followed what appeared to be the roadbed for several hundred yards before Aarne angled to his left and entered the trees. Vassar recalled that the road up to Malden was curvy as it ascended and assumed Aarne was forging a shortcut as he went through the trees, into the open, back into the trees, and back out into the open.

Occasionally the machine bogged down in soft snow. Each time, Aarne fed the engine and the sled plowed forward. Over drifts, down into low spots, between the firs, and upward they climbed with spectacular vistas increasing as they rode in the dawn of a new day.

Vassar was certain another adventure awaited Hank and him beyond the falls on Malden Creek. He had visited with their Father extensively about the timing and relayed his ideas and thoughts to Hank—but his Brother was cautious. *More to the point,* Vassar thought, *he's skeptical.*

Still, it was immensely easier getting Hank to embrace this venture into the spiritual realm than it was on our last trip, he thought. *There were times two years ago when I doubted whether he would follow me. Hank was within a hair's breadth of turning back shortly after we passed behind the waterfall and climbed up into the beginning of Gnarled Wood.*

Vassar looked back for his Brother, but could only see Robert. Vassar turned back around, *But Hank did follow. He trusted—ever so timidly—but that made all the difference. My Brother's a different man than he was twenty-nine months ago. It takes a great deal of courage to change, to transform—to abandon those things that aren't working for a new way.*

For the longest time he and Hank had only been brothers, sons of the same father. But now, they were cohorts and friends, warriors, commissioned together to carry out a special assignment given them by their Father.

Vassar knew what was to transpire would not be easy.

So did Hank. He knew snowshoeing nine or ten miles along Malden Creek in deep powder wouldn't be easy. He knew carrying a pack would be painfully hard, despite his preparation to get in shape by carrying his pack through the neighborhood with progressively heavier loads.

When tested, will I be strong and confident? Or, will I succumb— have to be rescued? The questions looped through Hank's thoughts. He squirmed on the seat behind Robert so as not to give the spasms a sitting target.

As they scooted up the hill to Malden Creek campground on the droning machines, their heads encased in the solitude of their helmets, Vassar and Hank collected their thoughts, their fears, their doubts, their questions, and their anticipations. For Hank, these were heavier than all the provisions in his pack.

They edged over a steep embankment. Hank bumped into Robert's back and Robert's helmet smacked Hank's visor. No harm done. The crack of plastic on plastic and chest to back returned Hank to the task at hand: staying on this bucking sled. He looked ahead at a steep incline out of the draw they were crossing. He gripped the handles under his seat and leaned into Robert as he gunned the machine forward. They were briefly airborne at the exit then landed softly in an explosion of deep powder. As they settled into a less raucous stretch of the ride, Hank reached around to where Robert could see him and gave him a thumbs-up with his mittened hand.

Hank returned to the fundamentals he knew. In a voice loud enough he could hear in his helmet, he said to the indwelling resource of his Father, "Magician, live through me, please." A fog appeared on his visor as he breathed out the desire of his heart, but then disappeared from the bottom up as the cold air filtered through the vent. Hank smiled. *I'm going to see Father, the High King of Glory.*

Aarne let off the gas and his sled bogged to a stop in a sizable clearing. Robert pulled up close. Vassar and Hank looked around at the snowy wonder of Malden Creek campground and trailhead. There were no signs, no picnic tables, no restroom, no Forest Service registration station...at least none that could be seen. They were all buried under inches and inches of white.

Aarne flipped open his visor. There was an awkward silence as the brothers waited for Aarne or Robert to say something—to welcome them to their destination, to signal that it was time to get off their respective rides—but Aarne and Robert were men of few words.

Hank thought back to their first trip: *We pulled into this same parking lot, or more specifically, the parking lot underneath us by however many feet of snow, and met the outfitter renting us llamas for our fly fishing trip.* He too was sparing with his communication, Hank remembered. *But he at least offered a few guidelines.*

The moment of truth had come. They planned, and studied, and interviewed cold-weather campers—all in preparation for this moment.

As the brothers swung into action, Aarne undid the straps holding their snowshoes on his rack. They took their packs off and leaned them together in between the machines, stood up, and unzipped the legs and fronts of their snowmobile suits, stripped them off, and handed them to Robert who stowed them in a duffle along with their helmets. Hank labored to get his snowshoes on, kicking Robert more than once, and bumping his head against his back. Finally, Robert suggested he turn around backwards on the seat. "See if that doesn't help," he offered.

Once their snowshoes were fastened, Aarne got into the helpful spirit. "Why don't you boys get off and we'll hand you your packs." Vassar clambered off of Aarne's machine, clearly possessing no skills whatsoever for this new experience.

Observing his Brother's awkwardness, Hank decided to try jumping off. He landed beautifully, but the snow compressed unevenly. Fearing he would fall backward into the snow machine, Hank over-corrected and fell face first.

Vassar came to his rescue, but neither his help nor Hank's getting up were graceful. Hank tried to recover, "For my next dive I shall attempt a full gainer." Vassar chuckled, Aarne and Robert remained expressionless.

As soon as Vassar and Hank achieved equilibrium, Aarne handed each his pack. Once they were strapped in and had their trekking poles extended to the proper length, Aarne took his mitten off and extended his hand toward Vassar first, "Vassar." Then to, "Hank." After his mitten was replaced, Aarne said, "You boys sure you're going to be okay up here?"

That's a trick question, Hank thought. *I've already proven I'm not proficient.*

While Hank thought about his reply, Vassar said, "I think we'll be fine, Aarne. I appreciate your concern.

"Robert, take care."

"Thanks for the ride up the hill." It was Hank's bravest posture. Aarne and Robert nodded, once apiece.

Robert flipped his visor down and started his sled. Following Aarne, they turned around, making a large teardrop scar in the snow above the campground parking lot.

The brothers stood motionless and silent until the sound of the machines was swallowed up in the deafening silence of the snow-entombed Absaroka wilderness. It was ten minutes to eleven. They were fifteen miles from the nearest plowed road, nine or ten miles from their destination, had no cell phone coverage, and it would be dark in six hours.

Unlatching his GPS from his pack strap, Vassar said, "You ready?"

Hank said, "You think we're doing the right thing, Vassar?"

"You tell me."

Hank thought a minute, sorting through his residual embarrassment and sore back muscles to collect the constructs necessary to answer Vassar. *Do I believe Father will meet me?* Hank mused to himself. *I'm doing my best, at great expense, hurting like a fool, and have fallen face first, first thing in the morning.*

It was a subtle accusation—that he'd already been let down—the implication being that Magician and the High King had already proven unreliable.

But the enemy of Hank's soul played his hand a bit too aggressively: *This is going to be a long trip for me.* Hank felt his emotions cascade and tumble into distrust. The thump at the bottom of his emotional gorge resounded in his heart and he recognized the voice of his nemesis, Jester.

Hank had prepared himself. He knew their trek back to Gnarled Wood would not be without conflict. He figured he and Vassar would be opposed, probably from the start. *And here we are. At the start, the very start!*

This isn't going to be a long trip, Jester. It's a grand adventure, and I'll be damned if I'm going to take my first step listening to your drivel. I won't back down! "Get away from me!" Hank screamed, swinging his ski poles about him!

Vassar jumped with Hank's explosion, but immediately raised both arms in the air and screamed his own valiant yell. Together, their shouts rocked the foundations of hell and served notice: We are back! We are warriors of light, serving our Father, the High King, with pure allegiance and utter loyalty!

"Alright! I feel better!" Hank whooped, as he took his mittens off to start his GPS. He put his finger on the button, crouched slightly, and looked at Vassar with the eye of a tiger. As quickly as he could with cold hands, Vassar caught up to Hank's fiery resolve.

And as was their custom, they started their GPS units simultaneously. They twisted around to get their compass heading, marked their course, and set off alongside Malden Creek.

CHAPTER 2

Malden Creek Campground

The brothers had saved the track of their previous trip in their GPS units, but remained suspicious of the technology in their hands. At home, Hank's GPS "pinned" his house where the Hooper's lived. And on their earlier trip to Montana, their units showed them walking on both sides of Malden Creek. Oddly enough, while they had marked the position of the waterfall, they were unable to reconcile the location later with the online maps.

A compass they understood, and they could read a map with the best of them. Neither required a battery. Neither was susceptible to cold. Neither relied upon unseen satellites—or map makers living in Silicon Valley or somewhere in India. Neither functioned by a conglomeration of circuits and software…that could fail.

But their doubt was short lived. They soon heard their navigation as they approached the edge of the clearing. Although shrouded in tunnels of ice, they heard Malden wriggling and running and dancing out of sight with the same enthusiasm it voiced in the summer.

The tumbling gurgle was a fantastic sound to Hank, escorting him into recollections instrumental in forming the character he brought with him now. He was exhilarated.

The snowshoeing was slow, hard work. In most places there was a crusty layer of snow under eight or ten inches of powder, but every now and then the crust broke and they sank another twelve or eighteen inches. When this happened, the effort to extract the sunken shoe often caused the other to break through, which then resulted in several high-steps in knee-deep snow until a firmer layer was encountered and they were once again "only" in half-a-foot of snow.

For the most part, their trekking poles, equipped with snow baskets at the tips, provided points of balance. But like the snowshoes, every so often they broke through the crust and left one of the brothers lurching to regain his balance.

Hank stopped, hands to his sides. "Whew! I should have done more lunges and fewer lunches."

Vassar was sucking air too. "Me too. How'd we overlook that this trail would be tougher in the winter than it was in the summer?"

"I don't know, but we did," Hank huffed. He had stuck his poles in the snow and come out of his pack. He unzipped his coat, rolled it up, and lashed it to the top of his pack, bent over and stretched his back for several seconds—until he felt the muscles ease their coil—and then shouldered his pack again. "I spent more time walking in the hood getting used to this blasted pack than I did riding intervals on my bike."

Vassar acknowledged with a grunt. He was preoccupied rolling and stowing his coat too. After he got his pack back on, he said, "Okay. It's my turn," as he moved past Hank to break trail.

A fir had succumbed and fallen across the trail, its boughs collecting copious volumes of snow and creating a formidable wall of branches and snowfall. The top of the tree extended to the edge of Malden Creek and its exposed base was a wall of roots and detritus. Vassar stood staring at the obstacle as Hank stepped up beside him.

Vassar eased toward the crest of the fallen tree, carefully separating branches to avoid tripping or being snagged. As he made his way, the sound of Malden Creek rushing through its tunnels of ice got closer to his feet. He stopped.

"What do you think?" Hank asked.

"I don't know. You'd think the ice would hold me, but falling into Malden would not be good." As he turned and began his retreat, the ice broke, and his snowshoe and boot dipped into the water. Vassar leaned forward and grasped a branch of the tree. He pulled his foot out of the hole he'd created and retreated. The wet snowshoe quickly accumulated snow and ice. In two steps, Vassar's left snowshoe no longer weighed a pound and a half; it was more like fifteen.

Hank laughed at his Brother, who feigned offense, then mocked himself good naturedly. His posturing soon turned more serious as he examined the task of cleaning his snowshoe.

Vassar wiggled the frozen binding until he got it loose and freed his boot. He handed the frozen snowshoe to Hank who whacked the shoe smartly against a tree. The brittle ice shattered, cascading in a crystal shower. Hank bent the binding against its natural inclination to break it free and handed the shoe back to Vassar.

While Vassar buckled his snowshoe back on his foot, Hank studied their alternatives. They backtracked a little and worked their way around the obstacle and back toward Malden Creek.

They traded the lead position after each break, snacked on trail mix to keep their internal fires stoked, and drank plenty of water to avoid dehydration. They used their hats and the zippers on their vests to regulate body temperature, attempting to stay a little cool and minimize sweating. Whatever was damp—socks, underwear—would freeze when removed, and once frozen it would be a challenge to thaw.

By 3:30 they dared not continue farther lest they find themselves unsettled and unfed in a dark world of dangerous cold. They had pushed harder and longer than planned, yet were not as far up the trail as they had hoped.

Hank pointed with his pole, "What do you think of that spot, Vassar?"

His Brother eyed their surroundings. The clearing was tight, snuggly circled with dense fir trees, but open enough to allow for a fire. "Looks good to me."

They side-stepped in their snowshoes and tramped down flat spots for their bivy sacks. The resulting, three-foot-deep holes looked like coffins without lids, but the walls would provide shelter from the wind.

They opened the valves on their self-inflating camp pads, unrolled their bivy sacks, and pulled their sleeping bags out of their stuff sacks.

While Vassar set up their small cook stove and prepared a place for a fire, Hank went in search of wood. Reaching underneath the fir boughs, he broke off small, dead branches for kindling along with progressively larger branches to feed the blaze. After setting up the stove, Vassar joined Hank gathering wood. They knew it would require an uncanny amount of wood to enjoy much warmth on a cold night.

Using the trunk of a fallen tree as a table, Vassar started the stove and began boiling enough water to hydrate their freeze-dried dinners. On top of green limbs prepared as the base for their fire, Hank built a small stack of kindling around a wad of dryer lint he had pre-moistened with Vaseline. Leaving a tail of lint exposed like a fuse, Hank flicked his butane lighter to light the lint. But the lighter didn't work. He had tested it—along with everything else—before leaving home, but it wasn't working now.

He borrowed Vassar's. He had used his to start the stove, but now his wouldn't work either. Hank squatted back on his haunches and thought backward. "Hey, Vassar. Where did you carry your lighter?"

"In my pocket."

"And after you lit the stove, you set it on the log?"

"Uh, huh. Why?"

"Huh. I guess these things have to stay warm to work."

"Interesting. We'll have to test them in the morning."

"Yeah. We'll see." Hank had already stuffed his lighter into his pocket and was rummaging around for his reserve of wooden matches. Shielding the tiny flame with his body, Hank held the match under the exposed tail of dryer lint, then added the match to his pyre.

Although he carefully nursed the flame with tiny twigs, the fire struggled. Getting onto all fours, Hank put his head into the fire pit and blew gently at the base of the feeble flame. It bent and growled against his breath, but was taller and brighter when he stopped blowing. He blew again, then again—a bit harder. He added fuel, studied his creation for imperfection, then breathed more life underneath its burning.

Hank snapped larger sticks and added them to the fire. When it was steadily burning thumb-size fuel, he felt secure enough in its future to turn his attention to dinner.

The brothers sat on their camp pads, having stamped and dug a rudimentary bench upon which to sit. Hank tended his fire while he chewed bites of beef stroganoff. As he neared the bottom of his bagged meal, the flames were reaching above the walls of their pit.

Vassar put the meal packaging into a zip lock bag while Hank fueled the fire with several fresh sticks of wood. Then, they turned their attention to replenishing their water bottles.

Downstream a few yards, Malden Creek sluiced through a narrow cut, jumping haphazardly over boulders, caroming off steeper-than-normal banks, and splashing with enough vigor to defy the formation of an ice tunnel. Getting to the open water would be tricky, but it was preferable to breaking the ice shrouding most of the creek.

Vassar grasped Hank's wrist and eased down the embankment. Lowering each water bottle by an accessory cord tied around its neck, Vassar patiently let Malden refill each bottle. After their bottles were filled, Hank pulled Vassar up Malden's bank.

Back at camp, Vassar started the stove again. Boiling the creek water for a minute or so ensured the death of all pathogens.

Hank steadied each bottle as Vassar filled them with boiling water, then put the lids on and buried them upside down in the snow to insulate them against freezing. He marked the burial spot with a trekking pole.

"You know, I read a book one time about this rancher. I think he lived in Washington. No. It was Oregon. The eastern part somewhere. Anyhow, he made friends with a coyote, which was an odd thing for a sheep rancher to do."

"Are you fixing to tell me a story?"

"Yeah. Well, not that kind of story. I really did read about this guy. It was a fascinating book."

"Do you remember the title?" Vassar asked.

"*Don Coyote.*"

"You mean *Don Quixote*, don't you?"

"No. That was the windmill guy. This fellow was a rancher." Hank knew his Brother was being intentionally cantankerous.

"Okay. So this man has a pet coyote."

"No. It wasn't a pet, but the guy did give him part of his bologna sandwich each day. Anyway, eventually he befriends this whole family of coyotes."

"These are wild coyotes?" Vassar asked.

"Wild as they can be."

"Where were they?"

"He kept them in a great big pen," Hank said.

"Don't sound very wild."

"Vassar. You probably ought to read the book for yourself."

"I'm sorry. I'm just kidding."

"I know."

"So, what brought *Don Coyote* to mind?" Vassar said.

"Well, this rancher comes up with an experiment. He was curious to know whether or not a coyote remembers where it buries its food, and he concluded that they did. In fact, they accurately remembered multiple burial sites. Squirrels, on the other hand, didn't remember where they buried anything."

Vassar saw where this story was going and had moved close to the pole Hank used to mark the buried water bottles. "So what you're saying is that you have the mind of a squirrel."

"No. What I'm saying is that *we* have the mind of a squirrel." They laughed.

They filled the final bottles with boiling water and Hank buried them in the snow bank next to the others while Vassar organized their stove for the night. They sat by the fire until their wood was gone, then headed to bed about 8:45.

Hank stood by his bivy, nestled snuggly inside the surrounding snow walls, and thought through his next steps. The cold prodded him.

Working by the light of his headlamp, Hank pulled off his gloves and gingerly unlaced his boots. He undid his pants, sat down on his camp pad, kicked off his boots, and rocking from side to side pulled his pants and underwear off. His bare bottom stuck to his camp pad, but he didn't stop to think about those implications. He changed his underwear and pulled his pants back on.

His fingers were tingling as he stripped his socks off inside-out and put on a fresh pair. He put his legs into his sleeping bag, placed each boot into a stuff sack of its own, and collected his cast-off clothing. He put a boot on either side of him, inside the sleeping bag, so they wouldn't freeze in the night, and placed his water bottle between his legs.

Not three feet away, Vassar engaged in the same ritual. Moisture was their enemy. Working as they had throughout the day, even though they religiously zipped and unzipped, shed clothes and donned them, all to avoid sweating, their bodies still expelled moisture—as much as three quarts given their extreme exertion. Granted, most of the loss was in their breath, but the clothes against their skin, even though designed to wick moisture away, still had to be changed to ward off cold.

Half-in, half-out of his sleeping bag and bivy, Hank removed his coat, folding and rolling it into a pillow, then pulled his mid-weight jersey over his head. He took a deep breath, crossed his arms, and pulled the long-sleeve shirt against his skin off, dropped it on the pile of other cast-off clothes, and wriggled into a fresh shirt. He quickly replaced his mid-weight shirt, adjusted his askew stocking hat, and put his used clothes in a stuff sack. He supplemented his coat with these to make a better pillow. His nest feathered and his body layered in dry clothes, the younger brother inch-wormed into his cocoon of down, relishing the almost-instant warmth. Working from the outside in, he zipped the bivy, then his sleeping bag, and last pulled the draw string to snug his hood around his head and face. Reaching between his legs, he retrieved his water bottle and put it on his chest to ensure it stayed liquid.

Hank purposely left the bivy over his face open; it was easily closed if needed. But he wouldn't need it tonight. The sky was brilliant and the air stunningly cold.

He knew from experience that getting to sleep the first night would take longer than the second night. And he knew that as the minutes passed, the fire would surely die for lack of attention, his eyes would acclimate to the dark, and the magical lure of the night sky would multiply.

With the anticipation of a child on Christmas Eve, Hank waited, encased in his mummy bag. For a while, he studied the firelight dancing upon the stage of firs circling the tiny clearing. But the fire struck its colors, defeated by its own hunger, and the shy stars emerged, points of light winking through the veil of heaven. Gathering courage in the progressive darkness, more luminaries showed their faces, peering down upon Hank, prostrate, observing their wandering across the ecliptic.

Wrapping its tail above Kochab, the ancient sky-dragon, Draco, arched his back along the celestial sphere. At the end of Ursa Minor, Polaris shone steady, brighter—the reliable one, the polestar, the one suitable for navigation. It struck Hank odd that this most-important star should be the outermost star, last, in the handle of the Little Dipper. *But the least will be greatest.* The thought reminded him of something Vassar said once.

The Big Dipper—the Great Bear with its seven, prominent stars—dominated the sky to the upper left of Polaris as it pointed back to the guide star. Hank recalled this constellation was mentioned in the Bible, and for that matter, in a number of ancient pieces of literature. In the hall of his mind he heard Don McLean singing, "Starry, Starry Night."

He compared the masterpiece above to van Gogh's famous painting of the Rhone, the Big Dipper featured prominently.

Hank twisted his head, his right eye obscured by the edge of the bivy, and he could see Cassiopeia—the "W"—with his left eye. Like the Big Dipper, but on the opposite side of Polaris, it too pointed to the North Star. If one of these constellations was below the horizon, he had learned the other was visible.

Turning, tucking his chin into his sleeping bag, and looking with his right eye Hank could barely see the twins of Gemini, Castor and Pollux; Castor mortal, Pollux immortal, and through the power of Zeus both immortalized in the night sky. *I don't know about that,* Hank thought. *It's a good story though.*

He stared again at Polaris, intermittently hazy in the cloud of his breath, and the other hosts of starry witnesses circling as if the sky was a theater-in-the-round. Vassar, famously comfortable anywhere, was breathing in quiet rhythm.

As he pledged to do at his commissioning by the High King, Magician spoke from Hank's heart into his thoughts, *You are like Polaris, Hank. Suitable for navigation. Steady. Dependable.*

The implication was clear: Whenever Hank looked into the sky, for all the myth and mystery across its expanse, Magician wanted him to remember that the High King thought of him like he thought of the polestar: steady, dependable, and suitable for others to navigate by.

I wonder if Father has already forgotten the sorry way I handled the spasms? Hank thought. As he lay still, his hip and back drew and convulsed to purge the lactic acid accumulated from the hard day's labor. It was too early to tell if they would relax or contract.

But Hank had learned that when Magician spoke, he needed to pay attention.

Polaris, huh? I'm the last person suited to that name, Magician.

I understand, but..., Magician began, before Hank interrupted him.

I know. I'm bad to forget.

You don't say, Magician goaded.

I am the person Father declares me to be, not the person I pretend to be with my performance. And the truth is, Magician, I don't want to pretend. I desire to live like who I am, not the hypocrite who plays a contrivance.

The parallel between "want" and "desire" did not escape Hank as he talked with his friend, Magician, the great Wizard of the Kingdom of Light. It had been a confusing, elusive distinction to grasp—at least initially. After he got the hang of it though, the difference between wanting and desiring was as distinct as sand and sugar.

Your Father wouldn't send you to the Round Tower if you were not suited and equipped for leadership and guidance, now would he?

No. No. He wouldn't do that, Magician. Father has a plan, and like a chess master, he's working his plan.

But you weren't prepared for the position he assigned you? Magician baited, and waited.

Hank stared at Polaris. Ursa Major, the Great Bear, was circling downward and under Polaris, the "W" circled upward and above. The Small Bear, Ursa Minor, was caught in between, its tail pinned in the night sky by the polestar. *No. I wasn't,* Hank confessed. *I appreciate Father's belief in me, but I still doubt, my conviction driven here and there by waves of circumstance. I want to believe…to believe I won't flinch when tested. I know a storm awaits my soul. But I don't know, Magician. I don't know. I feel more like a pawn.* He adjusted to ease the discomfort in his back.

So, what's in your heart to do, Hank? It was a familiar question, one Magician asked frequently.

Hank continued looking into the night sky. He was distracted by a shooting star, then by a satellite racing across the inkiness of space, wondering who it was spying on—wondered if the person monitoring its eye could see him bivouacked in their small clearing in the woods. Before long, he labored under weighty eyelids, and remembered

Magician's question.

He dozed. Slipped farther away. The Great Bear crept toward the horizon.

So, what's in your heart to do, Hank?

Hank heard, but his body succumbed.

CHAPTER 3

Beside Malden Creek

Hank awoke to the rustling of Vassar's synthetic swaddle as he inched his way into the morning, dressing in stages as he emerged from the splendid warmth into stunning cold. Hank looked at his watch: 8:20 AM. *It's been light for an hour at home,* he thought.

The last time they were here it was July and the summer days were noticeably long. But at this latitude, January's morning was late and its nightfall early. Last night it was dark by 4:45 PM.

Hank did the math. *A short day to accomplish a long list. Forget the goals. I'm going to stay in my sleeping bag.* He snuggled against the down mummy bag, but it was too late. His mind was in gear, pushing his thoughts into a semblance of order, then engaging the various levels of his conscious on sundry issues. As surely as if there was a rooster crowing, he was awake.

Hank lay still a few more moments thinking through the sequence of getting dressed. As he had learned to do the last time he was in Montana, or more accurately, during his previous trip into the spiritual world of Gnarled Wood, Hank expressed his thoughts to Magician while he stretched his difficult back, a task easier said than done inside a mummy bag. *Magician, live through me today. It's a big day, a demanding day; a day where I must stay focused.*

Hank recalled the question Magician left on the table last night. *Pawn or Polaris?*

Speaking confidently in his mind to his internal counselor, Hank thought, *Magician, I desire to live like the man Father says I am. The Polaris thing…I don't understand. But then, I don't suppose I need to understand. If that's who Father says I am, please help me live as he believes.*

Hank could feel the passion behind his sternum as his thoughts, in harmony with Magician's counsel, threw fuel on the internal fire.

Hank's back and hip plagued him with pain, sometimes poking, always prodding, frequently screaming at him from their persistent, insistent, nagging inflammation. That he had spent the night on packed snow, after carrying a pack, uphill, on snowshoes, following a rocking snowmobile ride, and a long plane ride the day before certainly didn't help matters. But he had gotten better at managing his infirmity. The morning stretches afforded him a perfect opportunity to meet with Magician regarding his challenge and the day's agenda.

After working his way out of his sleeping bag, Hank pulled the bag out of his bivy and vigorously patted and squeezed and fluffed the portions of the bag most susceptible to forming cold spots due to accumulation of ice. Although it was warm inside his bag, outside it was way below freezing. As the bag wicked moisture from his body, somewhere between the inside and the outside of the bag, the escaping moisture encountered freezing temperature. If Hank and Vassar weren't careful to break up this forming ice, within a few nights they would face the prospect of a cold spot where the down had lost its loft, and therefore, its insulating property. The areas around their necks, bottoms, and feet were the most likely to form cold spots since these areas of their bodies expelled the most moisture.

While Vassar started the stove, Hank fluffed his sleeping bag for him. Keeping the lighter in an interior pocket did the trick; Vassar got the stove fired up right away.

The thermometer read, minus nine.

Both brothers drank their coffee black from insulated cups after downing instant oatmeal supplemented with dried fruit and nuts. Vassar sat on his camp pad while Hank stood and stamped his feet against the cold.

They washed their cups with snow and started breaking camp. It took longer than they would have liked, about thirty minutes, but they reassured themselves they'd do better tomorrow.

Both tied yesterday's socks and underwear to the outside of their packs to air. Next, each tightened his boot laces and put on his snowshoes. They shouldered their packs, and with Vassar in the lead, followed Malden's path toward the falls.

What started as an overcast sky evolved into darker grey. The wind bore down with an earnest determination, as if setting its jaw for a serious task. It whistled through the tree tops, collecting atmospheric energy until it roared and raged through the spruce and fir. Early snow showers turned steady by mid-morning, and carried upon the windy vengeance, drove icy pellets into Vassar and Hank.

Stopping in the lee of a giant deadfall, Vassar said, "What do you think?"

"I don't know. I didn't see anything about a storm when we checked the weather. But, you know how it is in the mountains."

Vassar nodded.

"This doesn't feel right though, does it?" Hank ventured.

Vassar stared, one eye more squinted than the other. "No. I don't like what's happening."

There wasn't anything to be done, so after a few swigs of water, they resumed their trek to the falls. Hank took the lead breaking trail while Vassar recovered from his turn at the hard labor.

Minute by minute the snow and wind increased. It was getting hard to hear Malden Creek for the cacophony of the wind's tantrum and the forest's groaning. Slowed by the disorientation of the increasing snow, Hank kept moving while Vassar made certain his GPS tracked their location. Although he was less than ten feet behind his Brother, Vassar could barely see him through the blinding snow. Glancing backward, their footprints were erased in three paces.

They kicked the snow away from the base of a fir and crawled in midst the low branches to escape the disintegrating weather. Although protected from the storm's brunt, the tormented wind whipped around the tree in a dervish.

"If this keeps up...." Hank didn't finish saying what he was thinking.

They sat under the tree for thirty minutes and Vassar's pack accumulated about three inches of snow—an unprecedented snowfall.

"How could we miss a storm of this intensity, Vassar?"

"I don't think we did. I think this is an anomaly, a weather event no one saw coming. We've got to be close to the waterfall, but I'm thinking we need to find some shelter. This is getting dangerous."

"I agree. And besides, I haven't heard Malden in quite a while. Several minutes at least."

"Surely the GPS wouldn't be confused by a blizzard, would it?"

"Beats me," Hank said. "Not supposed to be. I Googled that question before we came up here. The guy who posted the answer sounded reassuring."

"Where was he?" Vassar wanted to know.

"Where was who?"

"The guy who said a GPS works in a blizzard. He wasn't in some place like San Antonio was he?"

"Good heavens, no!" Hank exclaimed. "What would somebody in San Antonio know about blizzards? And what kind of fool do you take me for? I might have been born at night, but I wasn't born last night." He paused. "I think he was in Texarkana."

Vassar laughed. "Texarkana, huh? You know, I think we need to find a better spot. I have a feeling this storm is going to settle in on us."

"I think you're right," Hank said.

They talked through their options. There weren't many given their ultra light equipment. Staying dry and warm wouldn't be a problem with their sleeping bags and bivy sacks, but if the storm persisted it would be measured in feet, not inches, and in days, not hours.

Two or three days in a bivy sack wasn't an option. Likewise, hunkering under the boughs of a spruce or fir tree, while more appealing than the bivy sack, wasn't a long-term option. They had to think ahead. No one would come looking for them. In all probability, the storm was sparing the lower elevations. Once the weather deteriorated into this sullen demeanor, with the mountain as an accomplice, the storm could feed on itself for several days.

Although it didn't seem possible, the brothers agreed it was snowing harder. After an hour—a relatively sheltered hour—their legs were covered with blowing, drifting snow.

If Hank thought his back and hip were in a foul mood last night, sitting on the ground for an hour redefined his sense of stiff and aching. "You know, Vassar. I hate to say it, but I can't sit here much longer. Sitting is hard anyway, what with my ornery ol' back, but sitting on the ground is about to do me in."

Vassar was quick to acknowledge. "I think we've been avoiding the inevitable. It seems to me our only option is a snow cave—unless this storm abates."

"I agree, but if it's going to let up, it needs to do it in the next couple of hours. Otherwise we won't have time to do what we need to do before it gets dark."

They rehearsed their course of action. In theory, they were prepared. But reading about snow caves and watching a couple of videos online were a far cry from what they were getting ready to attempt.

As luck would have it, there was a slope of snow adjacent to their sheltering tree. Judging by the terrain, there was plenty of snow to accommodate their project. Just to be certain though, Vassar cut a sapling about twelve feet long, skinned the branches off of it with his knife, and probed the snow bank for depth and density.

They had felt like fools carrying a snow shovel, and royal fools for packing a saw, but right now they considered themselves geniuses for their foresight. Much to their satisfaction, once they dug down several feet, the snow was densely packed. Vassar worked the shovel while

Hank wielded the saw.

They dug a vertical face about five feet deep in the slope, then began cutting, carving, and shoveling a tunnel from the face perpendicular into the snow bank. When the tunnel was four feet long, they began digging upward at a forty-five degree angle to form the roof of the cave. Taking turns, they formed a domed room with body-length benches on either side. In between the benches, just as they had studied in books and seen on the Internet, they left a trough for ingress and egress, gear storage, and for the cold air to settle into. Hank took special care to smooth the dome of the roof to prevent dripping. In the confined space, their body heat was already warming the interior; lighting a candle would create another four or five degrees of heat. Ultimately, it would be a balmy forty degrees inside their cave, according to the man on the video.

While Hank perfected the ceiling, Vassar took special pains to create vents. He discovered the ceiling was nearly three feet thick when he poked through it with a hiking pole.

It could snow all it wanted now. Apart from making them late to the waterfall, they were safe.

The Henderson brothers were proud of themselves. How many Texans had ever built a snow cave? And their effort was not wasted. The storm raged.

By late afternoon, the brothers were guessing the snowfall to be approximately two feet, maybe as much as three. Neither had ever seen anything like it and wondered if they were engulfed in some sort of record-setting weather event. They ate an early dinner and replenished their water supply with melted snow.

Reassured that their vent holes were working well as attested to by the health of their candle's flame, they broke out their sleeping pads, bags, and bivy sacks. Even though they didn't need the bivy sacks, they decided to use them for good measure just in case a drip should occur over them.

Having taken special pride in the interior appointments he created inside the cave, Hank was chagrined to discover his sleeping bench would work better if it were longer. He could make do, but he would be happier with another foot of real estate, especially if this was going to be home for a few days. Besides, what else did he have to do?

While he was at it, he lengthened Vassar's bench too, carefully carving and shaping. Vassar was occupied studying the vent holes. With such a heavy rate of snowfall, he was opening them every hour or so. He knew they had to be diligent to avoid a potential buildup of carbon monoxide.

Vassar insisted he and Hank stick their heads out the entrance of the tunnel periodically to get a breath of fresh air. Hank thought Vassar was obsessing, but since he didn't know any more about carbon monoxide than his Brother, he complied and crawled out for his turn in the snowy air.

After a couple of minutes with his head stuck out of the cave, appearing like a turtle with his head out of his shell, Hank crawled backward and Vassar took his place with his head protruding into the great outdoors. Hank, meanwhile, went back to tinkering with his shovel at the back of the cave.

"Well, whatever space we've got now is all we're going to get. Look here."

Vassar peered over his Brother's shoulder at bare earth. "I'll be. I didn't expect to see dirt. I'd say we judged the size of our cave about right, wouldn't you?"

"I'd say we did," Hank said, settling back onto his sleeping shelf. "Think we ought to go into the business?"

"Oh, probably not. Not right away anyway," Vassar said, going along. "Further study is needed, some market research, perhaps a focus group."

"We ought to form a committee," Hank said, baiting his Brother.

"Right. An exploratory committee. I know a guy in Louisiana who could chair it."

"Well, if anybody would know about snow caves, it would be a guy in Louisiana," Hank mused.

Still staring at the sight of black earth inside their dome of white, the brothers let their banter rest. The evidence was there, but both found it hard to figure how they had dug deeply enough to reach dirt. The measurements didn't add up to this exposed ground. But, it was only dirt; hardly worth spending too much time contemplating. It was odd though.

As bad as they hated to do it, just before bedtime they crawled out into the howling rage of the storm to relieve themselves. The blizzard was disorienting—disarmingly so—especially in the dark. Had it not been for gravity keeping them upright, there were no other visible indicators to orient them.

Hank experienced a brief panic when he turned to go back to the cave—not more than six feet away—but couldn't locate the entrance and couldn't see his tracks. After four or five steps in the direction he thought correct, he was relieved to see the faint glow of the candle illuminating the mouth of the tunnel.

He called to Vassar. Heard nothing. Called again, louder. Waited. Listened. Screamed. The shrieking wind snatched his voice into the storm's surge. Making certain of his bearings from the doorway, Hank ventured a few steps. Called out. Foreboding rose up, summoned by fear that his Brother was lost in the storm. Enough time had lapsed for Vassar to be beyond his voice if he happened to head in the wrong direction. And in these conditions....

Hank scrambled back into the cave, scattered his belongings as he frantically groped for his headlamp. Seizing it, he clicked it on, wrapped the strap tightly around this hand, and crawled quickly back into the maelstrom. Terror gripped him, closed his throat, froze his heart.

He shined his light at varying angles, trying to pierce the confusion. He called again—and again—into the turbulence and terrible cold. He felt himself descending into despair, sucked under by the overwhelming whirl that had dumped snow on them for the last ten hours. His composure turned to anarchy and his confidence to havoc as he reeled in circles calling for Vassar.

He stood midst the pandemonium, holding hope by a fraying gossamer thread. *If Vassar had provisions he could bivouac until daylight, but he has nothing—nothing to survive this chaos.* He hadn't taken his gloves, hadn't donned his wind pants, or bothered to layer his clothing.

It was a simple task. Nature's call. A routine necessity before bed. How could something so innocuous, so human, have turned into this grave danger?

Hank pled for mercy on behalf of his Brother. Prayed, but in panic was drawn toward the familiar conviction that his petulant God didn't give a damn about him or his concerns.

If anything is to be done, it's up to me to figure it out. It was the voice of Jester, taking advantage of the circumstance to accuse God, impugn God, and cast aspersion on His character.

Even though he'd made remarkable progress in building new patterns of belief about his Father, the High King, Hank remained susceptible to Jester's onslaughts, especially when sharpened by circumstantial evidence and emotional riot. He abandoned his prayers and turned his soul to reassess his meager options.

Caked with the brunt of the storm's fury, Vassar appeared like an apparition through the bedlam toward Hank's headlamp, running the last steps. He clung to Hank, wrapped in his Brother's embrace. They sobbed with relief that they were spared in their terrifying brush with natural elements monstrously greater than their humanity.

Without a word, Hank began dusting the snow off his Brother. It was pointless effort in practicality, but not to his heart. For that deep part of his psyche, the activity was cathartic, greater than any words or comfort.

They crawled back into the reverie of their cave and went silently about their individual business. They repeated the bedtime ritual they had done the night before, except they left their boots on the snow shelf rather than sleeping with them. Just before scooting into his sleeping bag, Vassar said, "I knew you wouldn't give up on me, knew you'd be there. Thanks."

Hank smiled at Vassar, nodded, and slipped down into his bag—out of sight—and zipped himself into his down cocoon, hidden and alone with his tears of relief, his doubtful faith, the shame of his distrust, and more fully aware than ever before of his deep, abiding love for Vassar.

Saying a blessing over his Brother and checking to be certain he knew where his flashlight was, Vassar snuffed the candle and wriggled into his sleeping bag. Outside, fueled by convection, moisture, and Canadian cold the storm intensified into a more boisterous gale. Branches broke, trees fell, and the wind moaned over the land as if enraged by some offense.

CHAPTER 4

The Snow Cave

Hank awoke, lying on his left side—the only side his temperamental back would let him sleep on—his head still inside his sleeping bag. *I shouldn't have my head inside my bag—all the moisture from my breath…the risk of cold spots.* Still, after Vassar's close call, he wasn't ready to stick his face out. Right now, he felt safer delineating his world as narrowly as possible.

He heard scratching. *Vassar,* he thought—*clearing the vent holes.* Even through four feet of snow insulating the roof of the cave, Hank could hear the storm rampaging in the Absaroka. The scratching stopped and started. *He's having a hard time. No surprise! It's a wonder the vent holes are still open at all given the mayhem out there.*

Hank tried to shut his mind off, but without success. Apparently his subconscious had been working while his conscious slept. All the things that drove him into the sanctuary of his sleeping bag were still front and center. He mulled upon these in the dark warmth, knees pulled up, hands tucked securely under his chin. In his fetal position, Hank worked through the outstanding issues.

The passage of time in a dark place is mysterious unless there is a clock to stare at. Although his watch was on his wrist, Hank didn't look at it. He pulled his knees closer, sinking deeper into his thoughts while the storm yowled around the cave. The intermittent scratching continued.

It occurred to Hank, somewhere in the night, that the scratching had gone on too long—too long at least for him to remain entombed in his bag while Vassar struggled to keep the cave vented. He felt guilty for not taking his turn poking the vent holes open. He rolled over, found the cord lock cinching his sleeping bag closed, loosened it, and stuck his face out into the black cold.

"You need help, Vassar?"

"Shh!"

Hank's senses went on alert. Lying perfectly still, hyper-attuned to his surroundings, he feverishly segmented the data feeding into his awareness. The scratching wasn't coming from the roof of the cave but the back of the cave.

Hank ran through his inventory of options. It didn't take long. Apart from his bare hands, the only thing remotely close to a weapon was his ice axe. *Where is it? Where did I leave it?* He mentally retraced his steps from earlier in the evening. *It's against the back wall—I think. Out of reach.*

The digging and scraping were far too heavy for a rodent or squirrel, or for that matter, a badger. *It can't be a bear—can it? Did we disturb a hibernating bruin, a sow with a newborn cub? What a nightmare!*

There is nothing more dangerous than a sow bear with a cub. The thought of mixing it up with a mad mamma in the confines of their cave—whacking at such a beast in the dark with a hiking stick, or even an ice axe—was a grim consideration. But the scratching had a metallic sound. *Perhaps the question isn't, what, but who?* he thought.

Fear and darkness are powerful when cloaked together. Hank thought of the dwarves in Tolkien's trilogy who were miners. In their greed, they dug too deeply into the center of the Earth and angered a demonic, dragon-like Balrog.

He tried to expel the notion. *Those are fantasies,* he thought. *There's no such thing as a Balrog!* For the most part his chiding dispelled the imagined ill—for the most part.

In his fearful scramble to construct a worst-case scenario, even the fantasy of a Balrog on the other side of the wall lurked as a possibility. He felt foolish harboring this irrational twist, but rather than dismiss the fear, he accommodated the consideration—to form a stronger plan of action. At least that's what he told himself, as he sat in the dark with his fears, listening. The digging progressed—toward them.

While he was still sitting in his sleeping bag—prudence would have retrieved his ice axe, or gotten out of bed, dressed, and at least been ready to run—the back of their cave fell onto the floor and a light shone through a hole the size of a basketball. The blade of a shovel carved and scraped the hole larger, energized by the breakthrough.

Too stunned to know what else to do, Vassar and Hank leaned over from their sleeping platforms, watching the hole grow in circumference. It was too late to intervene or take evasive action. The light increased and decreased as the shadowy form of the digger's body came and went with each expulsion of dirt onto the floor of their cave.

Eerie, dull light reached into the cave. Vassar and Hank mustered sufficient focus to crawl to their knees and lean against the back wall of their dome, hidden in deep shadow, awaiting their intruder with ice axes poised to impale whoever—whatever—was about to discover he was not alone.

Hank's heart beat furiously, a reverberating throb he was certain must be audible. But he was helpless to silence the rhythmic thumping or quell the adrenaline quiver in his hands. He slowly inhaled, no wheezing sound—exhaled obliquely into the back wall. Four seconds in, four seconds out. Again. No sound. *Perhaps with the element of surprise Vassar and I can overcome.*

A careful hand holding a candle reached into their space followed shortly by a left hand, knife at the ready—blade down, point forward. Stopped short.

He's considering the view he's dug into, Hank thought, the head of his axe poised.

"Well, I'll be!" the digger mutter aloud. "Vassar? Hank?"

Vassar switched on his headlamp and leaned over. The crooked nose scrunched up and withdrew from the blinding beam.

"Faith!" Hank exclaimed. "Vassar, it's Faith."

Vassar turned his light from Faith's eyes and watched as their distinguished friend crawled adroitly through the opening, knife still in hand, to be greeted by Hank's waiting arms. Unlike the first time they met, Hank had no doubts about this warrior whom he counted as a close friend. He let go, but only with one arm, turning him to face Vassar. "Look here, Vassar. Can you believe it?" Hank didn't allow room for Vassar to answer. "I can't believe it, but here he is. Right here. Faith. I'll be! How'd you find us?"

Vassar was shaking Faith's hand, sitting on the edge of his platform.

"You sure gave us a scare," Hank stated. "We were ready to impale you!" Hank held his ice axe at a menacing angle.

Faith struck the familiar, incredulous stance. "Hmph! All you would have done is made me mad!"

"We could have taken you," Hank stated. Staring. Striking an imposing posture. Then he broke down laughing, relieved that the tension was alleviated.

Faith put his arm around Hank's shoulder and turned him toward the hole in the back wall of the snow cave. "Check it out."

There, his face illuminated with light from their headlamps, was Love looking into the snow cave, a monstrous smile creasing his cheeks and surrounding his eyes. He struggled to get through the opening. Hank had forgotten how formidable a figure Love was. He was a third again wider than Faith, a walking tree-trunk-of-a-man, and solid as oak.

Sticking his head through the hole, Hope eyed the forest of legs and thought better of trying to crawl into the confined place. "I'll save my greetings for when there's more room," he stated.

Squeezed together in the tiny, domed room, with the fifth member of their number poking his head through the hole they had dug, the men picked up their relationships as though they'd never been apart.

Later, as Hank thought back on the reunion, it was as if their communication and unspoken understanding had grown substantially from what he remembered. He wondered if this was part of the solidification his Father had done. He was all but certain the indwelling Magician had something to do with the progress.

He knew Magician never missed a chance to advocate for his perspective. He wasn't heavy-handed, but with gentle persistence offered thoughts endowed with rich wisdom. He had proven himself a tremendous comfort, strength, and guide. Most of the time he offered his viewpoint telepathically with simple thoughts that could easily be mistaken as just that—simple thoughts—instead of profound guidance.

The conversation and catching up had been going on for some time when Hank realized he was shivering and standing sock-footed on the snowy floor of their cave. He began rummaging around in his pack for fresh socks. He thought he'd put them in a side pocket only to discover that in his haste to go to bed he'd put them in the top pocket with his wind shell.

Seeing what Hank was doing, Love said, nodding toward the hole at the back of the cave, "You know. The High King sent us to find you. Through that hole, just like when you crossed behind the waterfall on Malden Creek, the weather is different, and the time is different. No sense putting on fresh socks or getting dressed up in all these fancy clothes just to take them off again."

Hank had not contemplated that the hole in the wall was an invitation, his opportunity to continue the adventure begun two years ago. He wouldn't have to strap his crampons on and work his way behind the frozen splendor of Malden Creek Falls after all. Rather, his entry into the spiritual realm had been hewn out by Faith, affirmed by Love, joined by Hope, and awaited only his nod to proceed.

Hank stared at the opening, oblivious again to the wet cold seeping up through his socks. It was one thing to reflect upon his last adventure. But it was altogether a different matter to willfully crawl through this hole into the dull light beyond.

Knowing it was Hank's manner to ponder, the other four afforded him the time and quiet moments to contemplate what was before him. Hank looked at the hole, heard behind him the scurry of tormented snow, looked up at the ceiling, then down at his numbing feet, and back at the hole. He heard a thoughtful whisper, *If you thought it was hard the last time, just wait*, and recognized the circumstantial insinuation of Jester. Quickly, almost simultaneously, he heard in his mind's thinking, juxtaposed to Jester's threat, *Through there is where I belong. The desire of my heart lies beyond that opening.* It was the counter-perspective, Magician's trademark fidelity to speak guidance from Hank's heart into his mind.

Jester's temptation and Magician's affirmation collided in Hank's soul. Stress ebbed and flowed in him. Tension. Angst. He was ecstatic to rejoin Faith, Hope, and Love. He was tender and bruised from his losing bout with doubt.

Sitting with their hands folded in their laps, Faith, Love, and Vassar waited politely. Hope did the same on the other side of the hole. Hank looked around, assessing both friends and his Brother. "How long have I been standing here?"

"Doesn't matter," said Faith. "We've got nothing but time. Only thing that's important is what you've decided to do."

"I want to go with you all, through the way you've made, Faith. I'm destined to live on the other side." It was not a timid declaration, like so many of the fainthearted decisions he'd made when he was learning the ways of a warrior.

"Alright then!" Love exclaimed. "Let's do this." He eased past Hank, squatted, and crawled back through the opening where Hope waited. Vassar went next, followed by Faith. Hank looked around the snow cave. He placed his dry pair of socks on his sleeping bag, dropped to his knees, felt the labor of his back muscles, thought, *Magician, live through me, please*, and crawled through the hole.

Hank was greeted by four pairs of feet and knees, his three friends and Brother all squatting inside a rock alcove illuminated with a candle. Before he was fully through the hole, Faith crab-walked in front of him and into an adjoining passage. Love motioned for Hank to follow.

He crawled along on his hands and toes, more or less blind in the growing darkness, following the shuffling sounds of Faith. Within ten meters, a dull light guided him into a grotto festooned with decorous stalactites hanging from the ceiling as though remnants from a prehistoric birthday party. Careful to mind his head, Hank stood up, marveling at the enchanted room.

Once Vassar, Hope, and Love joined them, Faith explained that the next passage was wet, which Hank thought was reasonable for a cave, but then he noticed Love was undressing. *Oh! It's that kind of wet.* Just then, Faith handed him an oil cloth to wrap his clothes in.

He emulated Love's wrapping and bundling and tying, looking finally at his impromptu mentor for confirmation that he wouldn't be disappointed on the other side. "Hold the cloth like this," Love demonstrated, with the closure facing down to keep the water out. "Just don't let go."

Their clothes bundled, the five naked and shivering cavers waded into deepening water. It wasn't as cold as Hank expected. Still, he paid close attention to his stiffening back as the water rose to mid-torso, then to his chest, and up to his throat. His clothes bag snagged against the ceiling and he nearly dropped it, but he clamped his fingers deeper into the oiled fabric.

Ahead of him, Faith ducked under water, his bundle disappearing after him. Then, Faith's hand rose out of the water and summoned Hank to follow.

You've got to be joking! he thought. Hank took a deep breath, held onto his bundle of clothing, and used his other hand to protect his head as he went under water and felt the rock above him. *Who was the first person to do this?* Hank thought, as he submerged into the unknown behind Faith. He was under less than five seconds. Faith's hand grasped his, pulling him above water.

"Your Father told us about this passage when he sent us to find you and Vassar. I didn't know it existed," Faith said, as he and Hank scrambled out of the water onto an expansive rock shelf.

There's my answer, Hank realized. *Father! Only he would know about something like this.* "What'd you think when you first had to duck under that rock?" Hank said to Faith, as they watched the others make their way out of the water.

"Well, the King warned us ahead of time. Said when we got to this shelf," Faith motioned to the surrounding area, "we should line ourselves up with that stalagmite there and that stalactite hanging there." Hank eyed the angle Faith pointed out. "We'd never have known you could go beyond this pool if your Father hadn't given us directions. He's mighty particular about you and your Brother. Obviously, he's taken every precaution to be sure you're safe and make the transition back into this realm without incident."

"Without incident!" Vassar exclaimed, as he tossed his bundle of clothes onto the rocks and pulled himself out of the water. "To begin with, I have the ride of my life on that snowmobile. Then, I break through the ice and fall into Malden Creek. Then, a blizzard unlike any other sets in and my Brother and I have to figure out how to build a snow cave." Vassar looked at Faith, gesturing toward him. "You scare us half-out of our wits digging into our bedroom like a giant mole. And now, here I am, naked, after swimming through an underwater passage! Thus far, the trip has not been without incident. Oh! And I got lost in the snow too. Nearly died."

"Now see here, Prince," Faith began in mock defense. "I'm just following orders." The banter continued as they unbundled their clothes.

"Dry as a bone!" Hank exclaimed, elated and proud of himself. He put his socks on the rock and sat down on them as he began pulling on his long underwear. With his underwear bottoms pulled up around his thighs, Hank stood up, tugging at the recalcitrant fabric gripping his moist skin.

"Wait. Hold on just a minute," Love said.

Hank hadn't noticed that Love had disappeared. He was too amused by Vassar and Faith's repartee.

"I bet you'll recognize these things," Love said, placing a tarpaulin-wrapped package down on the rock.

With his long underwear halfway on and Vassar still trying to get dried off, Hank and his Brother watched Love and Hope unwrap the tarp. There—cleaned, folded, and adorned with a note—were their clothes, the clothes they wore during their first adventure into Gnarled Wood.

Hank waddled over, his underwear around his knees, and picked up the note written in his Father's familiar hand:

> Vassar and Hank—
> I'm glad you are here. Can't wait to see you!
> I love you both,
> Papa—

"It's from Papa," Hank said, handing the note to Vassar.

It was as though he had only taken these clothes off the night before. Without hesitation, Hank dressed and pulled on the splendid, handmade boots. He'd forgotten just how wonderful their fit was around his oddly-shaped feet. *These are a real pleasure,* he thought, standing up and looking down at the boots.

Vassar chuckled at his Brother.

"What are you laughing at?" Hank inquired.

"I was just remembering the first time you got dressed in those clothes."

Hank laughed. *Indeed. The first time—the last time—Vassar brought me to this world, I was stunned and confused, disoriented by the medieval world, the lurking evil, and the notion of my Father being the King and the armed guard being his troops.*

"You must have turned around fourteen times before you finally got dressed," Vassar stated.

"At least fourteen," Hank confirmed.

"Mustn't go without these," Faith said, holding their daggers, one in each hand.

Hank reverentially took his weapon, tears puddling in his eyes before spilling over onto his cheeks. *Father's gift to me. It's more spectacular than I remember.* He looked at the crest and his initials. He held the blade in the light, noting each mark and recalling the battle that scarred the blade. He felt the grip and worked his fingers around the leather. He eased his grasp and noted the balance of the custom-made knife. *It feels good—feels at home in my hand.* Deftly, ceremoniously, he strapped the dagger to his side and tightened his belt, tucking the loose end of the leather down through the waistband.

Stretching out his arms to form a cross, Hank clinched his fists and turned his face upward. *It's great to be back!*

CHAPTER 5

The Cave

In a blind hole behind a stalagmite, they stashed their modern clothing, bundled in the oil cloths, and followed Faith down a long, circuitous corridor of narrow walls and a high ceiling. Every so often, Faith stopped to be certain they were all together.

They came to an open area with several passages branching off in a variety of angles. Faith didn't hesitate. After walking some distance, they passed through another intersection of passageways and ante rooms. Again, Faith didn't hesitate. At the third intersection, larger than the others, Faith looked, nodded, and made his choice. He crossed, stopped, and turned around.

"There are three of these intersections," Faith said. "So, this is the last one. You find your way using the combination: 63-41-52." Standing in the threshold of his chosen passage, Faith counted the passageways clockwise from his left. "So that's one, there's two, three, four, five, and this one here is six. We came from there." He pointed to the third opening.

"If you will recall," Love chimed in, "the last intersection had four corridors. We came out of number one and turned right."

"Ah, I get it," Hank said.

"Good. Good," Faith encouraged. "Remember now, 63-41-52."

63-41-52. 63-41-52. Hank rehearsed the combination as they kept moving.

The ceiling got lower, much lower. They bent over, crawled across ledges, and over outcrops coming eventually to a gathering place where Faith stopped. "When you stop here, turn to face that seam in the wall. From that direction," he pointed as he continued, "move that way, or about 300 degrees from the seam in the rock." They all faced the seam and calculated where 300 degrees was on the face of an imaginary compass.

"OK. We ready boys?" Faith looked at each of his nodding compatriots. "We've got a little climbing to do before we get out of here. I'll go first. Hank?"

"Right behind you," Hank said.

"Good. Vassar? Hope? Love?" They agreed.

Bracing his feet against a succession of rocks, Faith climbed a steep incline and stood up, leaving only his ankles visible. Hank followed closely, stopping when he could see Faith staring up a formation of rock that looked like the inside of a chimney.

"What's that smell?" Hank wanted to know.

"Guano," Faith replied. "Bat poop."

Bat poop, Hank thought, letting the realization settle. The smell was strong. *Must be lots of it. Great. We're going to climb through this crap and get it all over us.* Then it dawned on him: "Hey Faith, where are the bats?"

"They roost here in the daytime. I doubt they're here now. Probably out hunting for dinner, or I guess it's more like lunch time for them."

"What if they're not all gone?" Hank asked.

"Oh, they'll just fly around. I mean, they'll brush up against you sometimes, but they won't hurt you. Just stay focused and keep climbing. They're not going to run into you."

"Yeah. They've got that echolocation thing going on, don't they?"

"Beats me," Faith said. "All I know is the King said they wouldn't bother me. They didn't and I didn't them. Worked just like he said, but they're weird little guys. When we came down, they were all piled in here on top of one another, thick as flies. You could hear them breathing, and everyone of them was hanging upside down."

"We've got bats at home. They say they eat a huge number of mosquitoes each night."

"More power to 'em," Faith said. "They can eat mosquitoes 'til their heart's content for all I care. Those little buggers chew me up something awful."

Faith pointed to the rope coil and the course of the rope against the wall. "I placed the tail of the rope with these specific bends. If anyone messed with the rope, in all likelihood these kinks and coils would not be like I left them."

Satisfied the line was undisturbed, Faith handed two pieces of rope to Hank, each about two-feet in length and less than half the diameter of the hanging rope. Following Faith's lead, Hank made a loop of each segment by tying the ends together with a square knot secured with half hitches.

Seeing the inevitable, Hank said, "You know, we free-rappelled into a cave years ago. It was a sixty-foot rappel."

"That's a great rappel!" Faith enthused.

"Yeah. It really was. We Prusik climbed back out."

"Harder getting out than it was getting in, wasn't it?"

"That's an understatement," Hank said. "So, tell me about this climb."

"Well, you chimney climb maybe eight or ten feet and then it opens up, wide enough that you can't chimney any longer."

"And that's where the Prusik knots come into the picture," Hank said.

"Right. Let me get to the top. I'll check things out and let you know when it's okay to start up."

Hank watched as Faith tucked the loops of line up through his belt so they were ready when he needed them. Lowering his voice to a whisper, Hank asked, "Faith, where are we going?"

"My goodness," he declared. "We're going to meet your Father, of course!"

Hank felt his face flush at what Faith believed obvious, but was certain Faith couldn't see the redness in the dim light. "And Father planned this route for us?"

"He did." And speaking casually to Hank's implied hesitancy, "There is an easier path out, and it is more direct, but you know your Father. He has a penchant for the way less traveled."

His Father's inefficiency amused Hank...most of the time. Then there were times like this, when his inefficiency was an irritant, mainly because it begged, "Why?" within Hank's analytical and strategic mind. "Why?" It felt linked to distrust. *I don't like that*, he thought. *Still. One has to wonder—or at least, I wonder—why?*

Putting his back and palms against one side of the rock chimney, Faith put his feet more or less at ninety degrees to his torso and began squirming-wriggling-inching his way with progressive wedges of his body and legs against the opposing sides of the vertical passage. Hank had tried this before. Faith made it look deceptively easy.

"Okay. I'm clear," Faith spoke down in a soft voice after a few minutes.

Checking to be certain his rope loops were secure in his belt, Hank emulated Faith's chimney-climbing technique. His effort was anything but smooth or graceful. He huffed and grunted, noting the gouges to his back and palms but not daring to lose his focus.

Where the chimney widened, Hank braced himself, using his legs to press his back against the rock. Grabbing his first coil of rope, Hank quickly made three turns around the climbing rope with the smaller rope, then put it inside itself to form a bite. He tightened the coils around the static line, making certain the turns lay neatly against one another, and repeated the process with the second loop. He slid the lower Prusik down until he could get a foot into the fixed loop, the beauty of the friction knot being that it slid easily until loaded with weight.

Sweating now, Hank feverishly but carefully secured his weight onto the first loop. Grasping the climbing rope, he pulled himself into a standing position. He held on and took a few deep breaths, recovering from his isometric sitting.

Hooking his elbow around the climbing rope, Hank adjusted the second Prusik. He put his other foot into the second loop, moved the knot upward until his knee was bent ninety degrees, and added weight. The knot bit into the static line and held. Squatting on the top loop while working the bite loose in the lower knot, he slid the loosened Prusik up the rope until the two knots were close together. Putting all his weight again on the lower loop, he loosened and slid the top Prusik up the climbing rope until his knee was at ninety degrees. He gingerly added weight until the knot bit decisively and began loosening the lower Prusik. Thus, he continued his ascent.

His knees shaking and his arms burning with fatigue, Hank scrambled up beside Faith who helped loosen the Prusik knots. "Nicely done, my man. Nicely done," Faith said.

The Castle and its Round Tower

Letizia Pintaro swore under her breath as she returned to the Round Tower from a midday appointment. Summer was her least favorite season, and her disdain was exacerbated today by the breeze. It only intensified the heat, and as the currents bent around the imposing edifice of the Round Tower and were forced through the confines of the castle buildings, the wind mussed her hair and pressed her clothes against her body. She didn't like hair in her face, let alone her mouth, and her dress wilted against her damp skin. Her job in the Round Tower required a professional decorum—that she be unremarkable, understated. Letizia dressed the part, but the wind pressed the fabric close, revealing a body endowed with enviable femininity. She felt exposed, noticed, by women and men alike as she moved deliberately toward the gates.

As soon as she passed under the last portcullis, Letizia ducked into a first-floor office, borrowed the key to the washroom, and stepped inside to compose herself. Glaring at her disheveled self in the mirror, she felt as though the wind had touched her with a thousand fingers. She took a deep breath and splashed water onto her face from the wash basin. She dried her face, then brushed the tangles from her hair, and retied the hair knot in her thick waves. She straightened her dress, running her hands over her curves as if to press the fabric by friction.

In the quiet of the water closet, Letizia composed her thoughts. *As soon as I step into the Tower, I need to be focused. Sharp.*

Although the Round Tower ran at a languid pace, Letizia didn't, and neither did her boss, Ennui. While appearing placid, Ennui was a torrent of determined shrewdness. As Ennui's closest, most-trusted, and most-relied-upon associate, Letizia consistently distinguished herself, not only for her efficiency, but for her similarity to her boss in thought and skill. Those close to both were of the opinion that Letizia was even keener and more cunning than Ennui.

Apart from being ruffled by the humid heat and unruly wind, she demonstrated remarkable control and wit. The more tangled the problem, and the higher the stakes, the more Letizia demonstrated herself a person in possession of extraordinary composure. Truth be known, others' appreciation of her physique and beauty distracted them from noticing her savvy intelligence. By the time they comprehended that they had been outsmarted, Letizia was well insulated from them. Nothing was traceable to her. That influential forces guided the in-house working of the Tower was evident to anyone with an ounce of curiosity, but that Letizia was behind these initiatives would be a dramatic revelation.

Occasionally someone assembled clues from across a spectrum of events and pointed their accusing finger at Ennui's office, but Letizia was rarely singled out. She came and went through side passages, didn't talk after work, and even stayed tight-lipped when having drinks with friends. She never flinched, self-promoted, or tipped her hand. For the little bit of desperation Ennui demonstrated upon occasion, Letizia showed next-to-none.

Letizia's staff said she had ice water in her veins. She heard the scuttlebutt and took it as a compliment. After all, a mistake could cost her life.

She had a select group of people she felt comfortable around, not because she could be herself, but because they didn't press to know what she did and with whom she worked. A few knew she worked in affiliation with Ennui's office, but assumed her job was classified.

What few knew was that Ennui worked for Zophos, the sworn enemy of the High King whose name the Round Tower proclaimed as their monarch. Yet not only did she come and go inside the Round Tower, she was considered one of its most powerful, respected, and venerated leaders.

Ennui and Letizia both knew the near-unchecked power Ennui granted Letizia was for Ennui's plausible deniability. The stakes were high. With the singular importance of the Round Tower to the High King, and thereby to Zophos, a mistake of any magnitude involving the Tower would mean a summons to Zophos' lair.

Letizia was privy to a few such summonses. Few returned, and the ones who did were never the same.

But she was wedded to power and hooked on the intrigue. While aspects of Ennui's job called for public glitz and visibility, Letizia was a shadow. She did oversee a credible office in the Tower that managed programming and coordinated initiatives. But she also ran a back office that enforced Zophos' projects. In this, she was invisible.

Letizia wore fine clothes, had help at home, ate at the best places, drank fine wine, and did so with powerful people. *Ennui makes public statements, and enjoys notoriety. She has veto power and Zophos' ear.* Letizia thought about these possessions of Ennui's, evaluating whether she wanted them for herself or not. She didn't dwell on the comparison long. *I control everything else.*

Ennui and Zophos didn't like each other, but had the utmost

respect for one another. Ennui and Letizia worked well together and communicated effectively. They balanced the interface between their front offices with exemplary management styles. Ennui knew of and understood the existence of Letizia's back rooms, but that was all she wanted to know.

They had the appearance of friendship, and spoke all the right words of affinity, but Letizia was never in doubt that Ennui was a ruthless governor. Too many times she had overseen one of Ennui's wishes, carried out an assignment that changed lives irrevocably, and done so witnessing no emotion in her boss.

Initially, Ennui checked up on Letizia after a clandestine job or unsavory assignment. But now—now Letizia had proven herself, and she had become powerful.

One can never be too careful. That was Letizia's mantra. No. It was more than that. It was her rule.

Ennui trusted Letizia, but Letizia didn't trust Ennui. As she honed her skills and deepened her contacts of those willing and able to carry out tasks off the record, Letizia accrued wealth, access, reputation, and most important, debtors—people beholden to her, people whom she had made, set up, rescued, and made all over again; people whose lives and lifestyle were attributable to one person: Letizia Pintaro.

She pursed her lips into a slight pucker as she scrutinized her image in the mirror. She took a breath, sucked her navel toward her spine, and pulled her shoulders back, enhancing her breasts. *Appropriate,* she thought, cognizant her allure worked to her advantage. She raised her chin slightly and prepared her mind to step from the sanctuary of the washroom into the public eye. A fleeting thought ran across her mind that she should empty her wash water into the chamber pot, but she thought otherwise. *There are people for that.*

Letizia moved discreetly through the labyrinthine corridors in the Round Tower. She knew the most familiar routes, but she opted for the less traveled. She'd been noticed enough for one day. And besides, *I have information to discuss with Ennui that mustn't wait.*

Ennui had endured dark rooms, more scary encounters than she could recall, and cautious informants—lower minions looking for cumshaw and favor—but now, she usually worked directly with the power brokers, typically in private meeting rooms, surrounded by other powerful people engrossed in their own deals. No one wasted her time, but when certain people—Letizia chief among them—suggested they meet, she knew they had something important for her.

Ennui was expecting her. The assistant waited momentarily at the door as she ushered Letizia into the office. Receiving no request from her superior, she closed Ennui's door and returned to her work station.

The two women spoke only briefly as they moved from the office to the more secure room where their confidential meetings occurred. Standing in the confines of the cloistered conference room, Letizia said, "Vassar is back."

Ennui raised her left eyebrow, only slightly, but enough to register concern. "Are you certain?"

"As certain as I can be at this juncture, but given my source, I think you can safely figure Vassar has returned."

Ennui put her left arm across her chest and rested her right elbow on it so her right hand could serve as a prop for her chin. "Anyone with him?"

"Yes. His Brother."

"Oh, yes. I've heard about him. What's his name?"

"Henry H. Henderson. Goes by, Hank. Lives in Fort Worth, Texas but has traveled into the spiritual world once before—a little over two years ago. Jester's people worked him over pretty hard. You know how the King likes to take the most unlikely people, pour heart and soul into them, and then believes they can perform at our level. Well, that's what he's done with Mr. Henderson. He showed some gumption when he was here last, but he's untested."

"Right, right. He is the man who murdered Significance. Correct?"

Ennui's precise speech, with nary a contraction, always struck Letizia as awkward, but that precision was part of Ennui's mystique.

"That's the man," Letizia confirmed.

"Okay. Put our special operators on notice. Vassar and his brother will turn up soon enough. They did not come here on holiday, so I am confident the King is beginning some sort of initiative. Keep me informed. In the meantime, I will visit with Zophos."

"I've already done exactly as you asked," Letizia said, with a wry smile. "I'll let you know as soon as I know anything."

Ennui looked blankly at Letizia. Her proficiency and anticipation didn't surprise her, but she was wary of Vassar and his customary companion, the Kingdom's Magician. She hated Vassar, and by association, anyone with him.

Letizia left through Ennui's private door.

On the sixth floor of the Round Tower, where the executive-level, administrative offices were located, the Committee of Twelve met with the incoming Chairman of the Tower, Mr. Pafford. As occurred in businesses located in the castle, Mr. Pafford rose through the Round Tower's ranks to its highest position, and as in other entities, it was expected he too would endeavor to secure his chair by surrounding himself with friends beholden to him and people to whom he owed favors. It was a reasonable balance of power.

Mr. Pafford outlined for the Committee his justification for the usual cleansing of higher ups and lower downs who had served in the previous administration. Nothing new about that—even though careers were ruined and lives wrecked. Their severance packages were thin at best, or if it could be arranged, nonexistent. This was for the higher good of the Tower, the new Chairman explained. And in accepted logic, he stated for the record, "The King understands these are difficult decisions for us who manage his affairs. He has his ways, which are higher than ours. He will care for those to whom he is indebted." Where Mr. Pafford was obligated by protocol, he followed suit, but where not he turned his discretion toward his personal priorities.

Mr. Pafford reconciled his responsibilities in concert with the power he sought, "…to effectively govern on behalf of the High King." He further justified what he portrayed as altruism with a general accounting of the money he said would be saved. "These budgeted funds, now stewarded by the fidelity of my management, should be reallocated for worthwhile projects in the Round Tower, beyond into the castle, and outward to the farthest reaches of Gnarled Wood."

The noble-sounding rhetoric was a customary touchstone of all those who had risen as he had. Everyone accepted that once Mr. Pafford served long enough, noteworthy projects throughout the Round Tower would bear his name in tribute. It was a perk of being Chairman.

Turning to implementation, Mr. Pafford spoke reverentially about the necessary dismissals and replacements of personnel. It was the culture of the Committee to care. "It is a justifiable sacrifice, an adjustment that we must make, for all that is good, decent, and of honorable repute," Mr. Pafford coached his trustees and directors. "Let us not shirk our responsibility, even though onerous, nor abandon our burden of leadership when heavy. Let us not grow weary in well doing or be faint of heart in securing the Round Tower. All else is subservient to advancing the High King's fame."

The longer-serving directors and staffers had seen and heard it all before. That Mr. Pafford was proving more thorough than his predecessors was an indicator they had chosen well.

As he explained to the Committee of Twelve, the personnel replacements were not because he felt threatened, but because he needed appropriate control. "I ask not for position. Rather, I am envious of the wisdom that is borne of placing loyal people at all levels, noble fellows at strategic interval to mollify or notify, especially in days such as these that circle us as wolves."

Mr. Pafford was nothing if not eloquent, and after a month as Chairman, his list of replacements was within the realm of acceptable. "After all," he reasoned further, "it is essential that the Round Tower be protected against subterfuge, foreign infringement, outside influence, and...."

He continued his rhetoric, almost in a harangue. To an outsider, his speech would have been strident and alarming. But not to the Committee. The threats Mr. Pafford named were abstract, but sufficient to approve his agenda. After all, he was sincere and they cared.

"It is my duty," Mr. Pafford declared, with passion and a clinched fist inside his opposing hand, "on behalf of the people, the Tower, the office, and the King to implement these essential adjustments. With this immediacy for action pressing upon us from without and within, I implore your affirmation of these ideals."

He didn't ask permission, per se. Rather, he informed. It was a subtle way—an effective way—of coercing the Committee. Coercion, of course, is not good—unless it works to your advantage and is your cultural norm. In the Round Tower, coercion and passionate caring were synonymous.

The Committee of Twelve nodded at the high moments and shook their heads at the low moments in their Chairman's speech. It never crossed anyone's mind to ask a question, or to consider if their actions aligned with their stated beliefs about the High King. They assumed and presumed the King's blessing aligned with their endeavors, oblivious to the leanness in their souls.

"In conclusion, I humbly submit to you, my trusted colleagues, this vision of the High King. These ideals, indicative of him, of his desires, and of the duty entrusted to me, are essential if I am to make him famous throughout the Kingdom."

When Mr. Pafford concluded, the Committee of Twelve approved by affirmation Mr. Pafford's measures and projects. In so doing, they avoided a formal motion, discussion, and the paper trail that would be otherwise recorded in Minutes of the Meeting. It was their culture to embrace responsibility lacking in culpability.

The lives of those let go went from secure to tenuous in the space of a short meeting lacking a written record. They came to work confident—and left demoralized, entangled with anger they couldn't vent, and without sufficient words to describe to their spouses why they were replaced. Jester took up their offense and ranted against the High King upon the platform afforded him by the Chairman and the Committee of Twelve.

And so it was that the head of maintenance was fired and replaced with Mr. Pafford's nephew, a farmer by trade who knew little of building management.

Of course, Mr. Pafford didn't fire the man who had been head of maintenance for two decades. That job was assigned to an assistant with a young family. After completing the wretched task, the assistant left work early, retreated to his private quarters, and got blistering drunk—for three days. His wife was horrified and took the children to her Mother's. The alcohol didn't cure his shame, but it did afford the subordinate the necessary time to convince himself the misery inflicted came with the territory, both for the man ruined, and the man who delivered the ruination.

Everyone, from Mr. Pafford to the fired Maintenance Director, and all those in between, invoked the High King's name. One couldn't discern if the invocation was an expected motto or a meaningful declaration. To outside observers, the King, the Round Tower, and the King's people behaved no differently than their counterparts in the castle.

Mr. Pafford didn't directly hire his nephew either. That too was assigned—for purposes of protocol. The nephew was ecstatic to have the job—more accurately, his wife was happy to have a steady paycheck instead of the seasonal, weather-dependent, market-driven money of farming. But a near-blind man could see the doubt on the man's face when he was shown the Tower's mechanical rooms and was introduced to a staff he hadn't the faintest notion how to manage. He wasn't qualified. The man hiring him knew it. The nephew knew it. But he was hired. Everyone said it was the King's will.

While the hiring assignment was better than the firing assignment, the professional shame was similar. Both assistants carried out orders they knew were senseless in order to protect—and hopefully—advance their careers. Both attempted to rationalize their actions with the opaque reassurance that they were not directly responsible—they were just following orders. Both received directives and carried out orders attributed to the High King. But like the man who did the firing, the man who did the hiring left early, retreated to a bottle of liquid comfort, and passed out in a puddle of his own vomit.

A piece of each man's soul decayed.

And the King's name was made famous.

Mr. Pafford was grateful—grateful for everything. He was grateful to be Chairman, grateful to the Committee of Twelve for selecting him—never mind that he was now beholden to them; he was grateful for challenges, grateful for opportunities, grateful to know people and be known by people, and he was grateful that he finally had the position and power to accomplish all that the High King had put before him to achieve for the Round Tower.

Grateful.

Gratefulness was part of Round Tower lingo. Gratefulness was expected. The term could be tossed about like a talisman to charm the inhabitants of the Tower, or it could genuinely convey a thankful heart. It was hard to tell.

The High King's name was invoked at each meeting of the Committee of Twelve and attributed to their every action, even the nasty work required for Mr. Pafford to secure his Chairmanship. After all, the language of the Round Tower expected a generous sprinkling of "King" references in all communications, whether official or personal. It was the custom and fashion of the Round Tower.

For many, if not most, their notion of the High King ranged from a linguistic usage to myth. When it came to practical matters, mentioning the High King's name was a cultural courtesy, certainly not a relevant consideration.

Yes. The King was famous, famous in deed.

Chapter 6

The Cave

Vassar was the third man to climb the rope. Hope followed him, then Love. It was hard on him. With his stocky build, Love outweighed the next heaviest, Vassar, by at least sixty pounds. But "hard" is relative. Love climbed with agility, removed his Prusik knots, and immediately began retrieving the rope into large coils.

"From here, we need to pay closer attention," Faith began. "We will recon down this passage," he said, pointing behind him with his thumb, "reassemble, and be on our way to rendezvous with the King. It will be tricky, though. The passage narrows and is only wide enough for one at a time."

Hank understood, as they all did, that leading reconnaissance would isolate that man and leave him vulnerable. He quickly volunteered.

"I was about to ask you," Faith said. "But thanks for volunteering. I think you know this area better than any of us."

Hank thought that an odd comment, but didn't ask any questions. His mind was already in the passageway, mentally working through various scenarios, adrenaline again coursing through his veins. He felt his senses heighten and his heartbeat increase, but his focus remained on the black hole behind Faith's right shoulder.

Hank lowered his voice and ran through his plan for scouting the passage. This leadership quality—effectively communicating to everyone dependent upon him—was honed during his previous journey into the spiritual world, and now it rose, spontaneously recovered from his earlier, repetitive training. "I'll follow the passage until it opens up in an area suitable for us to regroup. I'll observe, check the area, and…." He paused, stumbling over what came next.

Faith came to his aid. "The passage is supposed to be thirty to thirty-five meters long. Our rope is forty meters. Why don't you take the end with you? We will pay out the line. Once you are ready for us, give it a tug. What do you think?"

Hank nodded, put his arm and neck through the bowline loop Hope had already tied, edged around Faith, and disappeared into the passageway.

Crawling on all fours, he worked his way blindly. He moved anything that might hurt hands and knees or make noise to the side of the passage. He kept his head down and his back arched, figuring it was better to have a dinged back than a bruised head.

He didn't know how long the crawl lasted. On the one hand, time stood still, on the other, it passed in fleeting seconds. The rope tightened around his chest and against his neck. *Is it hung, or am I at the end of my rope?* he thought, missing the pun entirely. The passage had seemed like an extended "S"—no hard turns. And it was smooth, as though an underground water source had denuded it of hazards and detritus. *Must be farther than Faith thought. I can't have them stacked up behind me.*

Hank backed up a few feet to create slack in the line, ducked out of the bowline, which he then untied. Working blind in the dark of his tight confines, he piled the end of the rope into a heap he couldn't miss upon his return and moved forward un-tethered.

A dusky light shone ahead. There was a pungent odor, familiar but unrecognized given all that was on his mind.

He was extra careful, expending minutes to cover the remaining few feet before stopping short of the passageway's conclusion. He thought about pulling his dagger, but couldn't quite figure out how to manage holding the dagger, crawling tri-pawed, and being quiet. It crossed his mind to hold the blade between his teeth, but he dismissed the idea. *I'd look like a pirate*, he thought. He didn't bother to ask himself who exactly would be looking. Old habits die hard, even irrational ones.

The passage concluded at an awkward angle. He lay on his left side against the rock wall, straining to see and hear.

He sensed something, but it was indiscernible. Whatever it was, it troubled Hank, not because it was undefined, but because it felt magnetically dangerous. Part of him counseled for heightened caution and part of him was compelled to toss caution aside.

There was certainly an element of curiosity—*What's out there?*—and there was an element of responsibility: *I can't report feeling like the enemy is waiting for us. They're counting on me to scout the area. I haven't finished my reconnaissance.*

But this magnetic pull was something other than curiosity or duty. He felt drawn.

Crawling out of the tunnel, he stood with his back against a stalagmite. It wasn't formed in the customary conical shape, but was like a fin, perhaps twenty feet long and equally as high.

Once standing, he slowly extracted his dagger from its sheath, taking his time lest the dagger hiss with anticipation. His left hand ran lightly along the surface of the rock as he side-stepped forward. His right hand gripped the dagger and held it point-forward across his body.

He stopped, shy of the edge of the fin. Listened. Nothing. He took a deep breath for a count of four. Exhaled for a count of four. Repeated, then peered around the corner.

"Oh, no," he murmured, horrified by betrayal. "No!"

His recognition was instant. He did know this area better than anyone else. *My pit. The place of my falling and failure—the last time I was in Gnarled Wood. It's the place of my humiliation. No wonder it smelled familiar,* he realized. "I thought I was done with this," he muttered. "Thought I overcame it."

He didn't recognize Jester's voice—disguised as his own thoughts—feeding him implications of disappointment, betrayal, and disillusionment. He adopted them as his own. He didn't recognize Jester's voice now any more than he had recognized his compelling counsel while lying in the passageway. Nor did he associate the counterpoints as coming from Magician.

Thinking himself isolated, Hank stumbled around the corner of the stalagmite. The room was familiar—too familiar. *I've been setup,* he thought. *Now I get it: I'm starting over again. I only thought I had made progress. It's all an illusion. The one place I didn't ever want to see again. But here I am. I can't do this.*

He walked another ten feet, arms at his sides, pulled toward the center of the pit like a moth to flame. His shoulders slumped, his face drained of blood; the adrenaline fled from his muscles and he dropped his dagger clattering against the rock floor. Before him, bathed in appeal and ambient hues lay a mat—the mat! His mat! *My mat! Just where I left it, where I abandoned it. The one possession I had in the pit, my one place of rest, the one thing I could count on, the only place that was truly mine.*

The mental game—Hank's thought processes—shifted, ostensibly to create advantage for himself, to turn his disillusionment to self-determination. Here was his opportunity to retrieve that which was abandoned and supplement what he possessed. *The mat will work under my blanket. I won't ever spend another night on the ground...if I take my mat with me. I can take care of myself. I know what's coming, that's for certain. I can use this. I need this.*

A quiet thought occurred to him: *I promised to take care of you. Forget the mat! Listen! You are vulnerable. Pay attention!*

I understand why I had to leave my mat—the last time, Hank thought. *But not now. Now, I'm stronger. I can manage my mat. I can carry it.*

Hank looked around. *They wouldn't have sent me here—alone—if I wasn't supposed to look after myself. Given the sorry, wretched back I've got, I truly need a mat.*

He missed—or ignored—Magician's observation that he had jettisoned his dagger in order to grasp the mat. In the fog of the moment, Hank failed to remember all the ways in which the High King provided for him, cared for him, and never left him. All he could focus upon was the mat, the symbol of his own provision. Even in this Hank was confused. In truth, he hadn't provided the mat for himself. It was the capricious enticement of his nemesis, Jester.

He knelt down, touched the woven fabric, felt its familiarity, and spread his hands along the mat's edges to its width. He cherished the selective recollection of his days looking out for himself, reconstructing (with Jester's subtle assistance) memories of his days on the mat more grandly than they were in actuality. Knowing it is human nature to soften the degree of pain and the magnitude of grief, Jester took advantage of Hank's dull memory.

While Jester suggested thoughts, emotion, and action to Hank— the kneeling, the touching, the jaded recollections—Magician counseled Hank, *I was naked, destitute, alone, wounded, angry. I was afraid when I was on this mat. No hope. No outlook. I was convinced I was unloved— when I was on this mat. I made a courageous decision to abandon this pitiful symbol of self-reliance for the pledge of my Father, the High King, to supply every provision I need. I have the history to prove he did exactly as he promised. I don't need this mat.*

But Hank didn't believe, or didn't accept, Magician's input. The rules had changed between his last experience in the pit and this one. He reversed his earlier conviction and believed his mat had acquired value and that he was capable of taking care of himself.

Hank's eyes and ears told him he was alone. Never mind the forces of light and darkness rummaging through his soul. The man who had eaten at his Father's table in the high places, who had fought gallantly alongside Faith, Hope, and Love—a Prince in the Kingdom—adopted the limited perspective of Jester colliding with circumstance and his five senses.

Kneeling, he rolled and unrolled the mat. He rolled it again and held it close, treasuring the belief—the budding conclusion—that it held promise. He put his face against the fibers and inhaled the musty odor. He unrolled it. Looked at it with affection. With the sudden intensity most evident in a mother's eyes, Hank rolled up the mat again and tucked it under his left arm. Then, he carefully examined the ground for any pebble or protrusion that might damage the fibers. Once satisfied, he carefully unrolled and replaced the mat exactly as it had been. He provided for that which was supposed to provide for him. The irony escaped him—but it wasn't lost upon either Jester or Magician.

Remembering his colleagues, Hank stood—too quickly. His back and hip tightened. The pain could have served Hank as a mentor. After all, it was close to this very piece of rock that Competence inflicted upon him the grievous wounds that plagued him. Instead, he cursed his mutinous muscles and misfortune to be so constantly afflicted, and with his curse resented that his Father, the High King, who purportedly had the power to heal was not good enough to do so for him.

This too was a familiar theme to Hank. Jester knew exactly which emotional account to deposit Hank's distrust of his Father into. Just as planned, Jester could see his momentum gaining within Hank's soul as his subject revisited his old ways of living.

Hank limped across the room rubbing his back, went around the finned stalagmite, crawled laboriously into the passage until he located the rope, pulled it tight, and gave the line a strong tug. He held the tension until he felt a corresponding pull. Dropping the line there, he scooted back out of the tunnel into the hallway formed by the stalagmite and went to where he could look into the pit and keep a watchful eye on his mat.

He waited. Love was first to emerge. Hank watched as Hope crawled out, followed shortly by Faith. Once out of the tunnel, Faith began retrieving the rope into coils.

"Where's Vassar?" Hank asked.

"I'm here, Brother." Vassar's voice came from behind him. Turning quickly, Hank saw Vassar step from the shadows of the pit holding his abandoned dagger.

Love, Hope, and Faith filed past Hank. They began checking the perimeter.

Hank turned from Vassar and walked into the deeper darkness afforded him by the stalagmite. Vassar let him nurse his shame in the depths while the others secured the area.

Vassar could have rebuked Hank, could have left him, could have called to him and told him to make his way out from the darkness. He could have lectured—could have done anything that suited him. Instead, Vassar went to his Brother in his ungracious place of guilt, embarrassment, vulnerability, and dishonor. He came to him from behind, turned him around, and put his arms around him. He didn't make a speech. He didn't breathe deeply and sigh, as if engaged in heavy lifting or as though to express unspoken displeasure. He held Hank close for a moment, then walked with him from behind the stalagmite to where the others waited in a semi-circle in front of the mat.

The fog of the battle lifted for Hank. He recalled, *I've seen this formation before. They're waiting on a decision from me. They want to know what to do next: stay by the mat or step into the light?*

Vassar placed Hank's dagger on the mat and then stood silently beside him. Hank looked at the blue blade. The leather grip bore the dark imprint of his hand's oil and sweat. The King's crest on the pommel refracted the light into glints of diamonds on the fibers of the mat.

After all this, and I'm nowhere. After all I've been through, all I've done, and I'm still in the pit. My progress—my victory, my achievements as a warrior—can be measured after all. I'm less than a foot from where I started! So much for the King's ability to transform me into a warrior of light. What has all my suffering and trust in the King gotten me? Jester's subterfuge was aggressive, convincing, and it was proving to be a withering assault. Hank's resources were low—the spasms before he left home, the snow cave, the distrust fomented by each. The light in his eye was dimming.

"Oh, crud! Shoot, fire!" Hope exclaimed, breaking rank suddenly.

"I told you guys you shouldn't put me in charge of this," he said, in the general direction of Love. Coming around the mat while fishing inside his jacket, Hope produced the scarlet sash Vassar gave to Hank during their previous trek through the pit. Hope tied the red belt around Hank's waist, then returned to his place between Faith and Love. "I hate it when that happens," Hope said, again in the general direction of Love who only smiled.

I can nurse my pride and mine the depths of shame for something of redeemable worth. I can make excuses and project blame. I can slither like a human reptile, hoping that in so doing my friends will grant me the sour comfort of their pity. Or, I can regroup—confess my weakness, own my failure, declare my tryst with the old ways of my past, my proficiency, and my personal worth. I can step into the light—I know how to do that!—and re-place myself again in the capable hands of Magician. I can put myself at the mercy of my fellows. After all, as my sash reminds me, I am a redeemed man!

Hank recognized the voice he ignored earlier. Bolstered by Magician's internal counsel, he rapidly assembled in retrospect the clues he had missed.

With a spit on the ground and an indignant huff, in a voice barely audible, Hank said, "Go to hell, Jester. I am a warrior in service to the King. You have taken advantage of me, caught me flat-footed. Not again, damn you! With the strength of Magician and the company of my friends, I renounce you!"

Hank looked up. Faith, Hope, and Love stood before him, his mat and dagger in between them. Vassar remained beside him.

Hank was shaken by how precipitously he fell from the confidence of being in league with great warriors, working together to accomplish a mission, only to opt for the hollow advisement of Jester. *And I haven't even arrived at the Round Tower yet,* he noted. To think, *I was so close to throwing everything away. How could I have been so...?* Hank heard the condemnation in the thought and follow-up, recognized Jester's persistent, brazen persuasion, and rejected another half-truth—for the second time in as many seconds!

Instead of languishing in conversational exchange with Jester, as though Jester were reasonable, honorable, or had his best interest in mind, Hank blurted out a disorganized confession, "I lost my bearings, guys! I'm sorry. I wasn't expecting to. Got caught—flat-footed. I bought it. Everything, all over again. I see it now. Clearly. That mat!" he declared, pointing. "I reject it. Reject all the hollow promises Jester says it holds. I know better." Hank looked at his Brother and three companions. "Is there any way you can forgive me for my failure? I'm so disappointed in myself."

"Brother, we knew this would happen. We discussed it." Vassar said. "You were forgiven before you ever failed. In fact, we expected a worse failure. We thought the chances were pretty high you would have a catastrophic wreck! And, we forgave you in advance."

Faith bent over and picked up Hank's dagger. He turned the handle toward Hank, extending the dagger across the mat, and said, "To be disappointed in yourself is to have depended upon yourself. Your reliance is on Magician and the High King. Besides, your Brother had your back—all the way."

This time the irony of the circumstance was not lost on Hank. He looked down at his mat, then reached out and grasped the handle of the dagger. For a moment, he and Faith held the knife simultaneously. Obviously, Faith had the sharp end, and the lethal weapon could cut him if not respected. But Hank realized he too had a formidable end of the dagger. Holding it was symbolic of his identity—a warrior of light, son of the High King, Brother of Vassar, dwelling place of Magician. Prince!

Faith released the blade. Hank looked at the dagger, then sheathed the weapon. He heard Jester laugh derisively in a dark recess, but chose instead to adjust the scarlet sash of redemption around his waist.

Vassar said, "Do we have any further business here?"

"Nope," said Faith, backing away from the mat.

"Not that I know of," Hope declared.

"Me either," said Love, scanning the small circle surrounding the mat.

There was a pause. And out from that pregnant moment, Hank declared, "I'm finished here as well. There isn't anything I need in this place."

"Very well," Vassar stated.

Straightening his shoulders and adjusting his belt, Vassar said, "Hope, you and Hank—you're point. Lead us out of here. Love, you and Faith pull drag. I'll take the middle. Let's keep our formation tight and move along."

Hank stepped toward Hope and never looked back at his old mat.

They walked in the light, keeping their wits about them.

Hank had forgotten how hard it was to judge time in the dank, monochromatic dungeon. However, his legs and stomach clarified that he was tired and hungry. He didn't say anything, though. They were all in the same condition.

As Vassar instructed, they kept their formation tight. They were not careless, but kept a fast pace for a small patrol. Hank wondered what Vassar meant when he said, "Lead us out of here." *I don't know where we're going.*

But it was soon apparent: walk in the light!

They came upon a staircase hewn out of a rock face with treads of stone three feet wide. That they were to climb the stairs was evident: That's where the light came from.

The stairs weren't wide enough for two, and there was no handrail.

Where's the ADA when you need them? Hank thought. The others closed in behind them, staring upward.

Hope touched the small of Hank's spine. "I've got your back."

After his miserable failure doing point duty through the tunnel into the pit, Hank unconsciously concluded it would be a cold day in hell before the guys would trust him to be their eyes and ears. He didn't move out readily, looking instead at Hope to see if he was serious. Hope didn't flinch. Neither did he push or pressure. He intended his hand to be the reassurance his comrade needed.

Looking up the staircase, Hank began climbing. *Magician, live through me. Climb through me. Please give me the strength I need for this moment and what lies ahead.*

There weren't many stairs—just enough to ascend the steepest angle out of the pit—followed by a series of three landings that turned into a narrow corridor. The light came from the end of the hall.

This could be a real mess, Hank thought, looking down the confining passage. He felt a dark sensation. He knew he could be in the light yet not safe from the forces of Zophos' darkness. If his intuition proved accurate, and they were attacked in this corridor, it would be every man for himself.

Live by the sword, die by the sword, Hank thought. *That's the way it works, but my skills are rusty.*

I can't do this, Jester counseled in Hank's thoughts. *It's suicide. What's the King expect me to do? Something foolish—all by myself? And right off!*

The sense of darkness increased—to almost a sense of dread.

I can do this, a counter thought voiced itself in Hank's mind. *I'm prepared, trained, equipped, and backed by the best. Father won't abandon me to the darkness.*

He recognized Magician's advocacy on his behalf and in keeping with the High King's promises.

I can do this, he heard again in his head. *Trust me. I'll do it through you*, Magician persuaded, switching from the first-person to the second-person pronoun. *And I won't back down.*

Hank's eyebrow arched upon recognizing Magician's voice. He paid attention to every nuance in the corridor. Hope was three steps behind him, then the others, each in tight rank. With his hands skimming along each wall, Hank was alert to even a subtle vibration—anything that might give him a strategic edge.

The first attacker, with a face like a demon, claws for fingernails, and clad in purple and green stabbed at Hank with a short sword as he leapt from his hiding in an anteroom. The attacker's lunge narrowly missed, the blade passing through Hank's shirt a fraction of an inch from his ribs. Grabbing the man's wrist, Hank pulled him toward him, raising his knee a split-second later into the man's groin. Breath erupted from his lungs as Hope's blade slit his throat with a strong, upward slice.

Leaping after his now dispatched colleague, the second demoniac attacked with a downward stab. Hank dived for the man's knees, rolling. His adversary made the mistake of dropping his knife to break his unexpected tumble and was dead before he hit the ground, killed by Hope's dagger.

As Hank rolled under the second attacker, he pulled his dagger. The third attacker wasn't expecting an approach from the ground. His reflexes a second behind Hank's, he was pierced through his heart with Hank's blue blade.

Vaulting over the three fallen assailants, Hope met the fourth, momentarily off balance by Hank's thrashing legs as he lay underneath the man he had just killed. Grabbing the man's shirt at the shoulder while pinning his dominant arm against the wall, Hope plunged his blade through the base of the man's neck. With his blade stuck in the vertebrae, Hope pushed the dying soul against the demon-man who followed, knocking him off balance. Churning like an ox, Hope drove ahead using the dead man like a shield before gravity took its toll. Stepping on top of the fallen, he kicked the dead body off of Hank, who scrambled to his feet, slipped in the gore momentarily, regained his balance, charged behind Hope, and reaching over Hope's right shoulder stabbed the fifth attacker, slashing the side of his head.

With the grievous wound, the fifth reached to his face. He lost his focus. Dropped his guard. Hank's dagger didn't miss the second time and he crumpled, attempting to scream, but only blew bubbles as he drowned.

Hank's chest heaved as his desperate lungs tried to catch up with his exertion. He glanced back. Hope was working his dagger back and forth to extract it.

He was back on point. Hank listened, watched for movement. Many men have died during an ill-timed celebration of apparent victory. As he studied the situation, Hank recalled the fight in the narrows during his last venture into Gnarled Wood. *Had it not been for Vassar, I would be among the dead who celebrated too early.*

He stayed focused.

To his relief, one of his primary doubts was answered. He had not lost his skills as a warrior, nor was his discernment faulty.

He was back!

And what's more, he fought with greater confidence than ever before. *Magician, thank you, but we're not done yet. Live through me, please!* Hank adjusted the scarlet sash around his waist.

Slowly, he squatted down, never taking his eyes off of what lay ahead. He wiped his hand on the fallen man's pants and used his cuff to clean the handle of his dagger.

While Hank maintained his point, Love guarded the rear. The other three searched the fallen for clues and anything they could use to their advantage. It didn't take long to confirm that these were Zophos' people, perverted and mutated for destruction through alliance with the demonic.

Having completed their gruesome duty, and being assured they were unscathed beyond nicks and dings, Vassar kept the same configuration—Hank, Hope, himself, Faith, Love. "Good work Hank, Hope. These were bad guys, but you handled them!" He then reiterated, "Let's stay tight and keep moving."

Hank led in the light provided.

Emerging from the corridor, they were now above ground staring into a large room. Across the room, through a doorway, Hank could see into another room with windows bracketed by heavy draperies.

Hope peered over Hank's shoulder at the room. The parquet floors were immaculate, polished to a high sheen. Benches were spaced around the outside of the room, itself decorated with dark paneling and ornate beams in the ceiling.

"Looks like a ballroom," Hope offered.

"Uh huh," Hank confirmed.

"Light's coming from over there," Hope observed.

"Yeah. Going to be hard as heck to sneak across this floor," Hank observed, tapping the parquet ever-so-lightly with the toe of his boot. "We're moving from this corridor, where it's too tight for us to support one another, to a room that's too big for us to control."

While they studied the room, considering their options, an imposing figure filled the doorway across the room, obscuring the light and casting a giant shadow upon the ballroom floor. The man stood looking across at them, then began walking, his boots clicking a steady rhythm on the wooden pattern. He was smartly tailored in red and white trimmed with leather, a dagger on his left hip. He carried his sword sheath on his back, the butt and handle of his primary weapon appeared above his right shoulder awaiting his reach.

Hank watched the monstrous man approach and muttered to Hope without turning his head, "This one's yours."

"I think this one's going to take all of us," Hope muttered back.

Stopping fifteen feet away, the man said, "Are you Henry H. Henderson?"

The story of David and Goliath flashed through Hank's mind—the part about being called out by a giant.

"I am," Hank replied, wondering how the man knew his name, complete with middle initial.

"And is your Brother, Vassar, traveling with you?" the man inquired matter-of-factly.

"He is."

"Are you both well?"

"Yes. Yes, we are fine," Hank said.

"And those traveling with you: Are they well?"

"Yes, we are all fine. I'm fine. Vassar's fine. We are all fine, fine, fine," Hank said with some anxiety-fueled irritation.

Hank was just ready to ask a question or two himself, but the man preempted him. "Very well. I've been sent to escort you. Follow me, please." The man turned smartly and started back across the room.

Hank stepped out, following, but as each man emerged from the corridor, he motioned for them to fan out across the room. From above, they looked like a capital "C" laid over on its open side. They took nothing for granted.

They followed the man through a series of magnificent rooms connected by short hallways. Hank wished for time to appreciate each room, but they kept following the giant who maintained the pace of a man on a mission.

On three occasions the monster broke the symmetry of his formal march to point. At first Hank thought he was indicating something of interest, but in each instance, demon-attackers dressed like those who attacked earlier fell from hiding places onto the floor. Each was clearly dead, killed simply by the man pointing at them. There was no gore. No mess. Only the heavy noise of a deceased meeting the floor. The man never broke stride, never looked left or right, and never seemed threatened even though each time he pointed five to seven would-be attackers fell lifeless.

Glad this guy's on our team, Hank thought. *At least, I hope he's on our team. What if we are his prisoners?*

The man pushed through a set of double doors fifteen feet tall and they entered a rectangular room, too wide for a hallway, too narrow to do anything more than march through. Shoulder-to-shoulder, along both sides of the room, stood an army of men similar to the man they followed. As was his experience counting Colorado-bound railroad cars in the freight trains along Highway 287 back home, it didn't occur to Hank that he should count the soldiers until he had already passed too many of them. He simply knew there were a bunch, *And if they all possess the military prowess of the giant we're following, they're invincible!*

They marched to the center of yet another room, a perfect ellipse. Branching off like spokes were more halls, and as far down each as Hank could see, they were lined with warriors like the man they followed. *There are hundreds,* Hank guessed.

"Wait here," the man instructed. The small band, looking like a ragtag bunch compared to this magnificent army, huddled together like quail in the center of the room.

"This way," the man indicated with a sweep of his arm upon his return. They followed him part way down one of the spokes until he stopped, opened a heavy door, and ushered them into a common room—common compared to the rooms through which they had passed to this point. It was beautifully understated. The man closed the door, a solid "click" sounded as the door latched into the jamb.

They were alone, clustered together just inside the door, awaiting their fate. *No one even bothered to disarm us!* Hank noted to himself.

There was commotion outside. Running. The beating feet echoed down the confines of the corridor and grew closer. Pursuing. Approaching. The five men moved deeper into the room.

The man whom they followed, opened their door, and stepped back into the hall. Skidding across the wooden tiles, bumping into the door jamb with tremendous force, regaining his balance, and gathering momentum again, the High King launched himself into the arms of

Hank, Vassar, Faith, Hope, and Love. He was out of breath. Huffing. Gasping from his sprint, he hugged Vassar and Hank. Pushed them away and looked at them. Hugged them again. Kissed each on the forehead. Looked at Hank, and because he could swear by no one greater, he swore by himself, "My soul! You look awful! You're sticky! Blood all over you." The King frantically examined his youngest to discover his wound.

"Well Papa, we ran into...," Hank started explaining.

Without waiting to hear the explanation, as fathers are prone to do—having satisfied himself that the blood belonged to another—the King turned to the man by the door, "Get the special clothes I prepared for my sons!" he ordered.

The King ran to the door and called after the man, "Get them cleaned up, and find out how long it is until dinner! My sons are here!" he yelled down the corridor, and ran back to where they stood. He hugged each again, never minding that their soiled clothes soiled his in the process.

He greeted Faith, Hope, and Love, shaking each man's hand. He beamed a smile through teeth and pride and joy. "Nicely done," he said to each, touching all yet again, relishing their presence with him.

Looking back at Hank, then Hope, "You two look like you've been slaughtering hogs."

"I think hogs might have been harder," Hank replied.

Vassar interjected, "Papa, you wouldn't believe what he did."

Grinning at the sight of his two boys, the King said, "Oh. I don't think I'd be surprised. People accuse me of being prejudiced toward you—and they're right, come to think of it. But I know about you."

Vassar narrowed his Father's focus. "No. I wasn't in on this. Hank was point in a narrow corridor. Zophos laid a trap. A high-octane squad of his demons ambushed us in a very tight place."

"Isolating the point man," the King anticipated.

"Exactly," Vassar confirmed. "They attacked and Hank charged—

again and again. Hope supported him…."

"Hank fought a spectacular fight!" Hope interjected, interrupting Vassar's recounting.

Hank blushed and Hope tried to step back. Love pushed Hope over next to Hank where the four of them could shower them with admiration.

An entourage of the King's warriors—*I should have known,* Hank thought—entered the room following the man whom they had followed. It was the King's signal. He waved for them to follow the soldiers. "Go. I'll meet you for dinner."

CHAPTER 7

The King's Wilderness

It was a simple meal—venison and potatoes, garnished with mushrooms and cranberries. Slices of melon were dessert. The steward offered port as a *digestif*, but had no takers. The wine was robust.

The King heard a full report—blow-by-blow—of their adventures in the pit and the battle after leaving the pit. Hearing it, Hank felt removed from the eyewitness accounts rendered by Vassar, Faith, Hope, and Love. The King listened, made several hand motions—like a conductor wanting more from a particular section of the orchestra—but otherwise focused intently, nodding, smiling broadly. He basked in the pride of sitting with great men.

When the story was concluded, the King looked at Hank, and said again, "None of this surprises me. Hank, you have always had my utmost admiration. I believe in you!"

Hank appreciated the affirmation, but was uncomfortable with the superlative language his Father used—"always," "utmost."

"Papa, thank you for your kind words. I merely did what needed doing. Any of these guys would have done the same thing, only no doubt better. It's been a while—and what they're not telling you is…I saw my old mat. When I came into the pit, there it was, and I fell for it. Like a moth to the flame. It was like…."

The King interrupted him, "I know son. I know all about it. I was there."

Hank looked puzzled.

"You could see, couldn't you?"

Hank nodded sideways, a combination of affirmation and a point well taken.

"Doesn't change my opinion about you one iota! In fact, I concur completely with the affirmations given to you by these men who were there. I believe in you. I blessed you. I made you. And, I placed you there. I could have brought you back to this side of the time dimension from any number of places, but I chose the snow cave, the wet cavern, the narrow passage, and that exact spot in the old pit. An untested strength is a dangerous thing. All that solidification since you were last here? Not much use until you know if it is a reliable strength."

"Well, I was hoping I'd be stronger," Hank said, blushing again.

"I think what you mean is that you were hoping to control the outcome based upon your progress and proficiency."

Hank thought for a moment—and his Father let him. He had nothing but time for his son.

"I discussed things with Magician, just like you taught me. And, I was just thinking." Hank stopped talking.

"You were thinking you'd never encounter your mat again," his Father said. "Never find yourself in the pit again. That you wouldn't be so susceptible to Jester's wiles again."

Hank looked at the High King for a long moment. His jaw tightened as his teeth clinched. His eyes narrowed. "Yeah. Yeah, that's pretty close to it." Disappointment rose up from his gut like heartburn, dread choked his throat. Both were a toxic waste polluting his chest— the cavity containing his heart.

"Baloney!" the King declared with a sweep of his hand. The easy dismissal caught Hank off guard. A steward was in motion, apparently to fetch baloney, or the closest thing he could find. "No. No," the King declared to the steward. "It was a figure of speech. Slang. Language this displaced Okie-living-in-Texas can understand. While you're on the move though, I could use more to drink."

The King paused, thinking. "Where was I?"

"I believe you were talking about baloney," Faith offered.

"You're no help," Hank said sarcastically.

"Ah, yes. That's right," the King said, "Circumstances are an odd mix of experiences. Experience is important, don't get me wrong. Sometimes experiences are good and sometimes they are bad, but like sausage—or baloney—you don't always need or want to know the exact recipe."

"But it's important for me to evaluate," Hank began, before his Father held up his hand.

"I wasn't done. You need to hear this."

"Yes sir," Hank said.

"I appreciate your diligence to evaluate, and you are right: it is a valuable learning tool." Turning in his chair to face Hank eye-to-eye, the King leaned forward toward his younger son, "But Hank, I think your effort to correct course, adjust, learn from your mistake—whatever you want to call it—get it right, improve, I think it is hedging against any probability that I'll be less than good to you."

Hank shifted in his chair. His back muscles were tightening.

"Your primary method for evaluating my goodness to you is your circumstance. Your back pain, for example."

Hank squirmed again, crossed his other leg. "Yeah. My back is bothering me."

"I understand," the King said. "Here's the deal: If you are sure you're right, what justification—what possible good—could I have for not removing your spasms when you ask?"

Hank felt his Father closing in on his soul—wished for a deeper back on his chair. He realized too late that he was in between a rock and a hard place.

"Because you believe you have done everything right, and I have not removed your unpleasant circumstance, there is no alternative but to conclude I am less than good to you."

"Pain is a powerful motivator, Papa."

"I understand. And persistent pain without remedy leaves you susceptible to the notion that you suffer because I'm unhappy with you—that I don't like you. For no good reason! Otherwise, as a good Father I would change your situation. So, you work hard to be good—doing the right thing—so I will do the right thing, the good thing."

"I do try hard," Hank said. He didn't mean it defensively.

"You do try hard, son. Mighty hard. I like that about you. But that's not my point."

Hank looked hard at his Father.

"When you believe yourself right, anything that doesn't fit your right-ness—including your pain, including me—by definition is not right, not good." The King leaned back against the back of his chair, reached, retrieved his refilled wine glass, took a sip, and looked at Hank.

Hank dropped his eyes toward the floor. *No matter what he says, his standards are impossible.* The thought was bitter in his mind. *I have no choice! I have to be right. How else can I defend myself against his impossible expectations?*

The King sipped his wine and watched his son.

Hank felt scrutinized. *Even if I perform right, Father's goodness isn't a given—even though he claims it's constant. Not to me, anyway. If he liked me, you'd think he would be consistently good to me.*

Hank had been down this steep path before—the first time during his earlier trip to this side of Malden Creek. He felt himself sliding down the slippery slope. But what had taken him a long duration in the pit to realize, he had now developed the skills to more readily see. *I desire to look at life through his eyes. I don't want to look at it through the myopia of my viewpoint.*

Hank shook his head. "Papa, I'm sorry. I know what you're saying."

"I know you do, Hank. Look at me."

Hank looked at his Father.

"I love you. I accept you. I will always be good to you, always do right by you, but you can't evaluate my goodness by your condition or circumstance."

Hank stared at his Father. He looked away—toward the windows and away from his Father and circle of friends. He turned back, stared again into his Father's eyes, leaned forward. "I want to believe you," Hank whispered.

His Father leaned closer, "Then do. I will help your unbelief."

"You're okay with that—with my unbelief?" Hank asked.

"Of course! What more could I ask?"

"It just seems wrong to question—to doubt…you. To…," Hank hesitated.

"To believe I am less than good?" his Father wanted to know.

Hank nodded, his distrust peeled naked of its veneer.

"Thank you for telling me, son. I've known this for a while. So have you. It's good to get it on the table though, isn't it?"

Hank nodded, a bare agreement. "Are you mad at me? Disappointed?"

"For being honest? Good heavens no. I appreciate the care you have shown with your caution, but we are close enough that honesty becomes us." He paused. "One more thing, as long as we are having this discussion. Jester has suggested that I have the same expectation of you that you have for yourself. Because you passed through the pit today, after trying so hard to avoid it, he suggested that I abandoned you, that I haven't done good by you. He suggested that you were alone. Isolated—in that dark and ungracious place."

"He did, Papa. And you know what? I listened. I turned to my mat."

Hank's Father leaned back again in his chair. He eyed his son, waiting.

"I believed my circumstance was a referendum on your goodness and my trust. And that's where the baloney comes in," Hank stated.

The King slapped his knee as though his hand was a gavel and his leg a bench. "That's where the baloney comes in! Jester sells it as if it's prime," the King confirmed. "He's always selling something worthless—like that fellow back home still selling encyclopedias."

Hank's mind jerked from the medieval world back to the modern world of search engines and exponential volumes of digitized information, then to the worthlessness of an encyclopedia set, and the ridiculous picture of a door-to-door salesman selling the volumes. *How's he know about that?* Hank thought.

Speaking to the unspoken, his Father said, "Your Brother's been telling me all about that technical stuff. Electrons going here and there, circuits, and so forth. Great stuff. All measured by light, you know?"

It took Hank a moment to make the connection. His Father didn't wait on him, sucking him into the spectrum of his thoughts at warp speed. "There's visible light and electromagnetic light across the visible and invisible spectrum, and a few folks speculating that light is infinite. Imagine that!"

Hank was amused by this dramatic side of his Father—and Vassar—deliberately taking him into water over his head. He wanted to say something meaningful, but all that came to mind was, *"To infinity and beyond!"* He opted to leave his mind unspoken.

But of the fundamental point, Hank was certain. "Papa, I get it. Thanks for talking to me, helping me get my focus back. I love being with you."

"Hank, I would rather die than not be able to live with you. You are a fine, fine person. I'm so proud of you."

Once again, Hank was blushing—but absorbing every precious, important word of affirmation.

"Before we change the subject, give me a summary," the King requested.

Without hesitation, Faith said, "You mean about that quantum physics-fiber optics-EMR stuff?"

"Oh, please," said Hank. "Does anyone really need to hear a review of that?"

Faith raised his hands as if surrendering.

"If it will make you feel better, I'll go over it with you later," Hank said.

"Fair enough," Faith conceded.

Turning to his Father, Hank said, "To live successfully, I rely upon Magician. To live truly, I live from my heart. To live freely, I embrace your rightness, not my own. To live confidently, I trust your goodness, not mine. To live fully, I walk in the light. In so doing, my heart's desires are realized."

The King smiled, pointed toward Love, and said, "Remind me later to write that down. I'm going to use it in my next book."

Love nodded seriously, then chuckled at the King's thinly veiled recognition of Hank's professional life as a writer.

Holding his wine glass in one hand, the King put his other hand on Hank's shoulder. The touch was for affirmation, but using it in feigned support, he stood up. Thanking them with genuine appreciation, he dismissed the stewards, and instructed the guards to assume position outside the door. The King finished his wine, stepped away from the table, and motioned to follow him.

They entered a cloistered anteroom through a hidden passage. Inside were twelve guards—three spaced equally along each wall. At the High King's request, six chairs were place in a circle in the center of the room. That service completed, the guards stood back awaiting orders.

With an affirmative nod by the King the soldiers left the room in formation. Before the door closed, Hank saw them reassembling their guard outside the room. It was obvious to Hank that whatever was on his Father's mind was confidential.

The door closed. The six sat in silence until the King heard the sharp click of heels outside. Leaning forward, elbows on his knees, the King nodded slightly at his eldest and said, "Vassar."

Vassar reached into his leather satchel, producing a folded document that he handed to Hank. Hank eyed the wax seal imprinted deeply with

Vassar's signet and looked to his Brother for guidance.

With his palm facing Hank, he said, "Please, wait until you get to your room."

Hank tipped his head in deference and tucked the letter inside the pouch he wore against his skin.

Leaning forward, with their heads gathered in a clustered circle, Vassar explained with deliberate sentences the situation facing Gnarled Wood, the castle, and the Round Tower. He noted Zophos' modified strategy of working under cover, "...and while this is effective, he is still prone to overreach." Zophos' desperation and insecurity were well known weaknesses, but so was his formidable power of persuasion. In fact, his deception was usually only picked up by the discerning or well-trained.

It came as a surprise to Hank that Zophos had a regular audience with the High King. He was curious to know more, but given the intensity and pace of Vassar's review, he decided to inquire later.

Vassar worked from the general conditions in Gnarled Wood toward the specificity of what was transpiring inside the Round Tower. It sounded to Hank as if not much had changed in Gnarled Wood. Zophos' troops still patrolled both visibly and under cover.

With their status in the Kingdom, Hank's especially, they would be high-value targets. "So be careful," Vassar briefed them. "Everyone who looks innocent is not."

"As for the castle and surrounding area," Vassar said, "generally speaking, conditions are more intense based upon one, proximity to the Round Tower, and two, the urban environment. Zophos knows the priority we place on the Round Tower within the Kingdom," Vassar stated. "He is also of the opinion that 75% to 80% of the Round Tower's inhabitants are loyal to him. We believe that number is high."

"How high?" Hank asked.

"By 30%, give or take 5%," Vassar said. "As you know, we are evaluating the hearts of those in the Tower. Zophos' numbers are based primarily on performance. While performance is certainly an indicator of hearts loyal to Zophos, it is not necessarily a good indicator of a heart loyal to the King. That said, at any given time a majority of those in the Round Tower actively follow guidance originating with Zophos."

"Let me guess," Hank interrupted: "Jester's handiwork?"

"You nailed it," Vassar confirmed. "He has noteworthy momentum, so it doesn't take much persuasion for the unsuspecting to follow Jester like lambs to slaughter. But let me reiterate, just because these folks follow his counsel doesn't mean their hearts are disloyal to the King; they are simply deceived, and in their deception, behave contrary to their true heart-desire."

"Those percentages are still alarming," Hank observed. "It would be great if there was a way to help people act from their hearts."

"Well, that's where you come in, Brother."

"Oh, my. I knew I should've kept my mouth shut," Hank deadpanned.

"It wouldn't have made any difference," Love said, with equal lack of expression. "You were designated before you ever showed up."

"Hank, you know Jester's wiles," Vassar continued, "how he operates, how he frames his opinions…."

Hank interjected, "Boy! Do I ever. First-person pronouns, and so forth. He sounds just like me, and the way he correlates what he's advocating with my experiences—my whole life! If you're not careful he can make killing your mother sound like a good idea."

"You better throw the shovel out," Love counseled. "You're just diggin' your hole deeper with these insights. At this rate, Vassar's going to send you to the Round Tower to battle Jester."

"Now that you bring it up," Vassar began, "that's exactly where Father and I are leading. Brother, you know Jester; and Love, you understand redemption. Both of you are totally committed to the King, the Kingdom, and rescuing the King's people. You're a perfect team!"

"And of course, you've got Magician inside of you," Hope chimed in, looking across the tight circle at Hank.

Faith sat up straight, a bold snarl across his face, and said, "They're also warriors. I'd choose either one—any day of the week."

Hank had gone from concerned to embarrassed at Faith's accolade. *If I'm going to be affirmed by anyone, there's no one better to express confidence in me than Faith.* Hank carefully placed Faith's affirmation of him inside his heart.

The King spoke, "Hank, Love: I echo everything said. I believe in you without reservation. There is no one better suited for this mission."

Hank stared at his Father for a long moment. While appreciative of his endorsement, there was an omission, and fear was rising like a flash flood back home. "What about you, Vassar? Your name's absent from the assignment list."

"My duties will shift. I'm going to be Administrative Liaison, ensuring concerted action and clear communication between you, those whom you place around you, including those with whom you work, the Kingdom, and specifically, Father. For access and security purposes, I'll interface with you primarily via Magician in the secure chamber of your heart."

Hank didn't hear anything Vassar said after announcing his new title. *Administrative Liaison, huh?* Hank was unimpressed. *Shit!* he declared to himself. The inelegant expletive, final word of many doomed souls—however inarticulate—resounded in his empty mind.

Vassar's going away. What we began together, I'm now going to do by myself. All the noise in Hank's head ceased. *He's leaving, he's leaving,* was singular in his attention, like a dripping faucet in the middle of the night.

Memories of Vassar raced helter-skelter through Hank's soul as though he'd just been informed of his Brother's death. He felt energy drain from his eyes. Pale and speechless, without heart, Hank sat back, taking himself outside the circumference of the close-knit circle.

As long as I'm with Vassar…, well, I've got life by the tail. I can handle anything. Being separated, being apart from Vassar?

Life-at-a-distance from Vassar flashed across his mind. For years he anchored at a distance from not just his Father, but from Vassar as well. All that changed with their fishing trip to Montana and subsequent adventure into Gnarled Wood two years ago. He had drawn close. Like a skittish animal, he trusted—finally. He lashed his wellbeing to the strength of Vassar, and along the way, *I felt closer to Father. With this new assignment, there will be distance—no matter how Vassar spins his new job description. Administrative Liaison! Huh.*

He thought of the good-byes he'd said in life. He couldn't think of one without promises to stay in touch, promises of, "We'll be back soon." As a boy, bewitched with the naiveté of childhood, he innocently believed this was true when his best friend moved to Illinois. As life wore on, other relocations by friends were padded with the same vanity: "I'll see you again soon. We'll talk." And they did, for a time, and then distance won, separation prevailed, and life required reframing—in a smaller frame.

Vassar is reassigned. I am not. Their paths were parting, no doubt this evening. *That would explain the demonstration of military might.* The isolation to which he had grown accustomed in life—that he thought was forever banished with his reconnection to Vassar—settled upon Hank and was terrifying!

There were words around the circle, but they didn't register. Hank nodded at the correct moments and turned his face toward whoever was speaking, but he had retreated into the cleft of his soul.

Hank occasionally marveled—objectively and apart from himself—at his ability to withdraw, to insulate in cloistered protection, within walls and ramparts. In such retreat he could guard the naked susceptibility he felt inside from threats outside.

He was often accused of being stoic, and Hank knew this was indeed the case. People meant it as a criticism, but he was never too highly motivated to change his stoicism. *There are too many circumstances where a blank stare works to my advantage*, he thought. *Sometimes a man needs a secure place to hide until he can regain control.*

Of course this faux invincibility, this aura of strength, was adopted by the same man who earlier leaned back, taking himself outside the tight circle. Portraying himself impervious, he adjusted his posture, sat at an angle, legs crossed, arms folded over his chest, and chin down. Looking out from under his eyebrows, he clenched his teeth and tightened his lips.

Affording him the space he needed to collect his thoughts—and Magician the respectful latitude to work his magic—Vassar summed up his thoughts: "So Hank, I'll be in constant communication with you through Magician. Anything, anything at all that you wish to discuss, I'm available." Vassar knew his Brother well, knew it would take time for him to process all that was transpiring, and so he left his final words there and turned his face to the High King.

"So Hank, like Vassar said, he will be in touch, as will I," the King said. "But as the battle for the Round Tower ensues, it is best if he and I operate from headquarters. Faith, you and Hope are to deploy immediately to the castle. Love, you'll accompany Hank when it is time. Until you hear otherwise, Hank, I've made provision for you to stay here." The King looked around the circle. "Questions?"

Questions? Questions? Yeah, I've got a few questions. Hank's anger and fear boiled in caldrons over his fiery doubt and distrust. This plan dredged old beliefs and doubts up from a forbidden swamp as though he'd never cast them away. In his emotional funk, Hank missed Jester's persuasive argument, *No matter how they spin this, I'm alone.*

The King waited, which was always disarming. The world could be racing to hell on the midnight express—it was in fact, as far as Hank felt—but his Father seemed to never hurry

Hank assembled what words he managed to find, "Are you sure about this? All this?" he asked, with an ever-so-slight twitch of his head toward Vassar while swinging his hand in an arc around the interior of the circled chairs.

The High King smiled slightly, a genuine expression of compassion, and said, "I am, Hank. It's a good plan, and it will work. Believe me. I will take care of you."

Although not realizing Magician's assistance, Hank took his mentor's recommendation and spoke honestly and vulnerably to his Father, "Promise?"

"With all my heart."

Hank had no words for Vassar. Instead, he leaned forward in his chair, elbows on his knees, and looked at his Brother sideways. Finally, he said, "Well, Vassar?"

"It's all in the letter I gave you earlier, Hank. All the thoughts of my heart. If there was another way, I'd do it. I know you don't understand, and I've told you all I dare tell you right now. There's lots more to discuss, but not now."

"When?" Hank asked.

"Soon."

Hank stared at the floor shaking his head slowly.

Vassar knelt beside Hank. "I know about the anxious thoughts you're having, and rightly so. But believe me: I won't leave you. Trust me. Depend upon Magician."

"And read your Brother's letter," Faith offered.

Hank stood and reached for Vassar. The two brothers hugged, and then were joined by their Father.

The breakup of the family huddle was the awaited cue. Gathering their travel bags, the King, Vassar, Faith, Hope, and Love exited the circle.

"Wait a minute," Hank protested. "I thought you and I were a team, Love. Where are you going?"

Before Love could answer, Vassar said, "Faith and Hope are headed back to the Round Tower. Love is going to prepare the way for you. I'll let you know when it's time to leave here."

"And you and Father are going to headquarters?" Hank asked.

"That's right. You and Magician are here."

The five walked toward the wall. Stopping short, Vassar said to Hank, "I'll be in touch. Don't be afraid. Believe! And remember, you're not alone."

There was a brilliant explosion of light that glowed white against the wall—and Hank's Father, Brother, and companions disappeared into it. As Hank looked after them, the light waned but left the room brighter than before.

Engulfed in the aching silence, Hank thought—fought—to corral the competing perspectives of Magician and Jester.

He sat down. Stared at the empty chairs, the vacated circle, and beyond. He let his eyes roam through the cavernous room. *I'm alone*, he thought. Rather, Jester suggested.

"Hell! I'm not going to sit here," he muttered aloud. He got up. Moved. It was a small action, but sufficient to indicate that for the moment he rejected Jester's perspective.

Hank stepped into the hallway lined with guards. Their Captain stepped forward, saluted, and said, "Sir. At your service."

The formality caught Hank by surprise. He'd never gotten used to the royal respect, but at least now he could summon the wherewithal to speak his mind. "I presume my Father—or Brother, maybe—left instructions for me?"

"They did, your Highness."

"Tell you what," Hank interrupted. "Let's skip the royal titles. I appreciate your recognition, but I would be more comfortable if we were less formal. One can't be too careful, you know?"

"Sir." The officer gently clicked his heels and bowed slightly. "As you wish."

The officer waited. Hank realized the initiative lay with him, "Please. Pardon my interruption. Proceed."

"Yes sir. Your suite is prepared. It is my pleasure to take you there when you are ready."

"Good. After you," Hank said.

A security detail followed Hank and the Captain. Hank didn't bother to gain his bearings. It's hard to know where you are if you don't know where you were or how you got to where you are. *I'll figure it out in the morning*, he resolved.

The Captain stopped before a heavy door with guards posted on either side. Inside were a bedroom and a sitting room. There was a bath off the bedroom. The sitting room was comfortable with a wall of open windows. Hank looked out, but only saw darkness. The curtains puffed in a cool, sweet breeze.

"Sir, if you need anything, we are at your service. In the morning, I'll help you get oriented."

Hank smiled and nodded.

"If there is nothing further, then sleep well, Sir."

"Thank you, Captain."

Hank closed the thick door behind the Captain and latched it. He leaned back against the timbers and took inventory of his circumstances.

In the main room there was a table and chair. In the corner were two more chairs, one with a footstool in front of it. The appointments weren't fancy. Some would say it was Spartan, but to Hank's eye the stark room was inviting in its simplicity.

Of course, there was a bed in the bedroom, but what distinguished it was how high it was off of the floor. There was a step stool for climbing in and climbing out. Against the opposite wall was a massive armoire, simple in design, but of expert craftsmanship. Hank opened the doors and peered inside. In the low light of the candles he saw clothes hanging in preparation for his arrival and suspected his Father's thoughtfulness.

Hank walked to the basin and splashed water on his face. He held the towel on his eyes for a long time; the pressure felt good to him and the towel absorbed the leaking tears, some from sadness, a few from frustration, and others the leeching of resolve.

Collecting two candles from the main room, Hank sat down at the desk. He stared at the wood grain for a moment. He ran his hands across the surface from center to edge and let his fingers grip the outside corners. He smelled the night air, relishing the damp nose of darkness and all it carried, then reached inside his shirt to the satchel against his skin.

He unwound the leather cord that secured the flap and carefully, reverently, extracted Vassar's letter. Laying the satchel aside, Hank forced his index finger against the wax seal and unfolded Vassar's thoughts. Penned with his precise hand, Hank read.

My dear Brother, Hank:

Don't worry! I know you didn't anticipate this, but Father knows what he's doing—and I am near you, as near as your thoughts and the desires of your heart, like Magician.

Know that I am working in advance, preparing the way. I'll meet with you frequently, but don't ever hesitate to draw upon the tremendous resource inside you.

Magician is not only a great friend and comfort, he will never leave you. Even though it will appear you are abandoned, don't ever forget that he lives in you and that you are never in the dark. In your heart, the sunrise from on high is always dawning, illuminating everything Father has written on your heart's walls. Magician is committed to explaining all you desire to know. If you need anything— anything at all—just ask. I'll see that you have everything you need.

I think you know, but for the umpteenth time—because I can never say it enough—I love you, Brother! I'm so thrilled you have Magician to help you and guide you—no matter what. Rely upon him for everything.

I anticipate Jester's plan of attack is most likely to suggest that you are isolated!

Hank, I have two thoughts about this: First, our Father lives and his light will not be extinguished. Second, he won't abandon us. No doubt Jester will suggest that you are orphaned. Don't believe him, not for a moment. You are not left behind.

We are family, and as such, we are bonded and can never be separated. In spirit, I am in Father and Father is in me—just as I am in you and you are in me. We are in Father. He is in us. Magician is evidence of this. Father said so! We are a unit, a family. We are cut from the same bolt of genetic cloth and our lives are interwoven. We are inseparable!

I don't need to remind you that Father has written his priorities and perspectives on the walls of your heart—for perpetual reference. You know as well that there is no one better than Magician to counsel, reinforce, and align you with your heart's desires regardless of life's circumstances.

Speaking of whom, let me remind you again to rely upon Magician for everything. He will teach and guide you; he will help you remember everything that you, and Father, and I have discussed. He will explain the intricacies of the Kingdom, provide legal insight on the family's covenant, and as you know, he is a formidable force to have on your side when conflict arises. Look to him. If you do so, there is no reason to be afraid of what's before you.

No matter if all hell is breaking loose, be at peace, Brother. Greater is he who lives in you than he who rules Gnarled Wood and beyond. That's not hyperbole! Magician is more powerful than Jester and Zophos put together, so don't be afraid if they assemble themselves against you.

You are such a magnificent person, Hank. I'm really proud that you are my Brother, but I'm even prouder that you are my friend. I haven't pulled any punches with you. I've told you everything I know and I've shared everything with you that Father has shared with me. And, you've digested it. Amazing!

Thank you for believing—believing not only in Father, but also for believing in me. Thank you as well for your trust. I know you've been pushed hard at times, but you have risen to the challenge. You've done so consistently, and that is impressive. I trust you as well—as does Father, otherwise the current plan would be modified.

Father believes in you. After all, he created this plan and chose you to carry it out. He knows you will represent him well, and I have every confidence in you too. If I didn't, I would have advocated for a different plan, but here we are!

Things are not going to be easy, Brother! The stakes have risen since we were last in Gnarled Wood. While Zophos is utilizing his shock and awe capabilities in some parts of the castle, he has switched tactics in other areas; most of the shock and awe there is a diversion. Always the pragmatist—

and opportunist—Zophos is operating in a more clandestine manner. He's pouring exorbitant amounts of money, effort, and personnel into subversion, espionage, and subterfuge. Always there is his illusion of light. He is a deceiver.

The inclination is to engage him at his level, but there is a more powerful weapon. In everything you do, Brother, let your motive be love. Nothing is more powerful because love is the essence of who Father is. When you love, you portray Father, and the only way you can love as he loves is to live from your heart and let Magician's strength bolster you. Read that line again. I'll bet you felt your heart jump, didn't you?

Make no mistake though: Love will earn you hate. It will associate you with Father, and you know as I do that those who belong to Zophos utterly despise the High King. But while there is no pleasure in being hated—Zophos' folks feel the same about me as they do about you—there is nothing to fear. Nothing! Just ask Magician. He knows the drill.

Rely on Magician. I make no apology for reiterating myself. You know how to do this! And as you rely on him for strength and perspective, he will guide you, protect you, and keep you from stumbling. Even if your life is compromised and death is imminent, no worries; Magician will guide you to victory—not only in this life, but the next as well.

Hank, let me remind you: Magician has permission and power to speak for the High King. I have given him authority to speak for me as well. He knows us perfectly, and he knows exactly what you need at any given moment. So, if you want to get Father's or my counsel with only a second's notice, Magician's your man!

If I were you, given the weight of this evening's meeting, I would go straight to Magician and ask him to bolster your sense of wellbeing. This is a heavy-duty project. I'd ask him to bring peace to your soul. Before I sat down to write you, this is what I did with Father and Magician.

Brother, every circumstance is going to scream that you are overwhelmed, outnumbered, and that you will be assimilated into the castle, the routines of the Round Tower, and the lethargy of life in Gnarled Wood. Don't you believe it for a moment! While you live and work and fight in Gnarled Wood, Gnarled Wood is not your home. You live and move and have significance because you are a son of the High King!

I know Jester will try to tell you otherwise, but this is the absolute truth! It is true for me, it is true for you. Where Father lives, that is where you, and I, and Magician live as well. But right now, we are privileged to be on special assignment to Gnarled Wood as representatives of the King.

To state the obvious: If Father didn't trust you, and believe in you, he wouldn't have chosen you for this mission. He loves you, Hank, and he knows you love him too.

I'm back now where I started: with love. Love as he loves. Love like you are loved. Wow! You will be one powerful soul if you do so. Already are, now that I think about it!

Hank, as your Older Brother, I've written to put your heart at peace. What lies ahead will be tremendously *difficult. But don't fear. Have courage! You and I are victorious warriors!*

I love you. See you soon,

Vassar

Hank folded the letter and carefully placed it back in his satchel. He wound the leather cord around the button on the front of the satchel to fasten the flap, leaned back, tucked the bag neatly under his shirt, and walked to the open window.

He stared into the darkness. Wherever he was, there was no moon or other ambient light. He thought back to his bivouac in the Absaroka. It seemed an eternity ago that he and Vassar were lying next to each other in their sleeping bags. But even there, in the cold air, miles from civilization, there were noticeably fewer stars than the points of light from his window. Spanning the arc of heaven, the Milky Way was so thick with stars it looked like smoke wafting across the sky as though drafted from some giant chimney.

The night was alive with chirping and squeaking—*Crickets? Frogs, maybe?* Hank thought. While the weight and magnitude of Vassar's letter occupied his thoughts, he listened passively to the night songs. There was comfort in knowing he wasn't the only one still awake.

Jester's voice startled him. *They left me here, alone.*

He felt foolish afterward for looking, but the dark counselor's voice resonated so clearly Hank thought he must be in the room in bodily form. But no, he was alone with his thoughts. The night creatures' voices dulled as Jester spoke his observations.

It's hard to argue with Jester, Hank noted. *Occasionally, he approaches too abruptly, and when he does, I can readily dismiss his spin as malarkey. But Jester's too shrewd to make that mistake often—if it's a mistake at all.*

Sometimes Hank thought Jester deliberately overplayed, or overstated, or over did. *Just to keep me off balance.*

Vassar's letter is amazing, Jester intoned to Hank. His affirmation hung expectant. *But, he is with Father and the others—and I'm here. By myself.*

Well, the guards are outside, Hank countered.

The guards don't count. He looked around the room. *My soul is alone.* Even the compulsion of Hank's detail-oriented mind—to consider all the variables—didn't escape Jester's input.

I wonder what's next? The impracticality of the letter tapped his suspicion.

It's a ruse. They're just blowing me off. They said it didn't matter that I failed—when I saw my mat…. But I wouldn't trust me if I were them. Jester's condemnation was cruel, and as Hank agreed with him, the self-condemnation struck deeply.

He didn't realize his nemesis had him backed into a corner and was whipping him with these body blows. Punch after punch. Hank absorbed one after the other, all the while leaving himself open to more abuse.

Hank heard singing outside his door. *That's odd,* he thought. *Who would be singing this time of night? And a woman! Why would the guards permit this?* The voice continued. Hank listened. The beautiful, intoxicating voice of a black woman swept the cold from his soul, sensuous and warm with comfort.

He crept to the door. The soulful melody was just outside. Hank grew up listening to jazz. The vocal riff enticed him, comforted him—like listening to Ella, Mavis, Dionne, or Aretha. *Unmistakable. But who? And why, and why now?* he pondered.

He had been thankful for the massive door when he entered his room. But now, wanting to hear this woman more clearly, he was irritated with its bulk.

Leaning against the wood, his ear pressed close, the lady sang, "You're not alone." Hank recoiled at the lyric, not because it wasn't beautiful. It was! He recoiled at the pointed message.

I sure feel alone.

Jester's harping was silenced. The resonance of the woman's voice dispelled his notion.

Hank threw back the bolt, pressed the latched, and jerked opened his door. His abrupt appearance startled the guards' decorum, but they quickly regained composure.

The hallway was silent. Hank rushed out, looked up and down. He asked the startled guards, "Where's the woman who was singing?"

Clearly, they were confused.

"There was a woman—just now—singing here, in the hall," Hank pressed the guards. "Where did she go?"

Looking up and down the hall themselves, one of the guards said, "Sir. We've been right here all along. No one has come, certainly no one singing. Why! You would have been disturbed. We would have stopped them, Sir."

"You're telling me there wasn't a black woman—that there wasn't anyone—singing out here just a second ago?"

"No sir. Or, yes sir, I mean. That's what I said. Well, I'm…."

Hank waved off further explanation about what the guard meant. "You did hear singing, correct?"

The guards looked at each other, baffled by their interrogation from the Prince. "No, sir. We didn't hear anything. We can arrange singing if you…."

Again Hank cancelled further offers with a wave of his hand. He stood for a moment, looking again up and down the hallway. Turned. Looking through his open door, toward the curtains billowing in the evening breeze, he heard a quiet reassurance in his mind's ear, *I told you that you weren't alone. You needed some reassurance. That's all.*

Hank assembled the puzzle. *Magician! I should have known. Only you could pull this off. Was that you singing?*

Quick as a wink, the thoughtful reply came, *No. But I know a lady who helped me out.*

Hank laughed. He laughed at Magician. He laughed at the thought. He laughed at himself, at Jester, and at the bewildered look on the guards' faces. He started trying to explain, then gave up. "Hey, please accept my apology for disturbing you," he said, edging toward the sanctity of his room behind the massive door. "It's been a long day. Fatigue! Can really play tricks on your mind."

The Captain and his men affirmed. "Good night, Sir. Sleep well. Everything is fine."

"Yes, yes. I'm sure of it. Thank you."

She sang again more soulfully and heartfelt than before, and Hank was reassured, *I'm not alone.*

He listened until the serenade in his soul ended, absorbing every note into his heart. He thanked Magician for looking after him in his vulnerable place. *And whoever the woman singing was, tell her thanks. Her song was perfect.*

Turning to his bedroom, Hank undressed, extinguished the final candle, and climbed into bed.

He laid in the darkness listening, hoping. There! Waltzing on the wings of the wind, the soulful melody began again. "You're not alone."

Under the covers, wrapped in darkness, Hank stated, "No. I'm not alone."

He pulled the quilt up, under his chin, and held it in both fists. He rolled side-to-side until the covers were tucked under him, and held his breath to listen. *Night birds. Tree frogs, maybe. Wind in the curtain, the leaves. No. I'm not alone. I'm not alone.*

CHAPTER 8

The Round Tower

"Ms. Pintaro. Ennui will see you now," the assistant said. Letizia gathered her bag.

Proficient, shrewd, and one of the most pragmatic and resourceful people Ennui knew, Letizia was relentlessly persistent, modestly discreet, and competent. Her features were sharp and her complexion fair. She was an auburn-brunette who wore her hair shorter than Ennui's black, long-flowing tresses.

Ennui presented an affable, public persona—easy to approach and speak to—but behind closed doors she could be intimidating with her precise speech, staggering intellect, and unflinching resolve to get what she wanted. Those who got on her bad side were usually removed before the sun went down. At least that's how it was in the office. When it came to her enemies, Ennui was ever-more vigilant and careful that her retribution wasn't traceable.

Enter: Letizia.

Letizia demonstrated an uncanny knack for doling out Ennui's reckoning with astute prudence. What's more, no one would ever suspect Letizia possessed the makeup for making people disappear. She had a quick laugh, ready smile, and girlish innocence. But she had proven herself—time and again.

The loyalty Ennui felt from Letizia was comforting. She knew Letizia had a network of dark people loyal to her, but what bothered Ennui was that she didn't know who these people were, where they operated from, and just how duty-bound they might be to Ms. Pintaro. It was a fine line to draw.

She was no fool. This business was ruthless and desperate. What else could it be when your boss was Zophos and the goal was capturing the King's throne?

She had promoted Letizia over two years ago, and had no regrets. It was a clear decision. But how she should manage this brilliant and clever woman was not self-evident. *Best to keep her close*, she thought, again.

"Good morning, Letizia."

The ladies exchanged pleasantries, caught up on bits of gossip, and along the way moved from hearsay and rumor to a troublesome situation on the first floor of the Round Tower. "What can you tell me about this?" Ennui asked.

"It's odd," Letizia began. "Those loyal to the King call it a revival. The movement is almost exclusively comprised of young people."

"What ages?"

"Their ages range from 12-22, but the majority—85-90%—are between 14-17 years. Total number in the group has swelled to 200 in just under one month."

"And you say they call it a revival?" Ennui asked.

"That's right. Initially it appeared to be a fad. But it's too simple to chalk this up to youthful enthusiasm, a fad, or group-think. At least, that's my opinion."

"Okay. This is larger than I was led to believe," Ennui stated. "How did this movement—this revival—begin?"

"That's interesting. The group is led by a young leader, 31 years old, married, three children. Well educated—two degrees—handsome, well-spoken, and somewhat charismatic. He is also a devoted follower of the High King. The First Floor Group hired him to work with their young people."

"Explain what you mean by 'work with their young people.'"

"Well, the First Floor Group hired him—full time—to encourage the young people in morality, ethics, and honesty. And, he has proven quite innovative."

"How do you mean?"

"They go on field trips into the castle and surrounding area. He has formed study groups. He interfaces with their teachers and has proven a great ally in helping redirect kids with problematic behavior. The youth group even took three days, at their own expense, to travel to La Faim and work among the poor. But most of all, nearly all these activities, to a greater or lesser degree, are focused around the High King's teachings."

"Okay. I understand. Thank you for the background. Now, please continue with how this group began."

Letizia explained, "The young leader announced to the First Floor youth that he and his wife were hosting an all-night gathering at their home—the evening after school concluded for the summer. He told them there would be food, games, entertainment, music, and an intensive exploration of the King's teaching on social activism. He also told them all were welcome. Apparently the kids took him at his word. Whereas his normal group numbered between 12 and 15 kids, over 90 showed up for the all-nighter."

"Ninety! What were they doing?" Ennui asked, incredulous. "I mean, I understand what you are telling me, but surely there must be more to this. Was there alcohol? Sex? How do you account for 90 children showing up?"

"I'm not sure I can explain the number. Perhaps it is simply word-of-mouth, or the place to be. Maybe there was nothing better to do the last day of school. My intuition tells me the High King and his people threw their influence behind this event. I mean, the young leader is an able man, but he can't draw numbers like this. Kids love to be where the action is—where all their friends are—but sitting cross-legged on the floor all night? Studying? The night after the last day of school? I don't think so. There is a missing piece to this puzzle and I suspect the High King has it."

"I thought you might say that," Ennui stated. "So, 90 children gather at the young leader's home the night after school is out. They carry on as children do, but turn their attention to the King's teachings."

"I'm sorry to report that our agent on the first floor missed the buildup to this event entirely. Neither he nor any of his people were at this event, so our intelligence is sketchy at best." Letizia watched Ennui carefully. There was a slight narrowing above her right eye indicating that her message was adequately delivered. No doubt, the first floor would have a new agent by morning.

Letizia continued: "Somewhere in the wee hours of the morning, after lots of juvenile fun and games, the students were intently studying the King's beliefs. A few had fallen asleep, but not many. From everything we can gather, Vassar showed up at the meeting. He talked with the students, praised the young leader, elaborated on the portion of his writings they were reading, and continued his encouragement until dawn."

"I do not have any reports of a breech in security, nor do I have anything to indicate Crown Prince Vassar entered the Round Tower. How can this be true?" Ennui was as flustered as Letizia had ever seen her, and with good cause.

"I'm looking into it, but the inquiry is slow, and we must be careful. Especially, now."

"Meaning?"

"Well, as you would guess," Letizia said, "after this experience the kids in attendance started telling their friends what happened. Even though school is out, they are still socializing. Word has spread dramatically—and the group has swelled to approximately 200. And that's what the First Floor Group calls a revival. Whatever it is, it appears viral. My recommendation is that we intervene."

"These things usually die down." Ennui sounded as though she was in denial. For many months, years actually, her plan to advance tolerance, indifference, and relative harmony had experienced tremendous success. Apathy was the most distinguishing characteristic of the Round Tower. Now, all of a sudden, here was her most-trusted colleague reporting an inexplicable, passionate outbreak of fervor for the High King and devotion to his teaching. *It is as though my agents were intoxicated and I was asleep at the helm!* she thought, embarrassed, but not showing it to Letizia.

"Ennui, with all due respect to you as my mentor and with deference to your office, my assessment is that this movement is different."

"What do you mean, Letizia?"

"I have my doubts that this will pass quietly away. It feels different. The children's eyes are changed—as though a light has dawned. Besides, the young leader is not like the others who hold this position in similar groups in the Tower."

Ennui stared at Letizia. "Are you saying you believe this group is a threat to our stability and the program we have in place?" she asked, pointedly.

Letizia thought for a moment, then carefully replied: "Yes. That's what I'm saying."

"Have you devised a plan?"

"Yes, ma'am. I have."

"Very well," Ennui said, waiting.

With her customary proficiency, Letizia ticked off the points. "I believe you know the senior leader of the First Floor."

Ennui nodded.

"I believe he is as mystified about this movement—this revival—as you and I are. I propose that you visit with him about the disturbance this is causing. If allowed to continue, significant harm could come to many reputations. After all, we can't let a bunch of kids lead us, now can we?"

"No. I agree with you," Ennui concurred. "I will visit with him as soon as possible—probably later this morning. I already have ideas about how to approach him."

"Very good. Thank you."

"And what about the young leader?" Ennui knew as soon as the words left her mouth that she had asked for more information than normal—but Letizia's report worried her.

"I don't think he will be a long-term concern." Letizia smiled, stopped speaking, and sat with her hands demurely in her lap.

Ennui waited a moment—and was relieved that was the end of Letizia's briefing, at least the extent of the plan she was prepared to share. Ennui knew she could ask for more detail, but she appreciated Letizia's lack of specificity and the plausible deniability it created in the event something went awry.

"Very well. Anything further?" Ennui inquired.

"No. Nothing more. Thank you for your time," Letizia said, standing.

"Keep me informed."

She smiled, pleasant, knowing what Ennui meant. "I will. Don't worry."

Ennui contacted the senior leader of the First Floor Group and met with him prior to a lunch appointment. She inquired about the movement among the youth in his group.

"I've not heard about anything like this in modern times," he told Ennui. "There are historical accounts of revival, but most of my colleagues and professional peers believe those were emotional reactions—which were common to the mysticism of earlier times and a less sophisticated populace."

In her calculating and engaging manner, Ennui recommended that he visit with the parents of the key young people involved in the movement. "Express your professional concern," she counseled him. "Emotionalism is a youthful battle to be overcome and won by caring adults," she guided. "Maturity is essential to success, stability, and position. These are key lessons of growing up, and it is the duty of groups like this fine institution on the first floor to help foster this quality in the next generation," she shared.

The senior leader paid careful attention. He knew this wasn't a social visit.

Her last suggestion was that he must use his position to speak out about the pitfalls of the path these youngsters have chosen. "What happened late in the evening on the last day of school—this notion of Crown Prince Vassar appearing—is imaginary, no doubt brought on by fatigue, youthful imagination, and lack of proper education on such topics," she suggested, putting key words into the senior leader's mind.

The senior leader listened intently. Ennui was polite, and her words were thoughtfully couched in a modest, coy, and reserved tone. On the surface, her counsel seemed like the suggestions of an interested person, one professional brainstorming with another, but the senior leader knew better. He also knew, quite clearly, what he needed to do—right away.

When Ennui completed her feedback, the two sat smiling at each other—Ennui measuring the message delivered against the message received, the senior leader managing the tumult in his gut.

Always gracious as part of his professional persona, the senior leader stood and reached his hand toward Ennui. He helped her to her feet and extended his arm for her to walk beside him. As they approached the door to his office, he placed his hand on hers, smiled, "Ennui, thank you for coming."

The young leader trudged indirectly toward home in the Tower. He had been to a meeting in the castle with a group exploring outreach into the Southeastern part of the castle. They were hoping to develop small cells of people in the community to examine the teachings of the High King.

Unlike the youth movement on the first floor, this group of devotees was closely observed by Zophos' agents. While Ennui was only concerned with her agents in the Round Tower, Letizia Pintaro networked through both the Round Tower's agents and the agents in the castle. One never knew when a relationship might come in handy.

The young leader had been up late nearly every night for a week. His youngest child was sick and his wife was worn to a nub with fatigue. The added work load from the revival of young hearts toward the King's teachings had worn him down. It was great work! The sort of response a man in his profession hoped for, but he was overwhelmed with kids wanting to know more, hear more, talk more. And then there were the new kids, droves of them, and each needed to be contacted personally. Each parent needed to be met, reassured, and if open, invited to join the group on the first floor.

He was planning to stop by the home of one such new kid and his parents on his way home. While most of the kids in the movement came from the Tower, this young person lived in the castle. He knew basically where the boy lived, but it was an unfamiliar part of the castle with narrow side streets and narrower alley ways.

The weather had been dry and hot, but a summer thunderstorm boiled through earlier in the afternoon leaving puddles in the poor streets and quagmires in the gutters crowded with too much animal and human residue. Even though dusky dark, it was humid and sticky.

The young leader stopped at a corner, uncertain of which way to turn. A stocky man with closely trimmed hair and beard startled him from behind. "You look like a man who could use some guidance," he said.

The young leader was relieved. He told the man where he was trying to go. Quickly—probably too quickly, had the young leader paid attention—the man acknowledged, "Ah, yes. I know the place. It's hard to find," and looking around, "especially in the dark. Come on. I'll take you there."

The young leader thanked the man and told him he just needed directions, but the man insisted. The young leader resisted and the stocky man took him by the elbow in a vice-like grip. The young leader struggled, but he was no match.

They turned down a tight passage filled with garbage and standing sewage in the culverts. Two accomplices joined the stocky man from the shadows. The stocky man said, "You've been busy with meetings, haven't you, young leader? Got a whole tribe of young people following you, I hear. Well, you and your meetings are a disruption."

The young leader was terrified.

"What's in your bag, young leader?"

The bag contained names, names of young people—their addresses, their friends, parents, and even their notes and journals. The bag also held papers from his earlier meeting in the castle. It was information that shouldn't—mustn't—fall into the wrong hands. He held it close.

One of the others tugged on the strap of the bag. The young leader didn't let go. The thug jerked again, and the young leader resisted.

The stocky man tripped him, and as the young leader fell, the thug folded his arm behind his back. With his other arm grasping the precious bag, the young leader smacked hard against the nasty pavement. The stocky man grasped him by the hair on the back of his head, lifted, and smashed his face into the pavement. Again. Blood flowed from his nose, lips, forehead, and broken teeth.

The second and third men kicked him, breaking ribs, bruising his thighs, and breaking his fingers as he tried to deflect their abuse. The stocky man smashed his face into the pavement again, and again, bursting open the skin on his cheeks and chin. He almost lost consciousness, but the stocky man's professionalism did not grant him that reprieve.

They took his bag and went through his pockets. They found

the key to his home. "Look here what I found," the second man said, dangling the key in front of the young leader's bloody eyes. "Let's see. What did they tell us? Is it a pretty, young wife and two children or a pretty, young wife and three children?"

The young leader squirmed. Thrashed his arm. Tried to get up.

The stocky man wrenched the young leader's body sideways and submerged his head in the sewage-filled gutter. The young leader held his breath, but the stocky man had done this before.

They're drowning me, he realized.

He thought of his wife. His children.

There was the reflexive action—his brain assuming command and control. He inhaled, sucking a great gulp of refuse into his mouth, nose, and lungs.

The stocky man held him under until he passed out, then lifted his head from the gutter, and dropped his face onto the cobblestones.

Pushing against the young leader's body, the stocky man stood. He took the young leader's bag, emptied the contents into his own satchel, and tossed the pirated empty beside its owner. "Give me the key," he demanded.

The youth stood in the doorway looking up and down the darkening street. He suspected the young leader might have trouble finding his home, and as dusk turned to dark, he watched expectantly. Waiting.

Although he didn't live in a good neighborhood, it was his home territory, and he knew everyone. He didn't recognize the two men who emerged from the alley, one rushing to one side of the street and one to the other.

He waited until the strangers were gone, then walked to the mouth of the alley. He saw the body, but with it face down and almost dark he had no idea who it might be. He looked around. No one. Walked closer to the fallen, and recognized the young leader's bag.

Scrambling from the alley, the youth ran back home, screaming for his father's help. The man ran alongside his terrified son to where the young leader lay. Crumpled. Broken.

It was a blessing in disguise—the final drop of his face onto the cobblestones, the merciless shove by the stocky man forcing himself upright. The shock and compression purged enough of the tooth fragments, blood, mucous, and excrement from the young leader's breathing passage that he didn't suffocate.

It was late when the knock came on the young wife's door. She peered through the peep hole into the somber faces of a man she didn't know and a youth whom she recognized.

It wasn't unusual for there to be a late-night knock, not when your work is with young people finding their way through life's twists and turns at all hours, but mostly after hours. But it was unusual for a parent to knock at this hour.

The man tried to reassure her as his son watched ashen. There were no words—no words the man knew, anyway—to gracefully inform her of her husband's condition.

With his hands in front of him, the left holding the right's wrist, he told her of finding her husband, cleaning him, and caring for him in their home. He was honest about the young leader's grievous condition, but spared her the details. He noted the point when her eyes told him she had retreated into her soul's inner sanctum to begin sorting her mounting anguish. The light in her look dimmed as she withdrew. *I've told her enough for now*, he thought, and curtailed any further recounting.

Before he and his son left, the man asked the young wife if there was anything she needed, if there was anything he could do for her. He meant it.

He promised to come the next day and take her to where the young leader was recovering. *I'll prepare her then for what she will see—see what's left of her husband.*

News spread of the young leader's tragic assault. Among the youth, there was the predictable array of widely-varying and intense emotion as they attempted, in their immaturity and innocence, to manage the horrors of an ugly world. The parents, in their own shock at the brutality unleashed upon the young leader, didn't discuss the tragedy with their children. They didn't know what to say. Inadvertently, the message was clear: We have no resource, personal or corporate, sufficient to help in such a circumstance as this. By inference, since the High King's name peppered the language of the Round Tower, the inaction and silence of the withdrawn parents implicated the High King as equally absent and impotent.

The well-meaning reassured the young leader's wife that her husband would be fine, that she was blessed he was alive, that he would be back before she knew it, that the High King knew this would occur and cared about her, that this was his will, and that this would turn out for the best. Others presumed the young family's affliction was the King's karma because of something they did to displease him. They cared enough to counsel the young wife to get the family in right standing with the King as soon as possible lest a more grievous discipline be warranted. Some of these who seemed to know intoned the children would be next to suffer. Still others exhorted her that it was more important than ever for her to think positive thoughts and not waver in her belief that her husband would recover fully. They were also of the opinion that the reason this suffering had befallen them in the first place was their lack of faithful belief in the King's power and goodness.

The young wife expressed appreciation for these platitudes and warnings because it was what was expected of her as a member of the First Floor Group. Further, it would be unfitting for her as the young leader's wife to handle herself otherwise.

These hollow assurances brought closure for the disengaged and unthinking. By repeating the trite phrases to each other and the young wife, the speakers concluded their analysis regarding this tragedy. Their lives continued. She and her children were left to suffer and manage grief in solitude and vulnerability.

When she was alone with her laundry, or end-of-day dishes, the young leader's wife felt her soul was in danger of running aground. She was foundering and knew these waves of tumult could well ruin her on life's rocky coast. For all her bravery, she wasn't okay. Her children were acting out. The oldest was sassy, the middle turbulently rebellious, and the youngest—18 months—tearful and clinging. Not a night went by without nightmares. Not a night passed without her being up to assist her husband.

The elder who chaired the finance subcommittee for the First Floor Group knocked on the young wife's door at dinner time shortly after the unfortunate event, unannounced, and delivered the news. "Since your husband isn't working, the elders felt it poor stewardship of the group's funds to pay him for a job he's not doing."

She nodded, standing at the door in her apron, the toddler clinging to her leg.

The rest of his message, couched against the magnanimity of generously continuing with partial compensation of one-quarter salary, was that they could depend on this income, albeit reduced, for two weeks based upon the young leader's time of service, the extenuating circumstance of his illness, and the good will of the finance committee. "At that time, however, if your husband cannot fulfill his duties," he said, "the First Floor Group will have to fill his position. And of course, as you understand, we will need full funds to pay the new person."

She stared at him, his words marauding through her until they found purchase in her destitute emotions. There they staked a claim, demanding a bribe she was unable to pay.

"I hope you understand," the Chairman said, nodding, smiling—the kind of grin expected of them in the Round Tower—his body language suggesting she agree and smile tepidly too.

"Thank you for stopping by," she said, flatly.

There was a slight squint in the inside corners of the young wife's eyes as she bid him a pleasant evening. For both the bearer of the message and the recipient, the action of the elders was the seed of bitterness planted by mandate in the fertile soil of their hearts.

The man left her doorway, relieved his duty was done, but with a withering wind blowing through his soul. She returned to her stove, to potatoes that boiled over in her absence, the same withering wind driving her closer to ruination on the rocky shoreline.

Time passed, and the young leader's outward wounds were scabbing and scarring, but he was violently ill from ingesting the putrid contents of the gutter. His gums were healing, but his smile was forever altered by the snags hanging where whole teeth had been.

Initially, the young wife expected to help her husband move from the bed, to the chair, to the bed, to the toilet, to the bed, to the table, to the bed, to the chair, to the....

But the realization began ringing: *He should be more independent... by now. He's trying, but the dizziness.... It's more than he can overcome.* She felt hope drift in the current.

Knowing his wife was sinking, the young leader courageously attempted more responsibility. He navigated by crawling. No one in the family knew which was the lesser of the two evils: assisting him or watching Dad and Husband crawl through the house.

Ennui sent her condolences to the senior leader, acknowledging the terrible timing and resultant bind this crime against the young leader created for him as he carried out his professional duties. She affirmed his position and professionalism, and she expressed her confidence in his leadership and commitment to do the right thing reining-in this unrepresentative and indecorous youth movement within the First Floor Group. Ennui's note of condolence was no surprise to the senior leader, and he was diligent to carry out his duties. After all, he was only four years from full-pension retirement.

Letizia received a verbal report regarding the contents of the young leader's bag. The report was delivered and received while standing. It was to the point. Nothing was said about how the information was obtained. It did skitter across her consciousness, but she demurred, *It was necessary.*

Others beneath her noted the names from the bag and began tracking, observing, and as warranted, escalating suspicious individuals. All Letizia cared to know was if they discovered any surprises. With none noted, she determined the matter resolved.

There were new agents on the first floor—three to be exact, none of whom knew the others existed, although the savviest of the three suspected. Each reported to a different supervisor who assumed he was passing duplicate information to his own supervisor. *One of these days,* each assured himself, *I will be a supervisor. For now though, I'm paying my dues.*

But paying one's dues while assigned to the First Floor Group was proving hard. What initially had been presented as a hot spot in the Round Tower was certainly no hot spot now. In fact, there weren't even any embers.

The senior leader had managed the group with a deft and professional touch. Each agent independently reported the senior leader's messages— both public and private—motivating the adults to squelch the youth movement. It was simply not in anyone's best interest—not the group, not the families, and most of all, not the young people. The sooner they returned to proper decorum, self-management, and dispassionate, polite, and pleasant communication the more representative they would be of the standards expected in the Round Tower, the First Floor Group, and most importantly, the High King. After all, what would he think if he encountered them behaving in any way unbecoming the balance and tolerance indicative of the Tower?

The problem of the youth movement was resolved. The numbers quickly dwindled from a spike of 250 following the young leader's awful beating to a fairly consistent 13-17. That attendance bottomed out lower than it was prior to the revival was attributed to poor leadership. The young leader should have known better. It was a cancerous rate of growth. Unsustainable. Irresponsible, really. Not to mention, unbecoming, unprofessional, and unprecedented.

As their thinking resolved into consensus, the elders replaced the young leader with a new staff person. One in possession of stronger credentials—for the benefit of the children.

The parents didn't object. They too wanted the best for their progeny.

CHAPTER 9

The King's Wilderness

itting just to the side of a sunbeam, his mind rambling through faraway places as he stared out the window of his room at a sweeping view, Hank returned from his reverie with the tap at his door. A soldier greeted him when Hank opened the peep hole. "Good morning, Sir. We have your breakfast."

Hank unbolted the door. Two soldiers, looking much like all the other soldiers he had seen, marched in carrying trays, one bearing food, the other coffee and service. The first set his tray of food on the table, nodded to the other, and was dismissed. The second introduced himself as he set the coffee service and began arranging Hank's table for breakfast. "Sir, my name is Parra. I have the privilege of serving as your valet."

"Parra, nice to meet you, and thank you for looking after me."

Parra moved efficiently, finishing his preparation so Hank could eat. After all, there was hot cereal, and no one wants to eat cold cereal or drink lukewarm coffee. "Cream? Sugar?"

"Nope. Black. Thank you."

Parra replaced the lid on the sugar and placed Hank's cup of black coffee beside his plate, stepped back, and stood behind Hank's chair to assist him when he sat.

When Hank made his first visit to Gnarled Wood, he was confronted with a level of personal service to which he was unaccustomed. It completely bewildered him, and took some getting used to. Still, coming back to it after two years away, he had to pay attention as Parra did his job.

Hank was hungry, and wherever he was, he had concluded he

wasn't a prisoner. Any residual doubt was erased when he took his first sip of coffee. The King never served anything mediocre to drink, and the cup of coffee was exquisite.

Parra busied himself straightening, arranging, and laying out clothes. He moved stealthily, like a human cat. It was apparent that even though a valet by assignment, he was a man who could handle himself if need be.

As Parra came from the bedroom, Hank said, "So Parra, I know this is a stupid question, but…?"

"Sir, there are no stupid questions, especially from a man who came by the route you traveled."

Hank had liked Parra immediately, but his gracious answer solidified his initial sense. "Thank you," he said, shaking his head gently as he reflected. "So you know about my trip then?"

"Enough to know you require some orientation."

"That's an understatement!" Hank said, setting his coffee cup down. He scooted his chair away from the table, turned it, and casually faced Parra. "So, where am I?"

Parra chuckled, not with condescension, but delightful opportunity. Spreading his arms wide, he said, "Sir, this is the King's wilderness!"

Hank didn't know what he was expecting Parra to say, but "wilderness" wasn't on either his short list or long list. "Say again, please."

"You are in the wilderness, Sir. Your Brother used to come here all the time. And now, here you are."

On cue, from the shadows, Jester inserted his unsolicited opinion into Hank's mind, *He's punishing me. Typical. I made the King mad, so he's getting even. Sure, he said it was okay that I fouled up, but who does he think he's fooling? There are consequences to everything. I've been set aside—in the wilderness, no less.* The thoughts arrived in rapid succession. Hank turned his head to look out the window.

There was a knock at the door. Parra answered, and snapped to attention as the Captain from the previous night entered. He bowed his head politely and greeted Hank with a warm, "Good morning."

With the Captain's entrance, Hank was distracted from Jester's accusation and spin. He stood to face the officer. He and Parra both had pleasant, expectant expressions. As he stood, a new—different— thought entered Hank's mind: *Why did I just revert from thinking of Father as "Father" and refer to him instead as "King"?*

Hank got it!

Without being heavy handed, Magician did what Magician was so good at doing. It was the slight edge Hank needed to seize the advantage, and with a purely mental declaration, while returning the Captain's greeting, Hank thought, *Go to hell, Jester!*

There was a glint in both the Captain's and Parra's eyes at the exact moment Hank instructed Jester where to go. He noticed, and thought, *I'm in good hands—here in the wilderness.*

While Parra stood close, the Captain elaborated on Hank's location as if he had been listening to the earlier exchange. Motioning toward the window, the two men moved that direction.

"Coffee?" Hank asked the Captain.

Parra was already in motion.

"So, my Brother came here?" Hank said, looking out the window.

"He did, Sir. But he never just came to the wilderness. Once here, he entered into it, fully becoming part of it." The Captain looked Hank in the eye. "He embraced it, and was embraced by it."

"So Vassar didn't stay here?" Hank observed, imagining his Brother bivouacked in a wilderness camp.

"Oh, yes. He did. Almost always," the Captain corrected.

"Not in these quarters. Just down the hall," Parra interjected.

"That's right," the Captain confirmed.

The Captain's distinction between coming to the wilderness and going into the wilderness escaped Hank. Shaking his head a couple of times, he said, "I'm sorry. I don't understand the point you're making."

"When your Brother came, the first thing he did was synchronize himself with the rhythm of the wilderness—the dawn and dusk, the movement of the animals, the songs of the birds through the day and night."

"You've already done much the same thing, Sir—intuitively," Parra offered. "You are very similar to your Brother."

It was a high compliment. Hank smiled and nodded, but doubted.

"The 'settling in' that I was describing," the Captain continued: "It helped your Brother feel safe, and it enabled him to accomplish the work he came here to do. He had to feel secure before the desires of his heart could surface. He knew he had to be in a place without distraction."

"I'm with you," Hank said.

"Unlike the routine places of life, with their irregular pace, noise, and confusion—and you know, the general mayhem of Zophos' influence— here in the wilderness there is the predictability of solitude. Of course, just because solitude is available doesn't mean it is apprehended," the Captain said, thinking out loud. "The advantage of solitude must be seized. Deliberately. With determination, and that's what your Brother did when he came here."

"So, he came here alone?"

"Physically, he was alone, yes. But solitude is not lonely, Sir. Solitude is what the Crown Prince entered into while he was here. And embraced by the wilderness free from irregularity, your Brother met with the King and Magician and replenished his soul. While in the solitude of the King's wilderness, your Brother walked, and talked, and listened to your Father. I've heard the two of them laughing, seen them in contemplation, and observed them wrestling powerful issues to the ground until they succumb to a thoughtful plan of action."

That was Magician's cue. Hank recalled his request—actually, the plea he made—of his Father before leaving Gnarled Wood. *I asked Father to take me into his world, to speak with me about his observations, his thoughts, and his initiatives.*

Although he had not predicted this is how his Father would honor his request, thanks to the Captain, Parra, and no doubt Magician's subtle counsel, Hank understood—or at least comprehended—the opportunity at hand. *Father is affording me the same opportunity he afforded Vassar.*

The Captain studied the man before him. He noted the slight bulge of his jaw muscle, and knew their discussion centered him. He gently placed his hand on Hank's shoulder as he stood and made his exit.

When Hank turned from staring out the window, Parra handed him his satchel containing Vassar's letter. *How did he know I wanted that?* Hank thought. But he knew the answer as soon as the question formed in his mind. *Magician!*

He scooted his chair up to the cleared table and pulled Vassar's letter from the bag. Parra refilled Hank's cup, eyed his charge one final time, then silently disappeared.

In the solitude of his chambers, the breeze blowing gently through the open window, and the sunlight dragging the shadows across the floor toward him by degree, Hank re-read Vassar's letter three times. With each reading the letter was different, not in content, but in emphasis. Vassar's words echoed the words etched by his Father upon the walls of his heart. As he read, Magician counseled Hank, offering commentary regarding the words on the page and the words in his heart. The three persons and perspectives overlapped, blended, and merged into one.

Hank carefully contemplated Vassar's opening words: "Father knows what he's doing." And in the second paragraph, "I am working in advance, preparing the way."

Hank leaned back and stared across the room. *A declaration and a promise*, he thought.

Like eating a waffle and realizing between one bite and the next that you are full, Hank knew all of a sudden that his mind had taken aboard all it could carry. He reverently folded the letter and placed it back into his satchel.

Hank changed into the clothes Parra had laid out for him. He pulled on his boots, fastened his belt and dagger around his waist, and slung a canteen over his shoulder and across his chest. Walking to the door, Hank paused before touching the latch. *Magician, I realize you have been guiding me this morning. Thank you. Please continue.* Hank waited a moment more—listening for any other thoughts from his companion before opening the door.

The guards snapped to attention as the door opened. Parra was waiting. "This way please, Sir."

For all the twisting and turning down various passages the night before, Parra guided Hank to a simple exit from the building. Along the way, several soldiers fell in quietly behind them. At the exterior door, Parra said, "Your Father has given his soldiers orders concerning you, to guard you in all your ways, wherever you go. Although you will not see them, and it will appear to you as though you are by yourself, they have orders to protect you."

"I see," Hank said. "Thank you, Parra."

"Certainly, Sir."

Parra opened the exterior door, but Hank hesitated. Thinking. Reaching inside his shirt, Hank retrieved Vassar's letter from his satchel. He held it reverently, then said, "I was just wondering if I could ask a favor?"

"Anything at all, Sir."

"Would it be possible for someone to make a copy of this letter for me? I need it printed on a durable material and I need each major thought numbered for easy reference[1]."

"I'll take care of it personally, Sir," Parra said.

Hank thought again. The letter was clearly a treasured possession. He held the letter out to Parra. Both men held onto the folded pages.

---

1   See the Appendix, page 517, to read a copy of Parra's work.

"Don't worry, Sir. I'll take care of the letter and will have the copy for you by dinner time."

Hank nodded to Parra, then stepped into the light of the new day. It felt good to be outside. He took a deep breath and studied his surroundings. Even though he saw his Father's soldiers exit the building with him, just like Parra said, he couldn't see anyone now.

Hank's thoughts returned to Vassar's written declaration and promise. *So Vassar, you have prepared a way for me?* Noting a little-used trail, Hank went that direction—into a forest of old growth and sparse undergrowth.

The King's Throne

The High King could have insisted on a more elaborate throne. In fact, he could have ordered whatever he wanted to be crafted, but he preferred the more understated seat. Vassar sat to his right.

From throughout the Kingdom—far and wide, high and low—the potentates, rulers, governors, legislators, bosses, and powerful people, some legitimate and some illegitimate, paraded their projects and issues before the King and Crown Prince. They wanted this, wanted that, sought more, needed permission, wished for power they didn't have, wanted freedom from responsibilities they did have, asked relief from burdens, debt, and obligation. On and on the pleadings went. How the King and Crown Prince put up with it, no one observing knew. In fact, why they put up with it, no one observing ventured a guess. But they did, and did so consistently and repetitively.

Late in the morning, buried toward the end of the long line of plaintiffs, claimants, complainers, reporters, defenders, usurpers, and those believing themselves entitled, Zophos stepped before the King and Crown Prince. It was more than he could bear—this command to report to the King on a regular basis. But, his appearance was nonnegotiable. Worse yet? To appear before the throne he was seeking to gain was like salt in an open wound. Zophos determined long ago that the first thing he was going to do, when he overthrew the King and eliminated the Crown Prince, was to order a more fitting chair!

He could see it in his mind, *A grand seat on a raised dais. Large. Imposing. Intimidating as hell! Gold! Lots of gold. Gold so pure it's soft when I sit on it.*

"Zophos! Where have you been?" the King demanded.

Jerking his mind back from his denial, his hands in front of him deferentially, Zophos didn't look at the King. Instead, he stared at a spot on the floor—the same spot he had picked out to focus upon when first summoned before the throne for insurrection.

Years earlier, eons, his *coup d'état* failed, not because it was a bad idea or ill-planned, but because he underestimated the King. The consequence of his botched power-grab was swift. He was expelled from his position of leadership in the Kingdom and cast into Gnarled Wood. While the consequence of his failure to gain the throne was quick, the King's retribution was anything but.

Each time Zophos stood before the King, his first summons replayed vividly as if current. Standing on these very tiles, staring at the same spot then as now, the King ordered him removed as Star of the Morning, cast from the Kingdom, and promised him an eternity of flaming fires, constant noise from grinding teeth—his foremost among them—and copious worms with ravenous appetites to feed upon his perpetually rotting flesh.

While Zophos wondered why the King delayed his promised retribution, he knew that he must do whatever was necessary—make any sacrifice, require any expenditure, spare no one or nothing, seize every advantage—to successfully dethrone the King and irreparably compromise the Crown Prince. Otherwise, his fate was certain.

Why the King delayed was none of his concern. All that mattered was now...but he was curious. Still, no matter how many angles he examined, he always arrived at the same conclusion: The King felt it was to his advantage, and the benefit of the people whom he loved, to delay his vengeance.

Zophos believed this was the King's weakness. *The people the King loves—living in Gnarled Wood, the castle, and most importantly, the chattel living in the Round Tower—are his soft underbelly, his vulnerability, his ultimate shortcoming.* Consequently, as with the King, people remained Zophos' primary focus, not because he cared about them as the King did, rather because he saw them as the means to achieve his goal.

Granted, he couldn't help but afflict all of Gnarled Wood with his hatred—and his desperation frequently enticed him to overplay, over state, and over compensate. But even after a binge of hostility, he returned to focus singularly upon the King's beloved people.

Zophos jolted back to the present with an elbow to his ribs by a Kingdom guard. He grunted and twisted, his breath escaping momentarily from the unexpected jab. He eyed the guard with a sideways glare.

"Zophos!" the King demanded. "You are wasting my time, time I grant you only because I am merciful to the unmerciful. Answer me, now! Where have you come from?"

"Your Highness, I have been roaming here and there."

"Be more specific," the King barked.

"I have been walking through Gnarled Wood."

"No doubt, no doubt," the King stated, bored.

While the King was Zophos' ultimate foe and his throne the ultimate seat of power, the King found Zophos the least interesting of all creatures both sentient and not. To Zophos, the King possessed unlimited power, position, and intrigue. But for the King, Zophos possessed not one iota of depth or interest to command anything beyond his slightest notice.

"Have you passed through the wilderness lately?" the King inquired.

Not taking his eyes off the spot on the floor, Zophos nodded, said, "Yes."

"Then you've noticed that my son, Hank, is there. He's a fine man, a great man actually. No one else quite like him. Carries himself with confidence, poise, and resolve."

"Who wouldn't feel confident with your people looking after him? Send your soldiers away and see how long he carries himself with confidence."

"You think so?" the King baited.

"No. I don't think so, I know so! Isolate him from your guard dogs, your Majesty, then let me have at him. His confidence will vanish like a mirage."

The King huffed through his nose at Zophos, which caused the dark lord to look up from the floor. "Faith, Hope, and Love have already been reassigned."

Zophos was delighted with the implicit permission to go after Hank. He was incensed that none of his people had informed him about this.

The King motioned with his head. He was finished speaking with Zophos.

The soldier standing next to the dark lord grasped him above the elbow, squeezed tight, causing Zophos' fingers to tingle, and led him away from the throne. Zophos looked back—he always did—but the King, as usual, had turned his attention elsewhere. The King and his throne were all Zophos thought about, but Zophos got the distinct impression he never crossed the King's mind unless he was standing in front of him.

The guard didn't bother to escort Zophos from the throne room, let alone the palace. It was a blatant demonstration of how unthreatened the King felt.

Zophos didn't need an escort. He knew the way. But he desperately wanted a patrol for the appearance of being noteworthy.

Zophos let himself out a side door at the end of a remote corridor. His carriage and horsemen waited—just where they always waited. Zophos' frustration spiked ferociously, spreading across his chest as though he was being stretched on the rack.

He stood silent, fuming, his fingers clinched into fists so tight his long fingernails cut his palms, drawing blood. Angry humiliation brimmed along his eyelids. He ground his teeth and his face contorted under the duress of his stress.

Zophos loosed his pants and urinated on the side of the King's palace. He walked, peeing as he went until his bladder was empty. Then, with bloody smears on the crotch of his pants, Zophos strode to his carriage, coughed, spit, and departed for the wilderness.

The Round Tower

Without the leadership of the young leader, and wilting under the dismissive comments of the senior leader, the number of youth in the First Floor Group fell further to eight young people, all of whom attended youth functions because their parents insisted. The senior leader, the First Floor Group staff, the parents, and the stalwarts of the First Floor Group took pride in these eight young people. They affirmed each other and told the children they were the faithful. The implication for their 240 or so missing peers was evident.

The kids knew better. This delusion of the adults discredited them as role models or dependable voices and created confusion. As a result, the youth were left with only themselves to chart life's course. For all their independent, adolescent posturing, they knew a lack of mentors was a poor place in which to find themselves.

Of the eight, two were spiraling out of control, exhibiting uncharacteristic misbehavior. Three were known to be active sexually, sleeping with whomever wherever. One was showing a dangerous proclivity for consuming too much alcohol, even appearing at youth group and school tipsy. Two of the kids seemed sincere in their commitment to the tenets taught by the High King, but there was enough residual hostility among their peers due to the young leader's demise, the disintegration of the youth group, and the belittlement by the First Floor Group's leadership and parents that these two were viewed as suspicious by both their peers and the adults.

Isolated and ostracized, not only by their peers and adult role models, but also due to schedule and home address, these two young people couldn't even draw consistent support from each other. Predictably, Zophos' agents nitpicked the two young people who were faithful to the King—watching, waiting, taking any opportunity to trip, discredit, accuse, and discourage. Since they had no support from each other, peers, parents, or leaders the kids suffered in their souls. However, to their credit, both did their best to consider the King's teaching on a regular basis and tried to let his tenets guide their daily activities. But, it was hard going. The agents were shrewd and relentless, and the circumstances were onerous for anyone, especially a young person.

Since the new leader of the youth was anxious to make a good impression, he presented nothing of alarm to the senior leader or his staff colleagues when they met. He did brief them about the two young people who remained committed to the passions fired by the so-called revival. This was an ongoing concern, but he assured them he was paying attention.

Personally, not only was he concerned about the aberrant behavior of these two young people, he was concerned about the potential fallout their behavior could have upon him professionally. Not only this, but the youth revival—and how he would handle it—was the primary topic the search committee asked him about during his interview to work with the First Floor Group. Only a fool would fail to speak to this concern when in the room with a cross section of those who matter. Nothing was ever mentioned about the other six youth.

Since equilibrium had been reestablished, the parents and supporters of the First Floor Group seemed content. For good measure, and for the opportunity to promote his leadership abilities, about once a month the senior leader publically referenced the revival, the dangers of emotionalism, and the need to be vigilant in protecting peace. His references were both admonition and oblique self-promotion.

With what he felt was genuine courage of conviction, the senior leader declared that although the First Floor Group is a people who hold tolerance most precious, there are times when toleration cannot be tolerated. Tranquility within the group is too important, he declared.

This logic was usually followed by the senior leader's affirmation that the First Floor Group was the most balanced, the most exemplary—indeed, the most noteworthy group in the Round Tower when it came to holding aloft, for all to examine, standard-setting ideals. In these emotional lectures the senior leader usually included two or three quotes by the High King. The quotes substantiated his teaching and implied the King agreed with his position. While this lent credence to the senior leader's comments in the ears of most, it was confusing to the two young people faithful to the King's tenets.

They were an easy target. Too immature to sort through the nuances of adult logic and deal-making, and too intimidated and isolated to cause a ruckus, they were of little concern to Zophos' agents.

But Letizia Pintaro left nothing to chance. There was too much at stake professionally—with Ennui, with Zophos—not to mention that something about these two young people troubled her at a gut level. She wouldn't—couldn't—let the supervisor's unremarkable report slide. She had learned to trust her gut instinct.

Letizia berated the supervisor for his lack of diligence. She told him to dig deeper, to demand excellence from those under him, and to accept nothing—stop at nothing—until the desired results were achieved. "And don't give me a report based upon a report," Letizia lectured. "Go see for yourself!"

The supervisor sat quietly, enduring, learning his lesson, and hoping for the opportunity to redeem himself with Ms. Pintaro. He wondered what to do about the remaining items on his meeting agenda. She answered his unspoken question. In calm, calculating tones, she told him to leave her office and not return until he verified his report.

When the man had slunk away and the door was closed behind him, Letizia smiled. She liked this supervisor and had plans for him to rise through the ranks—her ranks. *Meetings like this will secure his allegiance while testing his metal. High expectations create superior performance.* Still, as her smile faded, she knew that how he responded to her test was crucial to his future.

The two young people from the First Floor Group who remained loyal to the High King were lonely. They decided to meet after school. Showing more poise than might be expected from people their age, they met at a popular hangout frequented by an assortment of business people and others meeting to chat.

Purchasing drinks and a snack, they selected a table not quite on the fringe. They visited about school and caught up on who was doing what before turning their attention to the real reason they were meeting.

They had never had a meeting like this, nor participated in one, so they fumbled about with inefficient words to state either their cause or noble purpose. They knew they needed to meet, to support and be supported, but neither had a concept of how a meeting like this could be supportive or lend itself to problem solving. But pain is a tremendous motivation, and both were hurting from emotional isolation.

Mostly they shared stories and discovered they weren't alone. They were being singled out, monitored, and compromised. They were under mounting pressure from their parents to moderate their passion for the High King and become more like their friends. They found this mysterious since their friends were self-destructing. Why would our parents want us to be like them, they wondered? As their conversation turned to their friends, they expressed deep sadness at how many friends they had lost and how many were worse off now than before the youth movement began. They shared what they knew about the young leader, sat quietly contemplating the suspected correlation between the revival and his assault, and then turned their discussion to their beliefs about the High King.

Watching the two young people, the man waited until he figured they had sorted through the chaff and made their way into the substance of their meeting. Then, he made his move. Carrying his drink, he walked casually, weaving midst the tables. The bistro was filled with customers and nearly every table was occupied—just as he hoped would be the case.

He had rehearsed his plan numerous times, even while he stood off to the side observing them. He stepped to their table, "Excuse me. May I have this seat?"

"Sure. Of course," one said, motioning for the man to take the chair.

Both were surprised when the man sat down with them. "Forgive the surprise, young friends. I've observed your discussion, know something of the pressures you are feeling, and would like to visit with you about your options."

They were astounded, but kept their composure. The man had counted on that as well, just like he had counted on the bistro being busy. He didn't really know what he would do if one, or both, bolted from the table and ran screaming to management. Still, he couldn't afford them too much time to think. While taking advantage of their youthful innocence, these two were no longer naïve. The stress of the preceding months, and the intense scrutiny each was enduring, was hardening them with cynicism.

The young people looked at each other for reassurance. Just as their eyes began to squint, the man seized his opportunity.

"The High King is aware of the difficulties you are facing," the man said. "I have been sent here to encourage you. There are several hundred young people like you, and even more adults, in the Round Tower and the castle who are devoted to the High King. They too are courageous souls who walk in the light and have not compromised. Be encouraged!"

"Several hundred?" one said, leaning forward.

The man nodded.

The two young people looked at each other and back to the man. Broad smiles lightened the load on their anxious brows.

"Furthermore, just so you will know with certainty: You are indeed being watched. There is much to respect about those who are against you, but nothing to fear. Nevertheless, conduct yourselves wisely. Guard your steps. Care for your hearts with continued devotion to the King. Meet frequently to encourage each other."

The two young people were more at ease. A palpable energy circulated at the table.

The man continued, "You have enemies, but you have friends too—powerful friends—who are paying attention to your coming and going. Be confident, and don't be afraid!"

Both young people were beaming. They felt resurrected. Neither realized the weight of the onerous burden upon them, but their heaviness abated. It was as though a sunrise occurred inside them.

One of the young people asked the man, "So, how do you know about us, and who are you?"

"I am a knight in the Kingdom of the High King, pledged in service to him and to those whom he considers his friends. My name is, Faith."

The Wilderness

Hank followed the lightly used trail for about an hour. He was surprised how quickly the skills he honed during his previous trip to Gnarled Wood returned to him, not the least of which was the pace he kept.

The trail was mostly through timber with a few meadows. He startled a small herd of deer grazing in one clearing, but stopped and lowered his head so as not to appear their predator. He watched from the corner of his eye. The deer ambled off into the woods and Hank felt rewarded that they hadn't bounded away in fear. He wanted very much to enter into the wilderness, like the Captain and Parra said Vassar did, and not intrude upon or disturb the natural solitude and rhythm of the woods.

He caught glimpses of a lake as he walked and thought about cutting through the woods for a closer look, but opted to stay on the trail. If he left the trail he would have to think about where he was going instead of focusing on Vassar's letter.

The path rose up a rooted and rocky incline, culminating in a fine view of the lake. Hank decided it was time to take a rest. Because sitting on the ground was uncomfortable to his intractable back, still woefully sore from the earlier spasms, he searched the area until he located a deadfall that had a level spot where he could sit. As he eyed his prospective place, the thought occurred to him, *This seat is a little too convenient.* He looked around. *A touch too obvious.* Turning around, *And possessing a view of the lake that's a bit too picturesque. This is no coincidence.* He acknowledged Vassar's thoughtfulness and Magician's awareness as he sat down.

By Texas and Oklahoma standards, it was a small lake, but big enough that it wasn't a pond. Hank figured there was an official designation that distinguished a lake from a pond, but he didn't know what it was. *This is definitely a lake, but more of a Minnesota-size lake,* he thought.

While in graduate school, Hank spent days and days paddling a canoe with his friend Hub through the myriad lakes in the Boundary Waters of Minnesota and the Quetico Provincial Park just across the border in Ontario. The ancient glaciers left thousands of trenches, holes, hollows, and valleys that filled with water and left an outrageous—almost comical—map of lakes, ponds, and marshes.

Staring across the lake, its shores lined with firs, spruce, and pines, Hank reflected on those canoe trips. *Fresh-caught Walleye for dinner, drinking straight from the lake, camping on islands to avoid the bears, and sleeping during storms as rain pelted the tent, thunder clapped, and lightening split the pitch-black-night of the wilderness.* Great memories!

To his delight, a loon swam into view from a cove. He had observed hundreds of these eccentric birds during his trips to Minnesota and Canada.

While awkward on land—nearly helpless except for scooting along on their breast—their swimming and deep-dives were magnificent to him. He never tired of studying their bodies of checkerboard, black and white feathers, topped off with jet-black heads and red eyes. That their Creator designed them with a spear for a bill gave them a profile Hank felt was unparalleled in nature.

For all the interesting and fascinating aspects of the north woods, the magical, haunting call of a loon was his favorite. The Foreman at the North Woods Trading Post, Papa Joe, told him there are scientists who devote their careers to studying the mysterious birds. Hank thought that interesting, and mused again, *That might be an interesting job. Paddle out. Wait 'til dusk. The north woods are the only geography with a signature. Nothing like the eerie, lonesome whistle of a loon over a glaciated lake to conclude the day.*

"*Crazy as a loon!*" The simile popped into his head. *Fitting,* he thought. *Warbling, yodeling. Hanging out in bachelor flocks. Swimming around like they only have one leg and wing. Diving. Surfacing. Flapping.*

Running across the water.

The loon in the alcove below him called—the warbling yodel. Hank watched, expecting the customary gyrations and erratic diving. But it floated in one spot, facing the main body of the lake, scanning the skies, and periodically calling.

This went on for several minutes—perhaps ten or fifteen. And then the loon began its splashing, diving, ducking, yodeling, and generally goofy behavior, pausing occasionally to eye the sky. *I've not ever seen this before,* Hank thought.

Taking his cue from the loon, Hank studied the sky. A bird circled high above the lake. Then, he heard the return call, and watched as the incoming loon began descending in ever-tightening circles.

Unlike ducks, whose feet are farther forward on their bodies and suitable to use like landing gears, the loon's feet are close to its tail and remain folded up against its body when landing. Once airborne, their short wings make them strong, fast flyers who migrate thousands of miles. But take offs require a long runway and landings are more or less controlled crashes.

The incoming loon, having made its spiraling approach, skimmed the surface of the lake. Touching down at high speed, the loon skimmed the water on its belly, its head held high—until the entropy between flight and float erupted in a tumbling spray of lake water. The newly arrived loon composed itself with wing flaps and head bobs, as Hank had seen hundreds do, and swam to meet its awaiting friend.

The two loons swam off together. There were no more calls or funky behavior. *Clearly, there was an invitation issued by the first loon to the second,* he thought, *and given the waiting and observation of the first bird, this was a planned event. That's farfetched for a bird. But seeing is believing.* More than once he almost reached for his phone to research loon behavior, but remembered, *I'm carrying a dagger these days, not a phone.* That freedom didn't escape his notice.

Hank took his time enjoying the view from his private bench—

listening, watching, replenishing his soul. Late morning, to his thrill, the two loons returned. The first loon, Hank assumed, since all loons looked the same to him, sat floating while the second swam farther out into the lake. As he had observed on many occasions, the loon began flapping and running in an all-out effort to gain sufficient speed to become airborne. The bird ran flapping for five-hundred yards before escaping the surface of the water. Circling to gain altitude, it eventually was high enough to clear the trees at the end of the lake and disappeared. Once out of sight, the first loon turned and swam out of sight.

Hank was enthralled. For all the loons he had observed, and all the crazy loon behavior he had witnessed, this was unique. *It's a gift*, he knew, and with Magician's promptings, took conscious inventory of how his emotional and mental capital had increased. He concluded the loons were an orchestrated gift from his Brother. His heart was full and he was grateful. He sat on his log, shaded by a blue spruce, and relished the solitude.

Surrounding him, a pitched battle raged over the territory gained by the King in Hank's life. The King's soldiers, unseen to Hank, defended his position against the desperate onslaught of Zophos' forces. Unbeknownst to Hank, his life was in jeopardy, but he was held in the hands of his Father's troops—just as Parra said.

Hank realized that had he not availed himself of the wilderness solitude he would not have obtained the emotional and mental rewards he accrued. What he did not realize was how important his retreat into solitude was to his Father. While Hank had stepped into the wilderness, his Father had ensured his security in the wilderness so they could gain the benefit of solitude together.

And Zophos raged in desperation against the High King. In his frustration, he ordered Jester to redouble his deceptions and attacks on the King's son, the Crown Prince's Brother, Henry H. Henderson.

Chapter 10

The Round Tower

Faith called the first-floor class of senior students to order. Several months earlier he applied to be a substitute teacher. As an historian skilled in rhetoric and philosophy, he had all the teaching days he could handle substituting in history, language, religion, and philosophy classes.

He didn't need the work; he wanted access to the young minds and hearts. It didn't take long before the full-time teachers realized Faith was an excellent sub. Further, when resuming class, most regular teachers received unsolicited feedback on Faith that was glowing.

Faith's lecture was animated and energetic. He didn't mind interruption and honest questions. He knew young minds were alive and creative, albeit immature. And he knew creativity is a tender seed, easily crushed or stunted, but needing challenge to flourish.

He was filling in for a longtime teacher away on a short leave of absence. Today's lecture was a comparative overview of ancient literary texts dealing with the subject of light. "We will have a written test tomorrow," Faith stated. "I will evaluate and grade your essays over the weekend. We will review the material and tests on Monday."

Three rows back, her green eyes alive, belying her quiet demeanor, sat Audie Vandermeer, one of the young people Faith met at the bistro. She had proven herself an astute student with an incisive mind capable of thinking in both abstract story and concrete fact.

Monday morning, Faith rapped his knuckles three times on his lectern. He carefully reviewed the test, spending the hour highlighting, embellishing, going deeper on aspects of the subject the students demonstrated aptitude to understand, and revisiting points the class failed to articulate clearly in their essays. Just before the conclusion of class, Faith returned the graded essays.

At the top of Audie's essay it said, "See me." She examined the pages. There were no marks and no grade. Her heart sank.

She took her time gathering her things and kept her head down, avoiding the inquisitive looks from friends wanting to know what grade she received. For his part, Faith kept the class longer than he should have, leaving them less time than normal to move from his class to their next class. In so doing, the students didn't engage in the routine banter. It was his gift to Audie.

Audie lagged behind, waiting until two other students visited with Faith before stepping up beside his lectern. She started to show him her test and his handwritten note, but he said, "Audie, I have four appointments already scheduled this afternoon. Can you meet me here at four o'clock?"

Faith's business-like tone was uncharacteristic, intimidating. She nodded, "Sure. Four-o-clock is fine."

She wasn't accustomed to being summoned for a meeting with a teacher and wished four o'clock wasn't five hours away, but she had no alternative. She had to carry the ill-defined dread for the rest of the day.

The hours passed like cold syrup. Only her best friend knew about the meeting. She had been able to avoid everyone else.

A few minutes before four, Audie peeked into the classroom. Faith was sitting with his back to the door beside one of her classmates—a young man with the notorious reputation of being a poor student. They were hunched over what she assumed was his unsatisfactory essay.

As she sat down on the bench in the hallway to wait, Audie felt ashamed to be classed with the likes of him. She mentally reviewed her essay, yet again, trying to comprehend how she missed the answer so badly. This had never happened to her before.

The school had an entirely different feel after hours. It was as though its life was gone and a hollow shell left behind.

The only bright side, the only possible good thing, to not having a grade at the top of the page was that Faith might give her a chance to rewrite her essay. But this faint hope wasn't something she clung to, not as she sat where she had never sat before. Waiting. Her dread now rose to the base of her neck more palpable than at any other point in her torturous day.

The door opened and her classmate emerged. There was an awkward silence. She was the last person he expected to see sitting, waiting for an after-school appointment. For him, these were routine. Audie felt small and inferior, looking up at her classmate. He nodded and spoke, "Hey, Audie." His inflection carried unmistakable surprise.

Audie didn't have any words to return his greeting. She knew her quietness would be perceived as snooty and she hated that, but her crisis was great enough to tie her tongue. She blushed and waved a self-conscious greeting.

She watched him walk down the dead-center of the darkened hall and wondered about the protocol of these situations. She didn't know if she was to wait for Faith to invite her in or if she was to knock and let him know she was outside waiting.

She didn't have to wonder long. "Thank you for coming, Audie. Please, come in." Faith held the door. She took three steps into the classroom and waited, feeling like a lamb led to slaughter.

Faith closed the door behind him and then turned the two chairs he and the other student had used to face each other. Motioning, he waited politely for Audie to sit before sitting down across from her. She held her test paper in her lap.

Faith held out his hand to receive her essay. He went to his lectern, and wrote with a flourish, "Excellent! Absolutely excellent!" and returned to his seat. He handed the paper back to Audie.

Audie held her essay and looked, stunned, at the bold words and exclamation marks. In the first place, she had never received this evaluation before, and in the second place, she had never received a test back that didn't have either a letter or numerical grade.

"I don't understand," she said. As soon as she said it, she wished she had couched her comment differently. "I mean, thank you. It's just that, I've never…." She stopped. After all her thinking throughout the day, this was her first attempt to say what was on her mind and her jumbled words revealed her jumbled thinking and emotion.

He had let her struggle—suffer even—long enough. In an astounding demonstration of his careful consideration of her essay, Faith reviewed her written thoughts without looking at the paper. He referred to such-and-such paragraph, the second line, and reflected insights, appreciation, and thoughtful editorial comments. In this way, he reviewed Audie's paper in detail from start to conclusion. She listened and followed, amazed, flipping through her paper as Faith talked and referenced. No teacher had ever done this before. She captured a lot of what Faith said, but her mind was still recovering from the fatigue of dread it had carried.

The review complete, Faith turned to the true purpose of their meeting. "Now Audie, listen carefully," he said, legs crossed, his face and its distinguishing crooked nose alight. "You have done excellent work. But I am of the opinion that you measured your words as you wrote—perhaps out of fear, perhaps making an effort to write a pleasing and satisfactory essay."

Audie shifted her eyes and tilted her head slightly. Faith was exactly right. She was flattered that someone was taking the time to probe her potential, was appreciative of the analysis to save her the effort required to understand this deeper aspect of herself, but she felt vulnerable with her possibility laid bare.

"You cannot let the editor in you show up for work at the same time your creative, thoughtful self is at work. You need both, but they don't work well together."

"How do you know this?" Audie asked.

"Because your writing lacks the bold, sharp perspective and conclusion your analysis indicates you are capable of writing. I realize you are being careful, and know that you must do that, especially when you offer insight about the High King's teaching. I understand that there are many teachers and students who would frown upon your inclusion of his tenets in a scholastic paper."

Audie had taken some risks in comparing the High King's writing to the other sources studied.

Faith uncrossed his legs and leaned forward, putting his elbows on his knees. "A lady as gifted as you must retain a shrewd editor, no doubt. But here's my point, Audie: A lady as gifted as you must not limit herself for fear of editorial scrutiny, especially when you have insight to offer. If you do, you will suffer inside. Do you realize that there is a great deal more in you than is reflected in this paper?"

Audie thought for a moment, then answered cautiously, but honestly. "I'm not certain."

Faith sat back. "I know. Thank you for the honest answer. Let me ask you this: As you wrote your essay, particularly the points about the High King and his teaching, did you feel alive? Passionate? Did you feel as though you were a bit outside your comfort zone?"

"No. Not really," Audie said.

"And when you think about the High King—right now, this moment—how do you feel?"

She thought. She closed her eyes, concentrated, and considered. Then said, "I want more than anything to know him better, to follow him with the desire and drive I feel, and to reflect through my life his life and teaching."

Audie sat for a moment with her eyes closed. When she opened them, a few tears trickled down her cheek. Faith's hands were clasped in his lap, a broad smile creased his face.

"Audie, I'm proud of you. You just voiced the desire of your heart."

She nodded vigorously, because she knew Faith's affirmation was true, and because he gave her a word—a concept—to define the source of this driving desire. Not only did he isolate her heart by naming it for her, but she felt something important pressing against her sternum—a tightness, a passionate intensity to pursue further.

"Here is what I would like to do," Faith said. "At your leisure, sit down with the essay question and write about it again. But this time, write from both your head and your heart, putting into words all that you can about your heart's desire to know the High King. Experiment within the safe confines of this question. See if there isn't a sharper edge on your writing. When you are ready, and if you wish, you and I can sit down again and discuss it. What do you say?"

Audie was excited and couldn't wait to get home and take pen and paper in hand.

"Very well," Faith said. "You are indeed as courageous as I thought."

She ducked her head and blushed with Faith's compliment and recognition.

Standing, Faith said, "Come on. I'll walk out with you."

It didn't take Faith long to gather his things, but as he assembled various papers, Audie said, "So what is my grade?"

Faith didn't look up from his sorting and gathering. "It's whatever you would like it to be. As far as I'm concerned, you have done excellent work, have learned, grown, and are on the cusp of greater learning and personal revelation as a result of your writing and work. You have passed the essay with flying colors and I will reflect that in my notes to your regular teacher—and in her grade book."

Audie quickly realized that Faith was more interested in her growth and learning than in standard performance. She took a step closer to his desk. Faith stopped his gathering and sat down in his desk chair to look up at the young woman before him.

"What you are interested in," she began, "is that I reflect in my essay the passion and desire and thoughtfulness you demonstrate in your lecture. Right?" She didn't afford Faith time to answer before continuing. "Especially about the High King. I realize now, looking back, that you are alive—different—when you lecture about the High King. When you speak about him, something is alive in me too."

Faith didn't say anything. It is moments like this that mentors live for.

As soon as Audie and Faith were off the school property, Faith stopped, and said, "Audie, there is a group of people, all of whom are loyal to the High King, meeting tomorrow night. I know you would be welcome."

Faith gave her instructions and thanked her for meeting with him. She watched him disappear around a corner and then turned her mind to her writing, her heart alive with insights and ideas, and her steps quicker than normal as she anticipated sitting down in the confines of her room to draft the desires of her heart.

Five people had already gathered when Audie arrived. A seventh arrived shortly after her. At first she was self-conscious, but she was so warmly received, and felt such affinity with these people that her reservations soon fled.

The meeting was informal at first, their talk encompassing predictable subjects. The hostess provided a light snack, and apparently this was unusual, as she said it was in anticipation of Audie's attendance. The snacks were cleared away, drink glasses refilled, and the small group assembled in a circle.

They talked about the King's influence in their lives. They shared about the pressures they were feeling. They discussed briefly a few concerns about life in the Round Tower. They laughed together, a few cried as they shared personal heartaches and trials, and each drew support from the other. As the evening concluded, they stood in a circle, held hands, and spoke to the High King as though present among them.

Audie was ecstatic! She walked home, but her heart skipped.

The Wilderness

Hank settled into a routine. Each morning he selected an important thought to consider from Vassar's letter. Before reading, he asked Magician to guide his understanding. When a particular passage caught his attention, he focused there, listening for Magician's counsel, and writing his own thoughts down on a sheaf of papers provided by Parra.

Just as he promised, Parra created a copy of Vassar's letter that had each major thought numbered[2]. In this way, Hank could reference the letter in his journal of insights.

It didn't take long for Hank to appreciate the discipline of journaling. While his thoughts were filled with assumption and generalization, writing did not tolerate assumption, generalization, or ideas otherwise lacking systematic logic.

The routine of writing was also a potent weapon against Jester's stepped-up assaults. He made accusations—loads of them, and powerfully personal. But Hank noticed that Jester's suggestions lacked cohesive truth, even when he quoted the High King, and the majority of his perspectives referenced the King. Hank realized this was Jester's

---

2   See the Appendix, page 517, for a copy of Parra's work.

way of casting aspersion on the King's character and creating doubt about his goodness. But through the labor of his written analysis, Hank noted that light was cast upon the darkness of Jester's assertions.

Jester was quick to declare that Hank was wasting his time—that he wasn't really benefitting from his wilderness solitude but was just enraptured by the location, and surroundings, and novelty, and gravity, and multiples of other things. Jester was verbose and opinionated, and simply stated, his viewpoint was that Hank was self-deceived.

Hank's journal, however, proved Jester wrong. The evidence was written in black and white. He was progressing, changing, gaining, and overcoming.

As his insights and personal revelations increased, so did his confidence. Just as the rigorous discipline with sword and dagger created confidence as a warrior, so his discipline of solitude in the King's wilderness resulted in confidence about his identity and position in the family.

Following his morning of contemplation, Hank was escorted downstairs by Parra and a contingent of the King's guards. As he began his walk the guards dissolved into the essence of the wilderness.

He always walked—sometimes not-so-far, sometimes a long way. There were plenty of times when he found a place to sit, and there were plenty of times when the balls of his feet were tender at the end of the day.

All afternoon he thought, discussed ideas and perspectives with Magician, and relished being within the solitude of his Father's wilderness. It felt as though his morning thoughts solidified during the afternoon of physical exertion and reflection.

While his record wasn't perfect, Hank routinely confronted Jester with his deception and confidently told him to leave him alone and go wherever Vassar and the King told him to go. He always cited Vassar's letter, Magician's counsel, or his identity as the son of the King. Jester never argued against Hank, but would often take another tack. Some attacks were more persistent, but Hank learned that his endurance and appeal to the King were ultimately more powerful.

After being out for the afternoon—rain or shine—Hank returned to his quarters, cleaned up, ate dinner, and settled back in a darkened room with a glass of wine to stare into the dusk and reflect upon the day's revelations. He would sit thinking and reflecting until he felt he had worked his way through all the outstanding issues in his mind and heart. Frequently, Magician provided summary and posed questions for Hank's consideration. Other times Magician simply affirmed and encouraged. Sometimes this meditation kept him awake until the wee hours of the morning, sometimes he was in bed early.

Each day he gained confidence, and after a number of days his practiced disciplines were seared into life-habits. Quiet. Contemplation. Reflection. Discussion of important things with Magician. Quiet. Contemplation. Each discipline stood on its own and Hank sensed this realization was as important as the forming of the discipline in the first place.

Hank knew—realized in his heart—that his time in the wilderness was coming to a conclusion, however. He didn't doubt that he would return, perhaps not to this physical location, but to the wilderness, just like his Brother, Vassar.

He figured his disciplines would not only be tested in the days to come, but that the skills honed within the wilderness would stand him in good stead in whatever location and endeavor his Father had in mind. After all, as Vassar had written to him, their Father had a plan and was working his plan.

On a number of occasions—any number of occasions—Hank said to Jester, "Leave me alone. Why can't you understand? No matter what deception you suggest, whether I catch it or not, I won't back down!"

As was his custom, Hank sat at his table with Vassar's letter spread open to his left and a piece of paper in front of him for journaling his thoughts. The index finger of his left hand marked his point of focus for this morning,

> *We are family, and as such, we are bonded and can never be separated. In spirit, I am in Father and Father is in me— just as I am in you and you are in me. We are in Father. He is in us. Magician is evidence of this. Father said so! We are a unit, a family. We are cut from the same bolt of genetic cloth and our lives are interwoven. We are inseparable!*

Hank worked as sunlight streamed through the window warming his back. Immersed in his writing, Hank snapped to attention, startled by Parra's knock on his door.

Parra entered with his congenial, "Good morning, Sir." He was used to Hank's table being covered in papers—had even commandeered another table for Hank's room. He set the breakfast service down, poured coffee, and arranged the food. He also knew this was not the time to engage his charge in too much conversation. One look at the writing table and it was obvious the man was engaged in some heavy lifting. Before stepping into the other room to organize and arrange, Parra reached into his pocket and presented Hank with a sealed note.

Sitting down, Hank placed his coffee closer, then used his finger to break the seal. In his Father's familiar hand, the letter read:

> Hank
>
> I have enjoyed–immensely enjoyed–the time we have had to visit, walk, and talk. Thank you for listening to me and valuing my thoughts. You make my heart happy.
>
> Magician is quite the commentator, isn't he?
>
> I know your heart has already alerted you that it is

time for a change. Please leave at once for the Round Tower. Don't be afraid. Just as my soldiers have guarded you here, so they will guard you on the way and after you arrive.

Pay attention! Zophos roams about, like a lion, looking for someone to devour. Jester is seeking any and every advantage. You are on their list because you are my son and you are powerful!

There is nothing to fear, but everything to respect. Be courageous! Be strong! Conduct yourself like the man you are! Carry yourself accordingly! Speak on my behalf—represent us.

I will guide you on the way. Remember this: We can never be separated. I am in you and you are in me. We are family. Magician speaks for both Vassar and me. He is the embodiment of us—the promissory note that you are never alone. Listen!

I'm proud of you, son.

All my love,

Papa

Hank re-read his Father's letter again as he sipped his coffee. He folded the letter and thought, then called Parra from the other room. When the valet appeared, Hank said, "I'm trying to think of a term—a title, rather—and I can't locate the word. It's on the tip of my tongue…, but just can't resurrect the terminology."

"Can you give me a clue or two?" Parra prodded.

"I read a biography of John Adams a year or two ago," Hank mused. "He and Benjamin Franklin were both given this authority—or title, or power, or whatever it is—to speak on behalf of the government while they were in France. They had full power—full authority—as diplomatic agents of the United States."

Parra's eyes were wide with mystery. "Sir, I'm sorry, but I don't know either Mr. Adams or Mr. Franklin, and sadly, I'm not acquainted with the United States you speak of."

Hank was immediately embarrassed. Immersed in his thoughts and musings he had forgotten the time change. "You're right. Forgive me, please. It's not important—neither here nor there."

"Well, thank you, Sir. You are most gracious. However, on occasion power plenipotentiary is granted here."

"That's it! That's the word, Parra. Good for you! It would have driven me mad trying to remember that term. Thank you."

"Certainly, Sir."

"Power plenipotentiary," Hank said, restating the title and accompanying power, promising himself in so doing not to forget again. "How do you use the term? Rather, what do you mean when you use that phrase?"

Just then the Captain entered the room following a courteous knock. Parra stiffened and nodded at the ranking officer. Hank waved.

Hank realized his query was lying in no man's land, so caught the Captain up on their conversation, "Parra and I were just discussing power plenipotentiary and I was wondering how you use the phrase?"

Pointing at a vacant chair, the Captain said, "May I?"

"Oh, sure. Please," Hank said, then followed that permission by pointing to another chair and instructing Parra to drag it over and have a seat as well.

As Parra carried a chair from the other side of the room, the Captain said, "Most people are thinking about the weather or whether to try cream in their coffee at this time of the morning. What ever in the world has prompted consideration of this high and mighty term?"

Hank said, "Oh, I was just reading a letter from my Father. Parra delivered it this morning."

"Ah, I see," the officer said. "And your Father has given you the power to speak on his behalf—full authority, no doubt."

Hank looked at the Captain. "How'd you know that?"

"Over the years I have noticed that the King is generous with the power he grants to his children. As a Prince in the Kingdom of Light, it is no surprise that you have been endowed with this blessing."

"And for the record, Sir," Parra inserted, "power plenipotentiary simply means that as your Father's representative, you are vested with full authority to transact business on his behalf."

"Well said," the Captain confirmed. "Suffice it to say, Hank, your Father believes in you. He trusts you to represent him and the Kingdom of Light. The King is not in the habit of writing for the practice of it, as if he has nothing better to do."

"Nor is he careless with his power," Parra added.

"Certainly not!" the Captain added. "Generous, but never careless. Your power plenipotentiary has been thoughtfully bestowed. Of this, you can be certain."

Hank nodded, contemplating the magnitude and implication. Returning to the task at hand, Hank said, "By the way, Papa—I mean, the King—has asked that I leave as soon as possible for the Round Tower."

Standing immediately, Parra said, "Very good, Sir. I will prepare you for your journey."

Standing as well, the Captain said, "When you are ready, I will provide the directions you require."

CHAPTER 11

The King's Throne Room

As the last supplicant was ushered away and the next approached, Vassar leaned toward his Father, "Have you noticed who is three back in the line?"

The High King glanced, huffed lightly, "Zophos is so self-possessed."

"If you ask Hank," Vassar replied, "he will declare Zophos eaten up with himself."

"Not a bad way to put it," the King acknowledged.

Zophos shrugged, vainly attempting to escape the prodding of the guard to move forward. He lifted his head to glare at the soldier, but then cast his eyes once again to the floor as he approached the thrones where the High King and Crown Prince sat. He bowed his head, clasped his hands in front of him, and stared at his usual spot on the floor. He hated these appearances more than all the things he had ever detested. In his mind, he ran through everything he planned to do when he wrenched the monarchy from the King—all the fiats he would issue his first day. He had been over his executive orders a million times since being relegated to Gnarled Wood. The dreams were his escape—his denial, actually—to manage the consequences of the precipitous fall he had suffered. The King considered his planning vain. Zophos considered it preparation.

Soon...soon, Zophos thought.

The King's question was predictable—his way of rubbing Zophos' nose in the degradation of his demise. "Where have you been, Zophos?"

Still focused on the spot, Zophos said, "Roaming Gnarled Wood, walking here and there."

"Yes, yes," the King acknowledged. "You're always going back and forth, aren't you?"

Zophos didn't answer. To do so would affirm the King's observation. Besides, he suspected the question was rhetorical.

"Have you been by the wilderness lately? Checked on my son, Hank?"

Zophos shifted on his feet. A guard inched closer to him, but the King held up his hand to stay the soldier.

Zophos was silent. The guard watched the King. He blinked permission. The guard grasped Zophos' bicep at his elbow. Pain shot up through his armpit and into his neck. Zophos jerked. It made his pain worse and did not loosen the guard's grip. He glared from the spot to the guard.

"I asked if you have checked on my son," the King repeated. "He's a good man. Your own tests have confirmed he is exactly as I declared him to be. And you thought he would succumb, didn't you? You're always missing the mark, Zophos."

Zophos fury rose up in him, stoked by envy, fueled with resentment. "Skin for skin," he muttered, hardly audible.

"What's that you say, Zophos?" Vassar questioned.

Zophos took his eyes off the spot on the floor, looked at Vassar, and back to the spot. "I said, skin for skin. A man will relinquish everything for his health."

"Ah, I see where you are headed," the King said. "You think if Hank suffers physically he will side with you."

Zophos didn't reply.

"I'll tell you what, Zophos. I know my son. In fact, you know my son. Have tested him yourself. He won't renounce who he is and he won't relinquish his destiny. By attacking Hank, you will only affirm your own desperation and defeat. You waste my time. Get out of here! Test my son if you want, but you may not compromise his life."

Periodically the King tossed these tidbits at Zophos to create further disequilibrium in his tortured soul. In time, he knew Zophos would implode under an escalating weight of hopelessness as his dream of wholesale defection by men like Hank shattered. In the meantime, Hank would shine in the light like a diamond set against a dark backdrop.

Departing the King's Wilderness

Hank headed northwest carrying a knapsack of clothing and food prepared by Parra. He knew his back would be sore and wished for his more modern pack, with waist belt and sternum strap, presumably still in the snow cave close to Malden Creek—in the real world of Montana.

Or is this the real world? Hank recognized the thought as Magician's. He thought about it for a moment before his mind became a tangled mess attempting to distinguish between the two time frames.

I don't know, Magician, he thought. *All I know is that I'm here, on a mission, and doing my best to trust you. First things first: The Captain said we would intersect a stream, that we should cross as soon as possible, and follow it downstream.*

Hank walked the better part of four hours before encountering the stream. He used his walking time to reflect on his days in the wilderness, assuming that whatever was in store for him would not permit the lengthy reflection he had enjoyed of late.

He turned downstream, found a tumble of rocks and deadfall that he used to cross the creek, and continued his trek. After another three hours, Hank began thinking about camp for the night. He also noticed—sensed within—that these woods were not as friendly as the woods he had been roaming. *I need to pay attention,* he thought. He looked up at the sky. He had been watching it all afternoon. *It's getting darker. Going to storm, I'll bet.*

Picking a sheltered spot twenty feet above the stream, Hank sat down and took inventory of Parra's provisions. To his delight, he discovered in the bottom of his knapsack, a hand axe and some cord.

He lashed the fallen trunk of a small tree, five-inches in diameter and eight feet long, between two trees and about three feet off the ground. Using the axe, he collected Spruce boughs and propped the cut ends against the cross piece with the branches facing downward, resting against the earth. He continued this overlapping of additional branches until he created a one-sided shelter to shield him from wind and all but the most persistent of rains. While he worked, he also stockpiled dry branches for a fire.

As darkness closed around him in earnest, Hank coaxed a small flame to life. He didn't need a fire for warmth as much as for comfort. He heated some tea and stared unblinking into the dancing, entrancing flames. He chuckled, thinking about his friend from Kentucky, Harold, who used to talk about being "mess'mrized" by a fire.

Hank and Harold shared a house together—"back in the day"—an airy log cabin that they heated with a wood stove, although "heated" was a relative term. Harold was older—maybe thirty-five or forty years. Hank couldn't remember. Harold dropped out of school when he was thirteen to go to work on the railroad. When he talked, which was a lot, he rattled off railroad-place-names as though Hank should know. Hank laughed again, recollecting Harold's tales. "Hank, we was running coal one time from West Virginia...," and sitting huddled around the iron stove, Harold regaled him with a tale.

I nearly froze to death that winter, Hank thought back to the drafty cabin. *My toothpaste was so stiff I had to mash on the tube with the heel of my hand to get it to come out—and my shampoo changed colors it was so cold.*

Harold progressed from an Electrician's helper, to an Electrician, eventually to Engineer. Somewhere along the way, Hank never was clear where, Harold left the railroad and became a coal broker. He made a fabulous amount of money and eventually had servants, a helicopter, a big house, the works. Then, he lost it all. Once again, Hank never knew how the great loss occurred, but it never seemed to matter to Harold.

Hank always thought that it would have been a grand experience to ride in the helicopter with Harold. He could hear him now, instructing the pilots in his butchered English where he wanted to land, the designated place no doubt determined by navigation of the rail lines, and never mind the sophisticated instrumentation onboard the helicopter. Hank smiled.

Sitting by the stove, Harold told stories that ranged from being shot while collecting a coal debt to losing his air brakes between switch forty-seven and the water tower outside some mountain town Hank never heard of.

By day, they worked together doing mostly electrical work. Harold taught Hank to bend conduit and run wire, but no matter how many explanations he gave—or how many napkin diagrams he drew over lunch—Harold's explanation of electricity never connected for Hank. *I nearly killed myself attempting to re-wire that ceiling fan in the den.*

When Harold and Hank were rooming together, everything Harold owned was wholly contained within a brown Chevrolet. Hank wondered again what was in the car, especially at the bottom of the trunk or back floorboard. The collection of tools, clothes, duct work, and papers was impressive. Even the speedometer was obscured, so great was the abundance of notes, business cards, and convenience store straws. *Harold always produced what we needed at the right time though. Don't know how, but he did.*

A mutual friend, Bob, called a number of years ago with the news that Harold had fallen dead of a heart attack. "He was mowing the grass," Bob reported. "Someone driving by saw him lying in the yard." It was one of the deaths Hank never completely recovered from—same with his friend, Kevin. Hank didn't begrudge Harold, or Kevin, his exit to a better place, he just missed him.

The thoughts drifted away like vagabonds, and Hank sat—mess'mrized by the dancing flames. He scooted a foot deeper under his shelter as the rain started. His fire hissed at the intrusion. Resisted. The rain pelted an all-out invasion, and as Hank retreated the fire succumbed in gallant emissions of steam.

Hank lay down on his cloak, propped his head on his knapsack for a pillow, and listened as the storm intensified. Out of curiosity, he held his hand to his face. It flashed and disappeared with the lightening. He turned onto his left side and closed his eyes.

Hank awoke with first light to what portended to be a clear day, a creek that had swollen dramatically overnight, and mostly dry bedding. He congratulated himself on the success of his shelter and set about his morning stretches to limber his back and hips.

Pulling from the dry wood he'd sheltered with himself, he built a fire, made tea, and dried out the toe of the one sock that hadn't made it entirely under the shelter. Standing with his back to the flame, Hank pulled Vassar's letter from the satchel kept close to his skin and read:

First, our Father lives and his light will not be extinguished. Second, he won't abandon us. No doubt Jester will suggest that you are orphaned. Don't believe him, not for a moment.

He folded the letter and carefully closed his satchel, making certain it was tied shut securely before replacing it against his heart. *His light will not be extinguished*, Hank reflected on the words, drawing an image of his fire the night before. *Unlike my hissing fire last night, my Father will prevail in light against the darkness.* Hank recognized the counsel and perspective of Magician.

He won't abandon us. Hank held onto that thought as he looked and listened. Apart from the rush of the creek and sounds of the woods, circumstantially it appeared he was alone. *But I don't live circumstantially,* Hank thought. *I live by the confidence I have in Father, Vassar, and Magician.*

"That is my theme for the day," he declared out loud.

Okay, Magician, he thought, *live through me today—whatever the circumstances!*

Hank stamped out the sputtering flame and remaining embers of the fire. He gathered his things into his knapsack, shouldered the weight, and followed the creek downstream.

His sense of impending ill grew as the day progressed. He didn't see anyone, but felt the onerous presence he associated with Jester and his henchmen. When the path was open enough for him to walk with a steady rhythm, he marched to his theme for the day—*I live by confidence in my Father, the High King, and my Brother, the Crown Prince; I am guided by my friend, Magician.* One word for each footfall, a quick recitation going downhill, a resolute one when he trudged uphill or navigated an obstacle. In this way he lived by his disciplines formed in the wilderness.

Just as the Captain indicated, the creek intersected a small road about mid afternoon. Exercising caution, Hank hid in the trees watching the road and studying the change in his surroundings. He was comfortable in the woods, but with the appearance of the road, he knew he would encounter people. He felt ready, but his guard intensified as he reiterated his request for Magician to live through him.

Stepping onto the road, Hank turned left. He made a mental note of where he exited the woods—just in case—and walked with a steady, strong step.

Soon, Hank came upon a wayside inn. The Captain told him it could be marginal, but when Hank asked him directly if he should camp or stay at the inn, the Captain felt the inn was safe enough.

He hid and surveyed the inn for half an hour before deciding to enter. He determined to eat, see how he felt about the place, and then decide whether or not to stay the night.

He was greeted warmly by the proprietor. There were eight tables, only two of which were occupied. He nodded to those who caught his eye and selected a table off to the side and partially obscured by a post.

When he was part way through his meal of venison stew, four men emerged from a meeting room behind the kitchen. Two left right away, the other two took a seat—front and center—and ordered drinks they didn't need.

One man got up to go outside and relieve himself. Apparently the exterior door close to Hank's table led to the customary egress for those in need of a tree.

When the man came back, he glared at Hank—the look of a man generally unhappy with life and carrying a chip on his shoulder. Noticing the pommel of Hank's sword, he called across the room to his companion, "Hey! This guy's carrying the King's blade." He stopped in front of Hank's table.

The second called, "You mean he's one of those knights of light?"

"Reckon so," said the first, with a haughty expression. "Sure doesn't look like a knight to me. Looks to me like he ought to be in back, washing dishes."

"Or mopping floors, maybe."

"Yeah, or upstairs cleaning rooms—with the maid."

"I've heard the King's knights are ceremonial," the man at the center table said loudly. "Makes 'em feel important to get called 'Sir,' and all that."

Hank made no move and offered no response. In his mind he called upon Magician to guide him and guard him.

The first man, holding up his hand and examining it theatrically, said, "You know, I forgot to wash my hand." He wiped it on his pants in exaggerated motions as he moved up to Hank's table. He picked up Hank's drink—with that hand—and poured the wine on Hank's bowl and plate. With the same hand, he picked up a piece of Hank's bread and dropped it in the ruined meal, sopping up the liquid. Calling to his friend, "See here? You were right about the King's people. This one's got no gumption."

As the man aimed to mash the soaked piece of bread into Hank's face, Hank grabbed his wrist with his left hand. The man tried to jerk away, but was unable to wrench his arm from Hank's hold. The man cursed Hank in the King's name, struggled again to free his arm, and unable to do so, kicked at Hank.

Hank jerked the man's arm toward him and struck him between his nose and upper lip with the heel of his hand, just left of center, splitting his lip against his teeth. The man's companion jumped from his seat, slinging his chair across the room as he rose. The man in Hank's grip blinked and reached for his knife.

Soon to be outnumbered, Hank stood and shifted from "fair-fight" tactics to "barroom brawl." Yanking the man toward him, Hank kneed him in the groin. As he bent, Hank grabbed him by the hair on the back of his head and slammed his face into the table. He rapped the man's face against the oak once more before his accomplice arrived, sword drawn.

Hank dropped the first man in the path of his next assailant and backed up a few steps, buying enough time to draw his blade. The second man was a street fighter—a bully—and lacked the skills Hank had honed as a warrior of light.

Hank defended himself while assessing his opponent. He knew he needed to be careful. Unorthodox tactics could be deceptively effective by soliciting an unorthodox response versus the discipline of sound combat. Hank made a split-second decision to not kill the man—affording him the benefit of the doubt that he wasn't one of Zophos' henchmen. *Maybe he's just a bully*, Hank thought. He could hear the first man retching on the floor.

The man swung his sword in an arching, hacking attack that Hank dodged. With his attacker's swing and miss, his strong side was vulnerable. In a quick thrust, Hank opened a deep gash on the man's thigh. He howled in anguish and slashed at Hank with a mighty backhand. The tip of the blade narrowly missed Hank's abdomen.

The man's undisciplined momentum carried his sword-arm wide to the right leaving him open to Hank's next thrust into his other thigh, this gouge deeper than the first. The man stumbled against the table as his leg went momentarily lame.

Hank waited, hoping the man would drop his sword in surrender. Instead, he slung a chair at Hank. One leg of the chair struck just above his knee! Hank almost collapsed.

Fueled with adrenalin, the man came again at Hank, jabbing his sword as he approached—cursing Hank, cursing the King, and with a clue that didn't escape Hank's notice, cursing his boss, Jester, for getting him into this mess.

That was all Hank needed. He picked up the broken chair by a leg, smashed the back into the floor, separating it from the seat. Advancing at Jester's pawn and using the chair bottom as a shield, Hank fended off the man's jabs. As soon as he backed the man out of the tight quarters, Hank stepped up his advance. Watching for his opening, he bent low under the umbrella of his shield, and cut the man's left knee out from under him.

Writhing on the floor, cursing more vociferously now than ever, the man swung and jabbed indiscriminately at Hank. Hank waited patiently, and seizing his chance, struck the man's sword low and close to the guard. The shock of the strike sent the sword skittering across the floor.

Showing surprising determination, and more proficiency than Hank anticipated, the man drew a hunting knife, rolled on his side, and slashed at Hank's legs. Hank struck the man's elbow with his blade. The knife dropped to the floor, its owner screaming in pain. Hank hit the man smartly with the remnants of the chair, knocking him cold while breaking his cheek bone and opening a sizable cut.

The first man got to his knees, knife in hand, as though to launch an assault of his own. Hank smashed the chair bottom into his already bloody face, striking him parallel to his nose, his right eyebrow accepting the brunt of the force. The man fell over backward with his legs folded under him.

The fight was over. Much to his surprise, the proprietor came to Hank, thanking him profusely, wanting to shake his hand. "These men, and the two that left earlier, have caused me so much trouble. They have hurt my business, threatened me, threatened my wife and children. Thank you, thank you."

Hank wasn't certain what to do. It wasn't like he could call 9-1-1. He stood thinking, looking. After a few moments, the inn keeper went to the other room for something. The other customers had left and Hank was alone with Jester's incapacitated goons.

Grabbing the second man by the right wrist, Hank dragged him across the floor to where the first man lay with his legs buckled under him. As he dragged the man, his body rolled over, face down. Hank dropped the man's right hand close to the right hand of his companion.

Hank went to the door and fetched the rock used to prop the door open. Retrieving the hunting knife, Hank placed both men's right hands together, one on top of the other, and using the rock, drove the knife blade through their hands into the floor. He pounded the knife blade deep into the plank, crossways to the tendons in their hands so as to permanently ruin their dominant hands for further attacks.

Hank picked up the second man's sword and struck the stone post with the flat of the blade, breaking it in two, eight inches above the guard. He dropped the broken handle in between the two bodies. *Maybe when they come to their senses, the broken blade will serve as a reminder that the light overcame their darkness.*

The proprietor returned with his wife at his side. Hank asked for some food. When they came back, he placed the bread and cooked meat they brought in his knapsack and apologized to them for the mess. He tried to pay for his meal and the broken chair, but they wouldn't take his money.

As he started for the door, the proprietor asked, "Are you really a knight in the Kingdom of Light?"

Hank nodded.

"We—my wife and I—are loyal to the High King. We've not known how to handle these people. They come here, scare us, intimidate us. It happens all the time. We're grateful."

Hank walked back to the proprietor and his wife, shook their hands, and said, "There's no reason for you to serve these men. Be courageous. Tell them you are servants of the High King and that upon his authority, they must leave."

The proprietor and his wife studied Hank. "We can do that?"

"Not only can you, you must!" Hank stated emphatically.

The proprietor's wife said to her husband, "This is what we have been talking about."

With excitement, the proprietor said, "It is. We have sensed this—thought we possessed authority, but we weren't certain. Now we know."

"Now you know," Hank said, smiling. "Be confident. While there are bad folks around, like these guys, the King's forces are here as well."

The proprietor and his wife nodded enthusiastically, the wife wiping tears of relief from her cheeks, her husband holding her hand. There was a new look in their eyes—a look of determination.

"I wouldn't worry about those guys," Hank said, pointing to the two men pinned to the floor with the hunting knife. "They will get desperate enough after a while to remove the knife. Let them be though, and don't offer any assistance."

"What about our customers?"

"Tell your customers who ask that this is what it looks like when the High King has had enough. Tell them light overcomes darkness. Let them know your establishment is dedicated to the High King and the Kingdom of Light."

Hank slung his knapsack over his shoulder and exited the inn through the side door. He stood silently in the dark until his eyes adjusted to the night. Reassured no one was waiting to ambush him, he turned from the predictable route and disappeared into the woods. Limping. Badly. Struggling. During the twenty minutes it took for his eyes to adjust, his leg stiffened painfully where he'd been struck with the chair.

He crept silently, deeper into the confines of the trees. From the position of the moon, he estimated it was midnight, and he guessed he'd been walking for three or four hours. Crawling underneath the low boughs of a spruce, Hank lay down with his head on his knapsack. He listened carefully, not moving a muscle, closed his eyes, and slept.

A disturbance awakened him. Without moving, Hank opened his eyes. The rustling was a squirrel, scrounging around on the forest floor at first light. Hank cautiously turned his head to assess his surroundings. For a man who picked a place to sleep in the dead of night, he chose well. He was concealed, and was protected at his back by a bluff.

Breathing more easily, Hank scooted out from under the tree. His leg was stiff and sore, mightily so. In fact, he could barely walk.

Before tending to his ailing limb, Hank ate the meat in his knapsack, knowing it would soon spoil. He drank from his canteen, and for the sake of drinking water and his leg, he knew the first order of the day was to find water.

He stuck a stick upright in the ground, marked where the shadow of it lay on the forest floor, then hobbled in search of a suitable limb to serve as a staff. He cut the branch, trimmed it, and skinned the burrs off of it. Returning with this assistance to where he marked the stick's shadow, he noted the sun's movement. With his bearings gained, Hank lurched along in search of a stream.

As he went, he got better using his staff, and the movement loosened his sore muscle. Within an hour, he came upon a small stream running clear and cold. He drank, filled his canteen, and drank again.

It was harder to get his boot off than he expected, but once removed, Hank stripped off his clothes and settled into a deep pool to soak his leg in the cold water. He knew nothing was broken, but his thigh, just above his left knee, was swollen and black at the impact. The bruise radiated up, around, and down in purples, blues, yellows, and various shades of red.

Hank thought back to the night before. He was glad he only roughed those guys up instead of dispatching them. *That would have caused more harm for the inn keeper,* he thought.

He turned his conversation to Magician, *Did I do the right thing— say the right thing to the proprietor and his wife?*

Thoughts formed in Hank's mind, which he took to be Magician's response. *You called upon me to guide you, to act through you, and then you handled yourself with confidence. And as far as the proprietor and his wife are concerned, I provide counsel and comfort to them as well, just like I do for you.*

How's that work, I wonder? Hank mused, as he sat in the water, slowly massaging his leg.

It's all part of my job description. Speaking counsel, providing comfort, and rendering assistance as necessary—I do all this for the King's people.

Hank felt the old sense of insignificance rising. It caught him by surprise, but the surprise helped him notice the presence of the unwanted emotion. He decided this feeling was because Magician wasn't his friend alone. *If he is in every follower of the King, then I'm one of his many friends. One of the masses. All this time, I thought I was unique, special, distinguished from everyone else. Significant.*

He hadn't anticipated wrestling the demon of significance again. Even though he had dealt Significance a fatal blow in the pit, the memory and emotion now rose like a phoenix to torment his soul. He felt guilty for the thoughts and emotions and reasoning, but he also needed to find resolution—yet again—to this fundamental question regarding his importance.

There was the clue he needed: "yet again." He had sorted this out before.

He reviewed what he knew, and as he did so, was certain he was not alone sitting naked in the stream, soaking his wounded leg. Jester was close. The internal struggle had all the indications of a battle between Jester, and Magician, and him. He'd fought a hundred—a thousand—similar battles and recognized the telltale tactics of Jester's persuasive creativity.

Speaking out loud, Hank said, "Alright Jester. Show yourself." Hank waited. "Jester! I said show yourself. Do it now! By the authority of the High King and my Brother, the Crown Prince, come here!"

Jester emerged from the trees.

"Anyone else with you?" Hank demanded.

Jester shrugged.

"Jester, upon the authority of my Brother, I command that you speak honestly with me. Is anyone else with you?"

"There are a few others." Jester answered, although trying desperately to remain defiant and independent.

"Here's the deal," Hank stated. "You, and all those with you, get away from me. Leave me alone. I have no business with you. Get out!"

Jester looked around pitifully. "Well, if you say so, Prince. Where would you suggest I go?"

"Let's be clear," Hank said, his eyes fixed. "It's not just you I am ordering away from here. It is you and all your colleagues. Capiche?"

"I understand," Jester said, turning to leave.

"Jester!"

His nemesis turned to look at him. There was fire in his eyes.

"You want to know where you should go? I'll tell you. Go present yourself before Vassar and ask him. Now get out of here!"

With that, Jester vanished. Hank sat motionless, trying hard to sense his surroundings. A tranquility returned to the woods, and his confidence had grown.

Hank looked at himself in the mountain water. His toes were blue, his skin covered with goose bumps, and his "special purpose" was drawn up short. With that observation, he decided he had had enough cold therapy and clambered out of the stream.

The sun felt good as he stood drip-drying. Naked, the woods empty of his enemy, Hank once again returned to what he knew of his personal significance. *I am significant because no one else occupies the same time and space as I do with my Father. In this, I am unique. In this, I am important, valuable. There is no one else who brings to the table what I bring—and, this makes my Father happy.*

Hank reviewed this several times. Satisfied his mind and heart were focused again on what he knew to be true, Hank felt confident to return to his discussion with Magician. *So if you are providing the same counsel to everyone, what is the nature of our friendship? I thought we were really close. What happened to that command Father gave you about living in me?*

Warmed by the sun on his body, quiet and focused, Magician's reply formed in Hank's mind. *I am the grace and mercy of your Father, Hank. I am the bond with your Brother, Vassar. The significance you have with them is compounded in me. I am the pledge of their faithfulness and lovingkindness. All that they are and all that is in you has its resolution in me. Given this magnitude, there is no one like you in the Kingdom. In fact, when you and I meet, it is the only meeting of its exact type in the history of time and eternity. That I provide comfort and counsel throughout the Kingdom indicates something about me. That I live in you says something about you.*

Hank looked around. He was alone. Standing naked beside the brook, he realized—through Magician's guidance—that he was integrally connected to his Father, his Brother, and to the Kingdom's resources through his constant companion, Magician. While others were similarly cared for by the King, no one was joined to this triumvirate of familial connection in the same way as he was—or, *as I am, this very moment.*

"Thank you, Magician," Hank said out loud. "I appreciate your patience."

You are significant, Hank heard Magician affirm from his dwelling place in Hank's heart.

"I am significant," Hank stated aloud. "I am significant and I am not alone. My Father has a purpose and my Brother is preparing the way for me." The recitation of essential points cleared the remaining fog from his mind.

His battle this morning, just as pitched as the fight the night before, if not more so, had been won. He stretched like a cat, arching his back in the sun's warmth, and turned his attention to getting dressed.

He had concluded that concealing his knighthood was pointless. It was probably wise that he retreated into the woods after the bar fight to let the dust settle, but now it was time to find the road to the castle and the Round Tower. *I have a mission to accomplish, a calling to fulfill.*

Chapter 12

The Round Tower

Bernard Bertram stepped to Letizia Pintaro's open door and knocked quietly on the door frame. Letizia turned from looking out the window, "Come in, Bernie."

"Thank you, Ms. Pintaro."

Bernard "Bernie" Bertram served as Letizia's Chief of Staff. Bernie was the person she trusted to help her think, organize, and manage. Although he was eleven years her senior, he was a reliable "Number One" and had reached the pinnacle of his professional life.

Every Monday morning, first thing, Letizia and Bernie met to review the upcoming week. Every Friday afternoon, last thing, they met to review the week, cover the weekend, and position themselves for the next Monday meeting. While this kept Letizia in touch, it gave Bernie latitude.

Each kept a running folder of notes from these meetings, complete with dates and assignments. The accountability served two purposes: First, it helped focus each on the real work that was to be done. Second, it maintained professional distance, not that Letizia had any designs on Bernie or him toward her. It was just good practice and typical of Letizia.

As Bernie entered, Letizia rose and moved to the side table, their customary meeting place. Both placed their notes conspicuously on the table. Letizia's other assistant waited judiciously until they were seated, then placed coffee service on the edge of the table. She waited momentarily to see if there was anything further, then dismissed herself and closed the door.

Their meetings rarely lasted longer than twenty minutes.

At about the eighteen-minute mark, both felt the rhythm of the meeting nearing its conclusion. The last item on Bernie's agenda was notification that he had hired an additional person for the office staff. "Her name is Caroline Ingram. She's being oriented now and I'll meet with her as soon as we are finished."

"Very good," Letizia said.

"Oh, and she pronounces her name, Caro-line, not Caro-lynn," Bernie noted.

"Caro-line," Letizia rehearsed. "I like that. It's unique."

Bernie looked at his agenda. "That's all I've got."

"Me too," Letizia said, rising.

"Have a good week, Ms. Pintaro. I'll let you know if anything arises."

"I know you will, Bernie."

He let himself out of the office, per usual, as she returned to the thoughts that had occupied her mind twenty minutes earlier.

The King's Throne

Staring at the spot on the floor, Zophos didn't answer. It was a small rebellion, but his passive aggression did little to appease his hostility.

"I said, how's the increased latitude I granted to you and your minions working out for you?" the King asked. "Hank coming around as you planned?" The King didn't exactly taunt Zophos, but it wasn't far from that condescension.

"Skin for skin. He will protect himself," Zophos repeated to the spot on the floor, not lifting his eyes.

The High King shook his head. "You bore me, Zophos." He motioned that he was done with the former Star of the Morning.

The door closed quietly behind Zophos as he was dismissed from the King's court. He stood for a moment, angst mounting, then moved alone through the Kingdom's halls toward his waiting carriage.

Exiting the little-used exterior door, his security detail snapped to attention as he hurried through the door toward his carriage. "Hurry up!" he commanded. "Get me back to headquarters." Pointing to one of his messengers, "I want Jester there, waiting, when I arrive. Go!"

The messenger departed, traveling upon the sound waves in the atmosphere.

Zophos fumed with humiliation, kicking the seat across from him, slapping his thighs, and stomping his feet to expel the acidic frustration. As the hostile energy oozed through his bloodstream and dissipated, Zophos refocused for his meeting with Jester. Still, he ground his teeth against the bit of his bridled limitation.

His staff always looked sharp, but never more so than when Zophos came back from his summons to the throne. Backs straight, chests out, chins tucked, heels clicked as he passed. Zophos entered his lair.

"Where's Jester?!" Zophos screamed, noting the vacancy in his office.

No one moved. No one knew. No message had been received.

Zophos ranted and raged, spat and kicked. He threw the crystal ash tray from his desk, smashing it into a leaded-glass, display cabinet. The crashing glass infuriated him and he screeched for someone to clean up the shards.

Jester ran through the door, his eyes wild with his own fury.

"Where have you been?" Zophos yelled. "I told you to be here!"

"I couldn't help it!" Jester screamed back.

"Couldn't is NOT in my vocabulary!" Zophos yelled, the blood vessels in his neck protruding, strangling, his eyes bulging.

"It is when Crown Prince Vassar detains you!" Jester screamed back at Zophos.

Zophos glared, breathing heavily. He didn't say anything, rather rolled his left hand aggressively in a forward-circle for Jester to explain further.

"I was working Prince Henry over. Hard! He's beat up badly, doubting—even on the edge." Jester embellished his success to appease the volcano erupting in Zophos.

"So? That's what you're supposed to be doing," Zophos derided.

"So Prince Henry commanded me in the name of Crown Prince Vassar to show myself. I had no choice. I had to obey! Just as you do." Jester knew he probably shouldn't have added that last bit, but it was true and he was angry.

"Go on. You've not yet accounted for why you are late," Zophos stated flatly.

"Prince Henry sent me to his Brother, Vassar. I stood in line. Waited. Waited some more. The Crown Prince wanted to know where I had come from, who sent me, and why I was there. Do you know how humiliating it is to be subject to the likes of Hank Henderson?"

It crossed Zophos' mind to lie, but knew Jester would realize he had no stronger position than him when compared to the King and his sons.

"And not only that," Jester continued ranting, "I also got bossed around by those two oafs who run the roadhouse and bar."

"What are you talking about?" Zophos commanded.

"The man and woman who own that miserable hostel on the way to the castle. They said a knight in the Kingdom of Light told them they had authority over me. Had to be Hank Henderson. Roughed up a couple of my people too."

Zophos hissed at Jester. "You still haven't answered my question. Where were you? Why were you late?"

"What part of having to report to the Crown Prince did you miss, Zophos?"

Zophos stepped toward Jester, his fists clinched. "Did they detain you?"

Jester turned away, lowered his voice, "Vassar sent me to the nether world to inventory sulfur."

"Inventory sulfur?"

"I didn't stutter!" Jester retorted. "You know as well as I do that I have to do what they say, when they say, how they say. And, yes! Sulfur! Great stockpiles of it. More than you want to hear about. And then I had to report back. More standing in line. More waiting. More interminable delay. More wasted time. When it was finally my turn again, I gave Crown Prince Vassar the inventory number. You want to know what he said, Zophos? Huh? Do you?"

"Yeah, sure. What'd he say?"

"He said, 'Why are you telling me this, Jester?' I said, 'Because you asked me to inventory your stockpile of sulfur and report back to you, your Highness.' He looked at me, and said, 'Oh.' Like he'd forgotten. He didn't want to know how much sulfur he had. He made me run a pointless errand."

"It's an abuse of power," Zophos stated.

"Yeah, yeah. You talk big. Do something about it!"

"Shut up, Jester! You're insubordinate and you're irritating me." Zophos got straight to the point. "I want the Prince to suffer, Jester! Physically, emotionally, mentally—most of all, spiritually. Break him! No more excuses. Do you hear me? Break him! Like you were supposed to do when he was in the pit."

Jester relished the opportunity to project his frustration and hostility upon Zophos. He disdained the dark lord, but they were still partners—desperate, driven partners. He'd had his say. In the end, they both had to have results. Arguing wasn't getting them anywhere.

"As you wish," Jester said, finally.

The High King and the Crown Prince stemmed the flow of those seeking an audience and stepped to their private chamber. "Zophos and Jester are discussing their disposition toward Hank," Vassar stated to his Father.

"Yep. You're right. It's a given: They will increase their initiative to deceive him."

"You worried about him, Papa?" Vassar asked.

The King thought, standing close to his oldest son. "No, I'm not worried. Hank's fine. He's with Magician and Magician's with him. But Zophos is going to increase the intensity around Hank."

"No doubt," Vassar concurred.

"Magician knows about this, though. So, Hank's okay. And, we needed someone who would bait Zophos into overplaying his hand. Hank's the perfect person. He's equipped, confident in his redemption, secure in his identity, and multi-dimensional in his comprehension of the Kingdom."

"Right," Vassar said. "Hank is all that—and more. He's a mighty warrior."

"Indeed he is! He got that from you. You are a lot alike."

"Thanks, Papa. Hank's a great Brother. Like you were saying though, Zophos can't keep over-reaching, overplaying, desperately over-investing. He's going to implode."

"True," the High King said, as he and Vassar moved back toward the throne room. "True enough. Zophos is going to collapse under his own weight. Well on his way, in fact. We will bankrupt him—trying to keep up with our investment in Hank and the family."

"He likes to think his resources are unlimited," Vassar observed.

"Yeah. Self-deception is his finest character quality," the King noted.

"You know, Papa, it's like Zophos is trying to get intoxicated drinking his own bath water."

With that, the King chuckled, shook his head, and placed his hand on Vassar's back. They walked together, exited through the door of their chamber, and sat again on their seats overseeing the Kingdom.

The Road to the Round Tower

Hank relied upon his walking staff to get through the woods and back onto the road. Once there he thought about tossing the staff aside, but carried it for good measure. Somehow, it felt right in his hand.

While his deeply bruised thigh was tender to the touch and looked atrocious, walking was working the soreness out. At least, that's the reassurance he gave himself as he labored through every pace. When he believed no one was looking, Hank practiced walking without a limp, but after a mile or so the compensating aches in his body were too much to bear. He decided to incorporate his limp into his swagger.

That worked better. Trying to not limp felt like denial. *After all, I got this wound battling on behalf of the King,* he reviewed with Magician. *I defended the defenseless—as a knight of light. This is a badge of courage. I need to honor it as such.*

The shift in thinking reassured Hank that he was embracing neither denial nor pity in his relinquished effort to walk without a limp. *That's good,* he thought. *Wounds are part of life—part of what forms my story. Vassar's got wounds,* he reflected, thinking. *Wounds are not bad. In fact, a man with no wounds lacks credibility.*

He thought back, while he walked, to his resolution under the spruce tree. *There's no point trying to hide that I'm a knight in the Kingdom of Light. I have position, identity, and place. I am a knight, a Prince, and I am the King's son.*

He walked—strutted, even—deliberate in his gait. In his soul, he was marching to the beat of his spiritual affirmations—each step a proclamation of his life's manifesto.

He marched, feeling the rhythmic pace in his angry hips and tortured spine. He marched, each step an electric jolt—lightning striking above his knee. Thought, *Yep. This is how such a person carries himself. I've seen it in Vassar a thousand times.*

Entering the castle, he decided the walking staff masked his knighthood, making him incognito, or perhaps the residents were too busy to notice. Whatever the reason, he moved through the castle streets in relative obscurity. Occasionally, someone stared, but he didn't know if that was because some people just stare, or if they recognized him as a knight.

Not knowing what to expect when he entered the castle, his plan was limited in scope. He found himself scurrying to determine what to do next. He didn't want to sit down, or stop to think, or do anything else that might draw unwarranted attention—so decided to return to a known location, the subterranean diner where he and Vassar and the others had eaten during his last adventure.

To his delight, he found Hoi Polloi right away. He stepped down into the sunken room and waited a moment for his eyes to adjust. The room hadn't changed, although the ceiling felt lower than he remembered.

Maybe you've grown, Magician offered to Hank's mind.

He smiled at his friend's humor—and the subtle reminder that he wasn't alone.

The same waitress was working the dining room. As she approached, Hank said to Magician, *Here we go. Live through me.*

While he recognized her, he couldn't tell whether she recognized him, which he considered a good thing. She seated him exactly as he would have asked: off to the side.

She took his drink order and returned. Just as he remembered, she was forthright in running through the available items on the menu, but then stating without apology that she'd order the day's special, "…if I was you."

Hank nodded his agreement. He'd forgotten how much he liked this lady. *She is who she is,* he thought, as she left to place his order. *I could take a lesson from her, couldn't I, Wizard?*

There was no comment in his head. Hank found that amusing. *Typical Magician.*

Sipping his drink, he decided his first move would be to inquire of the waitress. *She was helpful the last time I was here.*

She beat him to the punch, though. Setting another glass of wine on the table, she said, "I can see you're a knight, but you're a different kind."

Hank smiled. "You're observant," he said.

"It's my job, Hon." She waited, her weight resting on her left leg, left hand propped on her left hip.

"How am I different?"

"The crest on the end of your dagger," she said, pointing.

"You're good at what you do," Hank said. "It's a custom blade, given to me by my Father."

Before she could follow up with further inquiry about the dagger or his Father, Hank changed the subject. "It's been a couple of years since I last ate here. In fact, it's been that long since I was last in the castle."

"Well, not much's changed. Not as much fighting as there was two years ago, come to think of it. Guess the guys like you are gettin' things under control."

"I don't know about that," Hank said.

"I suppose you're headed to the Round Tower?" she questioned.

"As a matter of fact..." he was interrupted by the cook calling to her.

She excused herself to collect his meal, placed the ample portion before him, touched him briefly on the shoulder, and walked away, saying as she went, "Let me know if you need anything, Hon."

His meal was excellent, just as he recalled, but too much food. He pushed his chair back, crossed his legs, and enjoyed his wine.

She returned. "You finished?" She didn't wait for his reply as she began clearing his place setting.

"It was great!" Hank said, putting his hand on his abdomen. "I'm full as a tick though."

"Full as a tick, huh?" She smiled. "Not sure that's a good thing, if you know what I mean, Darlin'."

"Just saying," Hank said. "What can you tell me about the Round Tower?"

"Since you were last here…." She didn't finish her thought. "Did you visit it the last time you were here?"

She caught Hank mid-drink and swallow. He shook his head.

"Used to be the dickens to get into. Orneriest bunch of folks! Somethin' changed their minds, I guess. You can walk right in now, or at least that's what I heard. Haven't been to see for myself."

She picked up a few remaining items and stacked them on the plate. "Anyhow, a fancy knight like yourself ought to be able to walk right in."

Hank grimaced at the description.

She carried his plate and remainders away. He sipped and calculated.

When she returned carrying a damp rag, Hank picked up his wine cup. As she wiped his table, she said, "You know. There's a lady, a Ms. Pintaro. She's some sort of muckety muck at the Tower. Don't know exactly, but a real nice woman. You ought to get to know her."

"Interesting. What else do you know about her?"

"Told you all I know, Hon. She's one of those people who's open and approachable, but only so far. Then you kind a run up against a wall. Know what I mean?"

Hank nodded, "Uh, huh. I do."

"If I happen to see her assistant, I'll mention you if you like. She doesn't come in here, but a man by the name of Mr. Bertram does. He works for her."

"Oh, I see," Hank followed. "Thanks for your offer. I'll find her once I get to the Round Tower. Don't want to be an imposition."

"No trouble on my end, Hon. But whatever suits you."

Hank finished his wine, paid his tab, thanked the waitress, and headed back out into the castle. He didn't need directions. The Round Tower rose above everything else. Walking as he had practiced, Henry H. Henderson, son of the High King, Brother of Vassar, and knight of light made his way to the object of his calling.

The Round Tower

The young leader held onto the counter, chairs, and braced against the walls as he worked in the kitchen preparing the evening meal. His breaks and contusions had healed. There were scars and missing teeth, but his wife said they lent character to his face. He wasn't so sure, but what point was there in disagreeing with her? Besides, the pressing concern was to walk. It wasn't that his legs were unusable, rather that his equilibrium had been damaged.

In the early days after the assault, he improved and his family celebrated his recovery. But his progress slowed. He hadn't demonstrated significant improvement in several weeks.

He was getting better using his cane, but it was an awkward appendage. No matter how deliberate he was placing it within reach, the stick was predisposed to wind up on the floor. If he bent down to pick it up, the floor spun and he was face down before he knew it. Retrieving the cane required kneeling, going on all fours, and then using the stick to work his way back upright. He could count on working up a sweat before the trial was complete.

Because of his inability to work—or more accurately, his inability to find an employer who would hire him, the young leader and his wife were left with no alternative but for her to find a job. His dear wife had been an incredible help and a constant encourager. A real champion, no question about it! That's what he told everyone whether they asked or not.

He heard the door open. Anticipation and dread rose up in him. They were both trying to keep their spirits high, clinging to their convictions and commitments to the High King, but every day seemed to bring more disappointment.

The young leader would have liked nothing better than to meet his wife at the door, but sudden movements resulted in a tumble. Instead, he positioned himself in a corner where he was braced and could offer both arms to hug his bride.

The door closed hard, nearly a slam. She rushed into the kitchen, stopped short of him in a dramatic pose, tears streaming down her face, "Jake! I've got a job!"

Jacob and Caroline Ingram clung to each other in their kitchen. Kissing, holding each other, talking at once, the kids joining the family clutch—all celebrating in unison the great news.

Caroline helped Jake carry the meal from the kitchen to the table. After they'd eaten, they reviewed the last months of their lives. They affirmed—once again and to the nth degree—their commitment to the King, his teaching, and to the role they continued to believe they played in advancing the Kingdom of Light. We wouldn't change a thing, they agreed.

Time got away from them as they talked. The knock at the door startled them. Caroline looked at the table full of dirty dishes and leftover food. There wasn't any way to salvage a clean up now.

Two of the young people who came to their home every week were waiting on the other side of the door. Three others arrived shortly on their heels, Audie Vandermeer among them.

For Jake's sake, the weekly meetings usually took place at the table, but since it was full of dinner dishes, tonight they met on the floor. They laughed and cried and celebrated the provision of Caroline's job. They spent time discussing their faith and how it carried them through the difficulty. And, they thought hard about how such a terrible tragedy occurred in the first place to such wonderful people. The beating and the provision stood juxtaposed in their beliefs about the King, his care, and his goodness.

To his surprise, even though the waitress at Hoi Polloi told him so, Hank walked through each of the Round Tower's gates unimpeded and unquestioned. Once inside, he noted two signs placed prominently: one arrow pointed toward the Round Tower's offices, the other indicated the direction for visitors.

An older couple sat behind the tall counter, their heads barely visible. The sign above them read "Welcome Desk." Hank greeted them. They nodded, appearing a bit miffed that their conversation was interrupted. Reflecting upon it later, Hank decided they felt threatened. *But how could that be? All I did was say hi.*

He told them he was a guest and needed a room. While the man sat quiet, the female host produced a form for Hank to complete. As he filled in the blanks, she chose a room key.

Accepting his completed form, she double-checked the number of the room key, and was poised to write the number on Hank's form. She froze. Looking up at him, "You're Henry Henderson?"

Smiling, even though on alert that he had been expected, Hank said, "Yes, that's right. I'm Henry Henderson." He reached across the counter with an extended hand. "I go by, Hank."

The host accepted a quick handshake. The other, without saying a word, got up and disappeared through a doorway. Taking the original key, the lady replaced it midst the others, and selected a different key, one set apart.

As she handed him his room key, he noticed the number of his room wasn't recorded on the form. *Magician, something's up,* he thought. He looked up the stairs, and began climbing.

Magician's counsel was immediate and direct in his thoughts, *Be wise like a serpent, Hank, innocent like a dove.*

Wise like a serpent, innocent like a dove, he repeated to himself as he climbed. *Wise like a serpent, innocent like a dove.*

The hallway was vacant and silent. Hank watched from the head of the stairs for a moment before walking down the hall.

Stopping in front of his door, he knocked with his knuckle three times and listened. Nothing. Hank stuck his key in the lock and pushed the door open. He waited in the hall, looking into his room. Nothing. He pushed the door all the way back against the wall just in case there might be someone waiting behind it. Nothing. He stepped across the threshold and to his left, creating space—working space if he needed it. Nothing. He moved farther into the room, glanced behind him, and into the wash room. Nothing.

Hank closed the door and locked it, then began a closer examination of his accommodations. It didn't strike him as unusual that his room had a door leading to an adjoining room. But something drew him toward the connecting door. He eyed the door from a distance—but with the third sense of insistence, he went to it for a more thorough look. He noted the key hole was larger. He checked. The door was locked. He tried his key. It didn't work. He looked through the keyhole. Nothing. Dark. *Odd. It's still light outside. Maybe the curtains are pulled,* he thought.

He sat down on the edge of the bed and stared at the door. *What is it about this door?*

It dawned on him: *Connecting rooms are for families, and in this day and age, families don't travel.*

He presumed the persistent attention to the door came from Magician. *What should I do now? About the door?*

He thought for a moment, moved a chair against the door, and placed a wadded piece of paper into the oversized keyhole. He wished for a doorknob to jam the back of the chair under, *But the noise of the sliding chair will provide enough warning*, he decided.

He looked out his window. There was no view to speak of, but more importantly, *Unless someone rappels down from above, there's no way anyone's coming through my window.* He left the curtain open.

Hank wrote a fictional name and address on a piece of paper—in small print with a messy penmanship. He placed the sliver of paper in the center of the bed close to the pillows, then stepped back to see if it was legible from a distance. Satisfied that it wasn't, he wrinkled the covers just so, and studied his trap.

He looked through the peep hole and listened before opening his door, waited to step out, checked the hallway, locked his room, and walked heavily down the hallway. He waited at the top of the stairs to see if anyone emerged from the adjoining room. Nothing.

Hank walked for the better part of an hour, acquainting himself with the layout of the Round Tower, at least, the part of the Round Tower he could access. Most of it was locked.

Returning to his room, Hank was again cautious as he entered. While he didn't notice anything technically out of order, something didn't feel right. He stood at the threshold, unable to isolate his concern.

He closed his door and locked it, then turned his attention to the bed. A maid had come in, turned his bed down, and placed the address on the side table. *I wonder if that's customary?* he pondered. He knew it was in some of the better hotels he'd stayed in, *But this isn't a finer hotel and this isn't the twenty-first century.*

Although unsettled by his intuition, he got ready for bed. He closed the curtains. He placed his clothes at the foot of his bed and put his dagger and satchel on the side table.

He sat on the edge of the bed, his attention drawn again to the adjoining door. One last time, he walked over for a final examination.

He had twisted the piece of paper deep into the lock, to block the view and jam the tumblers. It was repositioned—without the twists.

He didn't sleep. He dozed, finally rising at first light to prepare for his day. Hank organized himself for a few moments of solitude, contemplation, and discussion with Magician. There was no writing table, so he sat on the bed and moved the bedside table over so he had a hard surface upon which to journal.

Just as he was about to withdraw Vassar's letter from his satchel, he thought to look at the adjoining door. To his amusement, the paper was missing from the keyhole. *Someone is observing me, and they're desperate,* he thought. *They're making stupid mistakes. I'll go along,* he decided. *Better they underestimate me than vice versa.*

Instead of extracting Vassar's letter from his satchel, Hank retrieved his writing instrument and paper. It took a supreme effort to focus—knowing he was being observed. But quietly, Hank retreated into the sanctuary of his heart for reflection and counsel.

He worked from memory. He called upon Magician, *Guide my thoughts this morning. I need a word for today, something special, something on point for all that this day holds.*

He listened thoughtfully. A memorized passage from the letter came to mind, and there Hank devoted his morning contemplation. Vassar had written…prophetically it appeared, given the circumstances:

> *No matter if all hell is breaking loose, be at peace, Brother. Greater is he who lives in you than he who rules Gnarled Wood and beyond. That's not hyperbole! Magician is more powerful than Jester and Zophos put together, so don't be afraid if they assemble themselves against you.*

As he jotted down his thoughts regarding Vassar's counsel, he wrote, I'm more comfortable in Gnarled Wood than I am in the "beyond"—

for it seems the Round Tower is located in the "beyond."

He stopped to think about "beyond." *But the Round Tower is where Father's people live—most of them, anyway—mingled with all of Zophos' folks. Like I once was, they are Princes and Princesses living beneath the status and privilege of their true identities. And Papa, you have selected me—honored me—to speak on your behalf to your family about you.*

Hank stopped to consider the implications of this honor bestowed upon him. *Papa, of all people, I am the least qualified, certainly the least worthy, to represent you. You have confidence in me, yet I stumble frequently. You trust me, yet I am prone to doubt you. You have equipped me, but my propensity is to go it alone. You do not condemn me, but I feel shamed by my shortfalls. You believe in me, but I don't. Father—dear Papa—and dearest Brother, Magician, help my unbelief.*

Hank sat thinking, noting the twisted piece of paper on the floor. *And if you could help my unbelief right away, that would be a good thing!* he added.

He wrote in his journal, "I concur! Magician's power is not hyperbole!"

Addressing Magician directly, *Did you get that vote of confidence?* Hank smiled, sitting on the edge of his bed. He liked Magician. *Live through me now—come hell, high water, or heaven.*

He folded his journal entry for the day and left it on the bedside table. He had been deliberately obscure. He didn't want to draw unnecessary attention to his satchel by placing the journal entry alongside the others—next to Vassar's letter. And as long as he was playing cat and mouse with whoever was on the other side of the door, *Why not require them to play at my level?*

Going naturally about his morning business was easier said than done. After the fact, he congratulated himself on a rather convincing performance.

Having casually laid several traps for his observer—mostly by simply noticing exactly how he placed various items, like the folded journal entry—Hank collected his personal effects and stepped to the outside door. Pausing before touching the latch, Hank asked, *Magician, do you have any counsel for me before I step into this hallway? All bets are off on the other side of this door.*

Thoughts formed in Hank's mind, *I am not hyperbole, and I am on your side. I'm with you. You are not alone. For the record, Zophos and Jester are assembled against you, but I am greater than they are. Let's get moving!*

And with that encouragement, Hank touched the hilt of his dagger, unlatched the door lock, and glanced outside. The hall was empty. He locked his door and went in search of breakfast.

A young man was seated at the Welcome Desk, and to Hank's pleasure, was more pleasant than the dour couple who checked him in. He had obviously been briefed on Hank since he greeted him personally, but whatever warnings he'd been given, he assigned them secondary importance.

With youthful enthusiasm—what his superiors would probably consider indiscretion—the young man bluntly stated what an honor it was to meet a real knight. "I've met knights before. They're scattered around the Round Tower, you know. But to meet a real warrior—gosh, this is just..." he hunted for the appropriate word, and then settled on, "...it's just great!"

Hank thanked the young man and chatted with him for a few moments. He eventually asked for a recommendation for breakfast. The young desk clerk gave high marks to a small restaurant not far away. Hank thanked the young man and turned to leave. But, he stopped in the middle of the lobby. He turned and went back to the desk. "You've worked the night shift I presume."

"Yes sir. I have," the young man confirmed.

"You about to get off?"

"Yes sir. As a matter of fact"—again with his youthful candor—"the next shift is here. I stayed because I wanted to meet you."

Hank reached across the space between him and the young man, holding out his hand. "I'm Hank Henderson."

"Mr. Henderson. It's my pleasure. I'm Ronan Chandler."

"Ronan. That's a good name," Hank stated. "Well, Ronan. I'm headed to breakfast. Want to join me? I'm buying."

"Wow! Thank you. Sure."

Hank and Ronan found a table at Hank's favorite location in public places: off to the side. Hank sat where he could see the door and watch the restaurant function while eating and visiting with his new friend.

The coffee was better than he expected. Hank was amused that Ronan was prepared to load his cup with cream until he noted the man across the table from him drank his black. Not trying to hide his changed mind, Ronan set the cream aside.

"So how long have you lived in the Round Tower?" Hank asked.

Ronan proved easy to talk to, which pleased Hank. He didn't consider himself much of a conversationalist. The subjects they explored were far-reaching, but Hank listened, probed, contributed, and carefully garnered Ronan's trust.

When the time seemed right, Hank asked, "Tell me what you know of the High King."

Ronan replied, spouting factoids intertwined with opinion and hearsay. Mostly it was the speech he'd been trained to give when he started working at the Welcome Desk in the Tower. He sounded convincing, but his assemblage of data didn't hold together. Whether he thought it did or not, Hank couldn't tell, but he suspected not. Ronan only regurgitated information, he didn't reveal any personal opinion.

Pressing closer, with an unthreatening tone, Hank asked, "What role does the King play in your life?"

"I'm not sure I know what you're asking me."

"Yeah, it wasn't a very clear question," Hank said, absorbing the brunt of Ronan's doubt to afford the young man a moment more to formulate an answer. "I mean, does the King exert any personal influence in your daily life beyond the high level stuff like rules and ideals?"

"Ah, I understand. No. Not really," Ronan said thoughtfully. "I've heard a few people say they know the King personally and follow his teaching, but I'm not sure I believe them."

"Why not?"

"Well, because he's the King and they're them. Like the King has time for them! Come on. I mean, even if the King's real, why would he give them or me a second thought."

"I like how you think, Ronan. You're analytical, honest, and thoughtful. I appreciate that in a man. Here's the thing though: Inside—deep inside, in your heart—there is a vacancy that only a relationship with the King can fill."

"Wait. You're saying the King exists and wants to know me?"

"That's exactly what I'm saying."

"No disrespect, Sir, but that's hard to believe," Ronan said. "How could that be true?"

"You sound interested in knowing more about the King's desire to meet you."

"I am, Mr. Henderson. I am. But are you sure the King wants to know me—and other people like me?"

"I'm absolutely positive, Ronan. After all, I know him personally."

"Yeah. I suppose you do," Ronan acknowledged.

"You know what?" Hank said. "There is a group of people, about your age, who meet each week. They explore this subject and are very serious about it. I know you'd be welcome. If you're interested, I'll arrange for someone to meet you and take you with them."

Ronan leaped at the opportunity. There was a hunger—in his soul—he'd not noticed until today.

"I'll make it a point to find out the particulars today. I'll look for you at the Welcome Desk."

Ronan and Hank parted company. Both hoped their breakfast was the genesis of a new friendship.

CHAPTER 13

The Round Tower

Hank knocked on the door—three distinct raps. "Give me a minute," he heard from inside.

The door opened, and Hank said, "Jake Ingram?"

Steadying himself on his walking stick, "That's me."

Still on the other side of the threshold, Hank said, "I'm Hank Henderson."

Jake switched hands with his cane and stuck out his right hand, "I figured as much. Love told me about you. Said you were in the Tower."

The men shook hands and Jake invited Hank inside. Hank complimented Jake on the warmth of their home. Jake pointed to a chair close to the hearth.

Looking around the room's appointments, Hank said, "I see you've got children."

Jake's face lit up. "Yeah, three. They're playing with friends this afternoon. Should be home any time. In fact, Caroline should be home soon as well."

"Well, I won't stay long."

The two men visited about miscellaneous things for a few moments. Hank told briefly about himself. He figured—hoped—he would have the opportunity to introduce himself to Caroline as well, so didn't download all his details on Jake.

Changing the subject, Hank said, "Jake, I know about the assault, about your injuries, and I've been told about your recovery and the ongoing struggles."

Jake nodded. As men are prone to do, he didn't offer commentary, only "Yeah, there have been some challenges."

"I can only imagine," Hank said.

Just as Hank was about to continue, a key rattled in the front door. Jake began the process of standing, taking his time so as not to lose his equilibrium.

A blond woman opened the door, medium height, nice figure, poised, with a quick smile, and a bag slung over her shoulder. She let the bag slip off, caught it by the strap, and set it on the floor as Jake was introducing her to Hank.

Caroline shook Hank's hand with a firm grip, then wrapped her arms around Jake. The couple hugged without embarrassment and greeted each other with a kiss.

Jake filled his wife in on Hank and the conversation to this point. "He knows all about the attack," he concluded.

Caroline produced a decanter filled with water, along with three glasses, then joined her husband and Hank at the table.

"If you wish," Hank resumed, "I think I can provide some detail about that fateful event that you may find encouraging."

Caroline and Jake looked at each other with looks that were a combination of anticipation and apprehension.

"First, let me put your minds at ease. I am a knight in the Kingdom of Light. I have been commissioned to come alongside you, and others like you, who are committed to the King and his Kingdom. Magician, the same comforter who guides you, has briefed me on your story. In fact, he has asked me to visit you so your strength and confidence will not wane."

Caroline reached for Jake's hand. Her eyes brimmed with tears. Jake noticeably squeezed her hand for reinforcement.

Hank reached across the table and placed his hand on top of theirs. He reassured them with a squeeze of his own and a light pat, then took his hand away and continued, "Jake, the attack wasn't happenstance. You weren't simply in the wrong place at the wrong time. You were targeted. Chosen. It was an effort by enemies of the High King to discourage you, to defeat you."

Now there were tears in Jake's eyes.

"All this time—ever since the beating—we've thought our suffering was pointless, that we were simply the victims of circumstance," said Caroline. "Our 'why's' have had no answers."

"I know. That's why I'm here. I've been sent to let you know your suffering is not without merit. In the first place, the King never lets suffering, whatever the cause, be wasted in the lives of his people. You were targeted because you are doing important work in the Kingdom. In other words, you were wounded in action. Both of you."

Caroline left her chair, knelt beside Jake, and hugged him, crying in his lap as he held onto her, rubbing her back. The relief of knowing their suffering wasn't pointless brought needed reassurance.

Hank stayed for dinner. The Ingram family insisted!

Jake, Caroline, and Hank talked late into the evening; Jake sharing insights into the dynamics of the Round Tower and the young couple talking animatedly about their work with the young people. Hank affirmed them again that their labors were not in vain.

Pledging that he would see them again soon, Hank headed home shortly before midnight. After they closed the door behind him, Jake and Caroline Ingram held each other for a long time. Their souls, nearing depletion earlier in the day, were overflowing.

Although they worked on short sleep the next day, their spirits were high. It was the day of their weekly meeting with the young people. First to enter that evening was Audie. She introduced them to her new friend, Ronan Chandler, who told them of his meeting with Mr. Henderson. Jake and Caroline didn't let on that they too knew Hank, but realized—from yet another angle—that Hank had indeed been sent by the High King.

Bernard "Bernie" Bertram assigned his star hire, Caroline Ingram, the task of organizing the departmental party. Once a quarter he pulled everyone together to pass out accolades, recognition, and provide time to socialize. Bernie's usual get together was over drinks and *hors d'oeuvres* of cheese and sausage in a private room, but yearly he assembled a more ambitious event that included dinner.

Caroline had distinguished herself. She was quick on the uptake, readily connected the working parts of the department, and made few mistakes, far fewer than any other new employee he had hired. She showed initiative and strong intuition regarding when to take responsibility and when to seek permission. And as if this weren't enough, even with her strong performance, and the competitive threat Bernie feared she would be to her colleagues, Caroline never disturbed the harmony of the office. If anything, she enhanced the working environment.

With a few questions, Caroline discovered what had been done at previous parties, what was expected, and what her budget was. *It's hard to be creative with* hors d'oeuvres *and drinks*, she thought.

She surprised everyone with a signature drink. She didn't declare herself the inventor of it, but when the Brandy-based cocktail received rave reviews, she called it, "The Bernard."

She was afraid naming the drink after her boss would garner accusations of "kissing up," but her place in the office culture was strong and the naming was in good humor. Bernie and Letizia both agreed they'd never seen anyone amalgamate themselves so seamlessly into a working group.

The staff didn't realize that underneath the daily office was a network of darkness only two steps removed from Zophos. Not even Bernie knew that. He did know there was another side to the business and took measures to manage within the boundaries set by Letizia. The staff assumed Bernie's practice of adjusting each staff person's job description and position every third quarter ensured critical processes were backed up. And, certainly that was a side benefit. But mainly Bernie moved people so no one gained enough professional insight to assemble the office's dark pieces into a puzzle and start probing.

Caroline grew more proficient and more reliable with each assignment. She made mistakes, but they were expected errors, and she proved responsible, honest, quick to correct course, and astute at not only fixing her error but growing from the mistake.

She was not only a good worker, but proved an able and natural leader as well. The efficiency and productivity of the entire office increased—and it did so harmoniously. In fact, the one staff member who was a burr under Bernie's saddle blanket resigned. Once departed, Bernie waited for the inevitable shuffling, adjusting, and territorial spats. But instead, the office's efficiency increased by another metric, and the only explanation, as much as he would have liked to take credit, had to be Caroline Ingram's influence.

As Bernard and Letizia reviewed the quarterly report, Letizia asked about the positive increases. To his credit, Bernard was forthcoming. "Ms. Pintaro, I would like to tell you I worked some magic, but I didn't, not beyond hiring Caroline."

"Bernie, that you hired Caroline speaks to your proficiency."

"Thank you, Ms. Pintaro."

The final item on the agenda was the annual dinner for the office. "I've asked Caroline to coordinate us. I've reviewed the budget with her and outlined the major components of the dinner and program. I've informed her that this will be an expanded occasion, with not only family, but additional guests, and formal dress."

Letizia nodded. Periodically, though not usually at the annual office dinner, Letizia liked to bring her colleagues and nemeses together and observe, glean, and change the status quo.

Caroline noticed, as she and one of her colleagues worked on the dinner invitations, that her friends, Henry H. Henderson and Love, were both on the guest list. She didn't indicate she knew either, but found their inclusion interesting.

Jake was putting together the family's dinner when Caroline arrived home. As she set her bag down, she picked up a sealed note lying in the floor. "Where'd this come from?" she asked, waving the note as she stepped into Jake's waiting arms.

He pulled her close, kissing her cheek. He let go of her and eyed the note more closely. "Beats me. Someone must have slid it under the door."

Before she could open the note, there was a knock. Caroline peeked, then opened the door. A courier, small box in hand, asked for her signature. After she signed, he handed her the box, "Be careful, ma'am. It's heavier than you might expect." And indeed it was.

Caroline closed the door and set the box on the table. The kids had come to see what was going on and were anxious to see what was in the box. Jake handed Caroline a knife and stood with his hand on her shoulder as she cut through the twine.

Inside was a bag, tightly wound, and padded so it wouldn't slide around in its container. Caroline unwound the tie, opened the top, and dumped the contents onto the dining table. A fortune in coins rattled onto the oak surface.

While the kids asked kid questions, Jake and Caroline were speechless. As they found their tongues, they too asked, "What on earth?" "Who could have?" "Why?"

Jake retrieved the sealed note from the counter. He broke the seal with his finger, opened the note without looking, and then turned his attention to the writing:

> You both need new clothes—suitable for a nice occasion—along with some money to look after the children.
>
> One of my couriers will arrive shortly with provision to cover your need. If I have calculated correctly, there should be some extra as well.
>
> Enjoy! I'm proud of you,
> Your King

Hank had given serious consideration to finding other accommodations, but was willing to put up with the systematic invasions of his privacy in exchange for an inside look into the Round Tower's watchfulness of him. Beyond this, he enjoyed crossing paths with Ronan.

Ronan told him that he had attended the meeting at Caroline and Jake Ingram's home. Just as he was about to go into detail, Hank stopped him and suggested they move their conversation to the breakfast place where they had their first in-depth conversation. Hank wasn't comfortable discussing the subject of the High King while standing at the Welcome Desk in the Round Tower.

Over a cup of coffee at the bistro, Ronan told Hank in the best words he could find how he and Audie stayed late after the meeting. He reported how Jake patiently answered each of his questions about the High King and how he came to a point where there was no impediment to making the decision before him. With a glowing countenance, Ronan told Hank that as the evening concluded, he got down on his knees—and with some coaching from Jake—pledged his life and allegiance to the High King.

Hank celebrated and affirmed Ronan's decision. Together, they retraced Ronan's pledge. Where appropriate, Hank offered a few words of explanation. It was evident that a new horizon had appeared for Ronan and he was enthusiastic about pursuing his new vision.

As they continued talking, alternating between Ronan's pledge and the implications of that pledge on his future, Hank asked him if he felt anything after he made his pledge. "Not particularly, at least not at that moment," Ronan said. "But, it's like my chest is full—or something. I know that sounds stupid."

Hank was quick to dismiss any notion of stupidity, noting to himself how quickly Jester takes aim at any light source. In simple terms Hank introduced Ronan to Magician. "He's the presence of the King in your heart. In time, you will get to know, understand, and hear his voice more clearly." He could see Ronan struggling to comprehend, so added, "Don't worry. We can talk more about this as time passes. Jake will be a great resource as well."

Ronan had digested all he could for one conversation. With a sly grin, he changed the subject, thanking Hank for introducing him to Audie. Boys will be boys, old or young, and the two of them discussed girls—Audie in particular.

As Hank returned to his room, the clerk at the Welcome Desk handed him a sealed note. He stepped away and opened the invitation to Letizia Pintaro's office dinner. He was curious about why he had been invited to a special dinner by someone whom he only knew by reputation, but concluded it must be part of why he had been summoned to the Round Tower.

Hank decided to use the invitation to create an advantage. He was satisfied by the seal on the note that the message had not been compromised. Stepping back to the Welcome Desk with a serious expression, he asked, "Can you tell me, please, who delivered this note and when?"

He got the same answer to each question, an indifferent shrug.

The morning clerk's passive aggression raised his hackles, but he controlled the urge to reach across the desk.

Looking again at the note for affect, Hank informed the desk clerk, "As you can no doubt tell, something important has arisen. I'm afraid I must leave right away."

"For good?" the clerk inquired, alarmed.

"No, no. I'll be back, but I'm certain it will be late—quite late. I suspect there will be additional messages. Would you keep them safe for me until I return?"

The clerk shrugged a lackadaisical affirmation.

Hank ceremoniously placed the note in an interior pocket to convey importance, donned a serious and determined expression, nodded once at the surly clerk, and quickly departed.

Hank allowed time for the Welcome Desk personnel to convey to whomever that he had departed for an extended period. After biding his time, which was harder to do than he expected, Hank returned via a circuitous route. In so doing, he bypassed the Welcome Desk and accessed his hallway via a maintenance corridor.

There was no place for the intruder in his room to go when Hank stepped through the door, unless he chose to jump out the window to certain death. The man was going through a stack of fake documentation papers.

As the intruder tried to muscle his way toward the door, Hank snatched him by his collar and flung him against the door. Turning him around, Hank threw him against the wall, never letting go of his collar. He demanded to know who he was working for. The man was silent.

Hank knocked the man's head against the wall. He blinked trying to clear the cobwebs, but still was not forthcoming. Hank punched him hard at the base of his rib cage and felt the lower two ribs give way.

After recapturing his breath, the man feigned ignorance, "I can't say," he gasped.

Hank demanded to know. The man shook his head. Hank struck him again on the damaged ribs.

The man made a feeble attempt to kick him. Hank noted the gallant effort—and appreciated the man's toughness through the agony of broken ribs.

Hank punched him again, same spot, twice in rapid succession. The man's eyes bulged with pain and he drooled on Hank's hand. Again, he shook his head.

Hank drew his dagger and placed the point of it just below the man's knee cap. He pushed until the pain registered on the man's face. The more the man squirmed, the more he inflicted pain upon himself. Hank demanded again to know who his boss was.

He hesitated. Hank pushed on the dagger, knew his blade penetrated the patellar tendon. The man's mouth opened wide as his pain escalated.

Hank waited. The intruder persisted in his enduring silence. Hank pushed on the dagger's handle. The leg flinched. The man gargled in the gutter of his throat.

He began confessing. He named a direct contact, a name Hank didn't recognize, but one he filed away for future reference. Figuring he knew more, Hank demanded the information. He whimpered Jester's name, which was no surprise to Hank. But knowing how Jester worked, Hank knew there was more. He kneed the man's thigh on his wounded leg. He howled and resumed his confession. Watching carefully, Hank recognized the man was empty of knowledge when he confessed that he thought his contact worked for Letizia Pintaro.

Hank half-walked, half-dragged the broken, bloody intruder

downstairs to the Welcome Desk. He left the man clinging to the Welcome Desk for support.

After collecting his things, Hank exited by the same circuitous and secret way he had entered earlier. He had already located a new lodging.

Hank arrived at his new place, checked in, cased his room, and sat down to reflect upon what he now knew. As the adrenalin ebbed from his bloodstream, he pulled the invitation from his pocket and thought, *Letizia Pintaro? I've heard about you. Apparently, you have heard of me as well. Now we will meet.*

Caroline and Jake arrived at the dinner venue early. She wanted to be certain everything was in order. Knowing Jake could take care of himself in a social setting, she left him to fend for himself while she tended to last minute details, although truth be told, there weren't many. The advance planning and communication, as well as her selection of location and staff, were again testimony to her proficiency.

Jake situated himself close to the back wall and enjoyed the quiet moments away from his kids. He loved them dearly, but like most parents, a night away was a welcome respite from their extravagant expenditures of energy.

Arriving early as well, Bernie noted the unfamiliar face. Jake began the tedious process of standing. As it was for most who met him the first time, the labor created an awkward moment, but once upright and stable, Jake extended his hand. "Hi. I'm Jacob Ingram."

"Oh, my gosh!" Bernie exclaimed. "Caroline's husband. I've been looking forward to meeting you. I'm Bernie Bertram. Caroline and I work together."

Jake was impressed. He knew Bernie by reputation, and knew he was Caroline's boss. That he would describe himself as her colleague indicated a great deal about the man.

Bernie had waved to a passing server who was now making his way to see what he needed. "Tell you what, Jacob. You and Caroline are seated at my table. Let's have a drink and get acquainted. What do you say?"

"Great," Jacob said. "And call me, Jake. I'm only Jacob when I'm in trouble."

"Jake it is!" Bernie repeated enthusiastically. "What are you drinking?"

While Jake hesitated, Bernie ordered a whiskey straight up. As the server looked to him, Jake said, "I'm having the same."

The two men found the table assigned to Bernie and sat down. Both recognized an instant affinity and their talk progressed rapidly below the surface of chitchat.

A few other guests arrived, fashionably early, and Bernie knew he should greet them, but he was too engrossed in conversation. After Jake referenced his disability a couple of times in passing, Bernie felt free to ask what had happened. He openly told Bernie about the attack, his injuries, and the resulting challenges he and his family faced. He also took the opportunity to thank Bernie for Caroline's job and told him what great reports she brought home each day after work.

As more guests arrived, Jake and Bernie recognized their conversation was on pause until the next opportunity they had to visit. "To be continued," Bernie said warmly.

"To be continued," Jake replied, using the table in collaboration with his cane to stand.

Hank stopped short of the door to the rented hall. Other guests were arriving, so he moved into the shadows to collect his thoughts and consult with Magician. *This is it. Any final words before I go inside?* Hank waited, listening.

Watch yourself, Magician counseled. *But, be yourself. You are secure. You are the King's son. Nothing can compromise you. You know this, don't you?*

I do know that, Hank replied in his mind and from his heart.

Good! Now, pay attention. I'll guide you.

I'm counting on you.

Perfect. Most importantly, love these people, Hank. Love conquers all.

Love? Hank thought. *I didn't love that guy very well who was ransacking my room the other day.*

Don't worry about him, Magician replied. *It was necessary to be able to love powerfully this evening.*

Hank hadn't thought of it that way before. *Anything else?* he inquired.

Walk in the light—as your Father and Brother are in the light.

Hank took a deep breath and stepped toward the door. Just before he entered, he polished his boots on the backs of his pants' legs, and reached for the latch.

It was a smaller gathering than he anticipated. His quick estimate was seating for fifteen or twenty. Caroline noticed him as he was introducing himself to the hostess and came over. "Hank, how nice to see you. I'm very glad you could come this evening."

As he kissed her cheek, Hank said, "I wouldn't have missed it. Thank you for the invitation."

"Well, I'm afraid I didn't have anything to do with it. You were on Ms. Pintaro's list."

"And is that a good thing?" he asked, smiling, and crooking his left arm.

"I can't imagine why not," she stated brightly and without suspicion. "You're here and it is going to be a great evening." Placing her right hand on his forearm, "In fact, you have the honor of sitting with the lady herself."

"Really?"

"Yes. I'm sure you will enjoy her. She is a wonderful woman."

They weaved through the dining room. The scarlet sash of redemption Hank wore at his waist complimented the bodice of Caroline's gown.

A cluster of people had gathered around the table where he was to sit. As Caroline navigated around the circumference of chairs, he noticed his name on a place card and made a mental note. Reaching back for his hand, she drew him alongside her, and waited patiently for her opportunity to make introductions.

"Ms. Pintaro. May I introduce you to Henry Henderson? Mr. Henderson, this is your table host, Letizia Pintaro."

The evening passed as most group dining experiences unfold—with small talk, smiles, and polite manners. The food was several notches better than Hank had expected, which was a delightful surprise. He hadn't been eating as well as he should have since arriving at the castle and Round Tower—but, he had pledged to change his ways…as soon as he got settled into a routine…and that was intended to be tomorrow.

Hank made a point of saying good-bye to each of his table mates with equal sincerity. He was being gracious, but he was also hoping the action might hide the fact that he knew more about his table host than tonight's dinner conversations revealed.

Working his way from the room, assuming he was being watched, Hank focused on maintaining an even, relaxed, and confident composure. Appropriately, he spent a few extra moments with Caroline. It wasn't hard to recognize her organizational efforts.

"The room was beautiful, Caroline. You did a wonderful job." He took her hand in his, "Thank you for a lovely evening. I hope I'm not being presumptuous, but I'm looking forward to the next time my path crosses yours and your husband's."

"We will make certain that happens sooner rather than later," Caroline reassured him.

He kissed her politely on the cheek, then stepped into the night air.

The doorman summoned Hank's rented carriage—a simple, black, one-horse conveyance, complete with a canopy. He rode toward the Round Tower, lost in reflection, the houses and buildings of the castle passing outside but not registering.

Seeing the Round Tower approach, Hank asked the driver to let him out before crossing the drawbridge. He paid and tipped, complimented the man's horse, and stood back as the carriage rolled into the darkness.

At the spur of the moment, Hank decided to take advantage of the evening. It was late, but most nights Hank resented having to waste hours in fitful sleep. Besides this, the summer days were uncomfortably warm, and the last few had proven miserably hot. When the sun disappeared behind the western hill, blessed cool descended—a welcome respite—and tonight, as he was riding home, a gentle rain began.

The carriage disappeared, the noise of the horse's hooves trailing some distance behind. Hank was alone with nothing but the city's slumbering noises and the patter of rain on the brim of his hat. Placing his hands behind his back, Hank strolled into the darkness, his head bowed, but not so far that rain dripped down his back. Within half a block, he had retreated into the confines and solitude of his heart to discuss the events of the evening with Magician.

I need wisdom, Wizard. I'm all but certain Ms. Pintaro has no idea I know more about her than I let on at dinner. Hank paused, envisioning Letizia and his proximity to her at the dinner. *She's formidable.* Hank was unconscious of shaking his head left and right, acknowledging the truth of his assessment of Letizia. *How the other people at the table fit into her sphere, I can't be certain. Of course, everyone was on their best behavior, which complicates my observations. But, I didn't get the sense anyone was either intimidated by her or indifferent toward her. Maybe everyone was playing the same guarded game I played. Hmm. I don't know, but I doubt everyone at the table is as good at that game as I am.*

Hank thought about that assessment, but dismissed the concern that he was blinded to accurate self-awareness by arrogance. *An honest valuation of my social skills isn't wrong just because I'm good at holding my cards close to my vest. There are plenty of situations where my guardedness is an impediment, but tonight's dinner was not one of them,* he decided.

The rain picked up its intensity and a cool front rode in on the stiffening breeze. Hank walked on.

He wondered why Caroline worked in Letizia's office. He couldn't put words to his intuition, but felt there was something more significant to her job than a paycheck. *Still, I don't have enough information,* he thought. Hank placed his observation on a shelf for later reference. *Perhaps something will come of my sensibility, perhaps not.*

As he came to the end of his personal debriefing of the evening, Hank made a mental note to pursue getting to know Caroline and Jake Ingram. He also knew he had not seen the last of Letizia, and while certain of this, he wasn't sure what that portended. *I know this. I've got to watch my step. In this instance, not trusting is a shrewd advantage.*

The irony was not lost on him as he walked. *Sometimes it is good to withhold trust,* he thought. *But it's never good to distrust Father,* he countered—or Magician suggested. It seemed like the better he got to know Magician, the more occasions there were when he couldn't distinguish between his thoughts and Magician's.

He had gone from being damp to being wet, which wasn't bad, except that it included his feet. Hank headed back, squishing as he went, but his heart was full.

CHAPTER 14

Gnarled Wood

Zophos sat brooding, which is what he did when he wasn't stalking. The activities were the same except for the movement. But whether sitting or roaming, his eyes had the same intensity.

Some said his gaze was resolve, some said it was anger. Others felt it was the look of fear.

Varnished with layers of denial, there was unspoken, hopeless desperation in every soul allied with the dark lord. Their eyes revealed the inescapable and terrifying sense that the High King of Light's promised consequence upon all in collusion with Zophos would indeed come to pass.

The consensus was that their premonition didn't really matter; they had gone too far. Their only option was to disparage the King and his Kingdom at every turn. Perhaps, in the end, Zophos would eke out a victory. In the meantime, determination, anger, fear, and desperation were tremendous motivators.

Zophos liked to believe he possessed ultimate power, and he often claimed to possess unchecked authority. He pointed frequently to the number of people who followed him, listened to him, and adhered to his leadership—even if indifferent—as proof that he was more influential than his avowed enemy, the High King.

However, no matter how much he blustered and posed and boasted, he could neither escape nor consistently conceal that he had to meet with the King. When he was summoned, he had no alternative but to report his activities, and his activities had to be in compliance.

He never told any of his subordinates when or where he was going when he was summoned to the King's throne. There was a pattern though. One of the King's guards would show up at Zophos' Gnarled Wood headquarters, usually during his second or third appointment of the morning, and tell him he had been summoned. This wrecked his calendar and destined him to have a bad day, exacerbating his frustration owing to a long string of bad days. But there was no acceptable excuse for his absence. He had to scramble, adjust. He had to order his staff to reschedule his appointments—beginning with the next one.

And for what reason? This question haunted him, bubbling in the heat of his brooding fire.

He knew he didn't owe anyone around him an explanation, and more often than not, he didn't explain. But after a while, he occasionally would say something. It was usually an outburst of intimidation toward whoever was closest as he departed to answer his summons. Insecure leaders are prone to such hyperbole as an overstated defense, but Zophos consoled himself as Hippocrates did, *Desperate times call for desperate measures.* He stated the mantra with each footfall.

Even when you are a god you are accountable, he counseled himself. *Being godlike has its burdens of leadership. There are secrets that must be kept for the good of the cause.*

It would be wrong to tell them I've been summoned by the High King, Zophos rationalized.

But the monarch interrupted him nearly every day! The King's summonses made him look like an errand boy. And, they reminded him of his limitations. Daily!

No point in worrying others over this inconvenience—this tactic the King utilizes, he thought. *When the tide turns against him, he will dispense with this petty posturing.* Like most who practice the dark art of projection, Zophos failed to recognize his irresponsibility.

So Zophos ruminated and skulked, brooding over what he could do to alter the balance of power between the King and him. *Surely there is something! Some measure that will change the momentum, give me the advantage. There has got to be a weakness I can exploit.*

That Zophos repeated this routine daily and asked himself the same questions, hoping for a different result than he achieved yesterday, only underscored his irrational vanity.

Inaction is unacceptable! He who hesitates is lost. Zophos committed a number of clichés to memory. They were his soul's fare. He never acknowledged that the tighter he clung to them for reassurance the more rapidly they leaked through his clutch, nor did he bother to reconcile why he, a god, quoted men for inspiration.

Thus he brooded, stalked about, brooded, roamed, brooded, created havoc and fear, brooded, attacked, brooded, created confusion, brooded, deceived, brooded, and so forth. Day after day, eon by eon. Regularly, he rededicated himself to try harder.

And at some point during his initiatives…he was summoned.

His hope for success was always deferred, and deferred hope created a vacuum in his soul that he couldn't assuage. His reaction was predictable: He tightened his controlling grip—with frustration both persistent and intense.

Many of the King's people felt they were targeted by Zophos, and felt they experienced the full force of his power, but the King limited what Zophos could do. It consistently worked to the advantage of the King's people while irking Zophos no end!

After reporting to the King, he inevitably returned to Gnarled Wood and took his anger out on his own staff and followers. It was the only place his authority went unchecked.

When prowling through the domain defined for him by the King, he fanaticized grandly of all that he could do—if only he were not governed by the King. But he operated in a confined space, with limited ability.

"It's enough to burn a god out!" he often complained.

In truth, the King didn't manage him. He typically delegated Zophos to Vassar, who in turn delegated him to people like Hank Henderson, who usually delegated him to Magician, who ordered him about like a pawn. The lack of deference to his god-status only fueled Zophos' hostility.

But per usual, he sat concentrating, hoping for a creative breakthrough while anticipating the interruption of his summons—his own anticipation an interruption in and of itself! He cursed his lack of focus, pinched the bridge of his nose, creating dull pain to weed out the extraneous, and redoubled his concentration.

His aide knocked on the door jamb. Zophos' anger boiled over. He spun in his seat and threw the knife-letter opener he'd been fidgeting with at his assistant. The aide had worked for Zophos long enough, and dragged enough unsuspecting souls away, to expect the hurtling blade.

The knife stuck chest-high in the door facing with a vibrating twang. Regaining his composure, the aide announced, "Sir. Ennui has arrived for your appointment."

Zophos let loose a string of expletives, then immediately regretted his outburst. Ennui was always so composed. *Desperate times call for desperate measures*, he assuaged himself. Never mind the corollary—that desperate people do desperate things.

Ennui took the letter-opener knife from the assistant and carried it to Zophos' desk. Placing it carefully atop a stack of papers, she sat down across from her boss. Before she leaned back, she moved her hair over her left shoulder. The epicanthic folds over her eyes smoothed her facial expression while allowing for her severity. She didn't like Zophos. Neither did he like her. But, they needed one another.

She didn't wait for permission, and knew better than to anticipate any introductory discussion or small talk. *He will ask questions if he has them. I will note his observations, weigh his wishes, and consider his commands.*

Zophos knew, looking at Ennui, that she was brazen. She knew he was ruthless. They worked well together.

"The Round Tower is stable," she began without fanfare. "The leadership is predictable. As in past summers, the Tower has instigated more programs for children and young people. They celebrate the same successes, all of which they religiously measure by their own standards, and all of which they attribute to the High King—and all of which they will forget shortly after the summertime report is presented." She delivered her report mechanically. "No standard measurement is carried forward unless it suits them. Thus, they account for their numerical growth."

"When's that report due?" Zophos questioned.

"The first Wednesday of September."

"It's July, for crying out loud!" Zophos fumed. "How can you sit there with a straight face assuring me of the contents in a report that is weeks away?"

"The summertime report has not varied for years." Ennui's tone had a touch of condescension in it which Zophos' noticed and resented. He motioned for her to continue, not that he needed to, but like her disrespectful tone, his hand motion was a subtle declaration of power.

"You are concerned about the consistency of the report," she continued, precisely. "There is one change I project. The fatigue experienced by the leaders of these programs will be a magnitude more severe this year."

"Be more concrete," her boss demanded.

"The leaders who work with the children and young people will not simply suffer physical and mental fatigue from their labors, but the narrowness of their work and the marginal nature of their results have eaten at their souls so as to burn them out. What they began with high hopes and *noblesse oblige* has become a small task fraught with interruption. Bottom line, they will not easily recover from this summer of service."

Zophos recognized from Ennui's explanation the burn out in his own soul. He quickly repressed it. Her incisive analysis of the summer program was a perfect example of why Zophos put up with Ennui. He would never dream of throwing a knife at her, or crossing her, or doing anything else to undermine the woman. The apathy she created, the unfulfilled longing she fostered, and the leanness in peoples' souls she advanced—all in the name of the King—was remarkably effective.

Nevertheless, he couldn't bring himself to recognize her ingenuity.

Ennui knew she had done consistently great work. It chaffed her that Zophos kept for himself what rightly belonged to her. Her stomach growled with hollow emptiness over his robbery of the recognition belonging to her, but her face did not betray the resentment she suffered.

A grin creased Zophos' face, revealing the winsome smile that was charismatic beyond comparison. "What becomes of these throw-away leaders—when they are burned out and disillusioned?"

Not batting an eye or condescending to the use of a contraction, Ennui stated flatly, "Their bankrupt souls are buried in shallow graves on the backside of the Round Tower. It is believed no one will notice. Besides, the work of the King, as they like to believe they are doing, is too important to take time out for triage, let alone the effort of genuine care to either the living or the dead."

This wasn't the answer Zophos was expecting. His faced showed surprise.

"Nor will anyone ask about them or seek them out," she continued. "It comes down to this: The Round Tower claims to care for the poor, the weak, the downtrodden—the widows, and the orphans. This is what the King requires. But in truth, the Round Tower does not care for their own wounded, let alone the wounded in society. They talk about it—a great deal. Hardly a meeting goes by but what they discuss this ideal. But they do not seek out the lost, and they do not extend mercy to the suffering—either inside or outside the Tower."

Zophos held his palms up toward the ceiling, wrists bent at ninety degrees, asking a question.

"Zophos, the Round Tower does not accommodate compromised people unless it suits them."

"There are walking wounded everywhere!" Zophos exclaimed. "What do they do with them?"

"They eliminate them." Ennui's face had no expression.

"Just like that?" he questioned her.

She shrugged, used to the incongruity within the Tower's systems. "Some are executed, many without trial, many more with convictions handed down by committees, boards, and kangaroo courts, and all in the name of the King and preserving the King's reputation. Numbers of them are ostracized because they do not fit in, do not have anything to offer that is valued by the Tower, or they are rejected because they are jeopardized in some other way. They are wounded. Flawed. They are damaged goods. The majority of these souls die from the starvation of neglect. Rarely does the Tower afford any casualty a proper burial unless doing so is unavoidable or seems beneficial to their reputation. The ones placed in shallow graves behind the Tower are the lucky ones. Many are put out through the back door. Most are simply forgotten. You should go behind the Tower sometime," she said. "The stench is insufferable."

"Why don't they clean it up?" Zophos asked.

For the first time, Ennui smiled. "They are in denial."

"Denial? The evidence is everywhere, at least to hear you talk."

"I have coerced them into attributing their treatment of the wounded to the High King. They believe they are doing him a service by ridding the Round Tower of all that is unsavory, less than satisfactory, unsuitable, and not representative of their standard—a standard they assert is the King's expectation. It is quite a coup! While the King appears unconcerned about reputation, the Round Tower has no higher priority. They ascribe to themselves this most precious standing and hold it dear—the very thing the King cares little about."

"Just as I hoped," Zophos stated.

Ennui couldn't believe he so openly took credit for her work, but she didn't say anything.

"The King is further discredited," Zophos gloated. He appeared to be talking to himself, but looked up at her. "You realize, of course, that the King cannot remain on his throne in the face of such accusations?"

Zophos slipped into his familiar harangue. "He must be overthrown, must be shown unworthy to rule. If that is not achieved…," Zophos didn't finish his sentence. He retrieved the knife, spun it in his fingers, felt the edge. "There will be hell to pay," he said, glaring at Ennui. She didn't know if he meant the King would inflict hell upon them or if Zophos would inflict hell upon her. Either way, they were both motivated to work, work desperately hard to achieve their essential goal.

Zophos changed the subject, "Give me a status report on the breakaway groups."

She replied with more confidence than she felt. "Like the summertime programs, the small groups are just another activity of the Tower. My people are watching though, just to be certain. Everything is under control."

"You better hope everything's under control," Zophos said.

She was unfazed—at least, appeared so. But still, she knew she had overstated.

There were indeed some small groups that were programs, fabrications of activity for appearance sake, but there were many more truly devoted to the King, the Kingdom, and the King's work and teaching. Truth be told, the small groups were flourishing, occurring randomly, inside and outside the Round Tower, and in such varying sizes and formats that she knew her people were struggling to monitor them all. And, these were just the groups she and her people knew about. Many groups were so informal they were easily confused with dinner parties or weekend get-togethers.

Ennui continued looking at Zophos in her poised manner. He stared back. "Would you like more information?" she asked.

He wanted to ridicule—say something demeaning—but thought

better of it, and said with condescension of his own, "Please."

"It is quite simple, really. The small groups undermine the stability of the Round Tower."

"How so?" he demanded.

"If people become attached to the small group, they are not inclined to invest either time or money in the large group. So for the sake of their own existence—their job security, reputation, and so forth—the large group leaders in the Round Tower are not supportive of people participating in small groups that are not sanctioned or controlled by them."

"I understand this. You said you had a simple solution."

"The leaders of the various groups in the Round Tower united, which was an interesting meeting, and passed a rule."

"A rule?" Zophos questioned.

"Yes," Ennui replied. "It is quite an elegant solution. The leadership decided that no group greater than twelve individuals could meet without their permission. In so doing, they left room for people to have parties and family gatherings, but they did not leave room for a group to assemble that is sizable enough to organize in a meaningful manner. The leaders formed a committee to screen applications for gatherings. My people work in concert with the committee.... This too is an elegant solution."

Zophos seemed satisfied.

Her plan seemed solid, and the solution seemed plausible, but something about it wasn't working. The small groups were flourishing in clutches of two, three, and four people. And further, when the groups reached twelve—the regulated number—they simply split into two unsanctioned groups, both of which quickly solidified into an effective hive of the King's tenets. She didn't understand why the numbers weren't working to her advantage, but she was laboring to figure it out. Until she did so, she would not report the anomaly to Zophos.

Just as Zophos' brow furrowed, formulating another series of questions, there was a bold knock. Ennui noted that he showed no displeasure, nor did he even pretend to cock his arm and throw his letter opener. Instead, he replaced the knife back on the stack of papers where Ennui had put it at the beginning of their conference.

The door swung open, and in contrast to the dark surroundings of Zophos' office and Gnarled Wood in general, a messenger of light from the High King announced Zophos' summons to appear immediately in the King's throne room to give account of himself.

Zophos offered Ennui no explanation. Their meeting was concluded—immediately—and for all their posturing and positioning of power with each other, both knew they were in subjection to the light.

Letizia's meetings with Bernard could hardly be construed as social occasions. Still, the Friday afternoon meeting wasn't normally as intense as the Monday morning meeting.

Bernie didn't reference Caroline Ingram in every meeting, but her name was mentioned frequently. Everyone in the office liked her. Even when she asked for sacrificial effort, or helped someone correct course, there was no grumbling. Bernie hadn't ever seen anyone so gifted with people skills.

He mentioned her again as he ran through his agenda with Letizia. At the mention of Caroline's name, Letizia interjected that she had heard nothing but glowing comments after the annual dinner. Bernie concurred, adding that Caroline's diligence with the budget he had given her was exemplary. "Besides that," he added, "we had a better meal for less cost than we've ever enjoyed. And further, the people who hosted us are begging for us to return. I don't know how she did it, but it's one more example of this lady's proficiency."

Letizia was a little uncomfortable with Bernie's infatuation with Caroline, but she wasn't far behind in her notice and admiration of Caroline. "She has distinguished herself," Letizia commented. "What do we know about her, Bernie—beyond the obvious, here in the office?"

Bernie ran through his information. "Married, three kids—seven, four, and a toddler. Moved a few months ago. Lives about ten blocks outside the Tower gates, poorer neighborhood, but solid people."

"What does her husband do?"

Bernie tilted his head once to the left—a combination of acknowledgment, thoughtfulness, and point of interest. "He's crippled. Disabled after a robbery and assault."

"Oh. I saw you visiting with him at the dinner. I didn't realize that was Caroline's husband."

"Uh, huh. Jake Ingram. His name is actually, Jacob, but he prefers to be called, Jake."

Jake hadn't jogged her memory, but Jacob did. Letizia pressed Bernard further. "Robbed and assaulted, you said?"

"Yeah. Said some guys mugged him while he was hunting for a house in an unfamiliar neighborhood."

Letizia grew more suspect of Bernie's story. He hadn't said anything, per se, to catch her attention. It was just her intuition—and the snatch of notice Jacob's name elicited from her memory.

"Beat him up pretty bad. Banged his head around enough that it messed up his balance. Then held his face in the sewer until they thought he'd drowned. Employer fired him."

"What's he doing now?" Letizia inquired.

"Odds and ends. Given his disability, no one will hire him."

Letizia was pensive.

"What's sad is," Bernie continued, "all they got was his address book."

With that tidbit of information Letizia assembled the puzzle pieces.

She didn't let on—at least, she didn't think she let on—but she was certain it was her people who inflicted disability upon Jake. She had given the order. Now, with this revelation, the consequence of her action faced her every working day with a smile on her face. While she—Letizia—had made Caroline's life miserable, Caroline made hers more professional, productive, and pleasant than it had ever been.

It wasn't the first time Letizia had encountered the results of her applied power. What was it about this occurrence that wormed its way into her conscience and caused her to pause?

She'd grown quiet. Bernie assumed it was the senselessness of Jake's assault. He was finished with his agenda, so folded his notes and waited for Letizia's signal. She was deep in thought. He thought about apologizing for the harsh news, but Letizia wasn't the type person you apologized to, neither was she the right person to interrupt when lost in reflection.

Bernie let himself out of Letizia's office, which was normal. What wasn't normal is that he turned to look back. Letizia looked stunned— like she'd seen a ghost or been told her Mother was dead. He pulled the door closed, but only to the jamb.

Hank was spending more and more time with Jake Ingram. The man was a compendium of information and ideas with a character forged upon the anvil of his suffering. Jake felt his suffering was associated with darkness because it was in darkness and from darkness that he was afflicted.

"Not so," Hank asserted. "I've discovered some of my greatest clarity comes in the night. Further, the King makes no secret of the fact that he has stashed hoards of treasure in dark places."

"You know, Hank, there are many moments when my suffering is dark as pitch. It's easy to panic in those desperate places, but you're right…if I listen, I hear the King's voice, calling my name in the darkness."

In another conversation, Hank said, "Suffering can be a remarkable mentor. Suffering permits no sloppy routines, trite declarations of comfort, cliché-riddled counsel, or cheap mercy."

"Agreed," Jake said. "It insists upon rigorous discipline—no excuses, no pity, no slack, and no day off."

During another discussion, Hank told Jake, "Suffering is like a stripping agent. It removes the varnish from life, revealing any flaw, any assumption, any delusion, any rationalization. Suffering guards, solicits, and ensures honesty—all the time, about everything, in every way."

"Suffering doesn't afford us the luxury of carrying unnecessary baggage," Jake declared.

Hank reflected upon the lesson he learned from his Father during his last visit to Gnarled Wood. "Only what is essential gets packed and ported," Hank declared.

"And on that score," Jake contributed, "suffering guides us candidly about what is essential and what is merely important."

"More than anything"—and as Hank said this to Jake, he was thinking of Jack Lewis, but didn't bother to attribute him. *Jake wouldn't know who I was referencing—not from the twentieth century, anyway.* "The King catches and treasures every tear and seizes each ache, turning the hardship to our benefit and his advantage." Hank spoke in a reverent tone. "What was intended by our enemies to destroy us, the King utilizes to form us, turning even that which is heinous to our betterment. It is as though he whispers to us in our pleasures, but shouts to us in our pain."

Jake and Hank shared great times sitting at his table. The kids had accepted Hank as a fixture, and he loved the energy of their young bodies. They laughed, kidded, wrestled, and did chores together. Hank also became adept at assisting Jake without diminishing his independence. As Hank knew so well, for all his input about suffering, pain was both a relentless mentor and a constant, torturous interrogator specialized in the abuse of human dignity. Whatever else one might say about pain, one quality was inescapable: Pain is persistent.

The thugs who demonized Jake in the alley had no way of knowing, first, the tremendous memory Jake possessed. Even though they stole his addresses and notes, he reconstructed the majority from memory, including no small amount of recall assistance from Magician. And second, the people in Jake and Caroline's life—primarily younger souls—cared deeply for their leader. Even though most of them were being pestered by Letizia's people, their loyalty to and love for Jake and his family were undiminished. The beating might have impeded Jake's ability to visit them as regularly as he once did, but it didn't stop them from coming to him.

As Hank and Jake shared life together, both Jake's and Hank's proficiency in hearing the voice of Magician increased and his wisdom solidified into their character. As Hank had been the beneficiary of his mentors, so Jake was the beneficiary of Hank. And as a grateful and responsive mentee, Jake stepped into Hank's life as a comrade.

Many times—hundreds perhaps—Hank asked Magician for reassurance that the lessons learned in his suffering would not be invested only in himself. It was gratifying to see Jake lapping up everything he put before him—and soon enough, when given opportunity, sharing what he learned with others.

There was a time when the traditional approaches of the Round Tower served the King, the Kingdom, and the King's people well. But those tried and true practices replaced the King himself. As incredulous as it seemed, one got the idea the High King could drop off the face of the Earth and the Round Tower wouldn't miss him.

Inside the Round Tower, there were myriad small groups. The majority of the groups claimed loyalty to the King as part of their group culture, but they were not appreciably different than any other affinity group that organized itself around a common interest or cause. They laced their conversation with King-lingo, but it was merely a dialect of Tower affinity groups.

The King himself was—unknown.

Hank, Jake, and select others spent hours discussing this dilemma. On the one hand, they wanted to be careful about tinkering with the Tower's systems. For all the ills within the Tower—all its inefficiencies, abuses, recalcitrance, and stubbornness—it was the King's love. More precisely, the people in the Round Tower were the King's love. But on the other hand, Hank and Jake and their colleagues knew the King didn't have any love affair with systems that didn't serve his people or advance his cause in their lives. While he had traditionally worked through the organization of the Round Tower, by all appearance and indication, he was breaking with that tradition.

Key people and families, all loyal to the King and the Kingdom, were quietly leaving the sanctioned organizations. Many assembled sporadically with clutches of closely aligned friends to discuss the King, his teaching, and the state of the Kingdom. Others stayed apart, independently taking charge of their own wellbeing in the Kingdom.

As Hank considered this, he decided it wasn't a bad thing, per se, *But it won't work for the long haul*, he knew. *Every person in the Kingdom needs a connection with others loyal to the King.* How to organize, what to offer, and how to support were the questions that occupied his thoughts and conversations with Jake.

The King was on the move and his followers were migrating with him. Where the King was re-forming his ranks, Hank and Jake couldn't always be certain, and they certainly couldn't quantify it, but that he had historically mobilized through informal small groups during periods of persecution was certain. That he was doing so again was apparent. The maximum-number-who-can-meet prohibition, designed to impede growth, actually fueled it!

This said however, something had to be done. The King's people in the Tower were suffering, not so much from Zophos' obvious onslaughts, but from apathy, indifference, and blindness to their plight. Their souls were wilting and they didn't know it—like frogs in the proverbial kettle. Even those who sensed their leanness weren't sure what to do. Seeing a deficit isn't enough. Action is essential—but action is the main casualty for those enmeshed in an apathetic culture.

Hank knew Ennui was the mastermind behind this dispassionate, utter boredom in the King's people. Since arriving at the Round Tower, he had crossed paths with her a few times socially. Her personal presentation and demeanor were easy enough, but he didn't like her.

Hank was all but certain Letizia worked for Ennui. But he didn't want to speculate, and he didn't want to discuss it enough to arouse interest. If he was correct, then these were two people to keep an eye on. He didn't fear them, but neither did he want to get sloppy and underestimate his enemies. He knew, and reassured himself, *Sooner or later, like their big boss, Zophos, they will over-reach.*

He could see the telltale signs of Jester's work. The stakes had been raised and Jester's sophistication increased proportionally. But like his boss, the one discipline Jester had not mastered was that of self. When he gained ground, he was never satisfied to leave well enough alone.

As Hank observed during his first trip to Gnarled Wood, it was immensely difficult to distinguish those truly living in the light from those professing to do so. The judgment call between the two became even murkier as Jester's deceptions and Zophos' pressures intensified.

Those walking in the light succumbed to the allure of darkness with discouraging frequency. To make matters harder, the people of the light often managed themselves by the standards of darkness. Meanwhile, those outside the Kingdom behaved more shrewdly, conducted their lives with more wisdom, and demonstrated more compassion than the true followers of the King.

In a further twist, while the King's followers talked about the light, those who walked in darkness claimed enlightenment. It was confusing enough to cause even the most ardent devotee to doubt.

But Hank's discernment became sharper, especially given Magician's ability to isolate incongruity between what people professed and what the King actually taught and personified as a ruler. Still, many senior leaders and long-standing members of the Round Tower could only be vetted over the time it took to assess the condition of their heart—light or dark, consumed with desire for the King or craven with want, pliable or hard, new or old.

Taking his time to figure out these people was all well and good. Hank was a patient man. But while he was assessing them, those who would prove mendacious were trafficking through the rank and file of the Kingdom, building connections, leadership dependency, and networks of people sure to be disappointed, disillusioned, or demoralized when their vaunted leader was revealed to be a wolf in sheep's clothing.

Magician's imagery was never far from Hank's consciousness: *Be shrewd like a serpent, innocent like a dove.* Like a serpent, he waited, concealed, until it was his opportune moment to strike.

Even when darkness was revealed, and the perpetrator dispensed, those wounded in the rouse had to be cared for, rehabilitated, and restored. At times the volume of casualties seemed overwhelming.

When he had time—took time—for an extended discussion with Magician, Hank often lamented that his enemies were not as easily distinguished as they had been when he first committed himself to walking in his Father's precepts. Always the patient mentor, Magician listened. But true to his own counsel, he too waited to strike until his opportunity was clear.

As Hank's power and influence increased, the High King sometimes baited Zophos into attacking. It was counterintuitive by the King—to entice Zophos to attack and suffer demoralization when the target was demoralized himself. But the King knew that in Hank's weakness his strength was most evident. He wasn't worried about Hank. He was engulfed by Magician!

And Zophos couldn't help himself. After every summons to the King's throne, his resolve escalated. He would return to Gnarled Wood with renewed fervor, marshal his forces, gain apparent ground, and suffer a demoralizing reminder that he was no match for the King. Then he would be summoned again, and the routine would repeat. The King felt no appreciable threat, but Zophos' frustration and desperation escalated disproportionately.

Just as the King planned.

The King's strategy made perfect sense, but in the midst of attack, Hank was susceptible to losing sight of his true identity. Working in concert with his old vulnerabilities to embrace pity, discouragement, independence, and self-justification Jester refined his approach to Hank.

When he was overwhelmed, Jester suggested, *I don't know how much more of this I can take.* Circumstantially and emotionally, it indeed looked grim for Hank, thus making Jester's insinuation seem reasonable.

When a key person disappointed him or proved unreliable, Jester suggested, *I should have done that myself.* Objectively, this made more sense.

As the circumstances accumulated, Jester intoned, *I'm trying my hardest. Why can't I get a break?* And any way Hank looked at his life, it seemed weighty, insular, inefficient, and unprotected.

The more Jester worked these angles, relentlessly pursuing, consistently disguising his attacks upon Hank as though they were self-analysis, and the more carefully Jester correlated his temptations with Hank's vulnerabilities, the more Hank was inclined to adopt Jester's perspectives as factual. The more Jester persisted—and the more ridiculous the shenanigans within the Round Tower became—the more discouraged Hank became. With discouragement Hank's momentum toward pity and inertia increased.

One night—late—Hank returned to his room. He went through the customary precautions to be certain his privacy was not compromised, but he did so without the sharp discipline necessary to pay full attention. It had been a hard day, compounded by a series of long, hard days. One after another the string of days and events accumulated until they reached critical mass.

Hank poured three fingers of whiskey, although he didn't really measure, didn't really care. He snuffed the candle and sat down before the open window. Holding the amber liquid, he placed his boot on the window sill and leaned back in his chair. He put his nose in the glass and smelled the sweet, buttery scent. He exhaled and breathed again, the scent more powerful this time, and took a sip.

This short moment of reverie was all Jester allowed his prey. Had Jester attacked with a sword, a stick, or a strike force Hank would have risen to the occasion. But Hank hadn't drawn his dagger in weeks, let alone his sword. Still, Jester's assault was every bit as dangerous and demanding as a fight with blades.

How is it the King requires faithfulness from me, but when I need him—and his people need him—he's nowhere to be found? I've done everything I know to do. He has yet to do anything. That's not good! You'd think if the King wants me to trust him, he would be more trustworthy. I suppose he'll turn up—probably at the last minute—and wonder why I've doubted. No matter what I say, he'll defend himself. Can't argue with him. Sure would think he'd prevent the losses. It's like he doesn't give a flip. Not good, not good.

Hank sipped the brown liquid, held it in his mouth, and was distracted from his thoughts by the stinging burn. Therein was the opportunity—the moment, the hesitation, the lull in the action. Magician struck! His onslaught was a flurry of measures and countermeasures Hank's mind only digested in retrospect but that his heart readily understood, embraced, and passionately joined. The speed and brilliance of Magician's strike was blinding.

Before he could swallow, the desire of Hank's heart rose up to defend Magician's declarations of his true desires, identity, and position. These truths, all of which were etched in the King's hand on the walls of his heart, were juxtaposed with vivid memory of how he used to conduct his life walking in darkness contrasted to his life in the light. Hank's ire rose up with indignation at Jester for taking advantage, but he was also angry at himself for listening and agreeing with his nemesis.

Magician guarded his friend closely to be certain his self-anger didn't get out of hand and become condemning pity, nor his self-disappointment become undue guilt. Focusing his resolution, Hank and Magician dictated Jester's defeat while repositioning Hank to refocus upon truth versus deception and regroup in the light versus the dark.

Fumbling in the darkness, Hank lit the candle on his writing desk. He dragged his chair from the window, fished his satchel from under his shirt, withdrew Vassar's letter, and sat down to review his instructions and known facts. He read:

Father believes in you. After all, he created this plan and chose you to carry it out. He knows you will represent him well, and I have every confidence in you too. If I didn't, I would have advocated for a different plan, but here we are!

Things are not going to be easy, Brother! The stakes have risen since we were last in Gnarled Wood. While Zophos is utilizing his shock and awe capabilities in some places, he has switched tactics in the castle. Most of the shock and awe there is a diversion. Always the pragmatist—and opportunist—Zophos is operating in a more clandestine manner. He's pouring exorbitant amounts of money, effort, and personnel into subversion, espionage, and subterfuge. Always there is his illusion of light. He is a deceiver.

The inclination is to engage him at his level, but there is a more powerful weapon. In everything you do, Brother, let your motive be love. Nothing is more powerful because love is the essence of who Father is. When you love, you portray Father, and the only way you can love as he loves is to live from your heart and let Magician's strength bolster you. Read that line again. I'll bet you felt your heart jump, didn't you?

Make no mistake though: Love will earn you hate. It will associate you with Father, and you know as I do that those who belong to Zophos utterly despise the High King. But while there is no pleasure in being hated—Zophos' folks feel the same about me as they do about you—there is nothing to fear. Nothing! Just ask Magician. He knows the drill.

Hank reread the prophetic lines from his Brother.

Indeed! Here I am, he thought, *enmeshed in a world of subterfuge, deception, and clandestine initiatives. And, Jester! What a nuisance! But, I've got to hand him his due. He calculated the circumstances and fed me one line after another until I nearly choked on my old inclinations. Whew! But Magician, you were right there, weren't you? Nearly late, but there.*

That Magician was almost late was a joke, but as with most humor, tinged with a barb.

Magician didn't let Hank's zinger go unacknowledged. *Give me*

a break. I had a committee meeting with your Brother and the King.
Hank knew he hadn't thought of that comeback himself. The quip was
signature Magician.

*So what gives, Magician? Clearly, I've been distracted—deceived. And,
I'm tired. Too tired. But, how are you seeing things?*

Hank sat quietly, listening, not with his ears, but with his heart.

*Had your Father not believed you were the man to lead this resurgence in
the Tower and the castle, he would have sent you home for good after your
initial visit rather than experience solidification in preparation for your
return. He has invested in you, and you have responded. He's proud of
you. Believes in you. Knows you are the man to lead the charge against the
principalities of darkness. Live from who you are, Hank. You are equipped
for this day.*

Holding another sip of the whiskey in his mouth, Hank thought,
*But Magician, I came awfully close to winding up where I started. I could
almost feel the lashing and abuse from disappointment, discouragement,
and depression. I could smell pity—could almost reach out and touch....*

Magician interrupted his thoughts. *I know you could, and your
Father and Brother know as well. That's the point. Your Father won't ever
let you get so immune to your vulnerabilities that you lose sight of your true
strength. Otherwise, all this becomes perfunctory. And believe me, this is
not an exercise. Our enemy is playing for keeps, but together, we are in good
shape. No fear! Nothing to worry about. You're fine. I'm fine. We're okay.*

Hank sat and let the realization—actually, the reminder—that his
Father believed in him sink into his heart. It took a while. His emotions
were running rampant. His body was crying for sleep. His brain was
feeling the effects of the amber infusion. His mind was grappling
to reorganize what he knew with the information gained. Magician
patiently superintended, guarded, and facilitated his rebounding
protégé.

*So Father guided me into harm's way, Hank thought. He let Jester—
and in all candor, Zophos—have a real shot at me. But after they threw*

everything they had at me, Magician rescued me while the kingdom of darkness suffered true disillusionment.

A thought entered Hank's mind. *Don't forget, your Father trusted Vassar with a similar mission of light.*

That's right! Hank recalled. *He piled the entire sum of the world's grievance, destitution, and debt upon Vassar and let Zophos drag him into the depths of Gnarled Wood's hell. Zophos must have thought he'd won! But no. Father rescued Vassar at the final moment, as he did me this evening, and as he led Vassar out of the pit, Vassar shirked off all the degradation upon him, flooding Zophos' hell in the overwhelming consequence of his deception.*

Hank felt the breeze touch his face. *But you didn't show up until the last, possible moment, Father.*

It makes for a wonderful adventure, doesn't it? The ultimate conflict between good and evil, and just when it appears evil will triumph, the hero is victorious!

Jubilation rose inside Hank. *I've seen that triumph a hundred times in Vassar,* he reflected. *He trusts Father without reservation.*

And your Father trusts Vassar like he trusts you, Hank. That's my point.

Father trusts me like he trusts Vassar, Hank considered. *I don't know about that, Magician.*

He inserted you into the enemy's camp. You carried light and life with you. Zophos and Jester and the rest believed that their darkness could quench light and life. But not so! Light dispels darkness. In your life there is a declaration of light that Zophos cannot overcome.

Whew! This is tough! Hank thought.

It's the mission in your Father's heart. As you asked, he included you in the advance against Zophos.

Though dreadfully fatigued and nursing a soul abused and wounded by the world around him, inside Hank's heart there was triumphant singing. He listened. He recognized his Father's favorite song.

The candle burned lower, the glass was empty, and the night air wafting in through the window was cooler. *What do you say we call it a night?* Magician suggested.

I hate going to bed, Hank thought in reply. But with the suggestion, fatigue flooded over his seawall. He resisted, nodded, shifted in his chair, and swam against the rising tide—to no avail.

Hank snuffed the candle—for the second time—and began undressing as he crossed the room.

CHAPTER 15

Hank was up early, his mind going lickety-split retracing the prior evening, drawing conclusions, seizing momentum. He stepped into the confidence of who he was, whose he was, who lived in him, and what he was called to do. He drank one cup of coffee and reviewed the section of Vassar's letter that captured his attention the night before.

Grabbing his walking stick, which he kept beside the door, Hank waited before touching the latch. *Magician, do you have any guidance for me before I step through this door? Not that it's your last chance, mind you, but it may be your best chance.* He smiled at the thought.

After last night's revelations, and kind rebuke for not taking better care of himself, he decided today was a day to slip away into the wilderness to recoup and regroup. He had things to think about, matters to discuss with Magician, some cleanup work remained inside his soul, and while he felt he was on the cusp of a plan for the Round Tower, it evaded him thus far.

Ordinarily, Hank would have taken a circuitous route out of the castle, stopping here, pausing there; turning this way, then that to see who was following. That he was being followed was a given. Who, and how many, he wasn't sure. But this morning he was lost in thought and departed directly toward the creek he and his compatriots followed during his last adventure in Gnarled Wood.

Turning from the road onto the trail beside the creek, Hank walked for a couple of hours until there was no more trail. He and Magician had carried on a lively conversation from the time he had gotten out of bed to this moment.

A gravel bar caught his attention, bringing him fully into the awareness of the creek's beauty and the allure of this particular spot. He sat down on a flat rock at the water's edge, tugged off his boots, and swung around, putting his feet into the water. Returning to his thoughts, ideas formed for how he and his colleagues might rally the faithful into enclaves of support and connection, certainly within the Round Tower, but primarily in the castle.

It didn't take long for the vision of leadership to crystallize in his mind. What he liked best about his ideas was the simplicity of the overall plan. He ran through the vision again, this time allowing his strategic gifts to populate the major components of the dream with practical steps for implementation and management.

Steps crunching the gravel behind him yanked him to his present circumstance. Five men approached in a fighting line. These weren't toughs, or bullies, or brawlers, but trained fighters.

Hank tried to control his fear, but he was disadvantaged. He was outnumbered, bare-footed, and backed up against the creek. He spoke, assessing, trying to create ease, "Good morning."

"You're causing problems." The man in the middle served as spokesman.

"Am I trespassing? Sure didn't mean to, and meant no harm. I'm not fishing."

"Problem's in the castle—and the Tower," the man retorted, focused on his subject, which only reinforced Hank's initial assessment that these were not your average thugs.

"How so?" Hank asked.

"We're not here to discuss things, Mr. Henderson. We're here to explain how things work when you get crosswise with the folks in charge."

Hank nodded, as if indicating he was listening for the explanation. But, he knew there would be no explanation containing words. This was to be an explanation by force.

The river and the rock where he had been sitting worked to Hank's advantage. Only two could get to him at once—unless the others wanted to get wet. He cut the first quickly and badly, causing the second to hesitate. As the third moved in, the second conquered his hesitation. Hank attacked the third man, knowing the second might well wound him, which occurred, but as Hank hoped, he didn't follow through.

Going to one knee, Hank turned his attack momentarily from the third man and lunged low at the second attacker, piercing him through at his navel. His sword met its mark, and with no bones to wedge against, was quickly withdrawn and brought about to defend against the third—not a second too soon.

The second man dropped his weapon, but did not fall. The subsequent attackers had to work around their staggering comrade. As he searched for a way to quickly dispatch the third man, who was proving a more formidable foe than the first two men, he noted the fourth and fifth moving to join the fray.

The third man took a desperate swing at Hank. It was the moment of lost focus Hank needed. The slashing blade grazed him and the weight of the sword carried the possessor's arm across his body before he could stop the momentum. His right side open, Hank stabbed the man above his belt and below his rib cage, again avoiding the risk of lodging his sword in bone.

Hank could feel the warmth of his own blood running into the waistband of his pants from the stab wound the second assailant had inflicted. Oddly, the greater pain he felt was in his bare feet as he poised, planted, and thrust against the river rocks.

The odds are more even, he thought. *One against two.* With his flanks no longer cut off, Hank moved laterally to create working room.

This was not a noisy fight. Men yell to intimidate or to dispel their fear. These were trained killers, used to silently doing what they were sent to do.

But the last man started yelling. "There's two of 'em! There's two! Come on! Get out of here!" As he yelled he retreated, leaving the fourth attacker to either follow his retreat or face Hank and his accomplice. Panic pervaded. He too ran.

In spite of the moaning around him as two of his attackers bled out and the third tried to crawl away, Hank glanced to see who his accomplice was. It was a fast look. He knew better than to take his eye off anything but a dead enemy.

There was no one. He called for him to show himself. Looked. Nothing, and no one.

His disciplines as a warrior beat in him like a metronome. *First things first,* he thought. *I need to secure the area.*

Still barefooted, he hustled to the crawling attacker. Holding his wound with one hand and crawling with the other, the man was like a tri-pawed animal.

Hank pushed hard against the man's hip with his foot. Toppling over upon his wound, the man tucked into a fetal position, bridging against the rocks with his head like a tortoise trying to right itself.

Hank peppered the man with questions. "Who are you? How long did you follow me? Who do you work for?"

He was forthcoming with the information he had, but as Hank guessed, he was the junior among the five. The leader was one of the two who escaped. However, Hank was able to determine that these weren't simply bad guys who stumbled upon him and decided to make sport of him. They worked for someone in the Tower. The man claimed they were only supposed to rough him up, not kill him.

He studied the man—quick glances, never taking his eyes off his larger surroundings. *There's no way this guy's following me.* Hank doubted the man would survive. And, he was wounded badly enough that if his friends returned for him, they would be slowed considerably.

"Roll over!" Hank commanded.

The man complied—not as quickly as Hank wanted, so he helped him with another shove. As the man grimaced, Hank deftly collected his dagger and backpedaled toward the creek.

Hank eyed his surroundings again—all three-hundred-sixty degrees. No one. Staying far enough clear to avoid a kick, Hank leaned toward the man, "Did you see the man fighting with me?"

The man nodded. His expression changed enough that Hank noted the man's realization that they misjudged their prey. From there, things had gone badly—very badly. He again rolled to his side.

"Where did he go?" Hank said.

The man shook his head.

"What did he look like? What was he wearing?" Hank probed.

The man collected his breath, trying to relax his chest enough to reply. Hank was impatient, but waited, then insisted again while threatening to strike the man. "What'd he look like? Where'd he go?"

Again, the man attempted to relax and speak, finally uttering in staccato, "Looked. A lot. Like you. Same sword technique. Bigger."

"Where did he go?"

"Disappeared."

"What do you mean, disappeared?"

"Into the sun."

Hank glanced up. Into the sun? It had been heavy overcast since mid morning.

This guy isn't making any sense, Hank thought, his mind working like lightning. *I'll sort this out later. Right now, I need to go—anywhere but here.*

He gingerly walked to his sitting rock. He took a quick look at his wound. While he was bleeding like a stuck hog, thankfully his assailant had missed anything vital. *I'm going to be sore, really sore. And, cleaning up is going to be a real mess. I'm not in immediate danger.* He looked around again. *Wow! My feet hurt like hell!* He examined his feet. Cuts and broken toenails, stone bruises. *Every step I take, for weeks, is going to be haunted with hurt.*

He studied his surroundings warily as he collected his socks and boots. Still no sign of the person who came to his aid.

While he pulled on his boots, he looked at the disturbed gravel bar. He wished for the tracking ability of Deets in the *Lonesome Dove* book, but knew he could sit for a very long time looking at the gravel and know no more later than he knew now.

He stood, feeling the effects of his fight. He drew his knife and cut a clean section of cloth from one of the dying men's shirts. He also took his belt. Hank folded the section of material, gritted his teeth, and pressed it against his wound, then fastened the belt around himself to hold the bandage in place.

Before sheathing his sword, he rinsed the blade in the creek, all the while keeping close watch for anything amiss. He looted the best of the fallen men's daggers and slipped it through his belt.

Hank worked his way alongside the creek for half an hour before stopping. He waited behind a fallen fir tree on the other side of three large boulders. After what he estimated to be an hour, he was relieved there were no signs he was being tracked.

Using the fallen fir as a bridge, he picked his way among the branches and crossed to the other side of the creek. As he did so, he recalled crossing this creek with Vassar, Magician, and their buddies during his last visit. *But it was winter then and the river's flow was higher.* Still, he was thankful for the tree bridge.

He moved stealthily farther up river, pausing in opportunistic places to read the forest for clues. Was he being followed?

Hank moved away from the river, far enough into the woods to be camouflaged from anyone following his trail. With the utmost care, Hank doubled back. Pausing. Watching. Listening. He moved slowly enough not to disturb the woods. He took his time, hoping he wouldn't meet anyone, but fully prepared if he should.

Nothing. He felt himself relax, which was a mixed blessing. He was glad to feel the tension ease, but with it went the adrenaline that masked the degree of his escalating pain.

Hank returned to the river and moved upstream another hour or so. He hadn't planned to spend the night in the woods, but he had what he needed with the river.

After following a stretch of the creek that was more or less straight, Hank turned to judge his line of sight. This was a good place to tend his maladies, he decided.

Shielding himself but not his view with a rock and clump of underbrush beside a pool, Hank stripped out of his clothes. He placed his sword and dagger within arm's reach of the deep pool and eased into the cold water.

He took his time, knowing he couldn't afford to surprise his finicky back and hip. And, he wanted to be as quiet as possible.

His feet throbbed with mighty pulses louder than the ache created in his bones by the snowmelt creek. He was surprised his boots came off as easily as they did. He'd expected more swelling.

The bleeding from his stab wound had coagulated in his makeshift bandage. That was the good news. The bad news was that the dressing had stuck to his lacerated skin and dried blood.

He massaged the material under the water. Slowly, the blood dissolved in a maroon-red current and the material came loose. He stood up and examined the exposed wound. It was bleeding again, but as he originally thought, it wasn't too bad. *Still, if I was at home in Texas, this would get stitched up. Since it's sort of vertical, I can hold it together with my belt—more or less—I think, perhaps.*

As he soaked in the river and watched downstream for movement, Hank rethought the battle sequence. All things considered, he was pleased with his performance, but he was disappointed in himself for not paying closer attention. It was a legitimate critique, but then the thought occurred to him, *I wonder why my Father didn't protect me?*

It was both an interesting question and an interesting observation. He soaked and contemplated and watched down river. As he mulled the question in his mind, *I wonder why my Father didn't protect me?* another interesting observation occurred to him. *What's with the pronoun before*

'*Father?*' *I don't call him, my Father. I call him, Father.*

Naked. Soaking. Observing. The nuance registered. He had moved from a legitimate review of a dicey fight to considering accusations of abandonment by his Father. The clue something was awry, was the pronoun, "my."

Speaking in a stage whisper, Hank said, "Jester! Get the hell away from me. As a Prince in the Kingdom of Light, I command you to present yourself to Vassar and do as he says."

Hank shook his head. *Jester! That sorry loser!*

Returning to his thoughts: *Magician. Please see to it that Jester does as I commanded. Should he come back, let me know. And while I'm sitting here and have your attention, who helped me back there—on the gravel bar?*

Now that it was numb from the cold water, Hank rubbed his wound.

It was your Brother.

"Vassar?" Hank blurted out loud.

Who else would it have been? Magician responded.

But I thought he was.... Hank didn't finish his thought.

But Magician did, *Not here? Is that what you were about to say?*

Yeah. That's it. I've been trying hard to go along—embrace this spin that Father is inclined to do with me. You know, about Vassar not really being gone, always present with me, and so on. But any way you cut it, Magician, I'm alone.

Don't you remember Vassar's pledge, Hank? He will never leave you! He can't! He can't abandon you any more than I can. You are part of him and he is part of you, and we are one with the King.

Hank listened, and even though sitting in icy water, felt warmth in his heart. The confusing comment by the wounded man suddenly made sense. "He disappeared into the sun," Hank repeated aloud.

Father, Vassar, Magician—they are light, Hank reminded himself, *indistinguishable from each other. Like staring into the sun. I get it. I get it!* he thought.

There had been no movement downstream—apart from a doe that stepped out of the woods to get a drink, and she wouldn't have shown herself if she had any hesitancy. His solitude was secure. Hank started out of the water. *Thanks, Vassar. Sorry I doubted you. Thanks for not doubting me.*

Standing naked beside the creek, Hank applied a freshly rinsed, homemade compress of shirt material to his wound. He again held it in place with the newly acquired belt, but tighter this time. Once doctored as best he could, he dressed, and collected his weapons.

There wasn't any point in hiking farther. He needed to secure his shelter and safety before it got dark. Not far from the pool, Hank found a suitable spruce to provide shelter. The tree was growing against a steep incline that curved in an arc from a rocky outcropping around the tree. Once under the boughs of the tree, he could enjoy two hundred and forty degrees of protection.

Working against the encroaching darkness, Hank gathered six arm loads of brittle branches and twisted clumps of dried twigs. It was perfect material for starting a fire, but he would have no fire this evening. Working in an arc, about fifteen feet from his sheltered spot, Hank distributed the dried material.

He saved one pile of the dried material. Before all his light was gone, he returned to the river, took a long drink, and refilled his flask with water. He listened carefully, and as much as the fading light would allow, studied the darkening woods.

Hank returned to his perimeter of dried twigs and used the remaining pile to complete his warning system before locating his spruce and crawling into his lair for the evening. He placed one of his daggers beside his shoulder where it was readily available. He unsheathed it so as not to make a sound if he took it in hand.

He had no expectations of sound sleep. The close of the day had been too eventful and he had too much on his mind, not to mention the pain tightening its grip on his body. But as he lay still, listening to the woods, like a ground fog creeping up from the creek, sleep engulfed him.

His eyes popped open and darted from side to side. They were useless in the pitch black.

A footfall on his warning system. Then, nothing more.

He held his breath to eliminate any extraneous interference to his ability to hear.

Another crunch.

Breathing—not his own.

Hank listened—took a shallow breath, ever-so quietly.

More breathing—or more accurately, smelling. *Can't be human,* Hank concluded, somewhat relieved.

But what?

There are bears in these woods. Blacks are of no concern, he thought. *But a Grizzly would be another matter.*

Breathing. Smelling.

Not a bear, Hank decided. *Not heavy enough—the breaths or the crunches.*

Still, *Something is there—right there.* He turned his eyes in vain toward the sound.

More breaths. More crunches.

There's more than one, he thought. *Can't be a catamount. They're solitary.* He listened again—to be certain his ears were counting correctly. There were multiple sources of breathing and smelling and stepping.

I'm surrounded by mule deer, he concluded. *Has to be.*

The breathing continued. The crunching stopped. Hank resumed his breathing and the adrenaline purged in increments from his blood stream. He tested his eyes. They were no better—and no worse—open or closed. He closed them. The fog of sleep again settled around him, wrapping him in its blanket.

Why shouldn't he wake up with the birds? He went to bed with them. To his momentary amusement, his eyes were working again. He stared up into the branches of the spruce.

Recalling the events of the night, he turned his eyes in the direction of the sounds he had heard. He was alone.

Hank stretched his back and hips while discussing the day before him with Magician. He was sore, but that was no surprise.

He crawled from his refuge and stood up. While his wounded side was vociferously unhappy, it was not as bad as he anticipated. But his feet made up for what his side lacked. He leaned on his hiking staff with both hands, slowly working his toes and arches inside his boots.

As he massaged his aching feet against the confines of his boots, he looked down. The impressions in the ground caught his attention. He counted five beds, each no more than three feet from where he slept. *Mule deer alright. They slept beside me—right beside me.*

I told you that you weren't alone.

Hank looked again at the impressions in the forest floor. He stared at them until an indelible image formed in his mind. *I think I'll draw upon these images the rest of my life.*

He turned to leave. *No. I'm not alone.* He savored the thought and its finish like the lingering of a fine wine.

Hank took his time returning to the castle. He didn't think his earlier assailants would have the gumption—or permission—to come after him again on the heels of their fiasco at the gravel bar, *But I'm not going to bet my wellbeing on what I think those jokers might or might not do.* What little he learned from the wounded attacker was enough to lead him to believe his next encounter would be more carefully scripted—*By them, on their turf and terms, not mine.*

Before each step, he placed his staff, stepped, looked and listened, then placed his staff again. His precautions reduced his pace over broken ground by over half, extending his return to the castle by double. *Better safe than sorry,* he counseled himself—disciplined himself. Besides, his feet appreciated the tenderness with which he walked.

Rather than crossing back over the river, Hank stayed on the less-traveled side. He only saw one person. The man was oblivious as Hank ducked into hiding. *I have to be more careful—all the time, no matter where or who—until I reassess my life and the people around me.* The individual on the other side of the river was picking berries. Hank watched until the birds returned to their normal routines.

He heard the castle before he saw its prominent feature: the Round Tower. Turning away from the river, he moved cross country, intending to enter the castle from a different road than the one he departed upon a day earlier.

Hank was blessed with a good sense of innate direction. Although he had never been in this section of Gnarled Wood, his internal compass guided his steps. He maintained caution, however.

The altered sunlight through the trees told him he was approaching an open area. Staying well back, he studied the field, and beyond that, the road that passed alongside. He worked his way along the perimeter of the field, staying several layers of undergrowth from the open, until his next move would put him on the road.

The day was changing from late afternoon to early evening. *Anyone who normally uses this road is sitting down to dinner,* he thought. Hank quickly moved from the trees onto the road. Once there, as part of his ruse—just in case—he pretended to check his fly as if he had merely stepped aside to take care of business.

Hank increased his pace, but not to normal. *I need time to take in my surroundings, not simply focus on my next step. Besides, my feet are hurting worse—if that's possible.*

He was confident he was headed toward the castle, but didn't recognize the road. He had been on it before—the last time he ventured into Gnarled Wood—but it was winter then. The world looks different robed in green and flush with blooms than when shrouded in grey and stripped to its bones.

Chapter 16

The Road to La Faim

Hank didn't recognize the road, but he remembered the smell. *I'm on the road to La Faim—the one that passes through that horrific dump.*

He tried to prepare himself, but the dump was magnitudes worse in the heat and humidity of summer than it had been in the frozen-dead of winter. He hated to demean the squalor of what hundreds of poor souls called home, but determined it was better to cover his nose than vomit and add to the stench. Even with his scarlet sash tied around his face like a bandit, he gagged every few steps, and probably would have tossed what was in his stomach had there been anything down there to bring up.

He quickened his pace.

La Faim wasn't much better than the stench of trash town—not then, not now. The same putrid stream demarcated its boundary. The same sorry sign announced its beginning. The same hunger was in the eyes of the people, and the same toughs waited to "greet" travelers.

Hank recalled the tense exchange the last time he was here and how Magician handled the situation.

As he crossed the footbridge toward the welcoming committee, Hank thought, *Magician, this doesn't bode well. Live through me as you see fit, and please protect me.*

Hank walked with all the confidence he could exude. While threat was all around him, he postured as though feeling no more concern than if he was walking down any other main street.

The young, dead-enders on either side of the street had seen it all. No sooner did Hank cross the bridge than they closed in behind him—

and he walked no farther than thirty yards before his way was blocked. The last time he was here he was accompanied by five others, all knights of light and capable warriors. Today, he was alone, save for the indwelling Magician. Stopping, as though just realizing his way was blocked, Hank recognized the young man that led their previous altercation. Hank stepped up to him with an extended hand. "Great to see you again!" he said. "How have you been?"

The young man was not expecting this. Hank pursued his quarry. "My friends and I passed through La Faim a couple of years ago. You made demands. Upped the ante. Things were getting out of hand. Swords were drawn, and you ended up at the mercy of my fellow knight. I can still see the scar where his dagger made his point."

The young man recalled, not so much because of the dagger point—he'd been on both ends of lots of knife fights—but because of Magician's promise. "Oh, yeah! You're one of the guys who promised to help us."

Hank nodded.

"Your friend said he was going to send somebody."

Much to Hank's surprise, Magician weighed in on the conversation definitively and unmistakably. *You're the man I'm sending, Hank.*

"He did indeed. And just as promised, here I am!"

The young man looked at his counterparts. First, he didn't know what to do. Second, he couldn't believe a man was true to his word when he didn't have to be. Third, he couldn't believe a knight in the Kingdom of Light would be sent. "Wait! You're the person he sent?"

"Uh, huh. That a problem?"

The young man laughed a tense laugh. "Nope. Not a problem. Just wasn't expecting this."

Hank pressed, backing the young man into the emotional corner of his doubts and pitiful expectation. "You weren't expecting my fellow knight to keep his word or you weren't expecting me to be the one to return?"

He wasn't used to being questioned, let alone confronted. "Well. Yeah both, I guess."

With the young man ever more vulnerable to his mercy, Hank moved in like a cat stalking prey. "You didn't believe there are really men of honor. And, you didn't believe you were worth having a knight sent to you. Is that what you're saying?" As he questioned, Hank moved within arm's reach.

"Didn't believe then. Not now. Didn't even hope." The young man's dark eyes lit up as the inferno within blazed. "Let's get something straight, knight: There ain't nobody gives a flying shit about us, so stop messing with me!"

Hank felt the heat of the young man's anger, and while directed at him, knew it belonged to others who had disappointed the young man—and his friends. "Well, you're wrong. Wrong on both counts," Hank declared, and as he did so, put his hand on the young man's shoulder and drew the tough alongside him. "Just as promised: I was sent and here I am."

There was awkwardness—for Hank and the young man. Hank wanted to take his pale hand off the young man's swarthy neck. It felt intrusive there. *Or does it feel bold?* he questioned in his mind. Hank stayed his hand, noted the muscles against his palm, felt the oil from unwashed skin at his fingertips, and the visceral energy coiled in the young man's body. He'd felt this energy before—in the snakes he'd held.

An eternity passed, the hardest eternity he could recall that required unflinching composure. Hank felt his private space evaporate as the gang closed around him. He worked furiously to stay calm and focused, but feared his hand most likely tightened, tipping-off the young man to his bluff. He held his ground. *I don't have anything worth stealing, and Magician wouldn't have sent me to these folks only for them to dispense with me—I don't believe. Maybe he would? If they were to do that, it would hurt like hell.* It was an odd thought. Never mind dying. Just don't let it hurt.

Hank felt hands on his shoulders, touches on his arms, and bodies close to his. For a long series of seconds he assessed if he was being apprehended or accepted.

As his novelty wore off, the gang divided into small clutches who remained in close proximity, but focused upon their own conversations and interests. Hank and the gang's leader talked, quickly running through the initial fact-gathering common with a new connection.

"By the way, I'm Hank Henderson," Hank said.

The young thug hesitated, then took Hank's hand, and said, "I'm Sjakal. Most everybody calls me, Jack, though."

"I see," Hank said. "And what would you prefer I call you?"

Sjakal thought briefly, shrugged a little, "Jack's fine, I suppose."

Hank motioned up the road, "Very good. Walk with me, Jack."

As they walked and Hank listened, he realized Jack didn't have the slightest idea what sort of help he needed.

Jack's two friends followed closely. The majority of the gang remained behind, although a few meandered after them at a distance.

When they came to the city limits of La Faim, it was as though Jack encountered a wall. To Hank, the road looked the same, but Jack had traveled the distance of his comfort and stopped. Hank made no effort to invite him farther. This was as far as Jack was going.

Hank again extended his hand to his new mentee. "Jack, as agreed. I'll see you in two days."

"Right," Jack said. "And Hank, I felt the bandage under your shirt when you had your hand on my shoulder. Take care of yourself."

Hank could feel the eyes of La Faim's derailed youth watching him as he walked up the castle road. After about fifty yards, Hank stopped and turned around. He looked for a long moment at the figures standing where he had left them. He held up his arm, waved, and turned toward his destination. His thoughts were a jumble of Jack, Jake, the Tower, his altercation beside the creek, safety, next steps, his family connections, and how his thoughts and desires aligned with the circumstances forming around him.

Every step was a trial on his bludgeoned feet, but he didn't limp. *I can't afford to. If Jack noticed, others will notice. Any weakness makes me a target, and until I figure out who is where and what is what, I have to mind every detail.* He used his hardwood staff until he reached the outskirts of the castle, but once there, he carried the stick by the shank—a statement of his swagger and unyielding defiance to pain's persistence.

Approaching the castle gate, Hank thought, *Okay, Magician. No telling what's going on in there. Live through me, will you please?*

Got you covered. And by the way, nicely done back there—in La Faim. You loved, in the same way your Father and Brother love. But of course, Love's in you loving.

Hank slowed his steps. This was a new thought, a significant thought. *You said Love is in me? Loving?*

That's right, the return thought came. *Just as I am in you, Love is in you. And just the other side of this gate, Hope will join us as well.*

So, in the same way you live in me, Magician, Love and Hope do as well? Right?

You've got it. The King is looking after you, just like he promised. You're not alone.

What about Faith? Hank inquired of Magician.

Oh, he'll turn up, I expect.

The walk through the castle was uneventful. He stopped at Hoi Polloi, had dinner, and returned to his lodging after dark. After his normal precautions, Hank cleaned up, examined his side the best he could by candlelight, and then checked his feet. Even in the dim glow of the candle, they were an assortment of cuts, scabs, and skin turned blue, black, purple, and yellow. He prepared himself for a marathon of disproportionate magnitude.

Safely cloistered in his room away from the public or spying eye, Hank hobbled like an old man across the plank floor. He sat down on the edge of his bed and placed the candle on the bedside table. He crossed his left leg over his right knee and gently massaged his foot. Then, did the same for his right.

He breathed deeply. Pain, he had learned, insisted that his whole body carry tension, like a petulant child requires everything of its parents. Deep breaths, he realized, were his Maker's remedy for expelling the unreasonable demands upon his mortality. With this awareness, he reclaimed territory taken by pain, and with each deep inhalation, also turned his heart to check in with Magician.

Hank took final inventory of his weapons, always placing them in the same location so he could find them in the dark if needed, blew out the candle, and lay down. He felt his body relax as the measure of gravity upon him dispersed across the breadth and length of his back. This was the most pleasant sensation of his daily existence, the ten or twenty seconds of his day when he was pain free. Tonight, the relief was more pronounced as the blood pressure waned in his abused feet.

Yet less than half a minute after lying down, his back and hip restarted their customary complaint in the lower register of the night versus the higher whine of the daylight hours. Once his moments of ease had concluded, Hank resumed his discussion of the day with Magician.

He reflected on where he was twenty-four hours ago, bedded down under the spruce. No doubt, a real bed was wonderful, but his heart longed for the hermitage of woods, the shelter of boughs, and the accompaniment of the creatures living there. With his mind in reflection and his body in bed, sleep again assumed control over the man whose Father was proud of him.

Jake and Caroline lingered over coffee as their kids shared a book given to them. Letizia unceremoniously gave Caroline the book before she left the office, not because the gifting of it was unimportant, but because Letizia didn't want to appear as though she favored Caroline's children over other employees with kids at home. Caroline was grateful for Letizia's thoughtfulness, even if she wasn't demonstrative.

Caroline's work was going well and she had received one promotion after another. While not thrilled to be in the workforce, she enjoyed what she did, and it was necessary.

Jake shifted his relentless determination and ingenious mind from the various things that consumed him prior to becoming disabled to include the demands of rehabilitation. No one knew much about the maladies and symptoms of nerve damage. After the medical community did their best, Jake became his own doctor and therapist. Patience, time, and hard work were paying off.

The kids had adjusted to the role reversal between Dad and Mom. They were secure in their parents' love, and since Jake and Caroline took his infirmity in stride, so did the kids. Once in a while they reported that a friend made a snarky remark about their Dad being a cripple, or uncoordinated, but overall it was neither here nor there to them that Dad used a cane.

Caroline and Jake frequently discussed the state of the Round Tower's commitment to the High King and his teaching. Each group had their lingo and unique programs, and each referenced the King in various ways, but few—if any—seemed to know the King himself. This was troubling. It is one thing to know about someone, quite another to know them.

Their conversations were frequent and followed a familiar format. Typically, Caroline said, "Jake, we need reform."

"I know, Caroline. I know. I'm as convinced of this as you."

"I know you are, Jake. But how?"

They would usually look at each other, the end of the conversation upon them, and say in near unison, "But how do you launch a reformation?"

This was the subject of their conversation when the knock came at their door. Their oldest peeked through the peep hole, opened the door, and let out a delighted whoop at the sight of Hank. He had become like an uncle—almost a grandparent—and was met with corresponding familiarity, which Hank loved.

Jake and Caroline received routine greetings, warm enough, but clearly they were second string to their kids. Hank engaged each child, catching up on their worlds and listening with interest to the hodgepodge from their minds. No matter the *non sequitur*, he treated each thought as if it was perfectly logical.

After the children's energy and enthusiasm subsided to a more normal level of insanity, Hank joined Caroline and Jake at the table for a cup of coffee. Caroline's watchful eye noted a slight limp, which she mentioned, and with her question the kids' curiosity was piqued.

He probably could have dismissed his gimp as nothing, but Hank loved to tell stories and the kids loved hearing them. It was a rare visit to the Ingram's home that didn't include a story—some true, a few fiction, lots a mixture of both.

Hank debated whether to tell them what happened, but not long. He resolved many stories ago not to withhold life's adventures from the kids. Of course, he edited aspects, but he made no pretence to shield them from victory and defeat, good and evil, the King and Zophos, and the kingdoms of light and dark. Neither did he withhold the role he played—that they all play—in these Kingdom conflicts.

He never embellished subtleties, but didn't shy from hyperbole. Of course, the kids loved an exaggeration and called his hand on the inserted extravagance. He feigned woe at being caught, backed up, and corrected course as he continued to unfold and navigate his tale.

This morning, to set the stage, he asked the kids to help him get his boots off. They worked on both boots simultaneously as he held onto the bottom of the chair to avoid being dragged onto the floor.

Everyone in the family, Mama and Daddy included, examined Hank's discolored feet. Of course the children, with their young eyes and lack of inhibition, studied each foot, toe, and toenail from six inches away. Hank felt a little self-conscious. He'd always believed his feet were ugly, but as long as the kids weren't bothered, he decided not to be either.

Having set the stage, he regaled the family with his latest tale as a warrior in the Kingdom of Light. He edited out the more gruesome aspects of his altercation, but the kids wanted to see his side when he got to that part of the story. Hank looked at Caroline for permission before revealing so much skin, but soon had his shirt up and his pants pulled down on his hip. There were "ew's" and "ick's" and "oh's" and head turns, but no one fainted away and everyone touched. Just like with his feet, the kids felt no more hesitation being personal with him than they did with their parents. Hank felt almost at home.

After the children turned their attention elsewhere, Jake asked Hank more about the assailants. He and Caroline held hands on the table.

Hank filled in the details he had omitted when the children were present. As he did so, he offered his conclusions. Caroline and Jake listened, asked a few questions, added some observations of their own, and agreed that the implications were troubling. More than anything, they were worried about Hank. "Clearly, you have gained the notice of someone influential," Caroline stated.

Hank didn't mention Letizia to Caroline and Jake. She remained a dark foreboding that he had yet to completely acknowledge, let alone categorize. That Caroline worked for her complicated Letizia and slowed his determination to focus, evaluate, and figure out what to do about her.

Hank turned his thoughts to the ideas he had for reforming life for the King's followers. "As I was sitting beside the creek, before the fight occurred…," Hank began explaining.

Over the next half hour, Hank laid out the plan he had been

contemplating. Three big ideas formed the pillars of his strategy: small groups of five to eleven people, organized by location, focused upon ten of the King's core teachings[3]. "Each week, every small group focuses on one principle—one essential aspect of the King's teaching. We can organize the groups by areas in the castle and Round Tower and oversee them with leaders we train," he concluded. "What do you think?" he asked his two friends.

The more the three of them talked, the more the vision seemed ingenious. What was an abstract concept—knowing the King better—could be simply defined, and for that matter, evaluated based upon the ten tenets indicative of him. Hank knew his Father well enough to know that ten tenets could not contain him, no matter how profound. However, as he explained to Jake and Caroline, "If people are proficient with the ten, core elements of Father's teaching, then they will have enough insight, confidence, and connection to engage him throughout their lifetime. And you know what else? These tenets will be like prisms through which Father's light passes and refracts. Magician never lets a ray of light go to waste."

At first, Hank's idea seemed too structured. None of the three had any desire to systematize relationship with the King, thereby making a similar mistake to the one the groups in the Tower were making. But on the other hand, it was essential that people know their confidence in the King was relevant, meaningful, and progressive. Of this, they were convinced. It was in discussing implementation that they ran aground.

Ideas of change and growth had been bandied about in the Tower for years, but actual evidence of change was hard to either come by or observe. Over time, many had come to feel that the King was conceptually a good idea, but practically irrelevant and discussion about him merely indicative of the Tower's culture.

There is nothing wrong with the myth of the King, Jester argued, *but*

---

3   For a complete list of "The Ten Tenets of the King," see the appendix, page 511.

to hold his reign as legitimate is delusional. He's a good idea, as are other principles in life.

No one said out loud that the King was irrelevant, of course. That was poor form in the Tower's culture. But the implication was inescapable. And further, the "myth of the King" or the "concept of the King" implied he didn't really exist outside the mind. So instead of the King being personal, legitimate, and his teachings profound, Zophos, Ennui, and Jester moved peoples' awareness of the King by degrees closer to the category of a broad-based principle.

To complicate the discussions Hank and the Ingrams were having, the Tower leadership was too heavily vested in the organizational structure of the Round Tower to be objective about change, presuming they desired necessary change and growth to begin with. In discussion, the idea of breaking with the status quo was fine, noble even. In fact, the Tower was proud of its reformation history. But that was then, when this leadership wasn't in power. This is now and few revolutions begin from within.

An actual revolution would mean the end of many programs and organizations, especially if the revolution decentralized Tower membership. If that happened, job security for many of the Tower's leaders would evaporate. Only the most courageous, honest, and passionate—or crazy, deluded, and emotional—would embrace such risk to their livelihoods.

Besides, to speak of reformation presumed the need to form again. This was irrational to the Round Tower's thinking. After all, the Round Tower was commissioned by the King! Why would he change it?

Meanwhile, the normally placid waters of the Tower were agitated. People were on the move, even sacrificing lifelong loyalties in search of something to mollify their heart's desire. Followers of the King were hungry for connection, change, and transformational growth. Their lives were far too complicated and life's demands much too great to accommodate organizations and activities that were irrelevant, inefficient, or worse. Under the duress of time, even the most sacred of idols melt.

Jake and Caroline knew that small groups were much more efficient and effective forums for guiding people's progress toward their goals of personal growth and relationship with the King. Buying into this aspect of Hank's vision—for them—wasn't a challenge.

However, the proposal that small groups be organized by location was more difficult to adopt, not because they didn't think it made sense, but because their current small group wasn't organized that way. By implication, the membership of their group, which they liked, would have to change.

The more they talked though, the more they agreed that groups organized by geography were an essential part of the plan's success. Jake said, "Since people tend to live in homogenous neighborhoods, groups organized geographically will be more or less populated with folks sharing common socioeconomic status, values, networks, difficulties, and dispositions."

Caroline added, "And just as important, if the King's followers know other believers who live close by, they will more readily connect in times of celebration, hardship, and need."

Jake nodded. "It seems worth a try. Something has to change. That's for certain!"

Caroline ventured to say what all three of them were thinking. "The simplicity of this is the key. In fact, it's remarkable—maybe revolutionary."

"Let's hope it turns into a reformation," Jake said.

Over the next few weeks they refined their strategy. Jake organized the substantial assortment of young people and adults within his circle of influence into groups of five, six, seven, and eight. The largest group had eleven. He reminded the members of this group of the maximum number allowed by the Round Tower without official sanction. "As soon as you are stable as a group, we need to divide the group by location," he counseled.

Leadership was more about hosting than leading. Jake and Caroline, and Hank when he could, prepared materials organized around the ten key tenets they selected from the King's teaching. Each week, they distributed these materials along with three or four questions for consideration. The leaders started their groups on time, concluded on time, and notified Jake or Hank if something wild happened in between.

As the groups settled into routines, meeting each week—on whatever night was best for the members of the group—Jake focused on making certain the group leaders stayed healthy as individuals and had the resources to support their groups. Just as hoped, the group members began taking care of each other rather than relying upon an organizational system. Accountability to each other, and the corresponding personal responsibility, increased. Within a few months, the leaders began reporting that they were observing greater devotion to the King, deeper belief, vibrant relationships, and practical application of the King's teaching.

The downside to this flow of good news was that Zophos and his loyalists increased their attacks and punitive actions. Sickness increased among leadership and their families. Financial pressure escalated, jobs were lost, and others were downsized in an otherwise strong market. As usual, there was the array of threat, invective, and hostility unleashed on the groups, the leaders, and sadly, upon their families.

While the escalation of Zophos' efforts was unpleasant, the small size of the King's groups made it more difficult for them to be tracked while enabling the members to be relationally close. Thus the groups, members, and leaders were more sensitive, capable, supported, and empowered to come against Zophos' deceptions and demoralizing attacks.

As the linchpin of the reform movement, the pressure upon Hank increased. There were additional outright assaults, such as those he had endured, but those efforts were deemed ineffective at the highest levels. While no order came countermanding assaults, it was decided that attacks against Hank should be refined to wear him down, discourage him, and isolate him. It was felt such efforts would cause him to lose focus. When this mental-emotional strategy gained traction in Hank's soul, then he could be truly marginalized—or, so went the logic of those arrayed against him.

The directives from higher up also mandated that Hank's team be targeted. While Hank had proven more resilient than anticipated, seeing his close associates suffer could actually render him vulnerable more quickly, it was felt. A multi-faceted strategy certainly couldn't hurt was the consensus.

Hank strongly suspected Ennui, and based upon the attack by the river, probably Letizia Pintaro were the driving forces behind the increased pressures. The escalating demands were profound, complicated, and confusing. Of course, Jester was a constant.

So great was the influx of needy people into the groups, Hank sensed "someone" was overplaying their hand. But even so—even if Jester and his boss, Zophos, were overreaching—the neediness of people was a prickly problem. Expressing the opinion that some of those with pressing or overwhelming needs were actually emissaries of the enemy was counterintuitive and seemed hardly loving or compassionate. It was a shrewd strategy, Hank realized.

No matter if he had the best interest of his leaders and their constituencies in mind, addressing the problem of "too much need" made Hank appear insensitive and uncaring. In addition, the King to whom they looked for provision was then easily portrayed as being less than good.

But the fact of the matter was, all it took to overwhelm a leader, or stall a group's momentum, or inundate everyone with besieging guilt was to insert a person with profound issues into a group. Leaders consumed by the overwhelming needs of a single person were unable to care for the broader needs of others. Members attempting compassion were engulfed by the magnitude of need and soon disillusioned with their calling and confidence in the King's teaching to care for those less fortunate or in distress.

Similarly, there was a numerical increase in people possessing decoy needs—needs that were indeed needs at face value but that the person didn't want resolved lest they lose their neediness...and thereby the pity of others which served as the counterfeit of genuine compassion and acceptance.

Acquainted as he was with the pitfall of pity, Hank spoke with Jake and the other leaders. "Just because a person is afflicted, doesn't mean they seek deliverance. One can despise affliction, but truly fear deliverance and the freedom of a new and responsible life."

They were all suffering similar drains upon their emotional accounts, but telling the difference between a person ready for help and a person sent to be a burden was anything but straightforward. In time, the distinction was evident—but by the time clarity was achieved, the damage was meted out in souls drained dry.

Hank's suspicion about Ennui and Letizia was correct.

Ennui sought to increase indifference and apathy. Leaders burned out their passion for people as their grand vision of compelling service to others was limited instead to the overwhelming needs of an individual. Letizia and her people sought to drain energy through the demands of increased affliction, hardship, and discouragement.

Together, Ennui and Letizia oversaw an escalation of job losses, sickness through exposure to tainted water, contagious people, and fatigue; they adjusted agreements and boldly modified contracts with impunity, compromised business alignments, bullied children, instigated irrational behaviors, and seized upon any other stressor that could work to their advantage. Allied with Jester, they brought all their forces to bear upon the King's people with the singular goal of undermining their confidence in his goodness.

As for Hank, Ennui and Letizia had no question that he was the instigator and linchpin in the growing fervor they were seeing in the King's people. As enemy-number-one they determined to do whatever was necessary to dull his focus, disrespect him, dismiss his significance, and otherwise demoralize his passion.

They tried everything in their power—including intimidation.

Hank met with two of the leaders whose small groups met in the Round Tower, one on the fourth floor, the other on the seventh. Meeting in the Tower meant these leaders had unique challenges that the leaders of groups in the castle didn't feel. But, they were doing well and their group members were flourishing.

The three of them had a light dinner of sausage, cheese, and olives. They encouraged one another, and as iron sharpens iron, honed their resolve to rely upon Magician in all things. After a quiet toast to the King, Hank said good-bye to his colleagues and departed for home.

Hank was surprised to discover the Tower's portcullises were closed. *This is the time of day when people are leaving the Tower, not trying to get in. What's the point?* he wondered.

The unprecedented security created a serious backup of traffic. The guards were using a single door to check people through as they exited the Tower. When the holding area was full, the line was stopped and the portcullis raised so the detained group could pass into the next holding area. The line didn't move again until the portcullis was lowered.

It's a charade of bureaucratic power, Hank thought. *If there was a genuine security concern, the guards wouldn't be so lethargic. But, there's no point in worrying.* He turned his thoughts to the events of his day and the day coming.

As he got close to his turn to exit, there was a stoppage. He didn't pay much attention. Guards arrived, adjusted, redirected, moved some people who were in front of Hank, and before he really realized what was happening, two guards grasped his arms and escorted him from the line.

They quickly ushered him through a door that he assumed to be a guard station, but the doorway led into a corridor running underneath the Round Tower's walls. The guards did not loosen their grip on Hank's biceps. He protested, but neither acknowledged.

His captors never laid a hand on him, at least an abusive hand, but for several days they deprived him of sleep. It was familiar territory for Hank. He had suffered sleeplessness since being wounded in the pit and discovered that the night hours were filled with solitude he couldn't find during the hubbub of the daytime. Even though the lack of sleep didn't rattle his composure, it was still torture and he felt the effects.

After five nights in a detention filled with interruption, little water, and no food Hank was hauled into a small room for questioning. He didn't know the man sitting in front of him, and had no idea Letizia was clandestinely observing.

His captors made him stand at attention for what seemed an eternity. Any twitch, nod, or shift was punished with a sharp strike by one of the four or five guards surrounding him. He wasn't certain how many there were, but the hits came from about that many different angles.

His feet and legs were numb with swelling. His tongue thick from dehydration and his mind a fog of fatigue. Each breath was sharp as his abused ribs expanded. The blessing was that the sharp twinges helped him stay focused.

They turned him from the wall and forced him to stand, smell, and observe as his interrogator ate and drank. His body had stopped sending hunger pangs to his brain, but thirst was driving him mad.

Only after he completed his lengthy meal did the interrogator lean back in his chair and commence with his questions. Most were innocuous, but a few were designed to elicit from Hank's fuzzy thinking incriminating information.

Early on, Hank called upon Magician to give him endurance, courage, and strength. Once the questioning began and the skill of the interrogator created the desired confusion, Hank changed his request of Magician and asked simply for wisdom.

After the initial questions Hank realized he would have to simply believe his thoughts were coming from Magician and respond. He discovered right away that taking time to think was a punishable offense.

He assumed they knew about the old wounds to his back and hip, as well as the recent injury to his side, since these were the favorite targets of their strikes. He didn't dare let them know how badly they were hurting him, but he could feel the scar tissue tearing, which if he lived, would prove a formidable soreness.

Whether his interrogator had another appointment or was losing interest, Hank didn't know. The man escalated his measures though. Rising from his chair, the interrogator faced Hank. Two guards secured his arms. The interrogator moved closer—coming face-to-face with his subject.

His teeth were an assortment of browns, yellows, and gaps. His breath stank with decay and disease. When he spoke his tongue waggled out beyond his lips and flicked spittle on Hank's face. It was purple from the red wine. His mouth was greasy, the back of his hand having served poorly as a napkin.

Hank tried to concentrate. The man's face was oily, his hair matted with unwashed dandruff. He exhaled into Hank's face, again and again. Hank knew the man realized the offense of his breath, but he had no recourse but to inhale the used air.

"I'm asking for the last time," the interrogator hissed from inches away. Hank could feel droplets of his saliva land on his nose and lips. "Tell me where the unsanctioned groups are meeting. Tell me who leads them. Tell me who attends. Do it NOW!" he screamed, the demand rocketing at Hank upon belched, undigested dinner.

The interrogator backed away. Hank was silent.

Shifting to a congenial manner and tone, "If you comply, right away, I will personally see that you are cared for." The oppressor paused as if considering. "It's a small thing I'm asking, hardly worth all of this." The interrogator motioned around the room. He paced two steps, waited, stepped back. "But if you continue to be difficult." The blunt force of the truncheon exploded against Hank's sacrum. His knees buckled. The room went dark. Pain burst across his ragged nerves.

Laughter echoed in the room. Derisive. Forced.

He heard it, knew he was the brunt of the wicked humor. Icy water hit the back of his head. Slapping his face side-to-side, the interrogator reset Hank's vision. The guards held him upright. He couldn't tell if his legs were working or not. He blinked. Focused. Smelled the putrid breath. "You weren't listening," the interrogator stated. Another slap.

Hank's mind cleared.

"Pay attention, Mr. Henderson. If you continue to be difficult, you will not leave here alive."

Hank straightened against the affliction, willing his legs to hold him. "Sir, I have no doubt that you hold my life in your hands," Hank stated respectfully. "You are a powerful man, and you deem me powerful as well or I wouldn't be standing before you." Hank felt weakness quiver inside his knees, noted the thought race into his mind, *I'm scared*, and didn't know if it was true or if it was Jester. He forged ahead, believing Magician was guiding him. "But as powerful as I am, I cannot unleash my greatest weapon until you use your greatest weapon."

"What are you saying?" the interrogator demanded.

The guards responded to their boss's hostile demand. Pain shot through Hank's shoulders as they wrenched his elbows at unnatural angles.

"Sir, your greatest weapon is to kill me. My greatest weapon is to die. Once I'm dead, your weapon will be spent while every drop of my blood will scream through the Round Tower, the castle, and beyond of my loyalty to the High King."

The interrogator spit on Hank and struck him with the back of his hand. Before he blacked out, Hank heard, "Take him away."

His arms hurt, realized he was being dragged. Hank thought about dying, coming to the end of his days, and recalled nearly doing so when attacked by Zophos' wild beasts the last time he was in Gnarled Wood. In his toxic brain, the vision of them leaping from the narrows and undergrowth was vivid. He ordered his muscles to respond, but there was no reply.

It amused him that his main concern wasn't in how he was going to be killed, or how bad the pain was going to be, but in attempting to die well. The internal resolve affirmed to him that Magician was his strength and his confidence in his Father wasn't misplaced. He knew his ability to trust was growing exponentially. *Odd that my belief in Father is growing now, when I'm captive, beaten, soon to meet my fate.*

They dragged Hank, hurting him and bruising him, until they navigated a series of passages and arrived at a door. *That's it,* Hank thought, finding his feet and standing up between his captors. *On the other side of this door is the killing field.*

As one of the guards—the ranking man, Hank figured—fumbled with an assortment of keys, Hank breathed deeply. Like always, the deep breaths were his signal to willfully focus on the light. It was a great test of his trust—a test he recognized and celebrated passing—knowing he was about to step into the darkness of death. He willed his heart to bask in the light. *I will finish well,* Hank resolved. *Magician! You promised to live through me, and if necessary, to die through me! I'm counting on you. I want to be a man of great courage.*

The door balked at the guard's tug, then swung open on ill-maintained hinges. The two guards on either side of Hank, grasped him, counted, and flung him through the opening into the darkness. Hank landed in a heap, hands tied behind his back. The door slammed closed, bolting and locking on the other side.

His brain registered the smack of his face upon rocks. Hank waited. *How will they kill me, now that it's time?*

He lay waiting, hearing distant sounds, smelling the familiar scents of the castle. Using his head and shoulder, he bridged enough to get his knees up under him, and rose to a kneeling position. Even in the dark, he could see there were no walls.

They tossed me out. Threw me away. Threw me out of the Round Tower—into the castle.

Standing spraddle-legged until his bone-tired brain rebooted, Hank whispered, "I'm free." Turning inward, he thought, *Magician, you protected me, negotiated another day for me. Thank you.*

Moving carefully through the dark, Hank worked his way deeper into the castle and farther from the Tower. He struggled to find a landmark, something familiar, but had no idea where he had been thrown.

Apparently it wasn't unusual in this neighborhood to encounter stumbling people with their hands bound wandering the streets. A passerby cut the ropes from Hank's wrists and helped him get oriented, never bothering to see if anyone was watching. He thanked the man, who only said, "You need to take care of your face."

Hank prepared himself for the worst as he walked in the direction told. Sure enough, within a few blocks, he recognized familiar landmarks and turned his feet toward home.

He slipped through his door and closed it gently behind him. He performed his customary check, and satisfied he was secure, went to examine the damages.

Overall, he was just banged up—nothing that wouldn't be okay in a few days—but there was a troubling cut on his face. Correction: a disconcerting gash! There were plenty of people in and around Gnarled Wood with scars you would never see in Fort Worth, Texas, but given that he anticipated returning to modern-day Cowtown, he decided it would be best to try and close the gaping wound.

Oh, for a tube of Super Glue! he thought. There were many advantages to the simplicity of the medieval world of Gnarled Wood, especially when it came to spiritual discernment, but when it came to medicine, it was indeed the Dark Ages.

Several weeks earlier he discovered a distiller who made a fine whiskey. However, in his search for a good whiskey he acquired a couple of bottles that weren't worth drinking. He got two cups, two bottles of whiskey—the good one and a poor one—a length of string, a needle, a knife, and placed the assortment on the table below his mirror. It took longer than it should have, but he was working with one hand because his left hand was dedicated to holding a compress on the cut.

Hank poured some of the poor whiskey into a cup, then placed the needle and thread into the gold-colored liquid. Using the tip of the knife, he submerged the string until it soaked up the liquid and stayed under. Removing the cloth from his face, he rinsed it out, wrung it, and poured some of the poor whiskey onto it. He gritted his teeth, closed his eyes tight, and with determination placed the whiskey-soaked rag over the cut. The burn was ferocious! Far mightier than he anticipated, but he knew that was a good thing. He couldn't afford an infection.

After his eyes stopped watering, Hank poured two fingers of the good whiskey in the other cup. Holding the compress with his left hand, he carried his drink with his right, and sat down to wait for sunrise and enough daylight to see what he was doing.

But after drifting off and dropping his compress twice, he decided enough was enough. He reapplied the whiskey to his compress, used his sash to hold the compress in place, and lay down. No sooner was he prone than his consciousness disappeared as though dropped over a cliff.

He awoke to the sounds of a world well into the routine of its day. It didn't take long to remember what had occurred. His body was stiff, especially his hips and ribs. He had a powerful thirst and an empty stomach. He touched the wound on his side. It was crusty with thick, dried blood. He winced with the touch and his face lit up with pain. With that, he remembered why the room smelled like whiskey.

After limbering up his muscles the best he could, he rolled out of bed. Standing, waiting to be certain he wasn't going to black out, he moved to the mirror to study his face. Looking at the gaping gash in the daylight, he was again satisfied he needed to stitch it.

He double-checked to be certain he had everything he needed. He retrieved the good whiskey from the night before, took a drink, and swallowed. It was insipid from sitting out.

The pain was bad, but not as bad as he thought it would be. Each time he inserted the needle through his skin, he thought of all the kids back home who were piercing their lips, tongues, eyebrows, navels, noses, and whatever else. *If they can endure piercing for vanity, so can I.*

He sutured the cut closed with twelve or fourteen stitches; he lost the exact count. After running his needle through the opposing edges of his wound, he cut the string, dropped the needle back into the cup of whiskey, pinched his flesh into a pucker, then gingerly snugged the cut closed, and tied off the thread. He debated what sort of knot to use, assuming the "surgeon's knot" he knew from fly fishing was the obvious choice given its name, but opted for the more secure square knot. *Don't want this coming loose.*

He left each knot with long tails of thread so he could locate the sutures after a few days of beard growth. He guessed the stitches should stay in for about a week. *Too short, and the cut will open again. Too long, and my skin will adhere to the thread and be the dickens to remove.* Both were unpleasant thoughts. *But the former would be worse,* he felt. *A week it is.*

After completing his surgical duty, he applied more whiskey to the finished procedure, forcing the liquid into the wound until it bled and stung. He decided to lie back down. He had a powerful headache, whether from being banged in the head or looking cross-eyed at his face, he couldn't be certain. He eased into bed, returned to prone position, and slept ten hours.

Initially, Hank's friends were alarmed at his ordeal, but their concern faded with the novelty of his face being sewn together. "How did you decide to do this?" was the most common question, followed by, "How long are you going to leave the stitches in?" And the inevitable, "How will you get them out?"

He felt a bit guilty claiming to have come up with the idea on his own, but trying to explain the time warp he was living in was fruitless. Of course, stitching wounds together had been around for a long time, but only the more affluent and those with access to medical care benefited from the practice. The concept of microbes, antiseptic, and sterilization were not yet known. So rather than attempt explanation, he took credit.

Chapter 17

The Round Tower

Letizia was curious to know more about Caroline and Jacob Ingram. Twice a week she heard a report about Caroline's work, accomplishment, steadiness under pressure, and so forth. But it wasn't just Bernie's reports. She saw first-hand.

Letizia didn't feel guilty that it was her order that resulted in Jake's disability, but she felt something unusual—an intuition she couldn't identify. This was part of her curiosity. She'd taken a few opportunities to work directly with Caroline in an effort to see if by proximity the mystery she felt would abate. If anything, it only got stronger, certainly not clearer.

She entertained the thought of discussing her curiosity with Bernard, but wasn't inclined to bridge the professional space she valued. In the end, she decided to leave Bernie out of her quest to resolve the curiosity that grew inside her.

Letizia thought about going straight to the source. Had the office been all there was to her professionally, she might have simply asked Caroline to stay late, and after everyone else was gone, quiz her until her curiosity was satisfied. But, the office was not all there was to her professionally. There was another side, and Caroline's husband was the victim of that other side of Letizia's professional world.

She didn't take uncalculated risks, she didn't build personal relationships with employees, and she didn't make mistakes. Letizia knew her contemplation of talking with Caroline was a break with the rules by which she survived, but she felt an urgency unlike any compulsion she had ever experienced.

As she walked, she chided herself for such a simple plan. She was acting on gut instinct, but the inclination and instinct were strong enough that she knocked on the Ingram's door shortly after the dinner hour.

Caroline peeked through the peep hole and let out a startled gasp. Unbolting the door, she said, "Ms. Pintaro. What a pleasant surprise. Please come in. Is everything alright?"

Letizia greeted Caroline and reassured her that she was in the area and thought she would stop by and say hello. "After all, I've never met your children, and I've heard so many nice things about them."

Caroline ushered Letizia into the family room.

It was Wednesday evening, and as he did most Wednesdays, Hank had joined his surrogate family for dinner. He and Jake both stood as Letizia entered.

Introductions were made, first for the inquisitive children. Caroline introduced each to, "Ms. Pintaro, my boss at work." The kids politely greeted Ms. Pintaro, and after a courteous number of minutes passed, retreated to the seclusion of the back room.

Both Hank and Letizia wore the seasoned expression of social poker players. There was no way to tell which was more surprised to see the other, but Hank greeted Letizia with the reminder that they had met at the office dinner. Letizia reassured him she remembered.

After Letizia greeted Jake, Hank said, "Caroline, I'm confused. I thought your boss's name was, Mr. Bertram."

"It is, but Ms. Pintaro is THE boss."

Letizia chuckled dismissively, and with a wave of her hand, elevated Caroline to prominence in the conversation. "I'm afraid I'm encroaching on Bernie," Letizia said. "After all, he hired Caroline."

Hank appreciated the recognition Letizia granted Caroline. *Very professional.* He watched like a hawk.

With mock gravity, Letizia said, "Don't tell Bernie, but I intend to steal Caroline for myself. In fact, I've already begun stealing her by degrees."

Caroline blushed, "Ms. Pintaro, I am thoroughly enjoying working alongside you."

Jake concurred. "She comes home every evening reporting that she has had a great day. Thank you for creating such a wonderful job for my wife. I'm grateful."

Caroline blushed again, smiled at Jake, and changed the subject.

The tightening connection between Caroline-his-friend and Letizia-his-enemy was troubling to Hank. In all the time he had spent with Jake and Caroline, they had not discussed her work in sufficient depth for him to realize she worked directly for Letizia Pintaro. He chided himself for not being more perceptive.

As the conversation unfolded, and Hank observed the professional camaraderie between Letizia and Caroline, he began considering anyone or anything—leaders, mentees, group members, meeting places—he might have unwittingly compromised by his close association with Caroline. Furthermore, he worried that she and Jake had such a close and open relationship. *Jake relies upon her to help him think through everything. What's he told her—who he's working with, initiatives? What all has she passed along to Letizia Pintaro?* Hank eyed Caroline. He admired her incisive ability to think and assess. *Surely she knows who this woman is,* he thought. *She has to know, and if she knows, then either she tells her everything or tells her nothing.* He listened to the conversation, smiling politely to disguise his guarded emotion, his mind working from a distance. *Everything or nothing? Which is it I wonder?*

As his thoughts progressed, he couldn't help but conclude Letizia knew what Caroline knew. Disappointment was certain and the inevitable sorrow cleaved his soul with a dull blade.

The Ingram's table was like a Viking craft containing his trusted ones—in many respects, his family. The funeral vessel drifted into the distance, but he knew it was not lost by a slipped mooring line, as though the knot of their friendship was poorly tied. No. The Ingrams drifted to sea because he cut the lines—sitting at their table. A cold indifference blew into his heart. Caroline was not a safe person.

While Jake opened another bottle of wine, Letizia asked Hank about his face. Her words and expression bore sincere interest. He had no proof she was behind his interrogation. It was just a hunch.

He was in a predicament. Did he lay his cards on the table—tell her he was interrogated over his commitment to the King—or did he create a story? With a quick plea for guidance to Magician, he opted for the story. Since Caroline and Jake knew what actually happened, and since his confidence in them was compromised by this professional connection, *A ruse might generate some interesting reaction*, he decided.

"You know, Ms. Pintaro, I wish I had a great story to tell you— some heroic tale of rescuing a child—but I don't. I was returning to the castle from La Faim a couple of nights ago and was fortunate enough to be given a ride on the back of a cart. However, I was unfortunate in that something spooked the horse, jerked the cart, and I was tossed out on my face."

Hank watched Letizia, Caroline, and Jake carefully. Caroline hesitated a split second, then went quickly to the kitchen, ostensibly to find a snack to add to the table fare. Jake sipped his wine and stared at the dark liquid. Letizia listened, watched Caroline excuse herself, let her eyes pass over Jake, and said, "That's terrible. I guess you're going to be okay?"

As composed as Letizia was, she looked away as Hank recounted his fable. She knew he was lying. Of course, that didn't prove she knew what really happened, but he knew her visit to the Ingram's wasn't purely social. *What's this lady up to?* he wondered, watching her across the table.

Letizia asked Jake, with the same caring and sincere tone she asked Hank about his face, what happened to him that necessitated the cane. Jake didn't pull any punches. He told her he was mugged, robbed, and beaten to within an inch of his life. He told her about losing his position with the First Floor Group in the Round Tower, which implicated Ennui and removed any shred of doubt in Letizia's mind as to her complicity in his demise. He described in general terms his work on behalf of the King. He told her briefly of his rehabilitative efforts and enthusiastically reported on his progress. After unfurling his story for five or six minutes, Jake concluded his brutal tale with, "That's probably more than you wanted to know, but there it is anyway."

Letizia reassured him that she was genuinely interested and thanked him for being so transparent. All the while, Hank watched Letizia's every nuance of movement. She asked Jake a few more questions about what he was doing now.

With great confidence Jake told Letizia of his relationship to the King, his devotion to the King's teaching, and his commitment to further the Kingdom and its ideals. He spoke passionately and honestly.

Letizia followed up with a question about Jake's devotion to the King and his trust in the King's ideals, "…even after suffering such a tragedy in your life."

"You mean, if the King cares about my family and me, and is indeed a good individual, how could he let something so terrible happen?"

Letizia nodded.

"We live in tough times, Ms. Pintaro. Gnarled Wood, the castle, and maybe most of all, the Round Tower need to return to the King's reign in the Kingdom. Zophos and his cohorts are hoping to overthrow the King, but he doesn't understand the transformation of a life touched by the King. Being connected to the King and the Kingdom isn't just about loyalty, although that is certainly an aspect. The relationship is more profound. Being part of the Kingdom means being the King's heir. It means being fundamentally transformed at the core of your soul. In short, being a follower of the King means you are part of his family. Instead of distant, you are included. The King's people are new people with new identities. They are people of the light.

"Just because bad things happen," Jake said, "doesn't call into question either my connection to the King or the King's to me. It simply means there is darkness that has not yet succumbed to the light."

"I see," Letizia said. "What do you mean by that last comment? About succumbing to the light?"

"Light conquers darkness. Every time. People have a choice, certainly. They can follow the darkness or live in the light. Of course, Zophos insists by use of force that his followers remain loyal to the darkness. The King, on the other hand, offers every individual the freedom to choose between life in the darkness or life in the light. But one day, the light will shine upon all who sit in darkness. It will be like a sunrise, but from on high."

"And at that point, the King will secure his reign?" she asked and stated at the same time.

"The way I see it," Jake said, "the King already reigns. He's just offering mankind the opportunity to get their choices clarified. He doesn't force anyone to submit to his rule. The fact that he offers every person this luxury of choice indicates he doesn't feel that either he or his throne are threatened—not by Zophos, not by darkness, and not by bad things that happen to his people. If he did, he wouldn't put up with the shenanigans."

She hadn't expected to hear all this. It was enlightening, troubling, haunting, and captivating. She knew deep down that this conversation was related to the mystery of Caroline and the pressing intuition that compelled her to the Ingram's home, but she had all she could manage, and she had stayed much, much longer than she intended. She was so captivated by the conversations and the dynamics of the evening that she'd absentmindedly drunk nearly two glasses of wine and had a buzz in her head.

Hank wanted some time to process the evening—by himself. Somewhere in his mind the fact of Jake's remarkable testimony to Letizia of the King's character and his trust in him registered, but he was fixated on the revelation that Caroline worked closely for a known enemy. Not much rattled him, but as he looked across the table at

Caroline, the revelation shook him.

He relished his Wednesday evenings with the Ingram family. It was one of the few places where he felt safe. But oddly, after this evening's turn of events, he felt more comfortable leaving with Letizia than he did staying with the Ingrams. When she made her move, so did he.

He expected to see someone waiting for her—perhaps someone he had "met" before—but no one appeared. Like any properly-trained, Southern gentleman, Hank walked Letizia to her home. Whatever she might be professionally, she was still a lady. Letizia was as uncomfortable as Hank, but she appreciated the escort.

They kept their distance, walking side-by-side, respectfully close, an arm's length between them. But Letizia stumbled. The streets were broken, the lamps in poor repair, and this was not her section of town.

Had he not been so focused on maintaining his guard, Hank probably would have suspected Magician of tripping her—and he would have been right! As he knew, but wasn't recalling at the moment, Magician never squanders an opportunity to advocate for walking in the light.

As vulnerable as it made her feel, and as uncomfortable as he was walking with the enemy, he offered her his arm and Letizia accepted.

It was a half-hour walk. They said little, but she didn't let go of his arm, and he didn't leave her until she was safely inside.

He wasn't ten feet away from her door when he muttered, "What the hell was that about, Magician?"

Hank wasn't really expecting an answer, but the thought popped sharply into his mind, *Which part?*

"The whole evening, but the last thirty minutes in particular," Hank answered under his breath.

The thought that came in reply bore Magician's signature logic, *Just working the edges and angles, Hank—all of them. It's what anglers do.*

That moniker—angler—caught his attention. Hank recalled his favorite author, Jack Lewis. The former atheist referred to God as the

Great Angler, describing in tight prose how He worked the multi-current waters of his atheism and hooked his soul. Now Magician used the same metaphor.

His mind swirled with the events of the night. He strolled toward home lost in thoughts of Caroline being compromised, Jake's courageous stand of faith in the High King, meeting Letizia Pintaro upon nearly-sacred, almost-family turf, and of all things walking her home on his arm. He didn't have the slightest notion where to begin in sorting this influx of information, circumstance, and implication.

Letizia had a nice home. It wasn't opulent like the residences of the men who worked for her on a cash basis, but then she didn't feel the need to compensate. When she spoke, things happened.

The only person who knew she had been out for the evening was her personal maid, Natalie, who knew when to speak and how to keep a confidence. She was a luxury, but Letizia could afford Natalie, so she did. She appreciated her pampering, her reliability, and even though their roles in life were vastly different, Letizia appreciated the comfort of someone whom she didn't have to manage, control, or suspect.

For her part, Natalie took pride in caring for Letizia. She had chosen service as her life and profession at the expense of family and friends. Hers was a world of nuance, discretions few would notice, but judgment that spoke of her attention to detail and unswerving commitment to Letizia's wellbeing and consummate excellence. Whether selecting the right broach, or the perfect scarf, making certain Letizia ate well, or providing a secure ear, her *raison d'être* was Letizia.

Natalie read Letizia's face as soon as she stepped through the door. It wasn't a look she was accustomed to seeing, but that she was trolling through deep currents was evident.

Natalie followed Letizia into the recesses of the home and was waiting outside her dressing room when Letizia emerged from the wash room. She helped Letizia undress, laid out her favorite pair of house slippers, and held a silk robe at the ready. It was late, well past Letizia's customary bedtime. Letizia smiled at her thoughtfulness and turned her back to Natalie, arms extended to receive the kindness. The silk was cool, but warmed to her body in an instant.

Natalie followed Letizia through arched doorways and across intricate rugs toward her study. Stopping short of the doorway, "May I get you a glass of wine?" she asked.

Letizia thought for a moment. "No. Thank you, Natalie. I'll have whiskey please."

Natalie now knew for certain that Letizia was engaged in some heavy lifting inside her soul.

Rarely was Letizia out of control. Rarely did she lose her composure. But when she found herself in a new place, Letizia's confidence enabled her to embrace the extraordinary circumstance with intellectual honesty and persistence until she grasped the details, comprehended the logic, and understood the dynamic. Tonight, this determination to wrestle her questions into submission included staying up later and drinking something different.

People didn't see this aspect of Letizia. They didn't see her lost in thought, didn't witness her reflective pacing, didn't see the personal marks she placed in the margins of whatever she was reading, didn't see her hands directing silent ruminations as if conducting Rachmaninoff, didn't observe the steely look in her eyes, or her lips undulating like waves upon a tumultuous sea.

People didn't see this in her because she didn't let them, didn't invite their company. If they had, they wouldn't have understood, or if they had any inkling of where she was going intellectually, their fear would have paralyzed them. The majority simply benefitted from her persistence, which wasn't complete until she was able to articulate in understandable terms what earlier was a mystery of sufficient grandeur to escape words and defy apprehension. The few who were self-aware enough to realize there were questions of the magnitude Letizia sorted through were intimidated by her uniqueness and kept their distance. For most people, what they don't understand, they fear, and what they fear, they dismiss, or if threatened, destroy.

But instead of keeping her distance, Letizia trod where angels feared travel. And if unable to resolve her conundrum, she returned—and returned again—until her mystery was solved, her inquiry answered, and any action necessitated by understanding was taken. If her professional life included duplicity, she never compromised her intellectual honesty. Most would be driven insane juggling what Letizia routinely considered. Indeed, some considered her obsessive; others thought her compulsive; a few believed her driven mad by her relentless quests. She noted their critiques, but to do otherwise—to not ask the questions, to not be inquisitive, to not persist—would be a failure of truth to herself, a breach of intellectual honesty.

That would be unacceptable. Letizia was not like most people.

Natalie delivered the dram and departed.

For all her brilliance, her careful attention to safety given the world in which she worked, and her ability to manage an array of details and concepts, had she been asked, Letizia would have sworn she was alone in her study. But she wasn't.

Just as he had done with Hank, and with others before him, Jester was present incognito. He utilized the same techniques with her as he did with everyone else. His approach was simple enough—disguise himself as her thoughts, complete with first person pronouns, weigh-in on whatever was happening to her circumstantially, and correlate his comments with her customary thoughts, emotions, and behaviors. The other ingredient of Jester's effectiveness was his unswerving attention to detail.

He had been playing this game since enticing Cain to consider murdering his brother, Abel. He was good at what he did, and like his boss, Zophos, he was driven desperate to succeed. Letizia hadn't given him a moment's worry, but after tonight's conversation at Caroline and Jake Ingram's home, Jester felt it necessary to make certain she wasn't alone with her reflection.

His adversary, Magician, the Wizard of the Kingdom and Sorcerer of Light, was also present. He was constantly working against Jester, subverting his ways, casting light upon his dark deception, and advocating on behalf of the High King. Yes. He too was a specter incognito in Letizia's study who spoke to her in first-person pronouns. But unlike Jester who dealt in deception, Magician spoke truth and true desire to her.

As she sipped her drink in the confines of her study, sorting through thoughts she considered her own, in truth Letizia was meeting in conference with Jester and Magician. All her considerations sounded the same—like her. Given the masquerade, it is understandable that she believed she was alone.

Jake Ingram's composure was disarming, she conceded. *Of course, he doesn't know what I know—that I am behind the disability he suffers.* She paused to consider Jake's impairment, to envision his crippled hobbling. *It would be interesting to see his response toward me if he had all the facts. I wonder? Would he be so noble toward me? So confident? So strong in his convictions?*

She had seen it around the office in Caroline—and she saw the same quality in Jake. *There's a peace I don't possess. What's that about?* she wondered. *And it's genuine? I've seen peace attributed to other people, but upon closer examination, it isn't peace at all. It's ignorance. Oblivion.*

But the peace demonstrated by Caroline and Jake...? That's not so easily dismissed. There has to be another explanation for their peace—the quiet confidence, the steadiness, the security. It was a compelling quality, not simply because it worked to her advantage at the office, but because she realized that what Caroline and Jake possessed in their relative hardship, *I lack in my relative prosperity.* "That's a disturbing thought," she muttered to herself.

Letizia admitted her deficiency to herself—her intellectual honesty serving her well. But having done so, she had to admit that she was intolerant of deficiency, especially in herself. She didn't do anything without reason and she didn't tolerate anything that could be improved upon or remedied.

Pondering this, whatever she possessed in qualities, skills, talents, power, and position, there was no question, *I lack the peace they possess.* If anything, she was not only deficient in peace, she was internally in turmoil. The tension wasn't a tumult, not by a long shot, but more like a nagging, dripping, persistent reminder that something wasn't right. She thought, *I would prefer a storm over this incessant erosion.*

This wasn't a new idea to her, but it was probably the first time she named the deficiency and considered it specifically. *Call it peace, or satisfaction, or fulfillment, or comfort, or security—whatever. I've thrown immense energy into assuaging this longing. And, I've come up empty. If anything, this, this inner vacuum is more pronounced now than ever before.*

Letizia paced. She thought. She grappled with unseen forces.

In spite of her formidable focus, however, the meagerness in her soul would not be sated. Now that she had named the deficiency—lack of inner peace, resolution—she realized her intuition, intellectual honesty, and integrity had been laboring to discover fulfillment for many years. In fact, the more she thought about it, the more she realized just how innovative she had been, in many different ways, in her quest for peace. *Every day my personal and professional lives are connected either directly or indirectly to the quest of achieving internal resolution.* The thought stunned her.

The more she thought, and the more she considered, the more astounded she became at the variety of things she had tried in an attempt to silence her soul's complaint of inner turmoil—the noise of internal dissatisfaction grumbling like the rumbling of her stomach when she was hungry. But for all the angles she had worked, all the achievements realized, and all the recognition awarded, her evaluation tonight led her to the same conclusion, *I lack the tranquility of internal security.* While she had taken the precautions available to ensure her physical safety, her soul felt dark, foreboding, insecure, and alone.

She had a mental image—like a wagon wheel—the circle of her life connected by spokes to a single hub. *The hub is lacking. It's insufficient.*

Once she arrived at this conclusion, Letizia began working her way outward in an assessment of risk. *How vulnerable am I?* she pondered.

A lesser person might have called for another whiskey—and another—until the plaguing query was quashed and her brain sufficiently pickled to be good for nothing more than fitful sleep. But not Letizia. She persisted, troubled more by the lack of an answer than her eroding foundation.

She paced barefooted, her hands clasped behind her back, head down but not bowed. Late into the wee hours she worked, walked, and wandered across her study and through the labyrinth of her dusky soul. Back and forth the internal debate was waged. Jester sparred with Magician, but his darkness was no match for the light.

Letizia accepted the sobering conclusion. *The only explanation for the peace I've observed in Caroline, the only accounting for Jake's confidence in the face of his fate, and the only conclusion for why they possess inner security and I do not is their allegiance to the King versus mine to Zophos. It's inescapable—the only possible conclusion.*

But to bow my knee to the High King. That would be the end of life as I know it. Personally and professionally. A profound sorrow seeped into her fractured psyche.

It was anything but peaceful.

Letizia stood frozen in the middle of her study. Her bare feet warmed the parquet. The night breeze drifted through the open windows carrying the sounds of the night upon its wings as she made her decision.

She was the most unhappy convert in the Kingdom. Her allegiance to Zophos was concluded, and most likely her work under Ennui as well. There was quiet in her head and a vacuum in her soul. Letizia was empty.

Her trembling allegiance to the High King had begun.

CHAPTER 18

La Faim

Hank changed his regular meeting time with Jack to late Wednesday afternoon. Even though it was inconvenient, and meant traveling the road from La Faim to the castle at dusk—not the best place to be—the schedule change provided a justifiable reason to miss his regular night with Caroline, Jake, and their kids.

The revelation that Caroline worked closely with Letizia Pintaro created more suspicion than he was able to get past. The implications were so profoundly far-reaching that he plummeted from the sublime joy of family and friendship into the depths of disillusionment.

Hank hoped Caroline was ignorant of Letizia's dark dealings—*Surely she must be*—but he couldn't be certain. Assuming she was ignorant about Letizia, he had no way of managing what she might mention in Letizia's presence. *I have to be sure about her, now that I know. The risk associated with slipping up—mentioning a name, a meeting place, the number in a group, even an idea that could be damaging if known—in her presence is too great to bear. I have to be careful—very careful. And this goes for Jake as well. I have to be guarded. I have no other choice.*

Of course, there was the option of asking Caroline what she knew or didn't know, and asking Jake straight up what all he had told his wife. *But if I broach this question with Caroline and Jake, and they are clueless, then I've opened quite a can of worms, and if I were them, I would be offended. If I question them and they know about Letizia, then I implicate them and they realize I know about Letizia and about their duplicity. Now the jig is up. This leaves them no option but immediate aggression toward me and the King's followers, unless they—that is, Letizia—hesitate and provide the King's people time to react. That's doubtful. Letizia would never stand for that, and certainly not her boss, Ennui—or her boss, Zophos!* The thoughts cascaded through his mind like an avalanche, taking down all in their path.

He retraced what he knew about Letizia. Huffed, *I know enough, in fact, to incriminate her and all who work closely with her.* He paused, not wanting to acknowledge the next thought in the queue. *Sadly, the implications now include Caroline, and in all likelihood, Jake.* Hank took a deep breath as he thought back through the logic of his considerations, arriving at the same conclusion. *If I reveal what I know, Ms. Pintaro will seize whomever she can without delay and without mercy.* Hank reflected on his recent detention. *There is no way I could warn everyone in time.*

His conversations with Caroline and Jake to date had been candid and comfortable, so honest that he truly felt they helped him shoulder the load he carried. He couldn't remember who all, or what all, he had disclosed sitting at their table, *But there's plenty*, he knew.

The only consolation Hank felt in this whole, disquieting revelation was that this was the first inkling he had something might be—could be—amiss. It was the first hint that the security of the King's people was compromised, that punitive action could be forming, or that people were in imminent danger. If Jake was revealing confidential data to Caroline, and if she was passing it along to Letizia Pintaro, then his consolation was that nothing had been done yet with the information. Yet. It was a small consolation, too small to cling to.

Hank felt like a fool for including Jake in his plans, for compromising his Father's trust in him to prevail in the battle for the Round Tower. *How could I be so stupid? But how could I have known?* he countered, recognizing neither Jester nor Magician.

And for all his time sorting possible options that might maintain their relationship, Hank's idea bank was empty. He wanted to ask Caroline—straight up!—what she knew, who she knew…. And, Jake as well.

That will never work, he argued internally. *Asking them reveals what*

I know, tells them too much.

It was a circular argument. Now he was right back where he started: saying too much, revealing too much, potentially to the wrong people. It broke his heart and depleted his energy.

Hank knew he couldn't simply disappear from their lives, but until he assessed the risk of Caroline and Jake Ingram's compromise, he had to distance himself. He had to protect those in his care. *Doggone! For that matter, I have to protect myself,* he noted.

Work. Obligation. These are reasonable excuses. For a while, he thought. *Hopefully, before they become too suspicious of my absence, I'll figure out what to do—whom to warn.* He thought about that idea. *How will I warn them? Where could they go?*

Caroline and Jake know I meet with Jack in La Faim. Of this Hank was certain. *I've mentioned others, but no one other than group leaders in as much detail—I don't think. But Jack? I celebrated Jack's growing inclination toward the High King with them—at their table. They were so enthusiastic!* he recalled.

I wonder if Letizia's reach extends to La Faim?

As he considered his options, Hank figured he could come up with a strategy to warn Jack. *And for starters, who in his right mind would want to mess with Jack? Or work in La Faim?* It escaped Hank's notice that he was working in La Faim and doing so directly with Jack. But then, he never included himself among those in their right mind.

Jack was a success story. He had not risen to the top of the gang in La Faim by brute force alone. He had a keen intellect to match his street savvy and horse sense. Each time they met, Jack asked loads of questions—and they weren't rambling inquiries.

There was way too much transpiring in Jack's mind to fiddle with trivialities. He was anxious to understand what made Hank different, how the King ruled, how the Kingdom ran, what part Vassar played—and why anyone gave a tinker's damn about La Faim.

That Jack would be skeptical was understandable. La Faim was a distant world away from the Round Tower and only separated from the dump at the end of the world by a polluted creek. It was a stinking, nasty, dead-end town, populated with dirty, broken-down people hemmed in on all sides by hopelessness.

The oppression of La Faim was palpable—a prison without walls. After each visit, it took Hank the long walk home to rid himself of its onerous weight, and once home, the first thing he did was strip out of his clothes and clean up. However, he knew that Magician had sent him to La Faim and he was certain Jack was his primary target.

Oddly enough, at least to Hank, the greatest impediment to Jack declaring allegiance to the High King was his personal satisfaction. He didn't feel like he needed anything from the King.

As Jack's reservation came to light, Hank's first impulse was to point to the degradation and dilapidation of La Faim and ask if he wouldn't like something better. But he realized such an approach cheapened his Father's desire for relationship with the shallow temptation of affluence beyond La Faim. Each time Hank thought about enticing Jack toward the Kingdom with the allure of a better life, Magician checked him. *Relationship with the King isn't about a better life,* he would hear Magician counsel from his heart. *Relationship with the King is about connection, transformation, and new life—his light overcoming the darkness of a human heart allied with Zophos.*

And then Hank would counter Magician's counsel: *But people do things for a reason, namely because it benefits them.*

Discussing things with Magician, even debating them, had seemed at first to be disrespectful to the great Wizard of the High Kingdom. But if Hank heard it from Magician once, he heard it a hundred times. "Come, let's reason this through together." And the more they sorted through things, the more Hank realized, *Magician isn't nearly as interested in the "reasoning" as he is in the "together."*

Why would Jack need anything from Father? Hank mulled over that counterintuitive thought during several commutes between the castle and La Faim.

If alliance with the King is about improving upon La Faim, then moving to the Round Tower makes sense. And it made sense at face value. From Hank's perspective, Jack needed everything new—from life, to language, to shoes.

But if connecting with Father is about relationship…? If that's the case, La Faim is neither here nor there. As Hank and Magician discussed the matter, it was clear Magician was of the opinion that relationship had nothing to do with location.

Father isn't necessarily interested in improving circumstance unless it serves his ultimate end! He's said as much to me, many times, Hank realized. *He's only interested in personal transformation that creates connection.*

The more Hank got to know Jack, and the more he observed his place in the culture of La Faim, the more Hank realized that Jack was the king of La Faim. *What he says, goes. What he wishes, is done. When he says, "Jump," everyone asks, "How high?" He has position, recognition, power, authority, and respect. He has money—by La Faim standards. He has women. He has fame. Jack's right. He doesn't need anything.*

Hank was more nervous than usual as he left the castle's outskirts. His suspicion about the Ingrams created necessary caution. But only a fool would fail to consider the signs. Once satisfied that he wasn't being tailed by anyone beyond the normal "keepers" assigned to him, he placed Caroline and Jake into a secure compartment in his mind and shifted his focus to Jack.

So what exactly is it that Jack needs, Magician? Why do you have me going to La Faim to meet with him and what exactly is it that you are proposing I deliver to him?

Hank took his time. He'd left early, planning in advance to meander, even detour through the woods if he felt the inclination. His mind wandered, taking in the sights and sounds around him. He knew that if Magician had something to say, he would flag down his roving mind in order for them to reason together.

At a bend, Hank ducked off the road into the timber. The handlers assigned to him were hapless thugs. He didn't feel particularly threatened by them. So, he dropped them and treasured the small delight he felt knowing they would have to give account of their ineptitude.

For a few minutes, Hank focused his attention on making certain they didn't follow and that he was indeed alone. He doubled back, and from a safe blind watched his two handlers engage in animated conversation. He couldn't hear what they were saying, but their gestures were obviously accusatory. After stirring up the dust in the road for several minutes, they retraced their steps in the direction of the castle.

Hank eased from his hiding and noiselessly crept deeper into the seclusion until he came to one of his special places of reverie. He paused for a few minutes to listen and observe. Dropping to all fours, he crawled through the underbrush into a hollow in the ground shaped like the curve of his back. The shape of the ground reminded him of his chair at home in Texas. Hank laid his walking stick beside him, adjusted his sword out of his way, and settled down to relish his solitude.

Like a falling leaf dancing with the breeze, Hank's mind fluttered upon a variety of thoughts, until it came to rest upon the question of why he was bound for La Faim. Quietly, like a settling leaf cradled by the breeze, Magician asked, *Are you alone?*

It was a trick question. On the one hand, *Of course I'm alone! I took great pains to be certain no one else is around.* But on the other hand, *No, I'm not alone. You are here with me.*

Exactly! And therein is why you are going to La Faim. That is what Jack lacks, what you have, and what I can provide.

Hank shook his head at the simplicity. *Relationship! Father—the High King—always prioritizes relationship at the expense of everything else. And why wouldn't he? The only thing I have that he doesn't is my heart. It's so obvious I tripped over it. Jack is alone.*

You know something about that, don't you? Magician interjected.

Hank smiled, not with happiness, but recognition. *Yes. I know something about that, Magician.*

So tell me where you are, Hank. Give me a summary.

Jack doesn't need a better life. He needs a new life, centered not in himself, but in the King. Right now, he's separated and alone, living by his own wits and devices. And, doing a great job, but doing so independently of Father. What's missing is connection with the King. That Jack resides in La Faim is neither here nor there.

Hank ran through various scenarios as he contemplated how to communicate Jack's true need to him. *And why is it so difficult to keep relationship prioritized in my thinking?* he questioned. *No doubt it has to do with Jester. If I were him, I would be pretty doggone desperate to confuse this matter.*

Hank was thankful for Magician, and told him so. His counsel, wisdom, and clarity were indeed remarkable, but more than anything, *It's just great having you close.*

He settled into the moment. The clarification of what Jack needed from him was a tremendous reminder of his own connection and relationship to his Father. *It's really tempting to view Father as a kingly resource and think of myself as an entitled dependent. Gosh! How often I revert to this belittling perspective.*

But again now, as he discovered was frequently necessary, he refocused upon the proximity of his relationship and the security of his place in the family. As his heart's desires surfaced, he noted, *This is the pivot point for whether I see myself as entitled or included, alone or connected.*

Hank felt himself slowly pulled from the recesses of his mental musing. He sensed, *I'm being watched.* He emerged fully from his thoughts into his immediate surroundings.

A set of yellow eyes stared at him from five feet away. Hank locked gazes with the coyote, knowing fully the wily animal sought him out. The longer he looked at the coyote, and the coyote looked at him, the more evident it was to Hank that the animal knew he had been sent—

sent as a gift, as a reassurance from the King to his son, "You are not alone. You are on my mind and I am here. Everything is going to be fine."

As silently as he had appeared, the coyote made his exit, satisfied he delivered his Maker's message. Hank crawled from his hollow place in the trees, brushed off the back of his clothes, adjusted his sword and dagger, and after picking up his walking stick, walked through the woods to rejoin the road to La Faim.

Audie Vandermeer and Ronan Chandler held hands as they walked to their small group meeting. Originally part of the small group that met at Caroline and Jake's home, they were now part of a group that met closer to their homes.

The splitting of the group had been challenging, but Jake did a stellar job of casting a vision for the new group, who were closer together geographically, and its host-leader. While Audie and Ronan continued attending their large group meeting in the Round Tower, they found their real soul-connections in their small group.

Although neither Audie nor Ronan had been able to articulate it, they felt lonely inside the large, First Floor Group. It was a well-oiled machine with multiple programs, committees, causes, and age-specific small groups. But for all the smooth organizational structure, there was a lack of correlation between what happened in the First Floor Group and their lives. Audie felt guilty for saying it, but she told Ronan she felt like the large group covered their human deficits with a veneer of organizational excellence.

Their small group had depth, relevance, transparency, and connection. It was without varnish—raw, grainy, unfinished. They knew each person in the group. Their discussions about the King and his Kingdom were meaningful, stimulating, and pertinent. And if someone missed the group meeting, it was noticed. A person could fall through a crack—or a chasm—in the First Floor Group and never be missed, but if someone failed to appear in small group, their absence was noted and explored.

It wasn't that membership in the small group was legalistic, or attendance mandated, or even expected. Rather, it was that membership meant friendly ties. Connection. Relationship, and relationship mirroring their relationships with the King. Just as the King, Vassar, and Magician were always closing the gap between themselves and others, so members of the small groups cared for one another.

The tighter geography and size of the group enabled the members to connect personally and meaningfully. They knew each other's strengths, weaknesses, wounds, and victories. If one had a need, the others rose to the challenge of meeting the need. If one had a success, they celebrated. If one had heartache, the burden was spread across the group's shoulders. If one had a dream, they shared, protected, encouraged, and promoted.

With the depth of relational connection came the additional benefit of seeing specifically how the King's teaching was personal and effective. Consequently, there was accountability and assistance that propelled everyone toward honesty, growth, and personal transformation. The shared stories of their lives affirmed to each other the King's loving touch upon them.

Audie's enthusiasm, confidence in the King, and relationship to him flourished. Growing by leaps and bounds, she demonstrated remarkable integrity. Since meeting with Faith when he filled in for her absent teacher, Audie continued to write journals with her observations about the King, his teaching, and her relationship to both.

Ronan's progress was not as impressive, and he recognized it. He hadn't said a word to anyone, most of all, Audie. He was falling behind.

More precisely, he was falling behind Audie. She was like a shooting star. As long as he was with her, he could play off her lead and cover the inadequacy he felt. But he knew he was bluffing his way through small group meetings and getting more and more uncomfortable around Audie. He felt himself withdrawing from her, not because he didn't like her, but because he felt intimidated by her.

He didn't like what was happening—not to him, not to them—and redoubled his efforts to distinguish himself. More accurately, to distinguish himself in comparison to Audie. He read. He memorized extensive passages of the King's writings in order to contribute to the small group discussions. And, he always looked the part, especially since he was associated with Audie.

However, he began to feel his association with Audie was hurting more than helping. A moderately white shirt looks white until placed next to a truly white shirt.

That's when Sonya surfaced. She was witty and fun, pretty, approachable, and smart in her own way.

He didn't stop going to small group, and didn't cut himself off from Audie, but the emotional distance between him, Audie, and the small group grew. He covered it nicely, continuing to talk the talk, and bluff his way through meetings and discussions both corporate and individual.

When he was with Audie and his small group, he felt inferior and intimidated. When he was with Sonya, he felt affirmed and confident. Lucky for him, his two worlds didn't overlap. He was able to juggle Audie and small group and Sonya rather effortlessly. What became increasingly more difficult to manage was the disparity between feeling he was nobody compared to Audie and somebody when he was with Sonya.

The more he hung out with Audie, the stronger his compulsion to rush into Sonya's arms as soon as he was able. And the more he hung out with Sonya, the more he longed for what Audie brought to him.

The growing distance between Audie and him became more apparent. She began asking questions. His denials escalated and his rationalization became more complex as her questions became more sophisticated. Not only did he feel intimidated, now he felt more and more that he was trapped.

He and Audie spent less time together, talked more about small matters (when they talked), and less about important things. They almost never walked together, and when they did, they rarely held hands anymore beyond the obligatory courtesy.

He felt stressed when he was with Audie, he felt invited in by Sonya. She was accessible. Audie was busy, her life full of extracurricular activity and the small group. Sonya was available. Audie traveled in an adoring crowd and Ronan felt he had to compete for her time and attention. With Sonya, he had plenty of alone time.

Sonya was responsive, conciliatory, and accommodating. She noticed him, affirmed him, and wanted him close. They worked well together and this helped Ronan reconcile the distance between Audie and him.

He noticed that he and Sonya didn't discuss the High King as frequently as they did when they first met, but he reasoned that this would remedy itself in time. Then, he promised himself it would—or at least, Jester promised.

For now, Ronan felt relieved to be free of the expectations Audie and the small group placed upon him. Relief had been a long time coming, and he clung to it—clung to her—like a drowning man holding to a life ring.

Sonya was sweet—like sugar—and the more Ronan had, the more he wanted, and the more he had, the less fulfilling Sonya proved to be. But like a horse running toward the barn in anticipation of a sugar cube, Ronan was in a gallop and there was nothing to do but give him his reins and let him run.

Each time they were together, they went farther. They were both in need of what they thought the other could provide. Sonya thought Ronan would confirm once and for all that she was desirable. Ronan felt Sonya would make him viable—wise enough to be acceptable to important, influential, intimidating people.

What they thought was desire, was lust. Slowly at first, but then faster, they removed the natural restraints. Once their shirts were off and Sonya felt Ronan's hands and lips on her breasts, their momentum escalated like a stampede. Covering each other's personal doubts with the intimacy of their physical nakedness, entwined in each other's arms and legs, she lost herself in his arms and he in her.

Before his throbbing stopped he knew Sonya was insufficient to the task he had asked of her. And while his chest still heaved upon her breasts, Sonya's heart sank realizing she had given all to no avail in search of desirability. Their exchange was in vain, pointless contributions.

Ronan felt ashamed, Sonya felt used. In their desperate quest to gain from each other what neither could provide, they offended each other for a lifetime.

Ronan was shocked. Sonya lay crying with the covers of the bed pulled tightly around her neck. He had no words for her and only expletives for himself.

He didn't bother to clean himself, just gathered his strewn clothes into a pile and dressed. The ache of disappointment in his chest was monstrous and the guilt upon his shoulders unlike any burden he'd ever carried.

He collected a kitchen towel, folded it, and placed it on the bed beside Sonya. He had done all he could—all he had left in him to do. It was a pitiful, woefully inadequate comfort, but he was depleted. That he folded the towel was all the thoughtfulness he could muster.

He said nothing, did nothing more, just walked from the room and left her sobbing, clutching the covers for comfort. He closed the front door behind him.

While they romped together with naked appetite, Ronan and

Sonya thought they were a twosome. But they were deceived. Their sexual entanglement was a *ménage à trois*—a threesome—with Jester pimping, enticing, cavorting with them, interpreting for them.

Deceiving them.

And Jester collected his win over the King.

CHAPTER 19

First Floor Group in the Round Tower

News of Sjakal's—Jack's—declaration of allegiance to the High King spread like a wildfire through the Kingdom's nooks and crannies. Because his story was sensational, it wasn't long before requests began coming for him to testify of his conversion from darkness to light.

Jack didn't have the faintest notion how the Round Tower worked, but assumed it had to be an honorable organization, as straightforward as the man to whom he had declared his loyalty: the High King. It was heady stuff for a man living in La Faim to be invited to speak at the First Floor Group's weekly meeting. He was a celebrity!

On matters related to his newfound faith, Jack depended on Hank's mentoring and guidance, but it never occurred to him to seek his counsel on whether or not he should relate his story to the First Floor Group. When the invitation came, he accepted on the spot.

Hank didn't know if he would have counseled otherwise or not, but as the two of them walked through the gates and under the raised portcullises into the Round Tower, Hank was anxious. There were any number of mistakes Jack could make with the First Floor Group. *But, how far wrong can he go relating the difference in his life today from his life previously?*

Hank didn't make a habit of attending the First Floor Group's weekly meeting, but he knew Jack would be a draw. Indeed, the auditorium was packed with people anxious to vicariously live Jack's life in the degradation of darkness and his conversion to the light.

Jack panicked when he looked into the auditorium. He stopped so abruptly, in fact, Hank ran into his back. Jack quickly reversed course pushing the two of them backward through the foyer for several steps before Hank could get out from behind Jack's wholesale retreat.

"Whoa. Whoa. What's the matter, Jack?" Hank had his hand on Jack's back.

"I can't go in there. With them," Jack hissed in a declarative whisper.

Hank looked at his friend. It was odd to see Jack absent his usual confidence. "Why not? That's why you're here. To speak to these people."

"But I'm not dressed right."

Hank's first inclination was to dismiss Jack's concern…but he quickly recalled those times in his life when he showed up at an event underdressed. *There's no good remedy for feeling like brown shoes at a tuxedo event*, Hank reminded himself.

Hank pondered for a moment. "Come on. Follow me."

Hank walked this way and that, looked here and there, thinking, *Magician, I could use some help about now.* Adopting the more-or-less secluded alcove down a hallway from the auditorium as Magician's provision, Hank started unbuttoning his shirt. "Give me your shirt, Jack."

Ordinarily Jack would have recoiled from such a direct command—just because he was Jack. But upon Hank's order, he complied, not bothering to protest until he was pulling his shirt tail from his pants.

"Don't mess with me," Hank ordered. He hustled Jack's shirt off his shoulder, stuffing his own shirt into Jack's free hand. "Here. Hurry up. We don't want to be late. Messes with your mind."

"Oh," Jack said simply, missing Hank's effort to relieve his angst.

As Jack buckled his belt, Hank stepped back to size-up his mentee's appearance. "You look great! Look like me," he stated matter-of-fact while putting his arms into Jack's shirt.

That got Jack's attention. "Damn. Don't say that. If I looked like you, these quality folks wouldn't be havin' me talk at 'em."

"Uh, huh," Hank acknowledged, working to get his new shirt

tucked in. He smiled. His intervention worked. Jack's pluck was back!

Hank finished buttoning his traded-for shirt as they walked back toward the auditorium. He pulled the collar up to his nose, noting that he had taken on the odor of La Faim. His reputation occurred to him, the thought lying stark next to the counsel he attributed earlier to Magician—the counsel that instigated swapping shirts. *I've compromised myself. They'll think I'm from La Faim—that I condone it. Don't know any better. What should I do?* A quick succession of justifications and explanations flooded into his worry.

His sacrificed shirt lay juxtaposed—contrasted—to his sacrificed reputation. *How odd is it that I was focused and Jack confused, but with the change of my shirt, he's focused and I'm confused!*

It was a short walk from the alcove to the auditorium. Jack chattered, Hank nodded, as though present and accounted for, but inside Hank's head, Magician coached in first-person. *Vassar has a solid reputation, but I can't think of a single time I've seen him protect it, or even cling to it as though it's important. In fact, he gambles his reputation with some frequency.*

As they stepped to the door of the auditorium and shook hands with the greeter, Hank recalled, *Vassar did the same thing for me that I've done for Jack. Changed shirts. He took mine, gave me his.* Hank shook his head slightly—unnoticeably—at the recollection. *At least Jack's shirt is clean. Mine was nasty!* Of all the profound memories Hank had of his last venture into Gnarled Wood, none was more graphic. In his heart, Hank winked his appreciation at Magician for the clarity he provided.

Hank grabbed Jack by the elbow, stopping him short while pulling himself alongside. He whispered in Jack's left ear, "I'm proud of you, Jack. Can't think of any place I'd rather be than right here with you. They'll have a reserved place for us down front. Lead out, I'm with you."

The senior leader of the First Floor Group was ecstatic to see his auditorium so full. As a result, he took longer to greet the audience than was necessary or than they wanted to hear. They had come to hear Jack, not him—but he wanted to pontificate upon his bully pulpit until he milked all he could from the expectant attendees.

There wasn't much to say in introducing Jack. While he was a big deal in La Faim, none of those accolades and accomplishments mattered much in the culture of the Round Tower. The senior leader was polite in his introduction, a nuance Hank missed but Jack noticed. He was already anxious about speaking, and the senior leader's measured introduction only added to his apprehension.

When people are nervous, some get quiet and reticent, some get loud. Jack wasn't loud, but given his nervousness he tried too hard, over-spoke, and that exacerbated his anxiety. He settled down after a few minutes, but only as far as the audience was concerned. Inside, Jack remained tight as a banjo string.

To his credit, Jack delivered his stories compellingly, especially for a person unaccustomed to public speaking. He related a few stories that were far enough outside the audience's routine to hold their attention— the story about his brother being stabbed, the one about his Father disappearing into the dump, as well as a few thoughts on how children in La Faim are protected from the packs of feral dogs.

Jack also described how he manages the people who work for him. "So there's runners goin' through La Fa all the time, carrying messages from my guys who manage blocks, to my guys what look after sections, areas, and so on. All the way to my guys that's close to me, and then to me. Top to bottom, within ten minutes I got everything I need to know."

As Hank listened, it struck him that while Jack was "talking about whatever," as he put it, he was demonstrating a team-driven, collaborative approach to business that would make almost any company more efficient. He also noted how similar Jack's organizational style was to the mafias of Eastern Europe, but sequestered that observation and its implication for later consideration.

Jack's engaging personality connected with the people, and mercifully, they accepted him and overlooked his marginal manners and butchery of good grammar. Jack took note and was grateful.

As he got into the crux of his story, he found his rhythm, moved more easily, spoke with some jargon, and humor, and related more of how La Fa got along. "La Fa! That's what we call La Faim. Those folks what named my town, whenever it was—if you take time to say the name like it's supposed to be said, you won't never get done sayin' what needs said before it's too late."

Jack amused Hank. Listening, watching, Hank thought, *He's got no formal education, but he's educated. Put him in a legitimate business and Jack's entrepreneurial talent would be stifled before the end of the week. Let him be Jack and he runs La Faim, a whole town, populated with renegades, and without a shred of government.*

Jack was doing a good job expressing himself. Not only that, from Hank's vantage point, he was doing a good job lining up the King's ultimate intervention in his life.

Still, what Jack left behind in life was more than most in the Round Tower realized independent man had invented—or at least, more than they liked to acknowledge. Considering the implication embodied in Jack and his tale—that the High King condescended to meet the likes of him in such a ruined place as La Faim—was troublesome to most of his listeners. If the progression of Jack's story was literally true—that the King traveled to La Faim in search of Jack, rather than vice versa—then the King's sense of propriety was less than the stellar standard attributed to him within the Tower.

Surely, the King wouldn't associate with the likes of La Faim! He couldn't, most in the Tower believed. But this is where Jack was leading them.

That Jack's old life was one of independence from the King, and his new life was one of reliance upon the King, he was crystal clear and said so with authority. He knew without a shadow of doubt that he had gone from separation to connection, had passed from dark to light, and from distance to relationship.

At his point of decision—to yield to the King's reign and relationship—Jack described what happened to the First Floor Group audience. "And so, it came down to this: I bowed my knee to the High King. You gotta understand: I ain't never bowed to no one, not even my head, let alone my knee. But I was done! Done livin' by my own wits. I was done tryin' to be somebody cause I was stronger, smarter, and meaner. I was done bein' my own man, all by myself. I didn't think I needed nothin'. I had everything—money, girls, power; a nice place. But somethin' was missin', and I knew it. My friend, Hank, sittin' right down here, he helped me. A lot. I wouldn't never have got it figured out. I needed to be changed inside. That's what Hank called it. So, I bowed down on my knees, back of my house where I keep my dogs. I told the King I was sorry for livin' apart from him. I asked his forgiveness—and I ain't never said sorry or asked forgiveness up 'til then. I declared to the King that I wanted him to change me, that I wanted to be in his family, wanted to be Prince Vassar's little brother. I asked him to live in my heart." Jack paused. "And then I told him I would appreciate it if he would honor my request."

Jack stopped. Stood shaking his head. Tears filled his eyes.

His pause was uncomfortably long—far too long for affect. Clearly, the audience realized, this man is serious and considers his story true. He believes the King condescended to meet with him in La Faim, by a dog kennel, apparently.

Jack didn't know it was the cultural expectation of the First Floor Group that he bow his head and keep his arms close. Instead, he lifted his wet face to the heavens and spread his arms in full reenactment of his wholehearted surrender of all that he was to all he understood of the King. With Jack's emotional demonstration of his abandonment to the King, the tension in the auditorium became palpable.

Jack regained a semblance of the composure expected of him. He eyed his audience with an intense look, not unlike that of a predator espying prey. Determined. Intense. Unblinking. Focused with the realization that life and death are at stake.

In words trembling under the weight of the King's response, Jack said, "I asked the King to give me a new heart and take his seat on the throne of my life." Jack leaned forward, his look piercing. "And I'll be a son of bitch if he didn't do it!"

Jack didn't understand what happened. At first, he assumed the meeting was over—that he had used up his time—but the gasps and irregular exit of audience members indicated otherwise. The dead giveaway that he had committed a foul was the senior leader's reaction to the exiting audience, and the disgusted glare he tossed at Jack.

He'd seen that look from his Dad during his growing up years. His Dad would come home drunk, or be angry for whatever reason, scowl at Jack, yell, curse him, take a swing at him, and stalk away.

Just as from his Dad, Jack deemed the senior leader's assessment as authoritative and accurate: *You disgust me.* Jack adopted again the inference and motivating message of his life—*I'm disgusting.*

What he'd done wrong was a mystery, but that he was wrong was evident.

Hank explained it to him later, but by the time their conversation occurred, Jester had had his way with Jack. According to Jester, the circumstances of Jack's life aligned once again—only more comprehensively, more definitively. Jack had it now on good authority that the High King felt about him just as the senior leader did, the First Floor Group, and his Dad before them. It all fit. *I'm disgusting.*

Jack was no fool. His shrewd mind assembled a comprehensive assessment of his former life and an indictment of what he had hoped would be true of him in the Kingdom. *It is a fantasy*, he understood. *Hank, all these others, the King—they're all bullshitting me.*

Jester drove the point home. Jack didn't miss the message.

Of course, it doesn't take a genius to draw the logical conclusion: *I belong in La Faim. That's all I'm worth. I certainly don't fit in the Round Tower, that's for damn sure. I'm a disgrace to the Kingdom.*

By the time Hank got to him, Jack's countenance conveyed all he needed to know. Hank cursed Jester and tried to stem the hemorrhaging of Jack's soul, but in the confusion and demand of the battle, there was little of substance to be done. He would have to wait for the fire fight to die down.

The senior leader marched toward Hank. Jack retreated. His shame was greater than he could bear, not for what he had done, but for who he perceived himself to be.

"I can't believe you brought that man here!" the senior leader began, railing at Hank, as if Hank were personally responsible for what someone else said. "He is an embarrassment. An offense to this group! An affront to the King! He has caused untold harm to...."

Hank bumped up against the senior leader's chest, grabbed his shirt with his fist to keep him from going over backward. "You listen to me! There is a world outside the Round Tower going to hell in a hand-basket. Meanwhile, you and your group are so self-absorbed that you are more concerned with how a man tells what has happened in his life than you are that his life has been transformed by the King. What did you expect? This man has emerged from the darkness and degradation of Zophos' kingdom and begun his walk in the light and you expect him to speak without offense? His whole life was an offense until the King reclaimed him! Mine as well. I was under the impression the same was true of you. Jack got it right tonight. You and your group have it wrong—and not by a little bit!"

Hank let go of the senior leader's shirt. The senior leader straightened and stepped toward Hank. But Hank met him. "Don't start with me. You have sacrificed a child in the Kingdom on the altar of your piety and precept. My patience is spent and your offense is great. Your behavior is repulsive!"

By now a couple of the First Floor Group's volunteer leaders had joined the senior leader. They didn't know exactly what was going on, but they helped the senior leader back away from Hank who smelled of La Faim and whom they figured must be deranged.

Hank turned to go find Jack and attempt some form of damage control. Before he left the auditorium, he stopped and searched out the senior leader with his eyes. Hank pointed at him for a few seconds, then left.

A couple of weeks after the fiasco at the First Floor Group meeting, as he was choosing plumbs at the castle market, Hank felt a touch on his elbow. Caroline Ingram was standing there. They greeted each other cordially before Hank said, "I didn't expect to see you here—during the middle of a work day. Is everything okay?"

Caroline assured him. "I'm just taking a day off to get caught up. You know how it goes—a woman's work is never done."

"So they say," Hank replied.

"You've been busy as well," she noted.

"I have," and Hank proceeded to update her on his endeavors. Nothing too specific. He hated meeting her this way—here. He knew he had to reengage with Caroline and Jake, but he had hoped it would be on his terms rather than fate's. The longer he went not seeing them the more his suspicion, distrust, and guardedness grew.

"I heard about the meeting with the First Floor Group," she said. "Doesn't sound like it went too well."

"No. It went fine early on, splendidly in fact, until Jack used an expletive to describe his enthusiasm over being in the High King's family. Kind of went downhill from there. How'd you hear about it?"

"They were discussing it in the office," she replied.

"I see," his suspicion confirmed. "What'd you hear?"

Caroline seemed evasive. Even in retrospect, he thought she would have been more forthcoming if she was not hiding something from him.

Hank feared anything he said might be used against him. As he looked at Caroline, the deep sadness he had been suffering since the night he realized she was working alongside Letizia Pintaro engulfed him. In the best of times, he didn't fancy himself a conversationalist, but in the dark times he pulled away and crawled inside his emotional cave. The more he distanced, the fewer words there were to speak, and the more loathe he was to try and find some.

He had nothing further to contribute. "Well, I hate to run off," he started. "If a woman's work is never done, then there is no rest for the wicked. I'm afraid I've got lots of territory to cover before the sun sets."

Caroline looked at him with unmistakable sadness. Nodded, a slight smile at the corner of her mouth, tears in each eye.

"Please greet Jake and the kids for me."

She touched his forearm. "Be careful. Will you?"

"Of course. You know me. I'm always watching my back, but why do you say that?"

Caroline ducked her head, looked briefly at the cobblestones in the street, then looked up at him. She shook her head gently from side to side as though conveying regret. "Just be careful." She squeezed his arm and disappeared into the market and shoppers.

"Sir? Sir? You going to buy them plumbs?"

Hank heard the calling, louder than the den of normal noise, and turned to see who was yelling at whom. His eyes met the face of the vendor.

"Well? Are you or ain't you?"

Hank looked at the plumbs he had selected. He'd forgotten what he was doing. He had no appetite, no interest, no motivation to continue. "No, I'm not. I'm not going to purchase the plumbs." He handed the produce unceremoniously to the vendor. "I'm sorry. Thank you anyway."

There was no question that Hank's handlers had become more sophisticated after Jack's presentation. But who exactly escalated the surveillance, he didn't know.

That the senior leader of the First Floor Group would have a security detail was understood. Maybe in addition to the guys watching his residence, Zophos had assigned undercover agents. Perhaps Letizia had stepped up her game, assigned the A-team to him instead of the thugs who had been tagging after him.

Until one of them makes a mistake, it's anyone's guess who the boss is, he thought.

He hated thinking such thoughts, but his Father had warned him that he was a marked man. No sense living in denial. Hank's strong inclination was to believe the spies worked for Letizia. *How else would Caroline have known to warn me?* And sadly, that Caroline knew to warn him also meant she wasn't ignorant of Letizia's questionable business practices.

The thought of Caroline working indirectly for Zophos haunted him worse by the day. He wanted more than anything to ignore it, but to deny the probability would be foolhardy. Magician's counsel echoed in his mind, *Be innocent like a dove, Hank, wise like a snake.* Back in the summer—back in Texas—he'd almost grabbed a Copperhead while cleaning out a wood pile. The image of the camouflaged, coppery-skinned, calculating snake lodged in his mind.

Hank nearly walked the soles off his boots thinking and worrying, running various scenarios through his mind, and crafting contingencies. He wondered if it was wrong to be so obsessed, but as he discussed the matter with Magician, he concluded it wasn't wrong. Rather, he was being diligent, bringing to bear upon the situation his entire mental, physical, and spiritual faculty.

He lost weight—six or eight pounds in one week, he guessed, judging by the extra notch he had to use in his belt. His mind was razor sharp, though. While he knew this degree of effort wasn't sustainable for long, he was thriving on the intensity. He reassured himself that when the dust settled, he would get away for some rest, maybe even go fishing. But for the time being, he ran his life without slack.

He read more than ever from Vassar's letter, mostly in the morning. In the evening, he considered what he had read. It was amazing how relevant Vassar's words were. *How does he do this?* Hank often wondered. His Brother never ceased to amaze him. *He's cunning—shrewd. The way he manages life is ingenious.* The image of the Copperhead in the wood pile appeared in his mind.

As life unfolded, Vassar's letter provided counsel and encouragement. For several days Hank spent every spare hour contemplating two paragraphs toward the end of the letter:

Things are not going to be easy, Brother! The stakes have risen since we were last in Gnarled Wood. While Zophos is utilizing his shock and awe capabilities in some places, he has switched tactics in the castle. Most of the shock and awe there is a diversion. Always the pragmatist—and opportunist—Zophos is operating in a more clandestine manner. He's pouring exorbitant amounts of money, effort, and personnel into subversion, espionage, and subterfuge. Always there is his illusion of light. He is a deceiver.

The inclination is to engage him at his level, but there is a more powerful weapon. In everything you do, Brother, let your motive be love. Nothing is more powerful because love is the essence of who Father is. When you love, you portray Father, and the only way you can love as he loves is to live from your heart and let Magician's strength bolster you. Read that line again. I'll bet you felt your heart jump, didn't you?

He hadn't reread the last line again as Vassar instructed—he had read it over and over again. He committed it to memory and recited it to himself as he sat in his pension, as he went out, and on his way back home. He encouraged others with Vassar's lines.

These were perilous times. While there remained physical risk for the King's followers in parts of the castle, the more pressing battle around Hank was for hearts and minds. His among them. So he paid attention, guarded his heart as Magician counseled, and stayed focused.

There was no question about the greatest weight he felt. He discussed Caroline and Jake, Ronan, Jack, and the leaders of the small groups with Magician. Concerns for himself were way down his list. His was a confidence forged in the pit, tested in the light, and commissioned by his Father, the High King of Glory. The others though, the younger ones near to his heart, *These are my primary concern*, he knew.

Hank looked up at the portcullis as he passed through the second gate leading into the Round Tower. When he first came to Gnarled

Wood, the Round Tower's administration was religious about controlling ingress and egress. Now though, loyalty to the King was optional for being a member of the Tower. It was impossible to discern who was of the light and who was of the darkness masquerading as light. One source whom Hank respected thought the population of the Round Tower might be half-and-half, fifty percent loyal to the King, fifty percent paying lip service to the King. Of course, no one knew for certain, but even if his source was off by ten percent—or twenty percent—that was still a disturbing statistic. He recalled that Vassar indicated similar numbers. Hank glanced up at the next portcullis, not wanting to appear too curious. The numbers were troubling.

However, while the allegiances within the Round Tower were speculative, Hank took great comfort in the robust growth and effectiveness of the small groups. There were groups all over the castle. There were even several devoted groups inside the Round Tower.

The members cared for one another, supported each other, and spurred each other along in their relationships with the High King. Because of the close-knit, neighborhood composition of most groups, if someone stumbled, was sick, fell on hard times, lost their way in life, or was absent the group responded. Every so often, an issue arose that required a more sophisticated action, but not regularly.

Young people, old people, and folks in between were growing more and more devoted to each other, to the King, to his guidance, and to the Kingdom. They were personalizing the ten tenets of the King's teaching, absorbing them into their lives and daily action, and they were sharing them with others as opportunity arose. No doubt about it, the vision Magician supplied was proving ingeniously effective. The King's battle line was advancing.

Hank made the turn at the last gate, passed under the final portcullis, and emerged into the Tower courtyard. Perhaps more than anything, the small group strategy had cleared away the mystery of the High King as portrayed by the Round Tower.

The message in the Round Tower was that the King resides in the Round Tower. That his standards and wishes are communicated and mediated by the Tower's leadership. That people living outside the Tower's cliques, certainly those in the profane castle, couldn't possibly know the King. Membership in the Tower and acceptance with the King were presented as synonymous. It followed then that the King's pleasure or displeasure was directly correlated to the pleasure or displeasure of the Tower's insiders.

Those endeavoring to find acceptance in the Round Tower—many had given up—labored to make themselves as acceptable to the King as possible, especially after a week working in the pagan castle. With varying degrees of confidence, the people came to the Tower to hear him discussed by Tower insiders and make necessary adjustments to their lives based upon the teaching of the Tower's leaders.

Once people left the Round Tower, or were otherwise outside the direct guidance of sanctioned leadership in the Tower, they proceeded through their days with general ideas attributable to the High King. But how they actually lived, loved, worked, and died was largely dependent upon their own resourcefulness. Most people did what was right in their own eyes because the King of the Tower was unknowable, his rules irrelevant, and his representatives onerously pedantic in their expectations.

He hadn't said it publically, but Hank thought some of the grandiosity and complexity the Tower's leadership created was more about job security than it was caring for the people in their organizations. How they conveyed the High King certainly bore little resemblance to the man Hank knew as Father and called, Papa.

While he knew his logic painted the Round Tower with a broad brush and was a bit oversimplified, these remained troubling themes in Hank's mind, and given the vision Magician had shared with him, apparently they were troubling patterns to him as well. Certainly, there were solid leaders and devoted members of the King's family intertwined with the Tower's culture. However, except for a few renegades, they were marginalized and hard to isolate. In fact, the only way most became isolated was through a misstep that got them expelled from the Tower.

Since being tossed outside the side door of the Tower after his own interrogation, Hank returned frequently to find others lying face-down, bruised, and bound. That was always disheartening, but the good news was that they were now free to know the King without impediment, their minds disabused of the Tower's fog.

You have to hand it to him, Hank thought. *Emulating the light, like he does. Zophos' strategy is ingenious. Devious and devilish, but, ingenious.*

And another thing, Hank thought, making his way through the Tower, *the formality within a number of the Round Tower groups— formality they put forward as representative of the King and his expectation for how we are supposed to communicate with him—is an impediment to close, intimate connection. Maybe I'm overly sensitive, given my history of placing relational filters between Papa and me rather than engaging him face-to-face. I don't know though. Filters aren't good, not with Father anyway.*

He knew his Father's heart could be found midst the formality of the Tower groups, but his light was often diffused by the routines, language, and attire. He knew better than to attribute all formality as sweepingly unrepresentative, but generally speaking he felt formality was the enemy of intimacy.

Clear away the mysterious language, the rules based upon performance and achievement, the high-minded and technical standards, as well as the formality wrongly attributed to the King, and the family had a chance of pulling together. *Get this done*, he thought. *Simplify. Clear away the mystery.*

Ronan was waiting outside the coffee shop—their usual meeting place. He looked like hell, and with Hank's observation of the fact, confirmed he felt like hell as well.

Thankfully, there was a sparse crowd. Hank chose a table in the corner and left the chair facing the wall for his young friend.

Ronan ignored his coffee, clasped his hands in front of his chin, and offered no preamble. He just started talking. Confessing, really. He didn't leave anything out, didn't attempt to diminish his failure, didn't throw Sonya overboard, and didn't pull any punches with Hank. He had no inclination or energy for a cover-up. He was depleted, knew it, and Hank was the only person he knew who might be able to rescue him.

Ronan hadn't lived long enough, nor did he have the self-awareness, to connect the facts of what happened and what he did to form either motive or consequence. All he knew was that he was in a self-made mess. He was confused, disillusioned with himself, and lost in a miasma of guilt.

Hank was disappointed, but he thought of his own tryst with Pity back in his pit of degradation. He listened to his young mentee. The more Ronan talked, the more vivid Hank's recollection of Pity's clammy skin was. Spurred by Jester's urging, he'd slept with Pity in search of relief from disappointment, anger, and loneliness. For that matter, he'd slept with Significance a thousand times in his fantasy. Ronan's confession of sex with Sonya was simply a variation on a theme—a tale of two loves.

He didn't need the details, but Ronan needed to give them. Naming what he did, detailing it, and identifying the fallout were necessary aspects of owning his failure, personalizing his offense, and quantifying the gravity of his mistake. It was a torturous confession, but Hank understood. He'd made plenty of similar confessions himself—to Vassar, Magician, his Father, and others. It was a necessary, awful purging.

As he had begun, without fanfare, Ronan simply stopped when he finished confessing the contents of his conscience. There was no conclusion and no request. He didn't expect anything from Hank. His failure was too egregious for forgiveness, let alone resolution or redemption.

Hank didn't go easy on Ronan. After making certain Ronan understood and concurred as to the gravity of the situation, Hank asked him, "So where does the High King fit in this tale of woe?"

"I know he's disappointed. Has to be. Has to be really disappointed."

"Is that all? Just disappointed?"

Hank kicked the last prop of delusion, pathetic as it was, out from under his young friend. Ronan's hands dropped from under his chin. He extended his arms, knocking over his coffee. His forehead landed on the tabletop. In great sobs he heaved out the tortured words of his lament. "I've gone too far. The King's given up on me, Hank. His light is gone. I don't blame him. I deserve it—deserve everything I'm suffering and more yet. I let him down. Disappointed him—disappointed him too badly to ever get back into his good graces."

Hank motioned for the waiter to toss him a rag. As Ronan convulsed in his chair, Hank stemmed the flow of coffee running back toward its owner. He held the second rag tossed to him in reserve.

Ronan looked up. His face was red, his eyes bloodshot and puffy, mucus drained from his nose, covered his lip, and bridged his mouth to his chin. He wiped at his face with the back of his hand, smearing the physical evidence of his grief from cheek to cheek.

Hank put his left hand on Ronan's shoulder, and with his right used the rag to wipe Ronan's stained face. Ronan heaved, his chest inhaling and exhaling in ungracious gulps and purges. He didn't resist. He didn't have pride enough left to worry about what others might think.

The waitress tossed Hank another damp cloth. He winked at her kindness, noting as well that she had guided incoming customers to the other side of the coffee shop. He wiped Ronan's face again, folded the cloth over, and let him take over.

"Ronan, there are multiple layers to what you have done," Hank began. "Are you listening to me?"

Ronan nodded.

"Look at me then."

It was the first step back from the brink, the first territory retaken from shame. To look another in the eye is to believe you have personal standing.

Ronan looked at Hank, then away.

"I said, look at me, Ronan." Once he engaged, Hank continued, "There are several layers to this situation. Sonya, of course, but also Audie, and perhaps your small group. We'll have to see. But first and foremost, is your relationship to the High King."

At the mention of the King, Ronan's tears flowed again.

Slowly. Carefully. Tenderly, like a father, Hank told Ronan of his own failure with Pity, Significance, and his journey through the pit. He told him of his prideful, arrogant, reluctance to relinquish his mat of self-provision, of how he had lifted his chin to the King in defiance of his authority, claiming instead his right to run his life as he saw fit. He described standing on his mat of self-provision, naked, bruised, and wounded claiming he didn't need anything, that he was capable of going it alone. And, that because of his capability the King owed him mercy.

Ronan listened carefully. Hank was judicious in his telling to be certain Ronan would see the parallels between their failures.

Then Hank pivoted on their common ground.

"Ronan, when you declared loyalty to the High King, you brought everything of yourself to him in response to his pledge to provide everything you need in abundance. Correct?"

Ronan nodded. "That's right, Hank. Everything."

"What about his pledge of faithfulness? Or his pledge of significance? How about esteem? Worth? Value? Position? What about belonging? What about his pledge to make you noteworthy?"

"That's right," he whispered. "He pledged all that."

"Then what were you doing searching for these things in Sonya's arms and thighs?"

Ronan stared at Hank, and Hank didn't blink.

Hank was patient, but unmerciful, as Ronan worked and reworked the problem, trying mightily to avoid the bottom line: irreconcilable, shameful unfaithfulness. To his credit, Ronan was a quicker study than Hank had been. Perhaps it was his younger mind, perhaps it was his mentor's determination to afford his adultery no mercy and his lust no quarter. Ronan's eyes again filled with tears, but these tears were accompanied with a look beyond pain or sorrow. His tears were droplets of horror.

It was bad enough that he stepped out on Audie, but he wasn't married to her. However, there was the astounding realization that his relationship to the King was like a marriage! Who would have thought? But shortly on the heels of this was the undeniable fact that he had slept with Sonya in lust of fulfilling his desires independently of the King's promised provision. One moment he clutched at the grandeur of being loved so completely by the King and the next was horrified at his unfaithfulness with Sonya while searching for what the King pledged was already his.

Hank continued. "Every need. Every desire. Everything you require to live life fully, completely, and victoriously is provided for you by the King. Every time, in every way, that you take matters into your own hand, seeking to meet your own needs or fulfill your own desires, you adulterously leave your first love, compromise your integrity, do violence to your reputation and identity, and screw with the enemy. Do you understand me?"

"I'm not sure."

If the young man was going to rise above this vulnerability upon which Jester capitalized, this principle had to be crystal clear. "What part of 'every' don't you understand, Ronan? Every need. Every desire.

Every thing in heaven and on Earth that is necessary for your wellbeing, the King has pledged on his honor to provide for you. Everything."

Ronan wiped his face and leaned close to Hank. "So anytime I take matters into my own hands—whether small or large—I'm doing again to the King what I've done to him by sleeping with Sonya. Is that what you're saying?"

"That's exactly what I'm saying."

Ronan stared at Hank a long moment. Sat back then, dumbfounded. His failure was greater than he imagined. It wasn't only a breach of his honor, a disservice to Audie and Sonya, and an affront to his reputation, but from the High King's perspective, it was an intimate disregard and indiscretion of his family fidelity.

"Independence is infidelity. Unbelief is adultery. Not only did I violate Sonya, I violated the King." Ronan muttered these realizations with a stricken countenance.

He looked at Hank. Shook his head. "Is there anything to be done?"

"Let me tell you something about the King. Where you are right now is a sorry place to be. You've created a royal mess. It is a poor time to come to the King, tell him how sorry you are, and pledge again your faithfulness when the bed's still warm from the body of another lover. If the King was proud, he would not have you on such terms, Ronan. But he is not proud. He stoops to conquer. I should know."

CHAPTER 20

The Castle

As was his custom, Hank sat at his writing table, drinking his morning coffee while considering Vassar's letter. This morning, he was focused upon the paragraph,

> *No matter if all hell is breaking loose, be at peace, Brother. Greater is he who lives in you than he who rules Gnarled Wood and beyond. That's not hyperbole! Magician is more powerful than Jester and Zophos put together, so don't be afraid if they assemble themselves against you.*

He picked up his coffee and turned around to face the window. The world outside wasn't stirring yet, except for the birds who were up before first light. *Peace?* he mused. *Makes no sense whatsoever, Vassar. Given the craziness of life—all the pressures, the stress within and the fears without—it is remarkable that you counsel me toward peace while all of us on this planet do what's right in our own eyes and create havoc. On second thought: It's not remarkable. It's audacious! Only you would have this perspective, Vassar. Only you. That's why I accept what you have written.*

Hank turned back around to his desk, closed his eyes, and folded his hands. *Magician, squelch my fear, if you would, and help me live in peace. Today, please! No matter what, let's begin now. And thanks in advance. If all hell has not yet broken loose outside this moment of reverie, then when it does, it will be quite an adventure, won't it?*

He folded Vassar's letter and was just placing it inside his satchel when there was a tapping at his door. Visitors at this hour of the morning were either in trouble or up to no good, and lately, the no-good type had increased. Snapping up his dagger, he stuffed his satchel inside his shirt, slipped the blue blade from its sheath, and walked to the door. He opened the port, keeping his face away from the opening just in case. A messenger stood waiting.

Still wary, but reassured by all appearance that the messenger was legitimate, Hank opened the door. He anticipated the worst, but it didn't occur. The messenger, however, recognized Hank's wariness and looked around to see what he was missing.

Feeling relieved, and a little embarrassed, Hank turned his attention to the messenger. The man handed him a sealed note. On the outside, written in a clean script, it simply said, Mr. Henderson. The messenger indicated he had been instructed to wait until the letter was read and responded to. "I will deliver your reply post-haste, Sir."

"Very well." Hank broke the seal and read:

Mr. Henderson:
I would like to meet with you—as soon as possible, please. I will adjust my schedule to meet yours.
Thank you in advance for whatever adjustments you must make.
Sincerely,
Letizia Pintaro

Of all the people in the world, Letizia Pintaro was the last person Hank expected to hear from—first thing in the morning or any time.

Hank stepped to his writing desk and sat down to reply, but his thoughts were scrambled with doubts and curiosity—and candidly, fear. He apologized to the messenger, "I'm sorry. This is going to take a minute. Please be patient."

After deliberating his options, Hank wrote in reply that he would meet her at Hoi Polloi in two hours. The short notice would limit her ability to set a trap and possibly upset her balance. The location was neutral, if not weighted slightly to his advantage as a regular customer.

He thought through the logistics one more time. His plan seemed sound. *I'll know soon enough*, he conceded.

He signed his name, folded the note, and sealed the paper with a glob of wax. He handed the messenger a generous gratuity along with the note, indicating with a stern voice and serious face as he did so, "My reply is urgent and time sensitive!"

By the look on the messenger's face, the money seemed adequate persuasion.

Hank watched the messenger hustle away stuffing the reply deep in his bag. He didn't know what to think next, but the words of his Brother came back to him, "Don't be afraid—even if they assemble themselves against you."

He closed the door and went straight to his bedroom. Taking special care to look professional, but not wasting any time, he dressed for his appointment. It was important that he arrive at Hoi Polloi before Letizia had time to set a trap. Unless she was somewhere other than her home or office, he should beat her to Hoi Polloi with a little time to spare.

He had deliberately not altered his routine in several days in hopes of lulling his handlers into a false sense of confidence that they had him figured out. Tiptoeing down the hallway, as though concerned he might disturb his neighbors, the watcher took note and rose to follow him. Hank started down the steps, being ever-so quiet. The man following assumed Hank continued downstairs, even though he couldn't hear his footfalls on the stair treads, and further assumed his counterparts in the lobby would pick him up from there.

Hank eased through an open window in the stair well and stood outside on a small ledge. More goons assigned to him were sitting thirty feet below, but unless he made noise, they had no inclination to look up. Deftly grabbing window casings, downspouts, and clothes lines he worked his way across the face of the building. Where the adjacent building's roof had an opening, he leaped across the four-foot chasm, landing like a cat. He congratulated himself for his Bourne-like escape, peeked below to see if his handlers had taken notice, and ventured across the roof of the building to find a way down to the street.

Hank approached Hoi Polloi from the back, taking care to check the surrounding neighborhood for anything out of the ordinary. Before going around front, he made certain the side door was unobstructed. He retrieved three bottles from the trash and broke them on the surface of the stoop. Using the toe of his boot, he scattered the shards of glass evenly on the stoop and the steps leading up to the door. He planned to occupy the table inside Hoi Polloi that was closest to this exit should he need it. The broken glass would crunch loudly enough that he could hear if anyone approached the side door.

The waitress greeted him warmly. He apologized for arriving before opening, explained his early meeting, and promised coffee was all he and the other person in his party would need. As he expected, the waitress reassured him he was welcome any time as she poured him a cup of coffee. He carried it to the table by the side exit to wait, listen, and watch.

The normal sounds of the restaurant prior to its opening were interrupted with irregular commotion. Letizia and two men emerged from the kitchen into the dining room. Hank stood from his table near the side exit. He didn't wave or speak.

Letizia pointed the two men to a table on the opposite side of the restaurant and made her way to where Hank stood. As she approached, he moved to help her with her chair. The waitress came, received Letizia's order, and departed.

"You made the appointment difficult for me, Mr. Henderson."

"I would offer an apology, but I intended to make it difficult for you, Ms. Pintaro."

"Why's that?" she inquired.

"Because you are a difficult woman."

"So you are aware of the dual roles I play."

He met her candor with blunt honesty. "I am."

His acknowledgment felt dangerous, but her revelation of the dual roles she played—one legitimate, one sinister—was sufficient information to confirm that his life was over whether he was aware of her dark business or not. Whatever else they discussed, his worry over traps and ambushes prior to her arrival was pointless now. *I know too much, whether I want to or not. She played a trump card before the waitress even brought her coffee—while I'm forced to follow suit. Very cunning, Ms. Pintaro. Very cunning indeed.*

Letizia was silent as the waitress approached, placed the steaming cup before her, refreshed Hank's cup, and departed.

Hank retraced the steps of his life—in the intervening seconds—as only the mind can do. *Will my passage be quick,* he wondered, *or will I succumb over time to torture? Do I have the wherewithal to meet my earthly demise with the confidence of a Prince in the Kingdom of Light? When will Magician depart, and prior to his departure, will he supply me with sufficient mercy for my final campaign? Would I change anything—if I could?* And in the caverns of his heart there resounded a resolute, *No! I wouldn't change a thing!*

"Mr. Henderson, you are a man of honor."

"I try to be."

"Tell me: Does your honor require you to guard a confidence?"

So my passage will be through interrogation, he thought. Hank's neutral gaze turned hard across the table from Letizia.

"Mr. Henderson? I need to know if you can keep a confidence."

"Damn straight! Ms. Pintaro. Wild horses can't quarter me to compromise. I'd forfeit the very character upon which my soul is built if I betrayed a single comment entrusted to me."

The strong response took her aback, but only momentarily. "I'm sure that is true, Mr. Henderson. I'm sure it's true." She was quiet for a minute, but never took her eyes off of his. "I was counting on that being the case."

What's that supposed to mean? Hank wondered. Her "counting on that being the case" didn't fit with her intention of dispatching him.

"May I ask a favor?"

Hank nodded.

"May I call you, Hank?"

He knew she was drawing him in. *Interrogators do such things— appear friendly, and after gaining your trust and hearing your secrets revealed, turn coldly away while the torture is meted out.*

"Sure, Ms. Pintaro. Call me whatever suits you."

She nodded, smiled demurely. "And please, no more Ms. Pintaro. I'm Letizia. Actually, my friends call me Lettie."

"Ms. Pintaro, can we forego this? You and I both know the game's up. Do to me as you will. Take a long time or make it quick. Either way, I'm not your friend and I'm not going to breach the confidences entrusted to me just to save my own skin."

Letizia turned her coffee cup between her hands and stared at the dark liquid. "You do know something about the backside of my professional life, don't you?"

He'd already incriminated himself plenty, but felt no obligation to further reveal what he knew. That would only necessitate in her mind a longer, more tortured exit until she was certain she gleaned from him all she could before his body was broken beyond remedy and released to the eternal.

As long as he was drinking his last, he might as well have another cup. Hank got up from the table and carried his coffee cup to the bar. While he was refilling, he carried the pot to where Letizia's body guards were sitting and refilled their cups. He replaced the pot and returned to his chair across from his executioner.

"I thought for a moment you were leaving," she said.

"Right. Like I could just walk away after this little chat."

"Hank, you have affirmed your honor, and I appreciate that. More than you know, in fact. I give you my word as well: I will not reveal a single word of our discussion, nor will I ever acknowledge you met with me."

"I don't follow you," Hank said.

"As you have implicitly acknowledged, quite shrewdly I might add, it would tarnish your reputation should anyone find out you have purposefully met with me. I don't want that for you, but I need help."

Hank chuckled at her. "And what sort of help can I possibly provide you, Ms. Pintaro?"

She hesitated.

For effect, Hank thought.

She looked around to be certain there was no one close.

As though I don't know what she's about to ask, Hank mused.

She looked up at him.

Like this is going to be a surprise, he thought.

Letizia took a deep breath, exhaled, and stated flatly, "Hank, I have renounced my service to Zophos and declared my allegiance to the High King."

"I beg your pardon."

"I'm not happy about it, but I'm convinced it was what I needed to do. I have no idea what's next. Where I go from this point…? I have no one to talk with about what I've done. I'm scared. Confused. Disillusioned. The conflict inside me is more than I can bear."

Hank interrupted her. "When did this occur?"

"Almost three months ago. I couldn't sleep. There were so many little things that accumulated, things I couldn't explain, that came to me out of the blue. Before I knew it, I was hemmed in. The weight of evidence on behalf of the High King's legitimacy was so great I couldn't deny his reign any longer."

"I see," Hank said, still wary of this powerful woman. "What did you do?"

"Do you remember the night I stopped by the Ingram's home and you were there?"

"Of course. I walked you home."

"Yes. You did. And I really was appreciative. I know you didn't believe me when I thanked you."

Hank waved off her apology. "Glad to do it. You needed a bit of assistance, was all. So that night, I escorted you home."

"That was the culmination. I couldn't stand any more conflict in my head."

"What sort of conflict?" Hank asked.

"Conflict between Zophos and the King. Conflict between how I was living my life and how people like Caroline and Jake are living theirs. Conflict over what I was doing and how my beliefs were evolving."

At the mention of Caroline's name, Hank asked, "How much of what you do is Caroline privy to?"

"You mean, the cash side of my business?"

Hank nodded.

"I live in two worlds, Hank, with a substantial barrier between them. Not even Bernie knows all that I do. Caroline is a wonderful woman—as sharp as they come—but she hasn't the faintest notion of my back-office business."

Hank was relieved to hear this about Caroline, but he was far too skeptical to swallow Letizia's assurance hook, line, and sinker. After all, thanks to her, he hadn't slept soundly since arriving in the castle.

Letizia continued. "In fact, a significant part of the conflict I feel—or maybe guilt is a better word—is that I'm responsible for Jake Ingram's disability."

That's a huge confession! He tested her. "I'm sorry. What do you mean?"

"Jake used to work for the First Floor Group. He was in charge of the youth program. In his enthusiasm, he led a resurgence of devotion to the King and his teachings that swept through the young people in the First Floor Group and spread to the schools and beyond."

"I've heard about that."

Letizia acknowledged with a nod. "My superior and I discussed what was occurring and knew we had to take compensatory action to get things under control. My boss, Ennui...." Letizia paused. "Hank, I am telling you so many confidential pieces of information, you and I will both hang if anyone ever finds out what I have disclosed."

Hank grimaced and nodded. "I know, Letizia. I appreciate your trust. What you say is safe with me. Go on."

She took another deep breath, and exhaled. "Ennui and I determined that I would work directly—or my staff would work directly—with Jake, the young people, and their parents. Ennui would work directly with the senior leader of the First Floor Group."

"I see," Hank stated.

"I'm not very good with names, and I didn't remember Jake's, but I remember details. I hadn't exactly forgotten about him, but I had no reason to think about him. I got what I needed, followed up, and reported to Ennui. Life goes on—even life on the dark side."

"I understand."

"I had no idea who Caroline was when Bernie hired her. I run a tight office. I need people who produce, and Caroline distinguished herself from the first day she came to work."

"How'd you find out about Jake and her?" Hank asked.

"After the office dinner party—the event where you sat at my table. You played your cards very close to your vest, by the way."

"I'll take that as a compliment, Letizia."

"Thank you for calling me, Letizia. This is so hard. I appreciate your graciousness. I know I deserve nothing but derision from you."

This lady is amazing, Hank thought. *She is either the most incredible actress I've ever encountered or she has indeed converted.*

"What you deserve is well beyond my pay grade and none of my business, Letizia. Please go on with your story."

She thought. "Where was I?"

"The dinner party. You were about to tell me how you made the connection between Jake and Caroline."

"Right. Bernie made the connection actually. He and I meet each week. Not long after the dinner meeting, his reports continued to contain more and more glowing comments about Caroline, and one day I asked him what happened to her husband. As far as Bernie knew, Jake was accosted, robbed, and beaten for the contents of his pockets, which were next to nothing."

Hank helped her. "But as Bernie related more of the details, you put the pieces together."

Letizia nodded. "You've got the picture. There are any number of others too, just like Jake. The burden is more than I can bear."

"I can only imagine, but we'll talk about that later. You've not told me about declaring your allegiance to the King."

"After you walked me home, I changed clothes, poured a strong whiskey, and retired to my study to think."

"Whiskey, huh? That may be the only thing you and I have in common, Letizia."

She smiled, nodded. "I spent several hours—into the wee hours of the morning—thinking through the implications of what I knew about the King, my life, other's lives like Jake Ingram, and what it would mean for me to switch sides."

Hank's nods coached her forward.

"There came a moment, standing in the middle of my study, after considering all the evidence to the best of my ability, that I concluded I had been duped. Deceived by Zophos, my own ability, and intoxicated with my power, authority, and position."

"What'd you do?"

"I knelt down and yielded my life and loyalty to the High King." She recounted her decision flatly.

"What happened then?"

"I don't know, really. I meant it, meant what I pledged, but I don't know what to do. I don't know how to sort out my life, don't know what's expected of me. That's why I've come to you."

"How'd you feel after you made your decision?"

"Truthfully?" Letizia asked.

Hank nodded.

"Truthfully, I was unhappy. I don't know what I expected, but I wasn't expecting to be unhappy. I was already unhappy. I didn't need to be more so, but I was—and still am. Everything is gone, Hank. Everything I've built, no matter how dark, is porous. There is no meaning. No joy. No matter what I pour into my soul since that night, whether things of Zophos or things of the King, it passes right through. I feel like I'm a shell. No one is home in my soul."

"I understand," Hank said.

"I'm so sorry," she said. "I know I've put you in a terrible bind coming here. But I didn't know where to turn. Didn't know what else to do."

Hank nodded. "Tell you what. I'll be a lot happier if I make a run to the men's room. I'll just be a moment."

Letizia turned to look at her body guards. One motioned, as if asking if she wanted him to follow Hank. She shook her head.

As Hank sat again, she said, "Thanks for coming back. If I were you, I wouldn't have."

While he was away, Hank talked things over with Magician. There were no words of warning from his companion, and his only words of wisdom were, *What have you got to lose by believing her?*

"First of all, thank you for talking to me. Thank you for sharing your story. As promised, your words are safe with me. Unless you choose to tell someone, no one will ever know we've met."

"Thank you," she said.

"Sure. No problem. Now second, there is a great deal we need to discuss—more than we could ever cover this morning. I've got a few thoughts for you to consider—plenty for one meeting. I'll let you digest them and then, if you wish, we can meet again and talk further. Fair enough?"

"More than fair," she agreed.

"Good," Hank confirmed. "Now, you've made a monumental decision to declare your allegiance to the High King. That means that at some level you've decided that what he teaches and how he governs is worthy of your loyalty and submission. Correct?"

"That's right. And I've noticed that since I made my decision, there has been a deep desire to know more about him."

"Very good. That means you are hearing—in your heart—from the Kingdom's Wizard, Magician. He's a profound, amazing soul. More about him later. Back to what the King teaches, okay?"

"I'm with you," Letizia said.

"When you turned from serving Zophos and the Dark Army, and declared your allegiance to the High King and the Army of Light, something profound occurred. More than just switching sides, with your declaration the King shined his light into your heart, Letizia. His light dispelled the darkness and left your heart vacant, devoid of the darkness that had been pervasive."

"That sounds like what happened, but what's it mean?"

"In the High King's wisdom, he chose to embody his light in his firstborn son, Crown Prince Vassar, whom he sent into Gnarled Wood."

"I know of the Crown Prince," she said.

"Your declaration of allegiance to the King is the first step, the statement of your intention. All that remains is for you to ask the light of the world—Vassar—to take up permanent residence in your heart, Letizia. Ask him to engulf with his light the void that your allegiance to the King created. If you do this, the Kingdom's light and life embodied in Magician will fill you."

Letizia's eyes were moist and she was spinning her coffee cup again.

"Hank, that sounds lovely. I would like nothing better." She thought, sadness consuming her. "Yes, I would like that," she mused. "But I could never do that. I could never make that request."

"And why not?" he asked her.

"Hank, if you knew all that I have done against the King, the Crown Prince—all the people I've hurt. I'm not a nice lady. Vassar is on my list—at the top, actually."

What list? Hank thought, then realized she probably meant her hit list.

Hank shook the thought of the list from his mind and focused on what he believed to be true about the King's redemption. "That's just it, Letizia. The King doesn't ask nor expect you to become nice in advance of placing his throne inside your heart."

"Something's got to change," she said. "He can't live within the dark confines of my soul, and I don't want him to. I want to be different. But of course, I know that's not possible. Can a leopard change its spots?"

"Lettie, listen to me. The King doesn't expect you to change. He intends to change you himself, and to do so as he sees fit. He assumes the task of redemption. All he asks of you is an invitation to take up residence within your heart."

"And then what, Hank?"

"Then, he will come in via Vassar and make your heart his home. He will shine his light in your heart and out through your life. He will inscribe his desires upon the walls of your heart, and through Magician, will counsel you regarding his desires until they become your desires. Lettie, the King will change you from the inside out through the provisions of his Kingdom embodied in Vassar."

"That's it?"

"That's it."

"And then?" she asked.

"And then I guarantee you that the porous, empty vacuum you described earlier will go away and the void will be filled to overflowing with the light of joy."

"I want to believe you," she said.

"Then do so, Lettie. I'm telling you the truth. What have I got to lose? There is no reason I shouldn't tell you what will make your life whole?"

"What about the darkness? The evil I have done?"

"I don't fully know. I know this though, the King is aware of what you've done, and he's made provision to forgive you for every offense against him, his Kingdom, and his people, including your years of service in the Dark Army. I don't know how he will work out the details, but he will."

"Hmm." She was pondering hard over forgiveness. It was an unknown concept to her. In her world, it was an eye for an eye and a tooth for a tooth.

"First things first. You need to decide what you are going to do with the light of the world, Crown Prince Vassar. Are you going to invite him into your heart and ask him to fill you with Magician's joy, or are you going to endeavor to create light for yourself through reparations and self-effort?"

"No. I'm not interested in that, Hank. There are insufficient reparations available for what I've done. As to self-effort, I've tried that."

They both laughed at her unintentional play on words. The laugh helped ease the considerable intensity at the table.

"It would appear I need to make another declaration of intent. I would be lying if I told you I understand all that you've said about the King, Vassar, and Magician."

"I would lie if I told you I fully understand," Hank said.

"Would it be okay if I stayed in touch, Hank?"

"It's more than okay, Lettie. I must admit, I was very skeptical about this meeting."

"And with good reason," she confirmed.

"I would be delighted to hear from you when you are ready," Hank said.

"Very well. Thank you again. I'll be in touch."

Letizia stood, as did Hank.

"Oh, and by the way," she said, "the men watching you?"

Hank cocked his head, listening.

"I've instructed them to make certain nothing happens to you."

He smiled. "Take care, Lettie."

She and her two body guards exited through the front door. Hank ate an early lunch and left through the back door. He walked home the long way, stopping by an out-of-the way shop to visit with a vendor he knew. The merchant's family made wine—from grapes on his Father's land. It was the best wine Hank had found in the castle or surrounding area. He bought a bottle.

Chapter 21

The Castle

Two small groups loyal to the King met in an ethnic area buried in the eastern part of the castle. Their neighborhoods were in transition.

The economy of one neighborhood was stable, but the population wasn't. Still, it was a desirable area filled with older people who had lived in their homes their whole lives, but as they died off, young families were moving in. The small group was comprised of neighbors whose ages covered a broad span.

The small group flourished and was soon three. With each division, the members' geographic proximity to each other tightened.

The older people cared for the younger like adult children, and the younger cared for the older like surrogate parents. When an older one became a widow, the group closed in around the grieving person with literal and emotional arms of support. Young marriages were bolstered by the steadiness of long-time unions. As financial downturns occurred, they shared the reversal. Children had the advantage of their friends, their parents' peers, and the life-lessons of grey-headed years.

If a family made a pot of stew and had extra, a family member went out and invited members of the small group to join them. If someone was in need, the small group supplied it. If there was a celebration, the small group joined with joy and recognition.

Within the small groups, the members shared life together. Their common bond was their place in the Kingdom and their relationship with the King. In all aspects of life, they demonstrated to one another the love, supply, and grace they knew was theirs as participants in the life and light of the King.

Opportunities to discuss the King and his Kingdom with neighbors came naturally; those not in a small group, heard and asked. There was little need to convince those not loyal to the King to consider his claims and invitation to relationship. The way the small group members loved and cared for one another stood in such stark contrast to life outside the Kingdom that they were inclined to accept whatever it was that created such affinity.

When the groups met, formally or informally, the conversation inevitably turned to one of the King's ten tenets. Each principle was fundamental to life, relationship, and wellbeing. Like all basics, the tenets were revisited regularly. As proficiency flourished, so too the members' lives.

Not far from this neighborhood was another that was in economic transition. With the struggling economy and financial stress came the customary issues. There was substance abuse, spousal and child abuse, and violence from frustrated people stressed to their breaking points. Some were working two, three jobs to make ends meet. Some survived tenuously as day-laborers. Others had given up hope of finding work. There were no luxuries. Financial need was rampant.

Like the more stable neighborhood, there was a small group of the King's followers meeting in this area. They studied the same materials and sought to form their lives around the same, ten principles as the other groups in their quest to live by and demonstrate the life of the King.

When they met together, they also shared life with one another and were acquainted with each member's struggles. Throughout the week, they supported the weak, encouraged the fainthearted, cared for the poor, and loved one another as they knew the King loved them.

Just as in their counterpart groups, their relationships and numbers increased. The greatest challenge they faced wasn't economic but the numbers of people coming to faith in the King. As their numbers increased, the density of King-followers increased in that geographic region, and the proximate closeness of the members grew tighter.

Reports of growth were imprecise. It wasn't uncommon for Hank or another leader to be contacted by a complete stranger who was facilitating a group. The pressures of life and the enemies of the King were certainly unpleasant, but the stressors were proving the greatest catalyst to growth in the Kingdom anyone had ever encountered.

Even within the Round Tower there was change. The committed followers of the King who were members of the Tower became part of the resurgence. They too met in geographically centralized small groups, experienced connection with other loyalists, flourished alongside their comrades, appropriated the King's ten tenets for themselves, and carried their focused zeal with them into the Tower's apathetic, staid routine.

That this was occurring, was known. How it was occurring, was also known. What to do to stop it was a conundrum that had Ennui and her staff stumped.

How can you stop life? People talk, live; they share, they meet on the streets, over drinks, and meals. One can't monitor every meeting, every conversation, every serendipitous encounter. Controlling the growth of the King's light and life was like harnessing the wind. Ennui couldn't even get an accurate count on group numbers, let alone group membership.

Zophos ranted and raved, and for her part, so did Ennui. The momentum they had worked hard to build was eroding and there wasn't a thing they could do about it. All meetings across the spectrum of the Dark Army's administration came to the same, frustrating conclusion: Until someone comes up with a workable plan, the only thing to do is increase stress across the entire castle and in all quarters of the Round Tower. "Men's souls will grow faint under the weight of this load!" Zophos declared.

Whether this was true or not, was irrelevant. In the first place, Zophos ordered it. In the second, no one had a better idea. Never mind that the history of the world did not bear his belief out as valid.

Quite the contrary. Increased stress always worked in the King's favor. However, Zophos' personal stress was so great he had no alternative but to project it onto mankind in hope of finding relief.

The most sophisticated aspect of Zophos' plan, he put forward as a new innovation. It was encompassed in his definition of "tension." It sounded like the same thing to his subordinates—the same initiative he put forward at their last conference—but who dared question? In corporate-think, a fresh label was as good as a new idea.

"There are many kinds of tension," Zophos lectured, during his plenary session with senior staff. "Use them all," he dictated.

Of course, Zophos' staff knew that this liberty-to-act actually meant, as long as it works and makes me look good—so I can take credit. Those things that didn't work were certain to be labeled insubordination. The staff knew they were damned if they did and damned if they didn't, but there was no other option.

"There are the obvious points of tension such as money, health, children's stability, and job transitions," the dark lord of Gnarled Wood rehearsed. "But there are other stressors—more abstract, yet equally effective." Zophos nodded at a terrified assistant to put the first diagram on the easel. "Apathy itself creates despondency, depression, and demoralization. I've instituted this quite successfully within the Round Tower. It is tested and tried. Utilize it to its fullest," he exhorted. Commanded.

It made Ennui mad that Zophos referenced her signature program—apathy—as if it was his idea. She raged against him in her depths—her disposition expressionless, her composition composed, her gut a cauldron.

"Next chart!" he demanded. "Try placing visionary people in dead-end jobs. Manipulate the bureaucracy, the hiring structure, and human resources. Do this to everyone, but target the King's sheep-people. Blind followers! Make stress pervasive. Create tension!" he recalled, resurrecting the operative term from his first chart. "Take control of the command structure. Position compartmentalized managers over outside-the-box thinkers. Stifle the human spirit. It is fragile, frail—the King fancies it created in his image. It is easily broken. Smallness and narrowness burn out the human soul. Instill doubt. Build limitation."

At no time was suffering to be left simply at the feet of fate. All hardship, stress, tension, and injustice, no matter how insignificant, were to be placed at the feet of the culpable King regardless of whether the accusation was direct, oblique, or even rational.

Zophos knew the freedom of human will was sacrosanct to the King. There was no situation, circumstance, or cause to justify the slightest infringement of his dominance upon mankind's freedom of choice.

Since conditions in the Tower, the castle, and Gnarled Wood were the consequences of man's best judgment, the King dared not routinely adjust the fallout of mankind's choices—regardless of how awful the suffering. For his part, Zophos pitted the atrocious suffering of humanity against the King's declared love, goodness, and personal ability to abolish their suffering. As a result, it seemed circumstantially as though suffering, tumult, and storm were acts of the King. In fact, many called calamity just that!

In Zophos' scheme, Jester was the logical person to speak to humanity, accusing the King for his duplicity—and accusing clueless mankind of being fools for believing that the King is good, like he claimed. There probably wasn't a soul alive that hadn't heard in their thoughts, *If he (the King) really loved me, then he would…*, and the sentence would conclude with Jester's correlation between the all-powerful King's alleged failure to alter circumstantial discomfort for those whom he purported to care about.

"Whatever it takes!" Zophos screamed. His staff knew to cheer at this point—with claps, whistles, rants, and raves.

But it wasn't all show and no substance. "There is no greater offense to the human psyche than seeing the least among them suffer," the fallen Star of the Morning instructed.

Children were neither here nor there to him. They couldn't make a responsible declaration of loyalty to the King until they matured, so until they reached that age, he abused them indiscriminately to offend the adults who were either loyal to the King or considering his claims.

Zophos created orphans, lame, abused, and malformed. Throughout Gnarled Wood, these defenseless children were abandoned to exposure, rejected, disabled, impeded, and compromised. They suffered horrific, wretched diseases over which they cried and clung to anyone for solace.

Others were aborted in the confines of their wombs, recoiling from the wires and rods that poked them to death in their mothers, the ones designated to nurture and protect them while dependent and vulnerable. And when their gaping gasps and tears were spent, unable to escape destruction, their eyes dimmed and their tiny lives concluded.

Thousands upon thousands, millions and millions—Zophos convulsed, dismembered, slaughtered, and broke them beyond remedy. Mankind resolved this suffering as "individual choice" that lacked either mercy or relent, but even the best and brightest were unable to reconcile except through blatant denial this genocide of the most vulnerable.

Humanity was caught in the middle.

At one end of the spectrum was the idea of absolute evil, at the other, the idea of absolute good. Zophos versus the High King.

Zophos marketed himself as figurative—a notion, a figment of imagination, a character akin to the fictional monsters of fairy tales. He branded the King as literal—professing to be good, loving, and omnipotent. The implication was clear: There is no culpability in a figurative, imaginary evil. To believe so is delusional, irrational even. But there is culpability in one who is literal, claiming to be good and all-powerful.

Why doesn't he do something? was the constant doubt, voiced by Jester, to the minds of humanity. Encompassed with arrays of unspeakable, irreconcilable, and senseless suffering mankind pointed angry fingers at the King.

The adults—young and old—were appalled at the abuse of the children. With the growing numbers of sufferers and heinous abuses, many among mankind were overwhelmed. Most didn't have any idea, presuming they even had the inclination, how to think about the plight of the marginalized.

In some sections of the castle, the infirmed were eliminated. In some parts, abortion was rampant. In other sectors, the children were left to fend for themselves and could be seen out and about on the streets begging. They lived in the sewers and caves and gutters, which to some minds, was unacceptable because it reflected badly upon their area of the castle. These tended to cloister their children into ramshackle dwellings, removed from society, and surrounded by walls where masses of unwanted were shielded from the public eye. On the other side of the walls, the vulnerable subsisted in their own waste, without bond, by whatever means; ruined humans, destitute regarding the glorious dreams of humanity.

A few organizations attempted to make a difference in the lives of the most vulnerable, but their capacities were soon overwhelmed by the stressors of budget, bureaucracy, crowding, insufficient staff, societal indifference, and…. The list was long.

Others—capitalists—sold the unfortunate and unwanted who were most desirable in a free-market economy not unlike other commodity markets. The less desirable because of color, impediment, appearance, origin, or age remained behind the walls or were wards within the overwhelmed system. Intoxicated by denial, the sweep of society deemed this the best that could be done and turned their attention to smaller matters inflated with grandiosity to assuage their consciences and obscure the discomfiture of need.

The cycle of Zophos' hopelessness spun like a gyro, creating its own direction, spinning under its own force. His plan was working. Only time would tell if his plan ultimately worked.

But in sectors of the castle where the King's small groups proliferated, the membership had the capacity to make a difference. And they did!

These groups courageously, and at great personal sacrifice, took in the orphaned, the abused, and the infirmed and cared for them—children, women, disenfranchised, diseased. At first, the burden seemed as though it would sink the tiny vessels of the small groups, and a few it did, but the majority flourished in matters important to the King and his Kingdom.

It wasn't long until those thrown away, marginalized, and rejected matured into those who wanted to know, "Why did you care for me?"

Zophos' strategy, as appalling as it was, backfired. His effort to discredit the King established the King.

When asked, "Why did you care for me?" the answer given was compelling, "The King cares about you and so do I, so do the people in the family of our small group. We have shown light to you because the light shone in us. Join us! Walk with us in the light."

From there, it was a short step for the rejected and compromised to throw the full weight of their souls into the King's waiting embrace. The groups grew in number as the King's followers grew in number. Zeal for the King increased exponentially in response to the personal and social pressures upon them.

The Round Tower was the only place where conversion to the King's Kingdom didn't explode. Largely shielded from outside interference, governed by strict and rigid standards, reassured that they were already engaged in the King's work when they made second-hand contribution to work in the castle, and languishing in the apathy associated with a limited vision for life, the culture inside the Tower continued collapsing under its own weight.

Membership stagnated, and with it, the precious numbers used to validate their success and justify their existence. Numerical growth! That became the rallying cry among the Tower's leadership.

But the belief that growth was merely stagnant was an illusion. When closely examined, most of the large groups within the Round Tower were experiencing higher death rates than birth rates. The growth they celebrated here and there was a shell game. In truth, Tower membership shuffled from sanctioned group to sanctioned group creating an illusion of growth. Since impressive numbers were the calling cards among Tower leadership, impressive numbers were reported when they mixed at professional meetings. To do otherwise was unprofessional. Anything less was said to reflect poorly on the King.

The Tower was in a death spiral. Perhaps they didn't know it—or denied it. Either way, they looked once again to physical plants and programs to rectify the discouraging numbers report that plagued their staff meetings.

The Round Tower's leadership rummaged through their archives and basements, dusting off the glories of yesteryear, and launched campaigns that in appearance and cadence were reminiscent of noble causes gone by. Consultants were brought in, experts long-in-the-tooth, who talked of what was once done as indicative of the King's will for what should be done.

Yesterday's strategy was inaugurated as today's cause, corroborated by a critical mass of leaders, each relaying thoughts to their colleagues via the professional grapevine. They attributed their plan of action to the King—even though he was not consulted.

The alternative was to go ask the King. Not say you asked, but go ask him. Not take a peer's word for it, but go visit with the King.

Who had time for that?

The Round Tower was in motion—constant, busy, a production of activities affirming viability. The band played. The leaders talked. Committees formed—and met, and met. Coordination. Themes. Printing. Banners. Special deliveries to membership. Event dinners. Participation was paramount, and the people followed. It was glorious—the program and production. Activity was indicator enough to demonstrate the Tower was engaged in noble endeavor.

"We are marching, marching, marching," they sang. The destination was not specified, only the goal for greater membership.

Leadership attributed the activity to the King. They said it was visionary. They called it a growth plan for today, tomorrow, and the future of the Kingdom. They said the King would be honored—which if one stopped to consider, sounded as if he didn't know about the Tower's initiatives and would be surprised—and pleased, but later on. At that point, one had to assume the King would be better equipped to achieve his Kingdom goals. The thought of what might become of the King and his Kingdom were it not for the Round Tower was inspiring.

"The numbers will be checked later—after the initiative is complete," Zophos instructed. "It isn't reasonable to track them during development and roll-out. Decline should be expected during the inconvenience of development."

In the Round Tower, contingencies were made to explain numerical discrepancy to the committees. Both attrition and activity in the Tower were attributed to the King. Everything looked and felt comprehensive. The Kingdom was under control.

Ennui carefully superintended the attrition. It was the one bright spot in her meetings with Zophos. That the Round Tower was filled with activity was neither here nor there.

Much to her surprise and delight, when Caroline opened the door, there stood Hank. It wasn't like old times; it was awkward. He had avoided them for several weeks, and his absence could only mean that they'd done something, or he'd done something—they didn't know which—to create distance.

"Why, Hank? How nice to see you!" Caroline said. Her greeting was warm and genuine, but knowing her as well as he did, Hank knew it was also measured. Stepping into the home, the familiar smell, the pictures, sounds—all of that flooded back and he realized how much he missed what used to be.

He presented her with the bottle of wine he'd purchased the day before, telling her it was the best he knew of in the castle. He intentionally arrived mid-afternoon—to test the waters. If they accepted him as a guest, he would stay for a few minutes and depart before the dinner hour. If they accepted him as family, he would stay for the evening, as he used to do.

Before he had the opportunity to say much of anything, Caroline and Jake and the kids were pulling him deeper into their home, immersing him in acceptance, testing him with unabashed affection to see if he was the same man he used to be. Overcome with relief, Hank knelt on the floor, wrapping his arms around the children, kissing them on the head, and whispering to them how much he had missed them and that he was sorry he had been away. "Never again," he promised.

Jake stood close, proudly observing his children extend his family's mercy in abundant measure. He who routinely accepted the strong arm of another to help him to his feet, extended his hand to Hank, helping him up from the floor. Before letting go of Hank's hand, Jake pulled him close and hugged him.

Caroline was last. The more cunning of the two, she had been more skeptical of Hank's absence, and now of his presence and peace offering of wine. She was a lot like Hank in that way. Slow to trust, shrewd, but once invested, loyal to a fault. If spurned, wary of investing again. She wrapped her arms around Hank's waist, hugging him tightly as if to make up for all the lost hugs.

Caroline was a complex person. Hank appreciated this about her. He expected she would suggest they sit in the living area, but instead she directed them to the kitchen table. That she invited him to the table was her sign of openness.

Hank wasted no time on small talk. "I've been absent, distant. I've avoided you and I've hurt you and the children. I want you to know I'm sorry and hope you can find it in your hearts to forgive me."

"What happened? Did we do something to offend you?" Jake asked.

"No. You didn't do anything. Nothing at all."

"What then?" Caroline pressed, as he figured she would—hoped she would, to help him purge the burden under which he labored.

"It was you, Caroline. I feared you, feared what you might know." He had struggled mightily with what to say about the cause for his distance. By revealing the source of his caution, he would shatter her innocence about working for Letizia Pintaro. He couldn't tell her about his meeting with Letizia and her conversion to the faith without compromising his honor and placing Caroline in a double bind. He resolved his conundrum by deciding to believe in Caroline.

"Feared me—and what I know? I don't understand," she said.

"No. I realize now you don't understand, and don't know, but it took some time for me to come to that conclusion. Let me explain."

Hank proceeded to carefully reconstruct the events of the last weeks, beginning with the night Letizia dropped by their home unannounced and he discovered she was Caroline's boss.

"But what's that got to do with anything? I thought you knew," she stated.

Hank explained that the proximity of their relationship hadn't been clear to him. "I knew you worked in her office, but I assumed you and Letizia rarely, if ever, crossed paths. When it dawned on me that you and Letizia worked closely, it undid me."

Caroline was guarded. "So why is that a problem?"

"As it turns out, it's not a problem, Caroline. But I didn't know that until recently." Hank felt his defenses rising.

"Okay?" Caroline said. "But what's the problem with Ms. Pintaro?

Why is she a concern to you—and me by association?"

He wondered if he should have waited to come to Caroline and Jake—until after they knew about Letizia. *But I thought about it, discussed it with Magician,* he reassured his mind. *Meeting with them now versus later is the better choice,* he concluded again, as he had decided a hundred times already. *I would rather be guilty of believing in our relationship ahead of time than confessing my doubts about it after they hear from Letizia and put the pieces of my absence together.*

"I want you to know," he began, "I've labored over how to tell you this. There's no good way to say what's on my mind."

"Tell us, Hank." Jake's admonition was forcefully clear.

Hank took a deep breath and began. "There's a back side to the office where you work, Caroline. Letizia is a high ranking officer in the Dark Army."

"You can't be serious!" Caroline exclaimed. "How do you know this?"

Jake chimed in, "How long have you known this?"

Hank recounted his suspicions of Letizia from his earliest days in the castle. He also reminded them of when he was attacked on the gravel bar beside the river. "I got enough information out of one of the wounded before he died to implicate Letizia."

Caroline was dumbstruck. Jake was worried for his wife's safety.

Hank reassured them. "I have additional information that I cannot share with you right now. While you should be careful, I have every reason to believe you are not in as much danger as you might fear from what I've shared."

"Then why in hell have you told us this?" Jake asked, anger and worry fueling his reaction.

Hank hung his head. He was halfway expecting the anger, but it landed heavy and hard. "I told you to demonstrate the value I place on our relationship. And, I didn't want you to find out later and discover I knew all along. You would have felt compromised—by me, not by…."

Hank didn't say Letizia's name. "I'd rather you...." Hank shrugged his shoulders. His hopefulness was sinking. He was losing Caroline and Jake to Letizia and his espoused integrity. "I told you because there was no way not to and adequately explain my absence from you and your kids. No way not to and be a good friend to you."

There was silence at the table. Caroline arose to check on the kids. Jake got up to go to the bathroom. Caroline and Jake moved around the house while Hank sat at the table.

Finally Hank said to Jake, "Would you like for me to leave?"

Jake snapped, "I think you've done sufficient damage for one evening. You've dumped your guilty conscience on my wife—to remedy your fouled up idea of loyalty!" Jake moved aggressively through the room, chair to chair. "Leaving us to clean up the mess is perfectly reasonable. Leave, damn you!"

Hank felt wretched. He was trying to do the right thing. Their response was his worst nightmare.

The lights in his soul blinked, flickered, dimmed. He felt the besieging, the surge. He heard the order to abandon ship. Looked, saw dark water rushing, boiling, swirling into his vessel's compartment. He cast about, sinking without so much as a thimble with which to bail.

He took a chair in the corner, as far removed as he could be while remaining in the same room.

He sat hoping for an opening that would signal he could reenter their lives, some indicator he could participate in cleaning up the mess. No opening came. He was ignored.

After a time, listing badly, he let himself out of the house. He stepped away, backward, looked one more time, and watched his fond memories with the Ingrams sink, claimed by deep darkness, to be entombed under tumult.

He closed the door after himself, checked that it was secure. A slight effort, granted, but it was his final responsibility.

Hank spent the evening packing. He was up early the next morning, and in spite of Letizia's disclosure that the men watching him were there to ensure his safety, he left through an undisclosed route and made his way through side streets to the outskirts of the castle.

He didn't know Jackson Gutmann personally, only by reputation. Ever since he and Vassar had first trekked up Malden Creek with llamas, he'd dreamed of taking another animal-supported trip. He had inquired here and there about pack animals—just dreaming—and one name came up more than any other: Jackson Gutmann.

Hank found Mr. Gutmann in back of his barn forging a repair to a wagon tongue. He introduced himself and told him he was looking to rent a donkey for a pack trip. Unlike the difficulty of finding a llama outfitter in Montana, Hank's request made perfect sense to Mr. Gutmann—except for the nonsense of renting. Mr. Gutmann had just what Hank needed, a five-year old jenny. "She's for sale though, Mr. Henderson, not for rent."

Hank wasn't in the mood to negotiate. He just wanted to get moving, and truth be known, the jenny was cheaper than what he was prepared to pay in rent. So after a handshake, Hank was the proud owner of a donkey named, Celia.

Hank followed Mr. Gutmann into the pasture where he introduced him to the newest member of the Henderson family. Celia was ugly as a board fence with a grayish-black back and head, a sort of off-white belly and muzzle, and more or less black legs from the knees down. Her coat was wooly, her eyes slanted, and her ears were ridiculously long but perky. More important than appearance though, Celia seemed compliant and came right up to investigate him.

Hank asked Mr. Gutmann a few pertinent questions about donkeys in general and Celia in particular. Her saddle was similar enough to those the llamas used that he felt comfortable saddling her and lashing the packs in place.

When he departed, the only thing in Celia's packs was a hobble.

Hank didn't feel like messing with Celia, and perhaps she sensed that, because she followed him without incident or complaint in spite of donkeys being cautious souls. By mid morning, Hank had purchased supplies for Celia and himself, including two tarps, one for her back and one to double as his shelter and the cover over Celia's load in the event of bad weather. Thankfully, he hadn't seen anyone he knew and hadn't noticed anyone watching.

He worked his way through back streets, jogging here and turning there, just to be certain his path was irregular enough to throw off anyone who might be following from a distance. He waited until no one was in view before entering the woods. Once in the cover of the trees, Hank and Celia made their own trail cross country until they intersected the creek he first followed with Vassar and their buddies. It was the same creek where he'd encountered Letizia's thugs.

Celia willingly followed Hank. He didn't stop, didn't linger, and she didn't balk. He didn't know if he was taxing Celia's energy or not. He figured if he was okay, she was okay. Even though she was carrying the bulk of the supplies, she was far from overburdened.

Because he didn't feel like walking in wet boots, Hank stopped at the crossing to remove his boots and pants. He thought about lashing both to Celia's back, but decided if she spooked he'd just as soon have his boots to put on and chase her down. He used his belt to tie his boots together and hung them around his neck. Naked from the waist down, he held Celia's lead in one hand, his hiking staff in the other, and proceeded to cross the creek without incident.

He pushed hard, hiking until nearly dusk. He didn't intend to build a fire, so only needed time to situate Celia. It was a full moon. *That's all the light I need to eat a cold supper*, he thought.

He hobbled Celia after watering her and left her enough lead to graze to her heart's content. There was no sign of inclement weather, but just to be on the safe side, he tied a line between two trees, made a quick lean-to from a tarp, and tossed his blanket underneath. As the moon rose, he and Celia chewed their dinners together. It was just like old times—apart from Celia not being a llama and Vassar not being present.

Hank awakened before dawn with the birds. He didn't know for sure, but figured they could see sunrise earlier because of their high perches. At any rate, he didn't need to see clearly to do his morning stretches and discuss matters with Magician.

Celia seemed content and hobbled to meet Hank as he approached, which if she hadn't done so already, won his heart. He scratched her behind the ears, and to his delight, she pressed her head against his chest. He had to brace himself to keep from being pushed backward. Celia's heart was also won.

Hank and Celia set off without taking time to eat breakfast. He doubled back on himself after half an hour, walked for fifteen minutes, and stopped behind a formidable deadfall. He listened, but mostly he watched Celia's ears for any sign she heard something he didn't.

Finally satisfied he wasn't being tailed, Hank meandered around until he found a grassy meadow for Celia. According to Mr. Gutmann, Celia would be well-fed on the mountain grasses. In fact, he'd said, "You'll prob'ly need to manage how much she eats, 'specially up in that high country. She ain't no horse, you know." Which Hank understood to mean, Celia's metabolism was slower than a horse's.

While she grazed, Hank ate some jerky and a piece of fruit. Both refreshed themselves in a nearby creek. Hank waited for Celia to pick her drinking spot, stepped around her, and drank from the creek as well, also on all-fours, but above her, to avoid the backwash.

Once watered and fed, Hank and Celia kept a determined pace, not like the day before, but without the normal number of breaks. Hank navigated by his wits and dead reckoning. He followed the same ridge he and his traveling companions followed the last time he'd been in these woods, but ridge or no ridge, he was more or less making this journey up as he went.

Hank was alone, but knew as well that wasn't entirely correct. Jester made the trip, and of course, Magician.

Magician's in my heart, Hank thought. *I wonder how Jester makes his way? Don't know that I care really, but yap, yap, yap!*

Hank reflected over Jester's string of recent rants: *The King this, the King that. Magician doesn't. Vassar won't, can't, isn't. What if? Shouldn't I? If only I could—or would have, or wouldn't have.*

Jeepers! What a pain.

As he thought, Jester upped his ante. *I don't know what I'm doing. Don't know where I'm going. I shouldn't be here. What a fool! You stupid, dumb....*

Hank quickly realized he'd been accommodating Jester's thoughts. He squinted, clinched his teeth, and stated with authority, "Shut up, Jester. Leave me alone."

Jester didn't leave, but he did pipe down.

Celia flicked her ears as her master's voice spoiled the silence-soaked timber. "Sorry, Celia," Hank said, noting her reaction and stopping to pat her face. "I didn't mean to scare you. Just getting focused. That's all."

Judging by the sun, Hank figured he had a couple hours of daylight. He kept walking while working backward in his mind to determine how long he would need to make a proper camp. "Celia, you tired? I am." She waggled her ears again with the sound of Hank's voice. "I think we both deserve some time to relax, eat a good meal. Take it easy. What do you think?"

There was no reply, of course. If there had been, it would have scared him to death, even though he had been thinking about the story of Balaam and his talking donkey. *That's a wild story. Wonder how that worked?*

"Celia. You got anything to say for yourself?" Hank chuckled. "Guess not. Tell you what. I think we ought to put in another hour. Tops. Maybe less if we find a good spot for the night."

He kept moving, looking, stepping over deadfalls and tangles, navigating the thick timber, ducking and dodging. He detoured a few yards left, but what he thought might do for a campsite would never do for Celia. He stopped to check his course. Listened. Watched Celia, and was all but certain they both heard a stream. Hank adjusted his course.

Sure enough, but it wasn't any stream, it was *the* stream he was looking for. Working from memory, he triangulated between the river, the ridge, and his recollection.

Hank quickened his pace until he saw the clearing through the trees. He moved carefully, watching his steps and guiding Celia's. As he had done many months before, he stood back from the clearing, camouflaged by the trees and undergrowth, and studied the situation. *I'm almost positive this is the same place. But it sure looks different without snow.*

Once satisfied it was okay to proceed, Hank led Celia into the open. The emerging view was unmistakable. Hank stepped lighter. *Papa's cabin is over that rise. I'm almost there.*

Celia stopped dead in her tracks—so suddenly it jerked Hank's elbow!

She was on full alert: ears forward, eyebrows twitching, tail swishing, and front foot lightly stamping. She lifted her nose, and just about the time Hank was set to encourage her forward in spite of her concerns, she let out a bellowing bray with teeth bared, tongue out, and head thrust forward. Her bray filled the meadow and beyond. With her second and third heehaws, the whole of Earth had to know Celia was present—and mighty unhappy!

Hank hadn't counted on the King's dogs being at the cabin—with the wolf pack, no less! But Hank saw them now, standing at the crest of the hill above the cabin, formed up in a line and spoiling for a fight. Hank thought of the taunts exchanged before the meadow fight scene in "True Grit:" *Bold talk for a one-eyed fat man. / Fill your hands, you son of…*. He was not amused by the image and was in no mood to pretend he was Rooster Cogburn!

Hank knew enough about donkeys to know dogs were their sworn enemies. *Negotiating a truce is about as likely as making peace between the descendants of Isaac and Ishmael.*

Standing between the barking and braying, Hank was besieged with disappointment. He found what he had set out to find, his Father's cabin, but it was unattainable. He couldn't get rid of the canines and he couldn't leave Celia. He could forego the cabin and retreat to the woods—but the disappointment associated with camping in the woods when he was so close to his Father's retreat was more than he could bear. *I'd just as soon return to the castle,* he thought.

He didn't know what to do and he couldn't think midst the barking in one ear and the braying in the other. Even Magician couldn't yell loud enough to make himself heard!

Until I get this figured out, there's nothing to do but retreat. It was a hard decision.

Celia wanted to stand her ground. In fact, Hank got the idea that if he dropped her lead, she'd march forward and teach the dogs a thing or two. *But then I'd have more explaining to do with Father than I want to take on,* he decided.

By making an arching hike to his flank, Hank eventually put distance between Celia and him and the dogs. Still, he had to hike backward a considerable distance before Celia calmed down.

While she had steadied, Hank was hungry, had no camp, and no plan with which he was content. He stopped and collected himself, gained his bearings, and made his way back to the stream.

He watered Celia, trying to be patient as she took her time between drinking binges. Finally sated, Hank hooked her to a Henderson-modified picket line, hobbled her, and in the waning light gathered the wood he needed.

He built his fire in the dark, but it didn't matter. He had built enough fires that he didn't have to see what he was doing. More pressing was the plight of his soul, turned like a gladiator into the coliseum with the wild beasts of disappointment, despondency, discouragement, and most dangerous of all, disillusionment. He was disillusioned with himself, with Magician's companionship, and even though it made no logical sense, with his Father for permitting the irreconcilable conflict of dogs and donkeys to derail his desperate hope for the solace of his cabin. Even the sputtering flame dispelling the dark night rendered little comfort.

After it served his purpose, Hank abandoned the fire to starve. He retrieved the one comfort he had, a bottle of whiskey. He planned to save it for the cabin—had envisioned himself sipping a dram seated at the King's table, staring off at the magnificent view. Instead, he sat in the chilly darkness.

The moon rose fifty minutes later than it had the night before and cast eerie shadows haphazardly around him and upon him. He corked the bottle and set it aside. He thought about lying down, but knew sleep was not in his foreseeable future.

After sitting for as long as he dared demand of his finicky back, Hank stood to check his meager camp. He was beyond tired, but not sleepy. He stepped over to check on Celia. She pressed her head into his chest and he reassured her. Hank lay down under the stars and watched the moon rise through its zenith. Somewhere in the night, sleep came and released him from his mental marauders.

He blinked awake, lying on his left side. *No point getting up*, he mused. *Got nowhere to be, nothing to do that can't wait.*

So he lay still, staring sideways through the grass. He drifted away, slumbered, and dreamed a dream he knew he wouldn't remember when he awakened.

Celia disturbed him, huffing. He opened his eyes to her hairy forelegs standing in front of his face. He rolled over and sat up. He paid attention for a while. Nothing. He checked with her. She was alert, swiveling her ears in search of a better reception, as if they were antennae. Hank went through his morning stretches, although Celia was in the way. *How ridiculous is this?* he thought. *A whole wilderness and I don't have enough room to stretch my legs!*

Even though nothing had changed, he felt better, but given the depths to which he'd sunk the evening before, that wasn't saying much. Still, he set about building a fire. There weren't any coals from the night before, so he started all over with tiny twigs.

When the water was boiling, he dumped a measure of coffee into the pot. It was his first time to use the kettle he bought before leaving.

He stood with his back to the small fire sipping his cowboy brew. There was cold in the air, the first inkling that fall was taking the handoff from summer, and none too soon as far as Hank was concerned. He never cared much for summer.

Celia again perked her ears. They craned comically over her forehead. She took a few steps toward Hank and assumed a defensive posture. She had his attention. Although they were relatively new traveling partners, this was unusual behavior.

Hank looked in the same direction as Celia. He felt to be certain his dagger was in its usual place and reminded himself of where he'd left his sword. His walking stick, a formidable weapon in its own right, was a few feet away. Celia stamped her foot a few times. Hank put his hand on her withers for reassurance—hers and his. *I probably ought to remove her hobble,* he thought—but didn't have time.

"Got enough coffee for another?" The question came from the direction Celia had been looking, but Hank couldn't see anyone.

"I do. How many of you are there?"

The bushes rustled, Celia stamped in her hobble and snorted with displeasure.

"Only one," Vassar said, stepping into Hank's camp.

There were no words. Only hugs would do. Hank introduced his

Brother to Celia, claiming she was his replacement. The brothers caught up briefly before Vassar asked the obvious, "What are you doing here?" (As if he didn't know.)

Hank filled him in, not sparing him much of the disappointment he felt with the conflict between, "…Father's dogs and Celia."

Vassar studied Celia as Hank explained the problem. She was grazing. "Doesn't look too jumpy now," he observed.

"No, but then Papa's dogs aren't around—and you're not lurking in the bushes."

"Yeah. I figure you're right on both counts," Vassar agreed.

Hank told Vassar how he had come by Celia and how long it had taken him to find his way from the castle to the cabin. He was proud of his backcountry navigation, and Vassar noted that as well.

"Well, tell you what," Vassar began. "Let's you and Celia and I head back to my cabin and see if we can't talk Celia and the canines into being friends."

"We can try," Hank said, "but I don't have much hope of that working."

"How come?" Vassar asked.

"Because dogs and donkeys are enemies. Haven't you noticed back home that the ranchers are keeping donkeys in their pastures?"

"I have noticed that," Vassar said.

"A donkey is a good guard."

"You don't say."

"That's right," Hank confirmed. "Seems they bond with the farm animals, whether sheep or cattle, and defend them against predators."

"Coyotes and wild dogs."

"Right," Hank confirmed. "They are also peaceful souls who don't tolerate conflict. So ranchers put them in with their bulls to keep them from fighting."

"I'll be! So Celia here would break up a fight between two bulls?"

"That's what I've been told," Hank stated.

"Well, one thing about it," Vassar observed, "if she and the dogs go at it, I don't want to be in the middle while they work out their differences."

Hank chuckled at the thought. "No. Me either. And if Celia does something to one of Papa's dogs, I don't want to have to do the explaining."

Vassar dumped the remainder of his coffee. Holding his empty cup behind his back, he said, "Well, let me help you break camp and then let's go reintroduce Celia and the dogs."

The wind had shifted. The day before it blew at their backs, but today it blew across the meadow as Vassar, Hank, and Celia crossed the field toward the King's retreat. That meant their approach to the cabin was shielded from the dogs' keen senses until they were upon them. Celia had been wary for the last fifty yards, but tagged after Hank without too much coaxing.

Even though he had prepared himself, the canine explosion still scared Hank half out of his wits. Celia reared up, jerking Hank backward, and began braying vociferously. Like the day before, only with even more volume and intensity, the growling-barking-braying with ruffs on end and hooves flailing launched a storm of mayhem beyond comprehension! Hank was yelling at Celia to reassure her, which in actuality was probably exciting her even more, and he was hollering at Vassar to do something about the King's dogs.

The situation rapidly deteriorated. Celia started toward the dogs with Hank in tow.

Vassar spoke.

Instantly the meadow was quiet. Birds flitted about, doing bird things. Celia lowered her head to graze on the meadow grass just as Hank had observed her do during their routine breaks from hiking. The wolves and the King's dogs casually jogged out to greet them, tails wagging, ears back, and tongues dangling over their jowls.

Hank noted that he alone appeared to be suffering with

apprehension, and he had plenty to go around. He wasn't breathing. His heart was in his throat. His mouth was dry and his hands were wet. Vassar was squatted down greeting the dogs.

"What about Celia?" Hank exclaimed.

"Is she troubled?" Vassar asked, turning to look in her direction.

By all appearances, she appeared never to have been better. The tumult of moments ago relocated to Hank's throat and rendered him mute. His Brother had surprised him many times, but never quite like this. Without editorial measure, Hank blurted, "How'd you do that?"

Ask a fair and honest question, get a fair and honest answer: "I made these animals. I can modify their disposition as necessary."

As was sometimes the case with Vassar, Hank realized, *I'm going to have to think about that for a while.* It was only four words—"I made these animals"—but there was a remarkable revelation in them.

Celia and the dogs had muzzles and noses together, sharing saliva, and whatever else they transferred licking each other's faces. Celia escaped the dogs' tongues easily by lifting her head. The dogs, however—their entire heads moved with the friction of Celia's tongue. *Amazing!* Hank thought. *You'd think they were litter mates.*

"Come on," Vassar encouraged. "Let's go to the house."

When they arrived at the cabin, Vassar busied himself with small tasks while Hank tended to Celia. He unloaded her, and even though her packs were not heavy, her coat was matted from the pack saddle. He used his fingers to fluff her fur until it stood up like a porcupine's quills. He dropped her hobble near the base of a porch post and was tying off her lead before hobbling her when Vassar said, "It's okay, Brother. Let her be. She'll stay close."

Hank looked at his Older Brother. It was a look Vassar had seen from his Brother before. "Trust me," he said.

Hank turned to Celia. He removed the lead from her halter and scratched her ears. She pushed against him with her face…before eyeing a clump of green that drew her attention.

CHAPTER 22

The Round Tower

Caroline tapped on Bernard Bertram's office door. "You wanted to see me, Bernie?"

As she entered his office, he moved from behind his desk to the small table he kept for more personal meetings. Getting right to the point, Bernie explained, "I have two matters to discuss."

Since Hank's revelation rocked her professional world, Caroline had paid extra attention to her work environment. No nuance, detail, or innuendo escaped her. She also ratcheted her professional demeanor up a notch or two, not that anyone would have noticed, but it was her way of reassuring herself.

Caroline always carried a sheaf of notepaper with her when she attended meetings. Every meeting was labeled, notated, and dated. Every action item had a unique mark so that it stood out at a quick glance.

"Ms. Pintaro asked me to meet with you, Caroline, in advance of meeting with you herself. She has been working on advance planning and succession. She would like you to become her successor."

Caroline's mouth fell open. "Her what?"

"You heard me correctly. Ms. Pintaro has selected you to be her successor, not right away mind you, but in the near future. She'll discuss the timing in more detail when you meet, I'm certain."

"But Bernie…," Caroline sputtered. "Why me? Why not you?"

Bernie chuckled. He hadn't seen Caroline flustered before, not even on her first day. "I'm not successor material, Caroline."

"Why not?" she asked, searching for relief.

Again he chuckled. "I'm too old, for one thing. For another, and more importantly, I'm perfectly happy in my current position. I have no aspirations to sit in the big chair."

"The big chair," she murmured. "I'm not certain I do either, Bernie. What should I do?"

Bernie reached across and squeezed Caroline's hand. "You should think about her offer, and you and I should develop some questions to pose to Ms. Pintaro that will help you better understand what she's proposing."

"Okay. I suppose you're right." Caroline looked at her papers, but wrote nothing and made no mark. She looked up, "Bernie, I don't have the faintest idea how to think, what to write, or what to ask. I'm totally undone."

"I know. I figured you would be. It's okay. I'll help, but before we compose questions to ask, the second item on the agenda is that Ms. Pintaro would like for you and Jacob to join her for dinner tomorrow evening, at her home, 7:00 PM. She will provide child care for your children."

"She wants Jake and me to come to dinner? At her house?"

"It's not unprecedented, Caroline. Besides, you all have a great deal to discuss that mustn't leak into the office until she is ready. Do you understand?"

Caroline nodded, "Yes, I do. Or rather, I comprehend. I don't understand. Oh, my! Jake is never going to believe this."

"I think he will. You underestimate yourself, Caroline. I suspect he has seen in you for many years what Ms. Pintaro and I have seen since you began working here."

"Thank you, Bernie. You're kind."

For the next hour, Bernie and Caroline—Bernie mostly—composed thoughts to pose to Letizia that would help Caroline understand her proposal. Once they had a long list of questions, they went back through eliminating those redundant and non-essential.

"Ms. Pintaro is a fine lady. I've worked with her for many years.

She thinks highly of you, so dinner tomorrow is not a make or break event. She intends to explore an idea about which she feels strongly. She believes you are capable of exploring it with her. Even if the two of you decide you are not the right person for the succession, the mere fact that she has chosen you to discuss this matter with her is a high, high compliment."

Caroline clung to that thought as she and Bernie concluded their meeting. She gathered her things, thanked him, and went to collect her personal belongings before heading home.

She informed Jake as soon as she was home, "We have got to talk!"

They worked together to put a simple meal together, eat, and spend a few moments with the kids before putting them to bed a few minutes earlier than normal. When the house was settled, Caroline and Jake huddled closely at the end of their dining table.

Letizia's personal assistant, Natalie, answered the door, but Letizia wasn't far behind to greet Caroline and Jake. Caroline presented her with a bouquet of flowers, and even though Letizia was a perfect host, the Ingrams were uncomfortable.

Letizia coaxed them to follow her into the kitchen where Natalie assisted her in locating a suitable vase for the flowers. Letizia arranged them herself and carried them to the dining table. On their heels, a servant came bearing before-dinner drinks, and the three of them retired to the veranda.

Letizia led the conversation, asking about the children, their families, and so forth. Jake and Caroline attempted reciprocity with comments about her home, its décor, and how honored they were to be eating a meal with her. They felt awkward, but not any more so than Letizia expected. That she was intimidating was no surprise—and that they were intimidated by the topic awaiting conversation was understandable.

Various topics were discussed over a delightful and delicious dinner of delicately pan-seared fish. To his surprise, Letizia seated Jake at the head of the table. While she didn't explain her rationale, she chose the configuration so she could see them both and so they would be close together for moral support.

Natalie brought the brandy service on a cart. She served each person, looked to Letizia to see if there was anything further, then disappeared into the kitchen.

There was a long pause as Letizia retreated into herself to collect her thoughts. Oddly enough, her hesitancy made her more human, spanning the gulf between her and them, and easing the tension Jake and Caroline felt.

Looking up, a rather severe look on her face, Letizia said, "Caroline, I know you and Bernie have talked. Thank you for coming this evening. I'm anxious to discuss the matter of my succession. But first, there is another subject. It is personal, but when your life and your profession are so intertwined, it is also professional I'm afraid, and therefore, requires the utmost confidentiality."

Caroline and Jake looked at one another, and said nearly together, "Certainly, Ms. Pintaro. Nothing will leave this room."

"Thank you. I knew that would be the case, but I needed to state it, if for no other reason than my own conscience." Again Letizia retreated, collecting her thoughts, hands folded before her, the white fingertips betraying her calm demeanor.

She looked up and began. "I know you are devoted followers of the High King, that you have a small group meeting in your home. Jake, I know you are responsible for training small group leaders throughout the Kingdom."

Jake stared at Letizia while Caroline looked first to him, then to her boss, then back to him. Their wishful denial that Letizia had a dark side rushed headlong into the theater of their lives screaming, "Fire! Fire!" Caroline reached under the table for his hand, and grasped his fingers. *We've been trapped,* she realized. *This evening is a setup. The whole thing! We're separated from our children!*

Jake squeezed her fingers as he too tumbled. *My kids are not safe— in the care of people paid for by this woman. It was too smooth—too good to be true. What a fool! What was I thinking? There's no succession plan.*

Although trying to appear calm and composed, fear consumed them, and for Jake, regret that he had led his family into so simple a demise. *People like Letizia don't have people like us to dinner.*

Letizia bowed her head and slowly turned her brandy glass. "I know as well," she began, her head still down, "that a few years ago you were the young leader of the First Floor Group." She looked up, "And, I know that you were directly responsible for launching the youth movement that became a revival for the King's teaching, spreading through the Round Tower, and beyond, even into the castle. Your leadership extended beyond your physical ability. The movement spread like a virus and there was a dramatic resurgence for the King and his Kingdom. His followers increased and his teachings were rampant throughout the castle and Tower."

Jake held Caroline's hand, as scared as she, and more regretful. *Why didn't I believe Hank? When I had the chance?*

Neither had ever felt so hopeless. They feared for their children's safety. It was more than either could stand, but Jake reassured Caroline with his grip and stared blankly at Letizia.

"Three men attacked you, Jake. You've told all who asked that you were robbed."

In chilling revelation, Letizia recounted what happened to him that fateful night. As she recounted the attack, with some aspects he didn't know, Jake and Caroline moved from terror-stricken to stunned. She knew details about his dismissal from the First Floor Group they didn't know. She knew nuances about the unraveling of the youth revival and the stemming of the King's reformation movement that could only be known by an insider.

Letizia's cold recitation caused the blood to drain from Jake and Caroline's faces. Once again she stopped speaking and bowed her head. Natalie stepped into the room to see if anything was needed. Letizia waived her off without looking up.

To Jake and Caroline's surprise, when she looked up, there were tears in her eyes. Letizia stared at Jake until he was even more uncomfortable. Tears ran down her cheeks, and dribbled from her chin. She made no effort to wipe them away. She didn't look at Caroline, but remained focused on Jake. Haltingly, but with clear words, she stated, "Jake, I ordered your beating. Your maladies are my fault and your impediments are to be laid at my feet. I am the cause of your suffering, and I am sorry. So very sorry."

"Why are you telling us this?" Jake asked.

"I have become a follower of the High King. I've asked him to reign in my life, declared my allegiance to him and Prince Vassar. I have invited the Kingdom's Wizard, Magician, to live in me, guide me into the King's truth, and convey the light through me. I've asked him to forgive me for all the ways in which I've offended him, endeavored to compromise him, and thwart his reign. I believe, because of his great mercy, he has extended forgiveness to me. However, I am convicted that there are certain people whom I have wounded egregiously that deserve my personal confession. Jake, you and your family are at the top of my list. As I look at your cane hanging over the back of your chair, I won't ask you to forgive me—cannot bring myself to even utter the request. But I can look you in the eye and tell you I'm sorry. I cannot mend what is broken in your body, but I can make financial reparations to you and your family. I hope you won't think me too prying, but I've instructed the ladies looking after your children this evening to assess any obvious needs and bring me their observations. And if you will permit me, I would like to visit with you in the near future to discuss specific ways in which I might assist."

Jake and Caroline were dumbstruck.

Letizia continued, again making no effort to compose herself. "It has taken me several minutes to lay my thoughts before you. I apologize. I know you have suffered from fear and doubt while I've set the stage for my apology. I'm sorry. If I could have devised another way—a quicker way—that spared you these moments of concern, I would have done so. But I couldn't. There is the matter of credibility that I could only establish with details, and sadly, details take time to articulate."

Jake and Caroline were relieved, sort of, but still wordless.

"Caroline, you are such a dear and wonderful woman. I admire you beyond words. I haven't forgotten Bernie's discussion with you yesterday. It was a legitimate meeting, not a ruse to get you over here so I could expunge my conscience. I'm anxious to discuss my transition plans, but I trust you understand, I need to get my confession out of the way first. An honest discussion of the future would not be possible otherwise."

Caroline knew nothing else to do but nod and mutter, "Certainly, Ms. Pintaro."

"I have laid a terrific burden upon you both," Letizia said. "Let me step to the washroom and leave you to visit for a few moments. No question you ask of me is out of bounds. I'm certain I look frightful." And with that, Letizia pushed her chair from the table, her tears flowing freely, and disappeared into the back of the house.

Ten or fifteen minutes later Letizia reappeared. She had changed her dress, brushed her hair, and washed her face. Tears still brimmed in her eyes, but she had composed herself.

Jake began. "Ms. Pintaro, if you wouldn't mind…"

"Whether I mind or not is not a consideration, Jake," Letizia instructed him. "Ask anything you like. If I have an answer, I'll give it, and if I don't, I'll find it. Now, forgive me for interrupting you."

"No problem, and thank you. Please, if you would, tell us about your conversion from the dark side to the light."

"This is still new, so my ability to describe my change of heart is not refined, but to the best of my ability, here is what happened. I believe, in retrospect, either the King or his Magician was deftly placing one straw after another upon my back. I didn't realize it, but the burden of proof that the King is truly the King was mounting through the voices and conduct of true believers and followers of his way. Sadly, but as you no doubt have surmised, you are not the only people who have suffered at my hand." Letizia dabbed at her eyes with a handkerchief. "There have been others, directly and indirectly, who have loved and lived and conquered my evil with the mercy and grace of the King. I thought I understood, but I believe otherwise now. I think my heart was noticing, and much to my surprise and delight, I have discovered that while I was busy running from the King and defending myself against him, he was carefully closing in around me. I swear! Over the last weeks I have felt like a fox cornered by a hound."

Jake and Caroline listened and nodded occasionally. Without doing so consciously, they were both searching for any hint that Letizia was deceiving them. But the longer she talked, and the more she revealed, the more they trusted she was telling them the truth.

"I don't know if my experience is normal or not, but my conversion was sort of a two-step process."

"How so?" Jake asked.

"Step one was the realization that the King was the legitimate ruler of the Kingdom and that his teachings were true."

"When did you come to this realization?" Jake asked.

Caroline continued gripping his hand like a vice.

"You will recall the evening I stopped by your home? Hank Henderson was there for dinner."

Jake and Caroline nodded that they remembered.

"I never intended to stay so long that evening, but I couldn't help myself. Your testimony of faith in the King, in spite of your infirmities, haunted my thoughts, not so much because I knew I was ultimately responsible for your hardship, but because I knew I had to face the truth of the King's declarations about himself and life."

"Caroline and I discussed that after you left. We thought it was a curious conversation and mysterious evening."

Caroline affirmed what Jake said with a nod. She still had no words.

"Hank walked me home that evening. It was dark and I didn't know your part of town. I had sneaked away. Not even Natalie knew exactly where I was."

"Hank walked you home?" There was a hint of skepticism in Jake's question, but probably not enough for Letizia to notice. Caroline certainly did, but she shared Jake's doubts and feelings regarding Hank.

"He did. The poor man."

"Why do you call him that?" Caroline asked.

Letizia shook her head as she looked at the table surface. "I've tailed that man—or had my people tailing him—since he arrived in Gnarled Wood. He is a Prince in the Kingdom and a knight in the Army of Light. I've hounded him, tracked him, interrogated him, and once I even tried to do to him what was done to you, Jake."

"You did this? To Hank?" Caroline asked.

"People who work for me did."

"People who work in the office?" Caroline exclaimed.

"Oh, my! No, no, dear. Not in the office." Letizia took in a deep breath and let it out. "There is a great deal for us to discuss, and we will. Soon. But no, not in the regular office."

Caroline breathed a sigh. This unfolding story was dramatic enough—and there was indeed another side to Letizia, darker and more sinister than even their imaginations had contrived.

"Anyway. Continuing on," Letizia resumed. "Hank is a shrewd and savvy man. When he graciously extended his arm to me that night, he knew without question that he was aiding the enemy."

"The enemy being, you?" Jake confirmed.

"The enemy being me, Jake. My people have stalked the man, spied on him, tried to trap him." Letizia stopped speaking for a moment. "I've even attempted to kill him."

"He told us about his mishap beside the river," Jake offered.

Letizia nodded and looked down at the table surface. "It was no mishap, Jake. No more so than what happened to you."

It was quiet for a moment at the table.

Jake swallowed, unconsciously shook his head slightly. "So you were saying Hank viewed you as his enemy."

"Yes," Letizia resumed. "He knew all of this that night, and yet, when I stumbled he gave me his arm, walked me home, and waited until I was safely inside."

She took a deep breath, collected herself, and continued. "I came home that night, knew sleep would evade me—didn't want to sleep, actually—so went to my study to consider my options. In the wee hours, the chess pieces of my life all over the board, I heard a voice in my head declare, 'Checkmate!' Whether I made that declaration myself or the King's Wizard stated it, I don't know, but it was true."

"What did you do?" Caroline asked.

Letizia sat up straighter. "I did what any defeated officer would do. I surrendered my sword. I knelt in the floor of my study—in this very home—and surrendered to the King. I stated that I had believed a lie, conducted myself treacherously and treasonously toward him and his Kingdom; I renounced my service to Zophos and my leadership in the Dark Army. And then, I bowed my head, declared the King my ruler, and pledged my allegiance."

"My God!" Jake breathed.

Caroline sat, mouth agape. Her hand had gone limp in Jake's grasp.

"I was the most unhappy person in all of the castle, I do believe!" Letizia stated emphatically.

"Most unhappy? How so?" Caroline managed to say.

"Everything I believed. Everything you see around you." Letizia swept her arms around the circle of the room, and by extension, her home and her life. "All that I worked for," and she looked directly at Jake, "and all I've done, was devotion to a lie. I hated admitting that I was such a deceived, wretched fool, but it was true. That night, one straw after the other was placed upon the formidable stack of evidence I was already carrying, and standing in the midst of my study floor, I realized my back was broken. Whatever the metaphor? I don't know how to describe it adequately. The hound of the Kingdom cornered me." Letizia turned her palms up, "I surrendered."

"Is all of that step one?" Jake asked her.

"Yes. I'm sorry for all my words. You are being so patient, but I really would like to believe that even though this is my story it is related to your emotional healing. I pray so."

Jake nodded. "And step two?"

"Several weeks passed. I was miserably unhappy. And, one conflict of interest after another was arising at work. I didn't know what to do or who to turn to for counsel, so I contacted Hank. He met with me, which is another story for another time, and I discovered I only knew half of the King's equation."

"I don't follow you," Jake said.

"I recognized the King's legitimacy and surrendered to his reign over me, but I had no clue about the role of Crown Prince Vassar. I didn't understand that the King establishes the hope of his Kingdom within me, within his people. I didn't know that his preferred throne is in my heart. I hadn't the faintest notion that the King, Prince Vassar, and the wizard Magician reside in me." Letizia shook her head at the thought. "Hank explained that Vassar lives in me to express himself through me." Again, she shook her head in disbelief. "It is still confusing, but as I sat listening to Hank—he was so patient with my questions—inexpressible joy filled my heart. It is there now! It is there in spite of the horrid conduct of my life and the gravity of my treachery toward the King and his people. I am a different person. What more can I say?"

Jake and Caroline looked at each other.

Jake said, "We've not seen Hank lately."

"No. He has disappeared, I'm afraid," Letizia stated. "I tried to tell him that my people—the ones tracking around after him, watching his every move—had been ordered to see to his safety. I don't know. I doubt I would have stayed either."

"What can you tell us about his disappearance?" Jake asked. He and Caroline had heard enough to realize their dismissal of Hank was unjustified.

"I sent word to Hank that I would like to meet with him as soon as he was able. He sent word that we could meet immediately, and named a place. We met, had the discussion I've reported to you, and that was the last time I saw him. My people reported mid-morning, two days later, that he had evaded them. None of my contacts has reported seeing him since."

Jake shook his head. "I threw him out of our home. It's a long and sordid story." He looked at Caroline. "We didn't know, but filling in the blanks with what you've told us, I realize Hank was in a bind. He was being a true friend, but I doubted him. Accused him. And…I threw him out for looking after Caroline and my family."

The three sat in silence. None had touched the brandy in front of them. No one took a drink now.

Finally, Caroline collected her thoughts and said, "Ms. Pintaro. I'm grateful for the belief you have expressed in me and my abilities. Under different circumstances, I would not be so forward, but I really must hear more about what you have in mind for me at the office."

"Yes, you must. More pointedly, you need to know about the dividing line between the office and the other work I've done—the work Hank so graphically refers to as my cash business." Letizia smiled, but it was a smile of regret.

Caroline squinted and nodded at Letizia. "Yes, ma'am. I think that's a good place to start."

For another hour, Letizia discreetly told Jake and Caroline what she had in mind at the office and what she didn't have in mind regarding the cash business. They knew plenty from Letizia's disclosures, but not enough to get in trouble, be held accountable, or determined culpable. There was never a more graphic demonstration of Letizia's remarkable mind than that evening.

She concluded, "Caroline, the front office is a legitimate business with beneficial purpose. With your skills, in concert with Bernie's assistance, and the modifications I've proposed in my transition plan, you can go to work each day with confidence, integrity, and purpose."

"Ms. Pintaro, you are a young woman professionally. Why are you building and executing a succession plan at this point in your career?"

Letizia knew the answer, but she'd never stated it out loud. She stared at Caroline. She knew she must answer her, one sobering word after another, in sequence, until the sentence was completed. "Caroline, when a person is enmeshed in the dark underworld, and they decide they want out of that life—out of that world—the likelihood of them safely working their way free is remote. Allegiance is absolute. Dear, you must understand. I am not simply enmeshed in that world. I am that world. If something should happen to me, I would like to know the office is in good hands."

"I see," Caroline said, softly. "But why so quickly? Why do you want my answer right away?"

"My conversion from darkness to light will not remain a secret for long. I can dodge, and deflect, and deceive for a time. I can even disappear for a while, but Zophos and his forces have their ways. Sooner rather than later, my house must be in order. Just in case."

"But what if you make it out?" Caroline asked, almost panicky sounding. "What if they don't get you?"

Letizia smiled. "The King will make that determination, won't he? According to Hank, and what I've read of the King's teaching, my life is in his hands. Whether I live or die, he remains and I am his."

Caroline was persistent. "Yes. I agree—fully. But what if you are successful? You will have given me your position."

"Yes. That's true, and if it proves to be the case, then we will run the office together. I have no doubt a person of your capability can effectively manage someone like me."

Caroline bowed her head and leaned against Jake. Letizia could tell the young couple had all they could manage for the evening.

But there remained a final detail.

"Before you leave, I have three final thoughts: Most importantly, know again that I am immensely sorry for the harm I have caused you. Second, we can work out the details later regarding financial provision for your children, but should anything transpire before we have that discussion, the account is established and sufficiently funded. Bernie knows the details. Finally, as a precaution, I have arranged a security detail for each of you, your children, and your home. They will also function as support staff around your home. The staff is distinct from my current security personnel, just in case there is discussion. And again, Bernie is aware of the account I've set up and funded to pay for their services."

The walk to the front door was awkward, and not just because Jake had been sitting for so long that his muscles were tight.

Leaping the chasm between professional protocol and societal position, Caroline embraced Letizia and held her tightly. Great sobs echoed in the foyer as the two women hugged. Jake stood respectfully, hard at work within himself.

When Caroline released Letizia, she backed up close to Jake, as if she'd just released a wildness. Letizia stood with bent shoulders, bearing up under the weights of her world. Her head was down and her face was wet. Her eyes were swollen and red, strands of hair stuck to her moist cheeks. She snuffed convulsively, so distraught was her soul.

Jake hooked his cane on his arm and stepped to Letizia. He placed his hands on Letizia's shoulders, and said, "Please look at me."

She couldn't.

Tenderly, Jake raised Letizia's chin. She blinked teary eyes at him. "Letizia, thank you for your apology. I forgive you."

Letizia tipped forward into Jake. He put his arms around her and Caroline joined him. Together they affirmed her, spoke the King's truths into her ears, and held her until she calmed.

"I don't know the future, but the King does. Our conversation is between us," Jake said, Caroline vigorously nodding her confirmation. "We will trust him one moment at a time."

Letizia thanked them for coming.

That reminded Caroline of unfinished business. "Oh, I almost forgot! Ms. Pintaro, I accept your offer. That's my answer. Thank you. Thank you for believing in me."

"I do believe in you, Caroline. I wouldn't have made the offer if I didn't believe in you. I'll see you in the morning and we'll get started."

Jake said as they left, "If you hear from Hank, please tell him I'm anxious to talk with him. I have some amends to make."

Letizia smiled. "I understand making amends. I'll do it. Good night."

The senior leader of the First Floor Group had given strict instructions to his Secretary that he wasn't to be disturbed. He was struggling to collect his thoughts for his presentation on the first day of the week. Every so often, even for a polished speaker, speeches refuse to come together. It didn't happen to him often, but this was one of those frustrating times.

He didn't try to hide his displeasure when his Secretary eased into his study, hands clasped before her in anxious anticipation of his anger. "I'm so sorry to interrupt, Sir. But, Ennui is here, and…"

"…and you and I need to visit," Ennui interrupted, taking the liberty of entering his office neither invited nor announced.

The senior leader greeted her—and her assistant. "Why, Ennui! How wonderful to see you. Please, please come in."

What else could he do? Professionally, he was beholden to her, which meant she held his future in her grasp. Always gracious, the senior leader thanked his Secretary, telling her she had done the correct thing by interrupting him. She smiled, knowing him well enough to know he didn't mean what he said, and closed the door behind her leaving him, Ennui, and her assistant to themselves.

While her assistant stood by the door, Ennui sat across the desk from the senior leader. He invited her to sit at his side table. "Please. My desk is like a fortress between us."

She stated flatly, "I am fine where I am."

Her stoicism couldn't hide that something was bothering her. The senior leader couldn't ever recall seeing this in Ennui, but he recognized it now, and he had an uncomfortable premonition.

She didn't bother to couch her comments in pleasantry, just came directly out and said that a number of First Floor Group members were regularly attending small groups in the castle. Of course, the senior leader acknowledged knowing this, "But what can I do? Forbid them? I don't have either the power or resources to stop them." He didn't say this defensively, but rather reasonably. *Surely she understands this*, he thought.

Ennui reminded him of the financial risks associated with these members' shift in loyalty from the First Floor Group to a renegade small group. In her inimitable way, she extrapolated the implications into the future, and the end result wasn't pleasant. Pointedly, she noted,

"The one thing certain to make the membership board dissatisfied with your leadership is a drop in revenue."

She didn't leave any room for discussion.

Ordinarily, if Ennui wanted something done within the First Floor Group, she funded it, staffed it, and he cooperated. But not this time. *This is an ultimatum*, he realized. *Plain and simple. She's bullying me.*

Ennui caught the senior leader at a vulnerable moment. Like her, he too could play the professional charade, put on his happy face, and exhibit a "can do" attitude. But he didn't this time. She made him mad—and she scared him.

On the one hand, she intended to scare him, but having done so, she lost respect and any confidence that he would get the job done. His weakness felt like insubordination. Taking note, she thought, *I do not tolerate disloyalty—from anyone.*

Ennui uttered no salutation. She got up, walked to the door, nodded at her assistant, and departed. The senior leader's Secretary waved nervously through the doorway, mouthed, "I'm sorry," and gently closed his office door.

Any hope of working on his presentation evaporated. It wasn't the first time his planning had been interrupted. He was a professional. *I'll rob time from somewhere else and work on it later*, he determined. He would use the sanctuary of his office to contemplate Ennui's threat.

He was at the top of his game. There was no higher place to go from here, which was a good thing, except for the nagging hollowness he felt. It made no sense! *How can I be where I am and not be fulfilled? I don't know*, he concluded for the hundredth time. *There must be more, must be another horizon.* The low-grade dissatisfaction had been growing in him. He was tired, could feel himself overplaying, leaning too hard into his expectations. This wasn't working out like he hoped in his younger days.

Pondering, pacing, referencing various resources, the senior leader was deep in thought. The door to his office opened. There was no knock. The Chairman of the First Floor Group's Board and two other Board members marched through the passage.

He didn't have to ask if anything was wrong. Everything right was sucked out of his office when the three entered. He offered no greeting, and received none.

It was a stand-up meeting—one of the shortest in his career. The second Board member to enter was a businessman in the castle. He held prominence, but it wasn't prominent enough for him. He was always striving to improve his standing, moving in and out of various circles in the community, and inside the First Floor Group as well. He hadn't been on the Board but six months. The other two, the Chairman and the third man to enter, were long-time members.

The rookie fished in his pocket, producing a folded paper. The three assembled themselves in a shallow semi-circle and the new man read, "It is the unanimous decision of the First Floor Group's Board that today be your last day as senior leader. Effective immediately, the vice leader is promoted. Thank you for your service."

The junior man folded his paper, stating as he did so, that the exact wording would be entered into the official minutes at the next meeting.

The Chairman of the Board spoke, "As is our policy, security will supervise as you collect your personal belongings. I believe they have brought a few boxes for your convenience. They will escort you from the premises. Given the nature of your departure, there will be no severance. Now, if you would be so kind as to hand me your keys, we'll let you conclude your employment."

He was speechless. But then, there was nothing to say. He shuffled to his desk and located his keys. He stood looking at them for a second, picked up the keys, and tossed them onto the floor. They clattered and skidded to a stop short of the Chairman who refused to pick them up. He looked instead to the junior member who bent over and collected the keys. The Chairman held out his hand to receive them, and the three men left.

As they left, two security personnel entered. The senior leader noticed the front office was vacant. His Secretary was sent home early.

CHAPTER 23

Letizia Pintaro's Office

As she had demonstrated when she was initially hired, Caroline proved a quick study. Letizia was anxious to equip her for success, and of course, Bernie was invaluable. That she had been promoted was all the office staff really knew. Titles would be announced later.

Initially, the most formidable challenge Caroline faced was familiarizing herself with the scope of the business. She devoted several hours each evening, after everyone else had gone home, to reading files. Occasionally, Jake asked if she had uncovered any hint of Letizia's other profession. Her honest answer was, "Not a scrap of anything remotely suspicious. It's uncanny."

Letizia included Caroline in every meeting, large or small, professional and personal. She knew Caroline would become proficient in the mechanics soon enough, and even without her tutelage…if circumstances dictated that fate. Letizia's larger concern was that Caroline capture the spirit of what she did, how she did it, and how she thought about it. She briefed her on contacts, carefully laying out history, fact, intuition, discernment, and future on every individual and group. The scope of Letizia's mind was formidable, but what was more remarkable to Caroline was the vast scope of her interests, abilities, and responsibilities, each systematically structured philosophically, professionally, and personally. There was very little that didn't have clear rationale, and those few things that didn't, Letizia readily referenced as outstanding items. The clear implication to Caroline was, "Should I depart and this be yours, I expect you to figure out where these outstanding items belong."

Unless they were sleeping, bathing, or indisposed the two women were constant companions. They talked about everything—from wardrobe, to management of house staff, to payroll, to the file drawers, to Bernie, to personal conduct, comport, composure, security, and back again. They laughed together, thought together, solved together, ate together, and most important to them both, they spent as long as necessary each morning discussing the issues before them with Magician.

Letizia was anxious to know Magician better, but she was hesitant to let the full weight of her life and intellect rest upon the Wizard. It wasn't that she feared sinking him, but that she was embarrassed by her hungry intellect. There were few in her circle that appreciated—or tolerated—her inquisitive mind and broad interests. To her, these were normal thought patterns. To others she was a burden, a challenge, a bore, and quite intimidating.

Unlike her boss, Ennui, and her boss's boss, Zophos, Letizia didn't use intimidation to shore up a sagging self-esteem, nor did she use intimidation as a control measure. That she was intimidating, she realized, but her esteem was fine and she had plenty of ways to gain whatever measure of control she desired.

She edited herself because she was a communicator. *Why use a complex or obscure word to impress when a simpler word communicates just as well?* When Letizia recognized an associate felt threatened, rather than push them into a defensive posture, she backed off and came at the issue from another angle. *Why ask questions until a person is speechless?* She didn't like the isolation her intellect created, but bearing its weight alone was better than breaking someone under the burden of her mind.

However, Caroline convinced her with repeated exhortations that Magician was plenty capable of keeping up with her. "Don't edit yourself. He can handle anything, from any direction, across any spectrum. After all, he created you. He can follow your thoughts. Be yourself! More than anything, he's anxious to spend time with you."

It was hard enough for Letizia to believe the High King and Prince Vassar, via Magician, reigned within her. But to believe they wanted to communicate with her—directly, heart-to-heart—was practically unreasonable. She readily admitted there was something powerful behind her sternum that wanted to believe this was true, but after all she had done to subvert the Kingdom…? "Caroline, why would either have anything to do with me? It's enough that they accept my devotion."

To a woman who lived ruthlessly, the High King's standards of love, forgiveness, grace, and mercy were foreign ideals. However, she couldn't deny that something was different inside her soul. Where there was darkness, now there was light. Where there was a vacuum, there was joy. Since she invited the spirit of Vassar to establish his Kingdom within her, something had fundamentally shifted—something inside her.

What Letizia did understand was loyalty. She expected it, required it, and punished any compromise of it. Over and over she examined the High King's pledge of faithfulness to her. From every angle, she considered his responsibilities against hers. She arrived at the same conclusion—no matter where she started from: *The King left himself no wiggle room. Should he fail, it will be apparent, and if he fails, the consequences—established by him and sworn by him—will be catastrophic! There's no way around this. No out for him. Clearly, the King either will do everything he promises or he will default. In that event….* She always stopped short to rethink her process. *In that event, he relinquishes his throne. No overthrow as Zophos advocates. The King simply abdicates.* No matter how she thought it through, the King's honor was irrevocably committed by his own pledge of loyalty.

But on the other hand—the other side of this agreement between us, she realized, *the High King provides for me to fail, even expects it, and promises mercy and forgiveness. The inequity of this agreement—this covenant pledge he has made—is striking!*

Letizia questioned Caroline relentlessly, and while Caroline provided many answers, they repeatedly returned to the inexorable fact of the King's love.

"The High King loves you with extravagant abandon!" Caroline declared, encouraging and exhorting her boss and mentee.

Letizia's struggles of faith were circular, and each lap began and ended with her choice to believe the King loved and accepted her. Caroline was a patient guide, but after a few laps around the circumference of Letizia's reasoning, Caroline grew more pointed in making certain her fellow member in the Kingdom family understood she couldn't reason her way into understanding why the King loved.

"You are back where you started from," she pointed out. "You can't think your way through this. You have to decide whether you are going to believe him or not?"

"But, why?" Letizia asked—once more. "Why must there be faith?"

"Because love is who the King is. It's the sum of his character, and no matter how you might think about love, love is more profound— much deeper—than your intellect is capable of reasoning. Love can only be comprehended and apprehended by believing in your heart."

There came the day—when Letizia and Caroline were having this discussion, yet again—when Letizia said, with no small degree of frustration, "But I don't want to just embrace love with my heart. I want to understand it!"

With trepidation Caroline said, "You don't want to embrace the King in your heart because deep inside you feel unworthy of his love."

Letizia eyed Caroline with moist eyes.

Caroline ventured farther. "You can't control his love, even though you are trying very hard. Bluntly, you are afraid!"

That got Letizia's attention.

The puddles in her eyes magnified her fierce response, "Afraid?"

"That's right. Afraid!" Caroline leaned closer to her boss. "Afraid that if you let the King into your heart, he won't like what he sees and will abandon you. Never mind the breach of his pledged loyalty. In his absence, there will only be hopelessness—hopelessness that you are beyond hope, beyond rescue, beyond redemption. Should you admit the King into your heart, he will leave in disgust and you will find yourself where he is not. That is the essence of fear!"

Letizia wasn't used to being confronted. She stared at Caroline a long moment. Fear wasn't an emotion—or a rationale—that she was accustomed to recognizing in herself, but now that Caroline pointed at it, she saw the face of fear.

Letizia didn't know it, but Caroline's words registered in her intellect and Magician underscored the truth of Caroline's confrontation inside her heart. After all, Magician never wastes the opportunity to seize an advantage, especially a courageous overture of love like Caroline's for Letizia.

Letizia thought about countering Caroline, but defense didn't resonate within her. Once again, she didn't understand the full dynamic of what was transpiring, but the enemy of all the King's subjects, Jester, was aggressively trying to discount Caroline's perspective and Magician's confirmation.

She rejected Jester's temptation, even though she couldn't articulate the decision at the moment, and said to Caroline, "You're right. Absolutely right. Now that I've met him, I'm terrified of finding myself apart from the King. But sadly, if I ever allowed him into my heart, he would leave and never return." There were tears in Letizia's eyes. The thought of the King's absence was indeed, terrifying.

Caroline addressed Magician with a quick thought, *Please give me the words*. Reaching across the table to grasp her boss's hand, Caroline said, "You're forgetting something crucial."

"What's that?" Letizia asked, tears in her eyes, but not without a flash of intensity.

"When you invited Vassar into your life, he made your heart his home. He, and the King, and Magician have explored every nook and cranny of your heart already and deemed it a perfect place to reside. Even if you wanted to prevent it, it is too late, Ms. Pintaro. The King is already in residence."

Letizia sat staring, studying her colleague. Her eyes pierced Caroline. "Caroline. I want to believe you, but if you only knew."

Leaning forward again, "Do you not think the King knows?" Caroline asked.

Letizia couldn't answer—at least, she couldn't answer rationally based upon the facts of faith she had in her possession.

"Ms. Pintaro, before you declared your allegiance to the King and invited Vassar to dwell in your heart, your old heart was dark, foreboding, and dedicated to Zophos. It wasn't a place fit for the King. But with your decision to serve the King, through Vassar's intercession on your behalf, the King dealt a fatal blow to your old heart, buried it in the deepest part of the sea, and gave you a new heart wholly dedicated to him, longing for what he holds valuable, and inscribed throughout with his desires."

"But why would he do this?" Letizia asked.

"The King knew he couldn't tolerate your old heart, but he loved you too much to leave you—or me, for that matter—destitute. Rather than live separate from you, he separated you from your old heart, gave you a new heart, and took up residence within you. Then, to seal the deal and reassure you, he pledged his faithfulness to you by placing Magician within. He cannot leave you without dishonoring himself and breaking both your hearts."

"What do I do, Caroline?"

"You decide to believe him, then do so. You grit your teeth, say no to your doubt, and declare your dependence upon everything he has pledged to you as true. This is the necessity of faith."

"How will I know this has happened—that he has accepted my declaration of faith?"

"Magician will let you know," Caroline stated matter of fact. "That sense you have behind your sternum? That's his presence."

"I do sense a pressure in my chest, like a force, a driving desire to believe," Letizia observed.

"On matters of this magnitude," Caroline stated, "Magician will give you thoughts that are in keeping with what you know to be true of the King, his pledge of covenant, and your heart's desire. That's the force you feel in your chest."

And in this way, Caroline and Letizia continued to discuss matters of the Kingdom. Caroline coached Letizia's life-change with honesty and personal transparency about her own life in the Kingdom. Magician seized every opportunity to confirm Letizia's desires. Letizia's faith in the King and his transformation of her heart solidified, and with Caroline's guidance and closeness, she discerned the sound of Magician's voice.

The High King's Refuge at 11,250 feet

Hank joined Vassar on the front porch of the cabin carrying two cups of coffee, strong and black. The view into the valley was more stunning than Hank remembered. The Aspen leaves were turning golden and crisp relief was in the air. The dogs sauntered over to greet Hank, as did Celia with her customary face-press into her master.

"Can't ask for a better greeting than that," Vassar observed.

Hank wanted to know how Vassar was doing in his role working alongside their Father, how he knew he needed help when he was attacked on the gravel bar, and why he didn't stay for the finale.

Vassar only shrugged when Hank pressed him about the gravel bar, but wanted to hear Hank's perspective on the Round Tower, the castle, and the state of the Kingdom. Granted, he already knew the status of these interests, but he wasn't seeking information. He was simply enjoying visiting with his Brother.

As the discussion turned to the Kingdom, Hank lamented that the

King was losing the battle for the Round Tower.

"What do you mean by losing?" Vassar asked.

Hank grimaced as he contemplated how to frame his assessment for Vassar. It wasn't a flattering report. Still, he told about the pervasive indifference within the Tower, the shunning and frequent persecution of the King's followers, as well as the quest for power, position, and notoriety by the Tower's leadership. He updated Vassar on Ennui's initiatives and the number of her staff deployed in and around the Round Tower. He concluded with, "So, Zophos' and Ennui's numbers are up, Father's are down. It's sad. Very sad."

"That is a sad report," Vassar stated. "In fact, it's pitiful."

Hank felt sorry for burdening Vassar and turned from his view into the valley to look at him. He was surprised to see Vassar's slanted grin. "What?" he asked.

"You really convinced Father's losing?"

"It's pretty obvious, Vassar. His numbers are way off."

"I see." Vassar looked serious. "How far off?"

"Oh, I don't know, maybe forty, fifty, sixty percent. Very hard to know."

"Those are big numbers," Vassar commented. "Big spread too. Demoralizing, in fact, isn't it?"

"Yeah," Hank responded cautiously. He sensed Vassar closing in on him. "What do you think, Vassar?"

Vassar sipped his coffee. "Father's numbers are beyond knowing."

"Why's that?" Hank asked, feeling relieved he had escaped Vassar's cunning.

"He doesn't report them. They aren't important to him, so he doesn't track them, at least not in a conventional way. Zophos and his team attach value to the unreported, unknown, and unimportant. Zophos spins this data then in order to create doubts about Father's legitimacy. Further, Zophos is inflating his own numbers to create a delusion of who is winning and who is losing. When you ask him, he justifies his numbers by observing the performance of those who are loyal to the King."

"I see," Hank said. "And since the King's followers are prone to underperform, Zophos asserts the validity of his numbers and his corresponding victory."

"Right," Vassar stated. "But just because Zophos has created a performance-based standard, that doesn't mean Father concurs. Father is interested in the heart, which as you know, escapes measurement."

Hank contemplated these things, holding his coffee close to his face. The steam curled around his nose and made his breath rich. "So is Father winning or losing?" he asked after a moment.

"Oh! He's winning. Decisively! Zophos is no match for him. In fact, it isn't even close. Hank, you don't have enough information to evaluate this like a profit-loss statement, nor are Father and Zophos drawn up against one another on a traditional field of battle so as to count territories, casualties, survivors, and prisoners of war."

"Now that you say it, I see that you're right, Vassar. I know that Father values the human heart beyond comprehension."

"You know, Hank. This is an interesting discussion, but it's flawed. We didn't begin with the right question. We began with Zophos' question: Is Father winning? The better question is, since Father has already won, how should we think and live? What should our perspective be? In other words, how should we conduct ourselves as victors?"

"I get that," Hank countered. "But what about the people who are suffering for their faith in Father? In some sectors of the castle, his people are being brutalized, martyred even. In fact, that number is way up. Worst it's ever been. That's hard!"

"It is hard, and it doesn't appear much like victory. But you need to be certain you properly define 'hard.'"

"Well, I know how I feel about it," Hank stated. "How do you feel about it?"

"The death of my people is important to me. It's precious, in fact."

Vassar was speaking as Hank's Father. Sometimes the three—Vassar, the King, and Magician—all overlapped, even spoke as one, and assumed a single identity. It was disarming, but Hank's admiration and respect for Vassar only increased during these exchanges. He thought often that he would never plumb the depths of his Brother's character.

"You listening?"

"Oh, yeah. Sorry about that. Got distracted for a minute."

"Do we need to move inside?"

"No, no," Hank replied. "I'm with you. You were saying?"

"I was saying that when my people die, their death is precious to me, but that they die is neither here nor there. All men die. As long as they're here—in Gnarled Wood—I live in them through Magician. When they die, they are with me face-to-face."

"So whether here or there, we all win—you, Father, Magician, and the rest of us," Hank summarized.

"Exactly. Zophos makes a big deal out of physical death, and it is a seeming loss for those left behind, but only for a short season. Father always works from and to eternity. While here—in Gnarled Wood's time dimension—the challenge is to embrace Father's perspective and live as he lives. To do otherwise is shortsighted."

"I see that," Hank said. "Father has a different way of thinking about death, suffering, economics, and winning. No doubt about that."

"That's true," Vassar affirmed. "You live in two time dimensions, Brother. You live in Gnarled Wood by the power of Magician and you reign with me in the Kingdom."

Hank thought about this for a moment, staring into the valley. "I hear you, Vassar. I go back and forth between the two perspectives."

"Very true. You're like an ambassador. Your citizenship is in the Kingdom but you are commissioned by Father to represent him and your homeland in the foreign place of Gnarled Wood."

"I know what you're saying is right. I just forget sometimes," Hank confessed.

"That's understandable. Zophos and Jester, and the others, are desperate to deceive you and discredit the King. But make no mistake. Zophos is a defeated foe, regardless of the statistical spin. He's working with one set of books, which he cooks. Father is working with a different set of books altogether, which he verifies, certifies, and underwrites. The deal is, you don't have enough information about either set of books to accurately audit them."

"So I have to take Zophos' word about his bookkeeping and Father's word about his bookkeeping," Hank summarized.

"That's right, and since you can't evaluate the books, you consider the source and believe accordingly."

"You know, Vassar, I may have told you, but when I was in graduate school—back in the other time dimension—I had to read a book titled, *How to Lie with Statistics*. I never actually read the book; I figured the title was all I needed to know."

Vassar chuckled at Hank's recollection. "Brother, could I give you an encouraging word?"

"Sure. I'll take all the encouragement you've got to give."

"The only way you are going to keep your focus is to know the heart of Father. He's good, Brother. And, he thinks the world of you."

"You remind me of Father, Vassar. In fact, I often think when I've seen you, I've seen Father."

"Hmm. Imagine that," Vassar noted, sipping his coffee and monitoring sunrise over the mountain top.

Hank spent a couple of weeks with Vassar at the King's refuge. They ate, talked, walked, laughed, sat, and strategized. Both were refueled during their time together. Vassar again exhorted Hank that Magician spoke with full authority on his and the King's behalf. "In him, I am always with you, Brother."

Hearing Vassar's exhortation reminded Hank of a paragraph from his letter that he had memorized.

> *We are family, and as such, we are bonded and can never be separated. In spirit, I am in Father and Father is in me—just as I am in you and you are in me. We are in Father. He is in us. Magician is evidence of this. Father said so! We are a unit, a family. We are cut from the same bolt of genetic cloth and our lives are interwoven. We are inseparable!*

On the morning of the fourteenth day, Hank departed with Celia for the castle and Round Tower. He stopped at the top of the rise in the meadow to wave to Vassar, but the light on the cabin was too bright to look at, let alone distinguish. There was consolation in his heart, however, as he walked in the light: *I'm not alone. I'm in Vassar and Vassar's in me.*

Hank and Celia entered the woods and followed what was now a familiar path. But at the trickling creek, per Vassar's instructions, they were supposed to follow the water flow until they came to a well-used animal trail. According to Vassar, the trail zigged and zagged with the efficiency only elk and deer could engineer, and was in the end a more direct course back to the castle. In fact, Vassar had assured, it would shave two days off the route via the ridge.

When Vassar told him about this trail, Hank asked why their Father originally instructed them to come by the ridge route when there was a more efficient way. Vassar's answer occupied Hank's mind this morning as he and Celia worked their way toward the creek. He repeated it aloud, for reassurance, as he descended, "Sometimes the most efficient route is not the best route. Occasionally, Father takes us the long way."

To his western mind, and truth be told, his modern mind, inefficiency was hard to tolerate. Hank associated inefficiency with irresponsibility and a low commitment to excellence.

Why anyone tolerated inefficiency was beyond Hank's comprehension, but that his Father was inefficient at times was obvious. *At least, he is inefficient by my values,* Hank reminded himself, sorting what he understood from what he didn't.

He mused as he walked with Celia, *Listening to Vassar explain Father's perspective of the long route versus the expedient route? I wouldn't have the patience for it. No doubt about that. But I can still see Vassar, leaning forward—toward me—intense, "When you first came here, Father knew you couldn't endure the more direct route. It was his mercy that directed us to travel the ridge route. And besides, Father has all the time in the world. You're the one who's always thinking about time."*

Hank stopped in the woods. Celia put her head against his back, her wet nose soiling the back of his shirt. *I'm the one who's always thinking about time. Vassar, Father, Magician? None of them seem too moved by the clock.*

As Hank's business mentor, Mr. Drucker, often did, Vassar had appealed to history for an explanation. Hank heard Vassar again. *"When the Israelites departed their bondage in Egypt and headed toward the Promised Land, the most direct route was an eleven-day walk. Eleven days! But instead, they spent forty years meandering in Sinai. It was a striking inefficiency. But the King knew his people were not ready for the efficient route because it led through enemy-occupied land. Plain and simple: He knew his people were not ready for war. So in his mercy and goodness, he directed them south into the wilderness, where historical retrospect reveals his gracious care and provision for them."*

That Vassar told me about the more direct route is a backhanded compliment. I wasn't ready for the demands of the direct route when I last made my way to Father's refuge. But now, he believes I'm ready. That's good. And I do see Father's mercy more clearly. Now it's time to trust him for protection and provision.

Celia shifted feet, bumping him.

Hank turned his thoughts to the reconnaissance Vassar supplied. *He was dismissive about the risks of the direct route. "Just more of the same. Nothing you haven't already encountered or can't deal with at the time." He sure seemed reassuring.*

As he stood thinking back on these things, he appreciated Vassar's belief in him. Still, he could hear the creek ahead, and with the sound, he could feel adrenaline seeping into his blood stream.

Jester suggested his adrenaline was anticipation, but Magician advised otherwise. *No. I think the adrenaline is about fear. Fear that I don't have what it takes to go the direct route, fear I will fail, and most of all, fear that Father and Vassar will be disappointed in me.*

Hank didn't do anything with his fears beyond recognize them. There was some sense that said, *Better to know where these are than dispel them and lose track of them.*

He produced a carrot from Celia's saddle bag and held it for her until it was a nub. She snarfed up the remainder from his palm and chewed while he rubbed her between her ears. She sniffed for more while Hank enjoyed her soft muzzle in his palm. He placed his hands at the base of both her ears, massaged her head, and said, "Okay, sweetheart. Pay attention. And look sharp." Hank patted her cheek. *Telling Celia to look sharp is like telling a turtle to hurry.* He looked at his trail partner. Perhaps it was his imagination, but she did seem to stand a little taller.

Not far down the fall of the creek, they encountered a distinct animal trail. After a drink, Hank and Celia joined the trail.

The path was indeed direct, but it was equally treacherous, almost a plummet. Hank's hip and back struck up their complaint while Jester howled about the King's unwillingness to remove Hank's affliction even though possessing the ability to grant him reprieve. *It's just not right of him,* Jester suggested to Hank. *It's not good.*

So incessant was Jester's harangue that Hank stopped to curse Jester on several occasions—for his accusation, but also for disturbing the peace. He felt better for the cursing, but it appeared to only goad Jester into stepping closer for his next assault, albeit from an adjusted angle.

Screaming pain, an unforgiving terrain, and Jester's repetitive attacks made for a horrendous descent.

As far as Hank could tell, Celia ignored Jester. But the deadfalls on the steep trail were more than dear Celia could manage. With each pile of fallen timber, she was too intimidated to keep moving. No amount of coaxing, even with a treat, could convince her to jump what Hank knew she could clear. "If a deer can get over this, you can too!" he exhorted. "Come on."

But she was having none of it.

Attempting to lead her around the fallen obstacle meant picking his way through dense timber. Of course, the whole reason for following the animal trail was to avoid navigating his way through the tangled forest, and besides, it made his pain worse to duck and dodge and high-step. He removed a few deadfalls for her, which she patiently waited for him to accomplish, but that made his back and hip worse. With his frustration mounting, he tried pulling Celia, but concluded right away that was in vain. He tried pushing, but she let him know with a gentle kick that she didn't appreciate being touched that way. *At this rate, the efficiency of this route is evaporating.*

Jester weighed in on the situation. *Vassar had to know Celia wouldn't like this trail. He knew these deadfalls and low branches would wreck my back, and still he sent me this way. Reassured me. Talked me into it—like this would be a good plan. Not good. Not good, Vassar. I'm not amused.*

Hank adopted Jester's perspective as his own. With sweat running down his rib cage, soaking through not only his shirt and pants, but even through his leather belt; Celia braying with all feet firmly planted—or kicking at him if he tried to persuade her from behind; and with pain shrieking through his body like a demonized banshee, Hank's composure was expended. "Vassar! You son of a bitch! You knew! You knew! You had to know!"

The forest absorbed his scream. His throat hurt with the sudden roar. But his rage was so pitiful there wasn't even an echo. He expended everything—noble and ignoble—and it made not an iota of difference, apart from creating silence, and that was deafening.

Hank knew the shame well.

Even Jester was quiet—finally. He had won.

For all the confusion and doubt and compounding discouragement he suffered to this point, the fog in Hank's world seemed to clear. *I don't have what it takes after all.*

Hank adopted the condemnation and it cascaded into self-condemnation. Joining forces with Jester, Hank also abused himself as the King's child, concluding from his cursing of Vassar as illegitimate that in reality he was the illegitimate child, especially now after impugning his Brother. Unwanted. Unloved. The offspring of debauchery, Hank sank under the weight of his failure and attributed identity. *I thought better of myself. Wanted to believe. I really did, but when tested, I failed—and not a little, but fatally.*

That word—fatal—caught his attention. It wasn't a common word in this medieval time dimension, but to a twenty-first century man well-versed in the technical world, he noted that "fatal" was an error that appeared on his computer screen: "A fatal error has occurred...," the dialogue box would grimly state. Scary stuff, granted. But whatever malady the computer suffered, *It isn't truly fatal,* he thought. *I have yet to throw a computer in the trash. A fatal failure is remedied by a reboot of the system.*

No sooner did he turn his attention to that task than a vision of Magician wiping his face with his scarlet cravat of redemption appeared in his mind. His plummet into the pit of Jester's dark accusations and condemnations was ungracious, to say the least, and his embarrassment at having adopted Jester's lies as truth grieved his soul. *There's no excuse for what I did, for what I said, or for what I declared about my Brother,* he thought, repenting of his wrong.

Jester suggested, *I need to understand Father's willingness to forgive. I can't just confess a grievous error and go merrily along my way.*

Hank dismissed Jester's complexity, thinking, *It would be nice to understand Papa's mercy and forgiveness, but I don't need to understand to know he extends the opportunity to start over—to reboot.*

Hank sat down on the deadfall that was the critical mass over which Celia would not go and he had imploded. *I'm so sorry, Papa, Vassar. I believed a lie, accused you, cursed you for not doing what I wanted, declared you not good, and abused myself as your child and Brother. I apologize. I would like to start over, please. But first, I would very much like to hear your thoughts on where I am and what's before me. Magician, if you would, please?*

You're disappointed in yourself, aren't you?

Disappointed is an understatement, Magician.

To be disappointed in yourself is to have believed in yourself, Hank. Your Father asks that you believe in him—trust him—not in yourself, your ability, your strength, or your resources. He is your resource, not you.

But the pain, Magician!

You know better than that! Magician's thought pierced him.

Yeah. I do. You've taught me better. I see it now. Again. Pain's a distraction.

That's right. Pain's a distraction, Hank.

I lost my focus.

You did, but that's why we're having this discussion. As you know, combat is confusing, and make no mistake, you've been in the thick of it.

Why? Hank thought in his mind. *Why is it always so damn hard?* Of course, given the direction this conversation was headed, Jester had to enter the dialogue. Hank sort of noticed, but not quite consciously.

Your Father believes in you! was Magician's quick reply and decisive counter to Jester's comment. *He's equipping you because he believes in you. He's investing the best of himself in you.*

Hank thought about that idea. *He equips me because he believes in me. Help me, Magician. I don't understand. You call it equipping and investing, but it feels like abuse.*

I know, but that's Jester projecting onto your Father what he is actually doing to you. Of course, Jester won't take responsibility. He's ignoble! So, he projects his failings onto your Father.

Your Father isn't abusing you with trials, as Jester accuses. Trials come. Trials go. Trials are what they are. They're beside the point.

Hank considered that for a moment. *Trials are beside the point.* He shook his head. Looked left, then right. *Seems like my trials are the whole point.*

They are!

"Magician, you're confusing me," Hank said aloud. "Are they the point or aren't they?"

Depends on whose perspective you're considering. Hank's conversation with Vassar returned to him. *If you're paying attention to Jester, trials are the point. If you pay attention to Father, trials are neither here nor there.*

Hank nodded. *Yeah. Yeah. Got it. Jeepers this gets confusing!*

Your Father is inviting you to join him on his adventure—as you requested, Magician explained. *But before you can go where he goes, you have to be equipped to walk where he walks. He descends to the deeps and hides his treasures there. He rides on the wind in bone-numbing cold. He inhabits all-consuming fire that eliminates all impurity. He treks in the heights where the air is brutally thin! Lack of oxygen may feel abusive, but walking above, where your Father walks, means gasping for air. It is what it is.*

I'm tired of my life. The thought landed hard in Hank.

Magician capitalized upon Hank's momentum. *You've said that a number of times. Your Father is taking you at your word. You're tired of your life and want to live fully in his life. Right?*

More now than ever before! Hank declared within.

You can't live where he lives by relying upon your strength and resolve.

And, you can't go where he goes and avoid pain.

Father travels the narrow way. He goes where none have gone before. While he is light, his treasures are invested in deep darkness. He steps into pain, embraces hardship, grieves where there is sorrow, and in all ways personally identifies with every failure. If he didn't, then there would be every reason to doubt him when he asks for my trust.

Hank ruminated on this: *If Father didn't understand every pain, failure, and grief then he wouldn't be trustworthy. He wouldn't be good. But that he does understand means he is absolutely, infinitely deserving of my unreserved trust.* Hank's eyebrows rose. *Sounds like Vassar,* he concluded.

But what about the pain? The difficulty? The disappointment? The losses? Doesn't he care enough to do something about this stuff?

Magician guarded Hank's heart while he processed, but he didn't shield him from the distraction of pain's shrieks and Jester's suggestions. Hank shifted on the deadfall, stretched his leg out, and tried unsuccessfully to reach the spasm deep inside the muscles along his spine. *Pain is a distraction,* he reasoned. *It is also a gift! After all, I wouldn't be here if it were not for pain's constant demand that I be honest about my weakness and Papa's strength. Father is not disengaged. He's in me, speaking to me. Father never shies from the narrow, hard, demanding, or ungracious. I cannot bear the thought of not joining him on his adventure. I've told him that, so he's honoring my desire and stated wish.*

Hank contemplated that conclusion for a moment before Magician weighed in. *It's more than that, Son. Sure, I'm honoring what you desire, but I believe in you. More than that though, I really want you with me. It would be unkind of me not to prepare you for what lies ahead of us.*

If your son asked to join you on a hike in the high country, wouldn't you prepare him ahead of time?

Sure I would, Hank thought. *It would be cruel of me to do otherwise, and if I had a son, I would long for him to join me in the high places.*

There you go, the thought in response came. *Trust me on this, will you?*

The pain in his hip and back had escalated, something he didn't think possible. It had started raining, which at first was refreshing, but the temperature was dropping as well. He had gone from sweaty-hot-miserable to shivering-cold-stiff. And Jester was in full rant, reminding Hank, *I've tried this before. It's never good enough for the King. Always expecting more and never offering quite enough resources for what he demands.*

Whatever. Get in the complaint line, Jester, Hank thought. *Your indictments are stale.*

Hank looked at Celia. She looked terrible! Her hair coat was dripping water and her head was down.

Magician called for the question. *What's it going to be, Hank? We going your way or your Father's way? I'm with you either way, up or down. But right now I'm cold!*

Hank knew Magician wasn't cold. *I'm the one who's cold!*

The question helped him focus though. Standing slowly—his best muscles like molasses, his worst like frozen tenderloin—Hank could feel the sweat of his labor against pain mixing with the rain on his face. Celia lifted her head. He stretched his arms out to his sides and tilted his face upward to receive the full brunt of the increasing storm. Speaking into the downpour, he said, "Papa, I don't understand all that we've just discussed, but then I don't need to understand. You owe me no explanations, but I want you to know I appreciate you entertaining my questions. You are truly humble and patient. Father, I desire to go where you are headed: up, down, sideways; backwards or forwards; through or around; in pain or not; storm or still; living or dying. I won't promise you anything, because to do so would be a declaration of personal belief in myself. What I do want you to know is that I'm with you. For the last little while, I've expected you to be with me, and you have been. Thank you. But I would much rather know I'm headed where you are going than take comfort in knowing you are going where I'm headed. I believe you and I believe in you. Please help my unbelief."

As he stood considering the ebb and flow within his heart, a thought came to him. He rearranged the tarps covering Celia's saddlebags, making do with one less even though it was raining cats and dogs. He took the tarp he'd gained and tossed it over the deadfall across the trail. He stepped to the other side, holding Celia's lead, and said, "Come on, sweetheart."

Celia cleared the deadfall with ease and waited patiently while Hank collected the tarp.

Thus, Hank and Celia worked their way efficiently down the trail. Hank's pain didn't abate. Jester poked and ranted and raved. The trail was slick from the rain. There were deadfalls, mossy rocks, and obstacles. Nothing changed circumstantially, but Hank turned the ears of his heart toward Magician for encouraging words, fresh perspective, and determined resolve.

And, it worked.

Jester insisted it would have been better—more loving, more thoughtful, more advantageous, more pleasant, *ad nauseum*—if the King had arranged his return to the castle differently. Endlessly, unremittingly, and ceaselessly Jester assailed the King's credibility and goodness because of Hank's circumstances. Never mind that this was normal weather for the mountains and normal behavior for a donkey.

Hank tried to ignore Jester as Celia appeared to do, but then adopted the approach of acknowledging his harangue before turning his circumstantial situation to his advantage and his Father's benefit. "My situation is difficult, granted, but Papa has promised his strength and I have that in abundance."

But why do I need abundant grace and strength? If there was just a smidgeon of relief, I would be better, Jester's counter came.

"What you mean," Hank stated aloud, "is that if the stressors were diminished slightly I could manage in my own strength. I reject that! My Father has said he is my supply and I'm depending on him to be just that. Nothing less."

But he's persnickety, unreliable, Jester accused.

"Father's timing and valuation are not mine, but he is faithful and good. His ways are not my ways, but his ways are my heart's desire. If my ways suffer in the process, then I am weaned from self-dependence. That is a good thing."

But he always pushes too far and demands too much, Jester asserted.

"If you mean to imply that Papa is unreasonable, that can be true. He is not always rational. But then, my thinking is limited to my physical senses and circumstances, and your input is rooted in the heart of deception. Father may take me with him to the edge, but I have no desire to live a life of safety. He may be dangerous, but he is good."

On and on this went. Jester was relentless. But Hank sparred against his nemesis in the power of the Kingdom's Wizard who lived within him. Magician seemed to relish the challenge, and Hank sensed within himself that he was gaining confidence and strength.

Celia stopped. Right now! Wouldn't go another step. Her ears waggled and twisted while her nose sifted the air to identify the change she sensed. Hank studied his surroundings, but couldn't discern anything amiss. After what he felt was a genuine show of respect for Celia, he tugged on her lead, "Come on, Celia. It's alright. Let's go." Nothing doing! Hank looked again. He encouraged his beast of burden again, with a slightly more insistent pull, but Celia wouldn't advance a step. *She's not being stubborn,* Hank thought. *She's bothered about something.*

"Mr. Henderson?" The call came from the woods fifty yards ahead.

Hank stepped back closer to Celia. *How did she know that?* he wondered.

"Mr. Henderson? Is that you?"

"Come out where I can see you."

Two men emerged from the thick woods. Celia huffed at them and stomped her front foot. Hank was amused at her irritation with them. *I'm glad she's on my side,* he thought.

"Who are you?" Hank wanted to know.

"We work for Ms. Pintaro. She said you would be expecting us."

Hank recalled Letizia's statement that she had assigned men to look after him, but… "How'd you know where to find me?"

"Ms. Pintaro told us." The speaker paused, thinking about the irrationality of that explanation. "There was a man in her office when she summoned us. Maybe he told her."

Hank didn't know what to make of this information. There was no way in the world he had been followed—not for seventeen days—and there was no way anyone could anticipate he would be on this trail unless they were tipped off. The only person who knew where he was going was Vassar. *Hell, I don't even know where I am*, Hank conceded to himself. The men didn't appear aggressive; they weren't even defensive. In fact, they seemed astounded that they'd found him.

Celia nudged him from behind, which Hank didn't find especially helpful. She might have decided they were okay—now that she could see them—but he wasn't so certain. Now it was his turn to not budge. "And what were Ms. Pintaro's instructions?"

"That we meet you, see to your safety and comfort, and that as soon as possible escort you to her."

"I see," Hank said. "And where exactly are you supposed to take me?"

"She said you should select the location and that she'll join you—at your convenience, and at the place of your choosing."

"You said there was a man in Ms. Pintaro's office—when she summoned you. Did you get his name?"

"Introduced himself as, Pistis or Pistos or some such."

"I see," Hank said. "Pistis, you say?"

"Something like that, yeah. Pisto, maybe. Why? You know him?"

"Perhaps. Perhaps." *So Faith's using a Greek pseudonym these days,* Hank thought. *Can't wait to gouge him about that.*

Hank appreciated the two men's efforts to look after him, but they weren't woodsmen. He let them think his life was more secure now that they were with him, but more than once he anticipated difficulty and tactfully guided them with casual recommendations. He got the distinct impression they were relieved to have found him and happier still to be headed back toward civilization.

The four travelers—including Celia—approached the castle outskirts about dusk. The sky was dark in the northwest. Intermittent flashes of lightening fluorescently illuminated a heavy overcast. As the sun went down, the changing temperature forebode a wet night. Hank felt a weight collecting upon his mind and bogging down his emotions. The burdens he left at the castle almost three weeks ago were waiting for his return. As he got closer, one-by-one he picked them up again and turned his mind toward finding resolutions. He felt like ignoring them, and more than once thought about turning around and leading Celia back into the forest, but his sense of responsibility and compassion wouldn't permit that. His Father's calling resounded inside his heart and commitment to his commission fortified his resolve. The closer he got to the castle, the more focused he became, and soon he was back in the zone of life on the edge.

They stopped outside the gate. Hank instructed the two men to go immediately and bring Ms. Pintaro to Levine's Livery. "They will provide for Celia," he explained. What he didn't say was that it was off the beaten path, which meant he wouldn't be watched or expected. In addition, the Levine's had a few rooms for rent. The appointments were Spartan, but they were clean. Maria Levine had a hearty menu of food and drink, although the menu was for show. You ate what she prepared or you didn't eat.

Hank had met the other half of the proprietorship, Jamison "Jay" Levine, casually. He was a no-nonsense man whom he liked at first blush. Word on the street was that Jay and his sons, Adam and Larry, didn't put up with rambunctious behavior from anyone. He wasn't expecting Letizia to pull a stunt, but he was still cautious. He felt guilty for doubting her conversion, but just because she changed her tune didn't mean he discarded as irrelevant what he knew of her former life.

Hank's two watchdogs didn't ask a question. He didn't really need further proof that they were indeed sent for his benefit. Nevertheless, their compliance with his instructions was reassuring. He watched them hurry off to fetch their boss before turning toward the livery.

He curried Celia, watered and fed her, and settled her into a secure stall in the stable. While he was caring for his traveling companion, an employee prepared water for him.

He took his time bathing and changing clothes. Even if Letizia was ready to dart out the door, it would be a generous hour before she arrived.

CHAPTER 24

Levine's Livery and Pub

Hank permitted himself one drink while he waited for Letizia. His stomach was empty and he wanted his mind clear.

He didn't know anyone in the pub-restaurant-roadhouse and he didn't recognize the man who entered through the kitchen, but he knew instantly he was there on behalf of Letizia. As wide as Letizia's network of assistants was, it amused Hank that her people were readily identifiable.

While her man cased the place, Hank rose from his seat in the corner and casually walked toward the kitchen. He didn't have to look to know the man was hurrying after him. Like a rodent running toward cheese, her service agent ran into Hank's trap. Before he knew what happened, he was disabled in Hank's grasp. The man grunted, first in surprise, then in struggle to free himself.

"Be quiet!" Hank demanded in the man's ear. "Stop squirming!"

Hank had warned the Levine's that such an altercation might occur, so Adam wasn't surprised. He quickly moved toward the hall where Hank had backed Letizia's guard into a corner, saying to his staff as he went, "It's okay. I was expecting this. It's okay. Get back to work."

Hank didn't relax his hold. "Why are you here?"

"I was sent to find you."

"Not so loud," Hank demanded. "Sent by who?"

"Ms. Pintaro."

"Where is she?"

"Out back."

Hank glanced at Adam. He shrugged and shook his head.

Hank tightened his grip. "Don't mess with me."

"She's in the grove of trees, behind the livery."

"How many are with her?" Adam required of him.

It humbled the man to have to answer a youth. "Three."

"And what were you supposed to do when you found me?" Hank asked.

"Tell Ms. Pintaro," the man said, grimacing.

"That's it? Just report back?"

"Yes. That's all. I swear!"

"You sure you don't work for Jester?" Hank asked.

"I don't know who that is. Honest. I work for Ms. Pintaro."

Hank had all he needed. "Very well. Don't try anything heroic and everything will be fine. I mean no harm to Ms. Pintaro."

Hank let go of the man while watching him for any false move. The agent rubbed his shoulder to relieve the spasm.

Adam escorted Letizia's agent out the back door as Hank followed. Adam's Brother, Larry, was just coming from the stable and hurried his pace. Someone had notified Mr. Levine—Jay—that there was a disturbance. He appeared from around the corner about the same time Larry arrived.

Hank filled Jay in on the situation...who picked up quickly and took over. "You go compose yourself, Mr. Henderson." Turning toward the kitchen staff, Jay said, "Susan, fetch Mr. Henderson a dram." Placing his hand on Hank's shoulder, "I'll see to your friends in the woods. No worries, Mr. Henderson. Off with you now."

Rain began to fall. Giant drops pelted the earth. Jay donned his poncho of waxed cloth from inside the livery door and worked his way along an arching route toward the clump of trees at the back of his property. The increasing downpour facilitated his surprise.

Jay studied the four, hunched-over figures during flashes of lightening. Not even the horses knew of his close approach. "Ms. Pintaro?"

"Yes? Here I am."

"Mr. Henderson's waiting on you, ma'am. No need for those fellows you have with you. They can wait in the barn."

As Jay watched, Letizia dismissed her guards.

After her agents were gone, Jay stepped from his hiding. "Sorry if I startled you, ma'am. I'm Jamison Levine. This is my place."

"Mr. Levine," Letizia acknowledged.

"If you're ready, I'll take you to Mr. Henderson. He's been waiting quite a spell for you. Good man."

"Certainly, please. I appreciate your guidance, especially in this weather."

Jay eased to her horse so as not to startle the animal and patted its dripping neck. He took Letizia to the livery and helped her from her horse. Larry approached to check on his Dad—and meet this woman who had created a stir. Jay introduced his son as he handed him the reins to Ms. Pintaro's mount.

Jay walked Ms. Pintaro to the house and held the door for her. As she passed him, he offered, "If I was you, Ms. Pintaro, I would hire some better people."

She nodded, then expressed appreciation for his respect and care. Maria greeted them, introduced herself, and volunteered that Mr. Henderson was waiting, but pointed Letizia first toward a room where she could, "…freshen up a mite."

Hank stood when Maria led Letizia from the kitchen. He greeted her with a kiss on the cheek, "Lettie, it's nice to see you again. Thank you for coming."

"I've been worried about you," she said, sitting as he held her chair. "We didn't know where you had gone."

"Yeah. Sorry. I needed some breathing room."

"You're making it hard for my men to look after you."

Hank was embarrassed. "I don't mean to be difficult."

Letizia raised her eyebrows.

He grimaced. "What can I say?"

Hank and Lettie visited for a couple of hours. Meanwhile, the weather worsened. Maria approached as the evening progressed, "Ms. Pintaro. I'm sorry for the interruption, but just to let you know, I've prepared a room for you. Tonight's no night to be on the road."

Letizia protested, noting that she wasn't traveling alone, "…and had to get back."

"We're happy to have you, Ms. Pintaro. As for your colleagues, Jay's bedded them down in the barn. They'll be comfortable there."

Letizia nodded her agreement and sincere appreciation.

Hank and Lettie spent the first part of their discussion on matters pertinent to her life. Once she got started, she didn't spare Hank from the load upon her mind. She told him about Caroline's promotion. Having managed a number of people, Hank recognized that Caroline's promotion was extraordinary, even for her. *But then, the risks are extraordinary,* he thought. *And, Lettie's concerned for her personal safety. More accurately, she's concerned for her life.*

They discussed abstractions about the King, his teaching, and also their relationship, but then reduced each abstraction to practical application. In this way, their conversation ebbed and flowed between theoretical constructs and personal focus.

"Either the King's life and teaching are relevant or they aren't," she said, voicing her internal debate to Hank. "I need to know—must know."

Letizia's questions revealed a hungry heart and visiting with Hank was the nourishment she needed. Their conversation reassured Hank that her conversion to the Kingdom of Light was legitimate. That eased his mind considerably, at least about her. *I've still got to be alert. Lettie's declaration of allegiance to the King will incite Zophos' ire.*

They agreed to meet in the morning for breakfast and further discussion. After thanking the Levine's, both retired to their respective rooms.

Letizia found Hank the next morning, sitting at the same table where they had eaten dinner, drinking coffee, and reading. So intent was he on the document before him that she surprised him with her greeting. He regained his composure, stood to greet her, and dragged her chair where she could sit next to him.

As she sipped her coffee, Hank introduced her to Vassar's letter. It was a bold thing, showing this treasure to someone so new to his life, someone who in her former life had tried to have him killed. But in his heart Hank deemed the risk apropos.

"Each morning, I read my Brother's letter," he explained. "As I read, I select a pertinent section for the day—a thought that grabs my attention. I figure it's Magician's way of focusing me. Then, I think about that central concept—until further notice from Magician or the end of the day."

Shoulder-to-shoulder, drinking their coffee, Hank and Lettie read Vassar's words.

Over breakfast they discussed what they read. Hank was amazed at how much Lettie retained from an initial reading. But what was even more interesting, they discovered they were drawn to the same lines. Once again, after the table was cleaned, Hank scooted his chair close to Lettie's and they read Vassar's words:

Don't worry! I know you didn't anticipate this, but Father knows what he's doing—and I am near you, as near as your thoughts and the desires of your heart, like Magician.

Know that I am working in advance, preparing the way. I'll meet with you frequently, but don't ever hesitate to draw upon the tremendous resource inside you.

Magician is not only a great friend and comfort, he will never leave you.

Letizia confided in Hank her personal concerns. While he knew what it was to be threatened, he knew as well that Lettie needed more than inspiration and encouragement. It was Vassar's words that inspired her transparency and confidence in his guidance. It should be reliance upon, and trust in, Vassar's words that provided her assurance.

Together, they aligned their hearts and thoughts with what they had read. "The reason I shouldn't worry," Lettie observed, "is because the King knows what he's doing."

"True enough," Hank concurred. "May I make an observation, Lettie? A personal observation?"

She nodded vigorously.

"It is true that when you bowed your knee to the King you declared allegiance to him, to his ways, and to his Kingdom. But when you accepted Vassar's invitation to join the King's family via identification with him, he became your Brother and the King became your Father."

She nodded, but the furrow in her brow indicated there was skepticism between her head and her heart.

"Lettie, as I listen to you talk about your relationship to the King, you avoid the implications of the second aspect of your conversion—your acceptance into the family through Vassar's intervention on your behalf."

"I'm not sure I follow what you're saying," she said.

"You consistently refer to the King, but you have yet to address him as family."

Tears puddled in Hank's eyes as he recalled the distance he maintained from his Father for so long, his distrust so violent he feared his Father. Addressing him as "King" maintained what he felt was a safe and respectable space. Reflections coursed through his memory,

The distance and label were foolish! But the fear! The fear that rose up considering the close name, "Father"? Whew. It was like discovering a rattlesnake crawled into my sleeping bag in the night. Fear is irrational, but it is as real as the table under my elbows.

Letizia grasped the irrational benevolence of a King on an undeserving subject. "I've done the same thing," she said. "I've extended another chance to an undeserving person. It was irrational," she noted, "even imprudent, but I've done it. Why wouldn't the King behave similarly?"

"I'm with you," Hank said. "Go on."

"Whether by reason or whim, I know in my heart the King accepted my declaration of allegiance." Letizia considered the soundness of her conviction before continuing. "I don't know why he accepted me, included me. I don't know why I'm a beneficiary of his estate."

She backed up, thought again, but was stuck. "I don't know," she conceded. "This adoption? Into his family? It's like my mind's a two-wheeled cart that's lost a wheel. I don't know—and I don't begin to know how to get rolling again."

Hank waited, listening.

"I want to believe. Long to believe, that I'm indeed in the family."

"It's almost too good to be true, isn't it Lettie?"

She sat looking at him. "Almost, but not quite. In my heart, I believe."

Hank smiled at her. "You know, Lettie. Rather than discuss this at the table, why don't we take a walk."

"I like that idea," she said.

The rain had returned all the dust and foreign particles from the air to the earth. Fall was in the air.

Hank and Letizia walked to the livery where her bodyguards snapped to attention. "I've met your friends," Hank said, motioning toward her agents, "but you have yet to meet my friend." They walked through the barn to where Celia had her chest pressed against her corral.

"Celia, this is Ms. Letizia Pintaro. Lettie, please meet Celia."

Celia acknowledged Letizia because she was a curiosity. Once she collected Letizia's scent—and checked her for food offerings—she pressed her head against Hank's chest. She noted the unmistakable whiff of a carrot coming from inside his jacket and began rooting for the treasure. Hank produced the prize, broke it in half, gave his part to Celia, and handed the other piece to Letizia.

Hank watched Celia, respecting her uncanny sensibility about other members of God's created beings. Letizia giggled like a teenager as Celia ate from her hand and nuzzled her neck. Hank noted it was an affection Celia extended to Letizia alone. Hank felt silly, placing as much stock in Celia's evaluation of Lettie as he did Magician's, but uttered in his thoughts, *Magician, you keep good company.*

Hank encouraged Letizia's agents to remain at the Levine's. She concurred. As he thought about it, *I have more confidence—far more confidence—in Celia's care than theirs.*

Hank and Letizia left by the road less traveled. With the rain, it was evident there had been no traffic. Celia followed.

As they walked, they were accompanied by their Father's finest symphony. In honor of their visitation, he assembled a broad array of whistling and singing birds, fluky breezes through fluttering leaves, and harmonious waters lilting alongside whispering grasses. The soft surface of the trail absorbed their footfalls so as not to disturb a single note.

Being out—away from the inn, away from the humanity, away from the guards—and into his place of respite and refuge, Letizia witnessed a side of Hank she'd not seen. As though enraptured, he pointed out the variations of sounds. Letizia thought he looked very much like a conductor—so caught up in the music he forgets there is an audience. The moment she noted his heart return from its elation to the physical proximity, he was embarrassed, or at least he blushed.

But Hank's joy in his Father's creation wasn't without purpose. From the noticeable comfort he derived from being in his Papa's presence,

Hank shared candidly with Letizia of his struggle to trust his Father. He talked with her about the tenuous balance between pain as his mentor and pain as his Achilles' heel. "Pain can focus me, but in those days and moments when I lose my way, pain is the precipice over which I tumble, invariably finding myself tangled in the thorny vines of distrust."

Letizia listened carefully. Not only was she not used to such transparency, she was closely observing her own propensity to distrust.

"Bit by bit, step by step," Hank revealed more of his life, encouraging and inspiring Letizia to follow with hers. "The place of trust is apprehended one torturous piece of ground after another. Two steps forward, one back. Two steps forward, three back. Three forward, one back. Trust is a desperate fight up the hill to the King's throne. It is ground littered with loss, sacrifice, disillusionment, ruin, glory, and close conflict. But every hard-won inch is crucial and critically important because each measures the victory of trust and is therefore hallowed ground. The battle for trust is perhaps the most important in the Kingdom."

"How so?" she asked.

"Because trust is the ultimate declaration of belief in the King and his goodness."

"Hmm," she mused. "Tell me more about that."

"History helps," he noted.

"History?"

"Uh, huh. History short-term and history long-term."

"The long view of history, as they say."

"Exactly. So let me give you an example of both," he proposed.

"Long-term and short-term mixed together?"

"Yeah. I'll assimilate my history with our ancient predecessor, Job, who struggled to trust the King and wrote it down for us to consider."

"Okay. Good. The long view of history supplemented with your story." Letizia leaned in closer.

"Job's fight was a brutal suffering—internal and external. Everything in his book hinges on the razor-thin edge of who was good. Was it him—an honorable, upright man of integrity—or was it the King?"

"I see where this is headed," she said.

"I figured you would. But circumstantially, the hardships Job endured pointed to the King not being true to his stated character, intent, and person."

"Why's that?" Letizia asked. "I was following you, and now I'm not."

"Job's suffering occurred because the King baited Zophos to test Job."

"Eww. I understand that. Job was caught in between the King and Zophos. Not good."

"Experientially, Job was in real trouble. In fact, it was life and death as far as he was concerned! He debated with the King, challenging him repeatedly, and carrying his argument to the foundation of the King's integrity. Eventually, he marked a deep line in the dirt with the heel of his boot and said, 'Even if the King kills me, I will still trust him.'"

"Oh, wow! You're saying Job called the King's bluff, daring him to kill him even though he was a good man. He was challenging the King's use of his power."

"Right," Hank affirmed.

"So whether the King kills Job or lets him live—either way, Job is good and the King is not. Interesting. Very interesting—very shrewd," Lettie said. "Go on. You've got me hooked, but for the record, I've not heard anything about you yet."

"I know. I'm getting there," Hank said. "Misery loves company, so I've got to get Job fully implicated before I confess."

Letizia laughed out loud. "By the time this tale is told, I think us girls are going to be the only ones standing," she said, nodding toward Celia.

"Yeah. You girls are going to rule the world, no doubt. Anyway, it was a setup: Job's integrity versus the King's goodness. One or the other."

"Both couldn't be right," Letizia said.

Hank acknowledged, then continued. "The hardship Job was suffering, he felt, came at the expense of the King's honor. 'How can the King be good and do what he has done to a man as upright as me? That was the nub of Job's argument and accusation.'"

"He felt his good behavior made him deserving of the King's favor and blessing, which he wasn't receiving in the measure he wished. You're saying Job felt entitled. Right?"

"In a word, yes," said Hank. "Entitled because he was a man of integrity. But providing what Job wanted would be an acknowledgement by the King that Job was right—and that he, the King, was indeed not good."

"I see what you mean," she said. "Quite a double-bind Job created for the King."

"I think it was unwitting on Job's part, but the truth of the matter is, he colluded with Jester and Zophos to trap the King."

"A good King wouldn't permit the suffering of an upright man like Job."

"That's the thesis of Job's story. The antithesis is that the good King did allow the upright man, Job, to suffer. In fact, he instigated the hardship. Job wasn't on Zophos' mind until the King mentioned him."

"I'm with you."

Hank continued, "Back and forth the conflict progressed, the prophet fighting to hold the ground of his personal integrity against the King who declared he was absolutely good. If Job was right, the King was wrong. If the King was right, Job would have to confess to being less than upstanding. Since his whole life was his integrity, this was a battle-to-the-death in Job's soul."

"The stakes were high for the King as well," Letizia noted. "Why didn't he just put an end to it?"

"Great question! The short answer is because the King was more interested in talking with Job than showcasing his power."

"Okay. I hear you," she said. "But I don't want the short answer—not regarding this. I want to hear the rest of Job's story—and you promised your story as well. You've got a ways to go, Hank."

"Right, right. Well, it gets worse before it gets better. Caught between Zophos, the enemy of his soul, some unwise counselors, horrendous loss, caustic circumstance, and the obstreperous King, Job struggled to stand and defend himself while the King refused to rise and show him deference. Over the razor's edge slicing between his personal integrity and the King's goodness, the upright man—Job—wrestled and writhed with the good King. Over and over, Job asserts that he is right and the King wrong."

"I'm still thinking the King should have just end it."

"But then the conversation would have been over, Job would have been eliminated, and doubt would persist over Job's accusations."

"I see what you're saying," Lettie acknowledged.

"So to summarize: Job trusted himself, and with good reason. Everyone, including the King, said Job was the most upright man in the land. In fact, it was upon this basis that Job approved of himself, but his reputation wasn't good enough to please the King. And this seemed unreasonable to Job."

"It probably scared the poor man to death as well," Letizia added.

"When it came down to it, the King demanded something more—something beyond reputation—from Job. Once all the self-justification is expended and it is Job and God at the crux of the issue, it came to this: The King required Job to abandon his reputation-based approval and adopt his—the King's—standard for approval rooted ultimately in his absolute determination."

"And that's where Vassar comes in," Letizia said.

"It is—but not right away. The King knew what he had in mind, but Job didn't."

"Ah. So the King challenged Job to trust his goodness…even though rationally, circumstantially, and experientially doing so appeared foolhardy."

"You've got it, Lettie! Job defined goodness circumstantially, primarily based upon reputation. The King defined goodness based upon character and his declaration."

"I understand, and truthfully, I identify," she said. "Well, Job must have survived. I presume he wrote his book or made a statement. Something. Otherwise, you wouldn't know this story."

"True, Lettie. I wouldn't know his story, which was a critical component in understanding my own story."

Letizia stopped walking. She looked Hank square in the eye.

Celia bumped up against her master, which Hank took as reassurance.

"The good King was patient with the upright man, Job. More patient than I would have been. And like he was with Job, he was patient with me too, Lettie. Job exhausted his arguments in defense of himself. Likewise, I expended all of my rather formidable, personal holdings in self-defense and self-justification."

"I see," Letizia whispered, knowing Hank was taking her into his life.

"Surprisingly, the King explained himself to Job—gave him the rationale behind his philosophy of leadership, governance, position, and relationship. Like my ancient mentor, the King tolerated my wariness and speculation as well. He reasoned with me. He never relented, never rendered an inch of territory to me based upon my self-justification, but he never once turned away either. And like Job, once the King had my undivided attention, he addressed my doubt."

"I didn't know we had that in common," Letizia noted.

"Oh, boy!" Hank exclaimed, acknowledging her identification. "He explained to me that my relationship with him, and my standing in the family, are not based in the slightest upon anything I have or have not done—no matter how good or bad—but are purely predicated upon the gracious and magnificent provision of Vassar."

"What did you say to him—when he explained this to you?" Letizia asked.

"Well, like Job, it wasn't one conversation. But when the real picture came into focus, I thanked him for his patience—for his indulgence, really. By any other standard, he should have had me dispatched to some eternal rock pile to do hard labor. In truth, that fate would have been more mercy than I deserved. But as you know, the King is rather extravagant when it comes to doling out his forgiveness and mercy. As I said, he explained himself to me. Vassar and Magician were immensely helpful advocates and counselors. Like Job, I realized that I knew a great deal about the King, but I didn't know the King's heart. In my anxiety to avoid him while justifying myself, I'd missed his personal advance upon my heart. Trying to secure and preserve the pitiful territory of self-justification, I discovered he occupied my heart—and by his residence confirmed me good because he is good. In this way the good King disarmed my self-determined righteousness and declared me right because I'm his son."

"What'd you do?" Letizia asked.

"I did what you did, Lettie."

"I don't understand."

"I jettisoned any notion of self-rule, self-defense, and self-justification. I told him that I was wrong about him. I thanked him for introducing himself instead of banishing me. I'd misjudged him. I was so focused upon defending myself as right that I had missed his true goodness. His divine humility to introduce himself to me, explain his reasoning, and then patiently do so all over again—well, suffice it to say, for the first time I saw his heart for who he truly is."

"And?"

"And I laid down my arms. Surrendered myself unconditionally."

"What'd the King do?"

"That leads us back to how we got into this conversation," Hank said. He took her by the hand, hoping that the touch would transfer to her the necessary reassurance for the decision that awaited on the other side of his answer. "He lifted me up, forgave me, restored me, pulled me close, provided his light for me, and asked only one thing."

"Yes?"

"He asked only that I call him, Father. By implication, that declaration of family title meant he was asking that I accept my place in his family."

"Now, we've returned to trust. Right?"

Hank nodded. And he waited, noting with amusement that Celia shifted her head from his shoulder to nuzzle Letizia.

"I don't trust anybody, Hank! Not really. I pose and posture in a charade of trust, but I rely precisely upon one person."

"Yourself."

"Talking with you is disarming, Mr. Henderson."

"And how's that, Ms. Pintaro?"

She chuckled at him. That he replied in kind acknowledged her loaded humor…and left her precisely where she had been.

"You're a fisherman, aren't you?"

Hank smiled. "No, Lettie. I'm not a fisherman. I'm a fly fisherman. Fishermen are uncouth, beer-drinking, bait casters, holding poles, and watching corks. A fly fisherman is a suave, debonair, handsome, and intelligent…"

"Oh, whatever," she interrupted.

"Why did you ask?"

"Because it seems to me the King is like an angler. Once he hooked me, alone in my study—such an unhappy adherent to his personage— he began reeling me in. First it was the revelation of his truth, to which I subscribed. Then, it was the news you shared of Crown Prince Vassar wanting to occupy my heart's throne, to which I agreed. Then followed the King's pledge of Magician as surety that I was his heir. I'm working to believe that, by the way. Now this. For the last weeks I've seen myself as fresh-caught and flopping about. I suppose, carrying the metaphor forward another step or two, now that he has reeled me within reach, I've expected him to gut me. But no! As you first told me sitting by the side door at Hoi Polloi, the angler has reeled me in, not to gut me or throw me back, but to bring me close, take me in his arms, bless me as his, and kiss me on the head."

Hank squeezed her hand.

"No matter how I've tried to resist—and oh, my! I have resisted some days." She paused. "I can't escape the sense of his lips on the top of my head." She looked at the creek, thinking, struggling with what was queued up next in her mind.

"That's all exactly true, Lettie. But that's not all. He has pulled you close and kissed you on your head, but he is also whispering in your ear. What's he saying?"

"That he's my Father. But above his whisper, like the shout of a warrior, I hear Vassar declaring that I'm his sister."

Like a deer who realizes it's spotted, Letizia stood perfectly still. Her heart was exposed.

Hank smiled. Nodded. "Yeah. That sounds like Vassar."

Hank hugged her around the shoulder, and subtly directed Celia and her forward. They walked a few steps, silence between them, but still accompanied by the King's chorus.

"So, Lettie. What are you going to do?"

"About what?"

"About what Father and Vassar are saying to you."

"I'm going to let myself be loved and cared for," she said. "I'm just not sure how to go about that. Any suggestions?"

"Well, I can tell you that part of my story if you like."

They sat next to one another on a log beside a gurgling brook. Aspen trees surrounded them, raining golden leaves as prompted by the fall breeze.

Hank told Letizia more of his story, more of his struggle, and more of his resistance to his Father's approach. "But you know, Lettie. It came to this, at least for me: Through his persistent goodness, no matter if I was suffering or in shame or enjoying celebration, he wanted to be close. Ultimately, even 'Father' was too distant a name to accurately capture my heart's desire and bond to his heart and Vassar's."

"Really? I don't recall hearing you refer to him any other way than, Father."

"No, you probably haven't," Hank admitted. "It's personal—very personal, almost sacred, in fact."

Letizia waited. Either Hank trusted her enough to share, to invite her into the private place where his heart dwelt, or he didn't. It was a place into which she hoped to be invited.

"One of these days," he began, "I need to take you to the King's Refuge. That's where I've been the last few days, by the way. But the last time I was there, a couple of years ago, Father and I were talking. As you've described, I felt him drawing me—inviting me—to a new place, a closer place. He was inviting me into his life and light—deeper, more intimate, tighter, and brighter than ever before. More than anything I wanted to be with him. The desire was so strong I thought my heart would burst. And of course, it was an invitation. All I had to do was accept, but my heart desired more than, 'yes.' I wanted a more personal declaration, so I asked him if it would be okay if I called him, Papa."

"Papa? What'd he say?" Letizia asked.

"What you'd expect. He was thrilled. And, I was too. No sooner had I asked him, than my heart was comforted. So, there you have it! End of story."

Letizia giggled, her joy joining the gurgling of the creek. "I like that: Papa."

They sat together. Celia ate grass, her munching occasionally audible above the sound of the water.

"So what do you call Crown Prince Vassar?" Letizia asked.

"Usually just, Vassar. Sometimes, Brother. But now that I think about it, mostly just, Vassar."

"Hmm. I've never had a brother. Didn't have much of a father either. He was a sperm donor who disappeared after his donation."

"I see. And your Mom?"

"Gone three years ago. All my life, it was just her and me. We made it, but to say we were poor would be an understatement. When I got old enough, I found work, and when Mom realized I could take care of myself, it was like she resigned from life. She declined, lost her job, turned to the streets, and lost her way."

"Oh, my," Hank said. "I'm sorry, Lettie."

"Yeah. Near as I can figure, her final resting place is a dump the other side of La Faim."

"I know the place," Hank said. "Know La Faim as well. In fact, I've got a good friend who lives there. He's a follower of the King too."

There was a moment of quiet.

"Your Mom made a tough exit."

"That she did."

"Have you been to her burial site?"

"You mean, the dump?"

Hank nodded.

"No. I've not ever been."

He thought a moment. "Well, I don't blame you, but if you decide at some point you want to visit, I'll go with you."

Letizia nodded. "You're kind, Hank. I need to think about that."

"Sure. I understand. Offer stands, though. Anytime."

Letizia returned to an earlier point. "As you can see, this family thing the King's got going on is bending my brain."

Hank chuckled at her description. "Yeah. I know that. Mine too."

Celia, Letizia, and Hank spent the remainder of the day wandering the woods, trails, and back roads. Letizia asked if they could do the same again tomorrow. Hank had nothing pressing.

They enjoyed a nice dinner, a fine bottle of red, and lingered until bedtime over a long conversation. The next morning after breakfast Letizia, Celia, and Hank repeated the day before, only in a different direction.

They returned Celia to her stall in the stable late in the afternoon and spoke to Letizia's agents. They seemed to be fairing well enough, although they smelled a lot like the barn. But then, so did Celia.

There was a horse in the livery and a simple carriage beside the barn that hadn't been there that morning. *Business is good for the Levine's*, and it pleased Hank. *These are good people*, he thought, happy to be here instead of his room in the castle.

Hank held the back door open for Letizia and followed her through the kitchen, greeting the staff as he went. He and Letizia planned to have a drink before cleaning up for dinner. Never one to let his guard down, Hank noted the new people sitting in the pub, but it was only after a double-take that he recognized Jacob and Caroline Ingram.

It was quickly evident that Letizia facilitated this meeting. He looked at her.

"Jake asked that I notify him when I heard from you," she said, looking him in the eyes. "I promised. We've all missed you terribly."

After the greetings, Letizia suggested, "Caroline, why don't you and I freshen up before dinner. Jake, there's a whiskey on its way. I'd appreciate it if you'd drink it for me."

The ladies departed, leaving Jake and Hank standing in the middle of the roadhouse dining hall. As Maria approached with the drinks, Hank motioned that he and Jake would move to what had become his customary seat.

Chapter 25

Levine's Livery

$\mathscr{H}$ank was cordial. He didn't have anything against Jake. Though it hurt, he had understood Jake's reaction, and he understood that he himself needed another prod before he would decide to retreat to the King's Refuge. All these things passed through Hank's mind as he and Jake moved to their table. But still, Hank reflected, *What Jake did wasn't necessary. It hurt my feelings—embarrassed me in front of Caroline and the kids. Friends aren't supposed to do what Jake did.*

Hank didn't like his feelings, but neither did he regret them. While failing to trust was a weakness, trusting too much—or too quickly—was also a malady to be avoided. He struggled with the first, but not the second.

Jake wasted no time once they were seated. "Hank, I was wrong the night you came to the house. Wrong in my treatment of you, wrong in my reaction, wrong in my assumptions. Just generally wrong all the way around. Of course, you had information about Ms. Pintaro that I didn't have. But still, I never should have doubted you, and worst of all, I never should have let you leave the house with unfinished business of such gravity. I threw you out. That's totally unacceptable! I apologize. I'm so sorry, and if you will—if you can—I ask for your forgiveness."

Hank was quick to forgive, to clink glasses with Jake, and to enjoin the task of putting their relationship back on solid footing. He was on guard as well.

He wished it wasn't so, *But better safe than sorry,* he thought, visiting with Jake. *Trusting and not trusting? It's so confusing. However, when in doubt, trust but verify.* That was Hank's self-counsel. *I don't know if that's right or wrong, but my relationship with Jake merits scrutiny. It would devalue both of us to do otherwise.* The thought helped his confidence.

Hank also didn't know if it was right or wrong to fling the tangled mess toward Magician in hopes he would make sense of it. But that's what he did, figuring, *I'll sort it out later—when I'm by myself.*

As he willfully tossed the conflict and resolution in Magician's direction, he left Jake at the table and stepped outside to wash his face. While he was there, he checked on Celia. What he really needed was the warmth of reassurance. *No offense, Magician, but I need somebody with skin on them.*

Hank recalled the confusion and insecurity he felt not long after first arriving in Gnarled Wood, not long after he and Vassar crossed behind the Malden Creek waterfall into the spiritual world. *Talk about confused!* he reflected. *We rode to meet the King at Erymos, and by the time we arrived, not only was I apprehensive about meeting Father, whom I didn't trust any farther than I could throw him, I was stunned by the time shift, the location, the cold weather, the medieval weaponry.* Hank chuckled, thinking back. *Everything was foreign. Seeking reassurance—*he could still sense the experience—*I reached to touch my horse, to feel its warmth.*

Reminiscing, he patted Celia's neck and rubbed her ears. *I wouldn't change my experiences for the world. But neither would I wish to go back through them!* Before leaving, he produced the carrot he'd robbed off the cook's table. Celia was appreciative.

Hank stopped before he opened the back door, pausing to consult Magician. *Any words of wisdom for me?*

Love these people, Hank. Lead them. Guide and encourage them.

Okay. Got it, Hank replied in his thoughts to Magician. *Anything else?*

Just one more thing, Magician's thought placement in Hank's consciousness was strong and clear. *I believe in you!*

Thanks, Magician. That means a lot coming from you.

Hank was standing on the back stoop when Larry Levine came

around the corner. "You alright, Mr. Henderson?"

Hank waved. "I'm fine, Larry. Thanks. Just thinking. Can't walk and think at the same time, you know?"

Larry laughed. "Me neither, Mr. Henderson. Me neither."

The ladies had joined Jake and were seated at the table when Hank returned. He greeted them, complimenting both on how pretty they looked. "You too, Jake."

"I've been told lots of things," Jake replied, "but never that."

As he sat down, he said, "Lettie, thank you for arranging for Jake and me to meet. We had a good conversation. I think all is well. Do you agree, Jake?"

"Everything's fine, Hank. My emotions are still wound around the axle, but they'll be okay in time. Thank you for understanding."

Dinner was primarily devoted to catching up, but when everyone was done chewing and left only with something to drink, the conversation turned to more serious matters. There was talk of Caroline's progress in understanding Letizia's job, discussion of how Jake's work with the small group facilitators was going, and celebration over three new groups inside the Round Tower. Much to Hank's delight, Jake and Caroline reported that Ronan and Audie had reconciled their friendship. It was a hard conversation, but Jake and Caroline facilitated it around their dinner table. Ronan had asked if Jake would assist, Audie agreed in advance discussion with Caroline, and then the four met. "It was a late night," Caroline stated.

Hank decided to bring up a subject that had been weighing on his mind. He had resisted introducing it during the personal conversations he and Lettie were enjoying, but with business matters on the table, *Now's as good a time as any,* he decided.

"If I may stick my nose into your business, Lettie."

"You're concerned about my safety, aren't you?"

Hank studied her. "Yes. I am."

"I knew this topic would come up—knew the moment Mr. Levine

sneaked up on me during the storm. Scared me spitless!"

Hank defended himself. "I didn't sneak up on you."

Letizia put her hand on his arm, a gesture that escaped neither Caroline or Jake. "I know you didn't. You sent Mr. Levine."

Hank shrugged. "Here's my point. That you need security is a given, but the security you have now is too obvious. Besides that, their skills are, shall we say, lacking."

She knew she needed to make adjustments in her staffing, so Hank received no substantive push-back.

He pressed on, "I hate to be so blunt, but I must be certain I communicate clearly. Lettie, you're a powerful woman, but you're too powerful. You are used to operating with impunity. As a result, the people around you aren't as careful as they need to be."

"Give me an example," she said, her business head working.

"I've evaded your agents whenever it pleased me to do so. They stick out like sore thumbs. They're clumsy. Even Celia notices them," he added.

Letizia breathed deep, exhaled. "You're right, Hank, and in trying to look after me, you're almost dismissive of the fact that I've tried to harm you. Like the altercation on the creek bank. That could have turned out very badly for you."

"We've heard some of this story," Jake said.

Letizia shook her head, "I sent five men to find him. Two returned. The report was horrible, including that they wounded you." She looked at Hank. "I'm sorry. They weren't supposed to do you permanent harm, only convince you to back off."

"I'm comforted," Hank deadpanned to ease the tension. He touched Letizia's shoulder in reassurance.

"Did they wound you?" she asked.

"I've got a scar. But it's not the first, and I suspect it's not the last."

Turning from the grim events on the gravel bar, Letizia said, "So Hank, you are a knight in the Kingdom of Light."

Hank felt the sheath of his dagger against his elbow. He recalled the doubt and shame associated with the weapon when he first carried it at the King's banquet, and haltingly, apologetically showed it to Significance. He hated the memory!

Hank straightened his back, set his chin, fixed his eyes, and placed both hands palm-down on the table. "I am indeed!" he stated clearly, confidently.

"I've never asked you," Jake said, "but I've heard that the King and his knights exchange personal pledges. Is that true?"

"It is," Hank replied.

Jake, Caroline, and Letizia waited. Finally Jake said, "Is your pledge something you can share with us?"

Hank smiled. He cocked his head ever-so-slightly and declared, "My name is, Henry H. Henderson, advocate for my Father, the High King of Glory. I walk with him, I talk with him, I listen to him, and I cause him to laugh. And he has said, 'I will bless you, I will make you, I will place you, I will build a platform for you, and I will cause you to succeed—on my own terms. But, it will cost you your life.'"

It was hard to know what to say after that. The King's declaration took the air from the room.

"Thank you for asking, Jake," Hank said. "It's a long story—how that came about."

"You ought to write it down," Caroline suggested.

"You should," Letizia encouraged. "What would you call it?"

Hank thought, then said, "I think I would call it, *No Mercy*."

"That's interesting," Caroline said. "Why?"

"Because that's what I've learned to this point in my life—or at least, what I'm learning. On the one hand, I subconsciously believed that the battle of life is a sanctioned match governed by clear rules. I believed my enemy fights fair. I believed that when I stumble, fall, or otherwise get down that Zophos and Jester will back off until I regroup. I believed that if I was hurt or wounded they would turn their attention elsewhere, and in so doing, extend to me the mercy of recovery.

"But these beliefs were wrong. Dead wrong! My enemy extends no mercy to me. Ever! As long as I believe otherwise, I remain delusional about my enemy's intent and underestimate him. That is a grievous mistake!

"And along the way, I discovered another belief, also false. I realized that I believed the King was not merciful—believed he was not good, that he didn't really have my best in mind even though he said he did.

"But I have come to realize that my Father is full of mercy—endlessly full of generous lovingkindness. Irrationally so! Every day, in every way, he extends his mercy to me. His mercy is new every morning—simply to demonstrate and remind me of his great faithfulness.

"My belief system was backwards. I believed Zophos and Jester would show mercy to me when I needed it and that the King would not grant me mercy because I failed to live up to his expectations. I listened to Jester's accusations about the King and judged him circumstantially, and in the end, I agreed with Jester and turned my philosophy of life upside down from what is really true.

"While loved by my Father, and dutifully espousing my love for him, I loved my life and gave precedent to it based upon Jester's deception. I lived as if it was tolerable to be devoted to two loves—life in the family and life on my own, independent of the family.

"But Father was patient—mercifully understanding to me. In time, I learned that I cannot grant Jester and his accomplices any measure of latitude; not under any circumstance. There can be no provision made for Jester. He grants no mercy, no mercy can be shown, certainly none assumed.

"And then on the other hand, because Father is a man of boundless mercy and I am heir to all that he is, I who deserve no mercy am filled with it and privileged therefore to extend mercy to others through his great provision.

"So yeah, if I were to ever write my story down, I think I'd call it,

No Mercy."

Again, there was quiet at the table.

Maria approached. She cleared a dish or two and set a bottle of wine on the table. "Compliments of the house," she stated without fanfare.

After Jake poured red in each glass, Hank returned to his earlier concern. "So Lettie, we really must improve your security. You need people around you who are trustworthy, not because you hired them, but because they are loyal to you, and pledged on their honor to guard you with their life. These need to be people of considerably more skill than the people I've encountered to this point."

Letizia agreed and promised to start working on that first thing. She and Caroline exchanged a couple of "inside" thoughts, and then the conversation at the table turned to more pleasant topics. They chatted until bedtime, then called it a night.

Hank was sipping coffee the next morning when Letizia came to breakfast. He helped her with her chair, and as she sat down, she said, "I hope you don't mind that I invited Jake and Caroline."

"No. I don't mind. In fact, I'm glad you did it. We needed someone to help us close the gap. Thank you. You're a thoughtful person."

They visited about the weather and other small talk, but then revisited the evening's conversation about her safety. She thanked Hank and discussed a couple of options with him. She was thinking in particular about an associate named, William Stephenson. Hank agreed that he sounded like the sort of man she needed, but he was careful with his opinions. This was something she knew more about than he did.

Jake and Caroline joined them for breakfast, then they were off for home. As Hank and Letizia saw them off, they promised to get together soon for a meal.

It was a beautiful day. Hank and Letizia passed through the barn and got Celia, then walked until lunch. After they had eaten Maria's cooking, Hank waved good-bye to Letizia and her guards. He watched until they were out of sight.

Hank found Jay tending the garden and discussed the matter of what to do with Celia. Of course, she was welcome to stay with them, but Jay referred Hank to a livery much closer to the castle.

While they were visiting, Maria joined them, listening, and picking up on the elements of their discussion. One thing led to another, and after considering the locations to which Hank regularly traveled, as well as his professional needs and personal desires, it was decided Celia would stay at the Levine's. In recognition of her "business" for the livery, her master would have a place to stay anytime he wished. For that, Hank was grateful. He and the Levine family were bonded in friendship. Reducing his wishes and their generosity down to practicalities, they agreed upon a deal for Celia and estimated Hank would split time between his place in the castle and "his" room at the Levine's sixty-forty.

"How about we reevaluate monthly until the details are worked out?" Hank proposed.

"Fair enough by me," Jay agreed, looking to Maria for her input.

"It's a wonderful plan," she declared, and sealed the deal with a hug of Hank's waist as he and Jay shook hands.

"We're agreed then," Jay declared, whistling to Adam and Larry, motioning for them to stop what they were doing and join them.

No other guest gets this treatment, Hank noted to himself. It was a load off Hank's mind—knowing Celia was cared for and that he had a safe place among solid people.

While it made for a long walk and a late arrival back in the castle, Hank departed the Levine's early, and walked cross country to La Faim to visit Jack. He found him holding forth upon the road from the dump before his group and an unsuspecting traveler. Knowing Jack's new heart, Hank couldn't help but chuckle at the unanticipated pressure the poor traveler had to be feeling. *Vintage Jack!* Hank made his way through the bodies to the middle of the crowd.

Noting movement in the ranks, Jack espied Hank and lost interest in his prey upon the road through La Faim. "Hank!" he yelled.

The group forgot the traveler, much to his relief as he escaped toward the castle, and reassembled around Hank and Jack. There was the customary banter—about Hank's walking stick, his clothes, and educated speech—along with the complete disregard for personal space. With each visit to his friends in La Faim, Hank always felt he'd been touched a thousand times by a hundred people. Initially, it was disarming. But now he thrived on the affection. Humanity bumping against, touching, invading, standing alongside his humanity, smelling bodies, affirming, reminding him, *I'm loved. I'm not alone.*

Many elsewhere, it seemed to Hank, appreciated him for his mind and cunning logic—aspects of him accessed from a distance, if desired at the moment and deemed beneficial. *I'm liked by them for what I bring to the table,* he thought.

But here, in La Faim, I'm loved for me—a simple, straightforward, struggling member of humanity. I like it here, he thought. *There's no room for pretense. We all smell the same—except for me,* he conceded. *But they accept me anyway.* He looked around as he and Jack walked. *Everybody here knows we're all in this together—and we best stick together,* as he was touched and patted in sincere greeting by two people heading the opposite way.

Per usual, the majority turned their attentions elsewhere after a while, migrating through La Faim like clutches of birds. Locating their customary spot on a broken wall down a side street, Jack and Hank sat down.

"Jack, I know we've talked about it already, but they worked you over pretty hard when you spoke to the First Floor Group. I've worried about you. How you doing?"

"That Jester fellow came after me for a while. Like you said he would. He's something, now. Stays with you—like white on rice. Tried to tell me it was the King's fault—all that happened at the First Floor. Then he tried telling me it was my fault. Then that it was Magician's."

"What'd you do?"

"Told him to go to hell—about a hundred times, maybe. I guess he finally went."

"You angry?"

"Yeah, I was mad for a while." Jack looked up and down the street. "But more than anything, I was mad for you. They ought not treated you like they did. Why hell, Hank! Wouldn't have been no program if it wasn't for you. Made me mad—that main man chesting up to you like he did. Damn straight! It did make me mad for you! And then I was mad for me, cause I wasn't there for you. Lost my way in the confusion. Not right, you standin' up to the main man by yourself. Should've been there."

Hank was surprised to hear Jack's perspective of the fateful evening. *I wasn't demeaned*, Hank thought. *Jack was, but he's hurt on my behalf. Nice to have a friend like Jack.* "Thanks, Jack," Hank managed to wedge into the conversation before Jack continued.

"But hell, Hank. I know you're okay—and I'm okay. We're tough, you and me. I got to say though, I feel bad for those folks up there in that Tower thing they've built. Livin' there, like they do behind them walls and doors. They don't know no better. May as well live in a cage— like my sister's bird does. Can't hold somebody responsible for what they don't know nothin' about, can you?"

"No. No, I suppose you can't," Hank answered, curious.

"Way I figure it, we're rich men, Hank. You and me. Filthy-rich men! You and I are brothers—and Vassar—and everything the King's got is ours. Can't get no better than that."

"Well, that's a fact," Hank confirmed. "I hadn't thought of it in those terms before. But, you're right."

"Damn straight I'm right! Wouldn't have said it if it wadn't so. But here's the deal: We're like fat cats in the King's family. We got Magician inside us—working his wizard-sorcery stuff like the King commanded. Know what I mean, Hank?"

"Yep. I do, Jack. I'm with you. I'm following your thinking."

"Well, if we got all that, there ain't no reason for us to worry or be mad cause some bunch of somebody's don't know any better. No sir! Way I think is, we're livin' above Hank, livin' the life like Vassar lives." Jack paused to ponder. "I been talkin' to Magician about these things that I'm thinkin'. Fact is, I think my thoughts are really his thinkin'. I'm not smart enough to think this stuff up. Got to be his ideas, and cause he likes me, he told his mind to me. That's what I think."

"I'd say you're on target," Hank said. "Thank you for talking with me. I'm encouraged, and I was a little under the pile when I got here. Not anymore."

"Yeah. I could tell," Jack said. "You looked poorly out of your eyes when you walked up where we was there on the road." Jack nodded backwards toward the road from the dump.

Hank chuckled slightly. "You are a good friend, Jack. Thank you for keeping an eye on me. I wasn't in the healthiest of places, but I've regained my perspective—thanks to you."

"Sure. Sure. You'd do the same for me," Jack said. "I figured as much. Wished I'd known where you was and I'd hunted you down to be sure you had your head together. But, didn't know. Knew you wasn't in the castle. Figured you went to the woods. Not right for a brother to be alone. "Jack put his hand on his friend's shoulder. "Hell, Hank. Even a sparrow's got friends to fly with."

Jack was investing in him from the great storehouse of riches he believed were his as a child of the King. *Remarkable!* Hank thought, inspired by his friend, the most unlikely of sources.

Out of the moments of silence passing between them, Jack returned to the beginning of their conversation, said, "After while, my mad started eatin' me from the inside out."

Hank acknowledged. "I know about that."

There was quiet while Jack assessed the status of La Faim and absorbed the moments sitting next to his friend. "So, I crossed the bridge and walked out through the dump where Magician and I could visit—man-to-man."

"You went to the dump to visit with Magician?"

"That's right. That's where I go when I've got thinkin' to do. Won't nobody notice I'm there."

"What did Magician tell you?" Hank asked.

"Told me about how the King forgave me for the sorry way I've done—and still do, come to think of it. Said the King made a decision before he ever met me to forgive me—for everything. All in advance. Told me the King believed it was in his best interest to handle forgiving me that way."

"I see," Hank said.

"I got to thinkin'—later on—about the First Floor Group. I decided if forgiveness was for my benefit, then hangin' on to my mad only hurt me."

"What did you do?" Hank inquired.

"I decided out there in the dump to forgive them people. Did it too! Asked Magician to help me, left my mad at the dump, and come back here. Went to the house."

"That's an amazing story, Jack."

"Well, I don't know about that," Jack said. "But I'm fine. Couldn't be no better. Hell, Hank! If I was any better I'd be too good!"

Hank laughed. "Couldn't have that now."

Jack didn't laugh.

Hank thought, *I suppose he really believes he could have too good a day. Who am I to argue with Jack? What's important here is that I leverage Jack's inspiration to live like my mentee lives.*

Hank had a late dinner at Hoi Polloi. While he was there, he discussed the option of renting the private room in back for a special dinner.

When he walked into the lobby of his apartment building, the manager welcomed him back from his travels and handed him a sealed note. Hank thanked him, acknowledged with a nod Letizia's agent on the premises, and climbed the stairs to his apartment.

He went through his customary precautions upon entering the rooms of his apartment, but with a bit more intensity. He felt an escalation in the air, an intensifying of the conflict between dark and light, and knew intuitively he was in the midst. As best he could tell, nothing was disturbed in his quarters. Hank stripped out of his clothes, left them in a pile, and cleaned up.

He noted the smell of La Faim from the pile of cast-aside clothes, shook his head at the notice. Hank sat down and opened the note. To his surprise, it was from, Walter F. Michelson, expressing that he wanted to meet Hank as soon as he was able. *What could the senior leader of the First Floor Group possibly want to see me about?* Hank noted that his anger was not nearly so far removed as Jack reported his was. He also noted Mr. Michelson provided an address other than the Round Tower. *So it's personal—or off the record,* Hank's curiosity was piqued, as was his apprehension. *If there was ever a wolf in sheep's wool, Michelson's it.*

True to his practice of doing the unexpected, Hank knocked on Walter Michelson's door at 7:15 the next morning. The senior leader peered suspiciously through the viewing port of the thick door. It took him a moment to recognize Hank, especially given his disquiet at having such an early visitor, but once recognized, he quickly opened the door and greeted Hank.

While Mr. Michelson hustled around in the kitchen to prepare coffee, Hank took the liberty of looking around the study. He noticed a book of the King's teaching open on Mr. Michelson's desk. Stepped to look. *There's no way Michelson could stage what books are open. Not at this hour.*

Carefully placing the coffee service on a side table, Mr. Michelson prepared coffee and guided Hank to a sitting area with comfortable chairs.

"Thank you for your note, Mr. Michelson. Forgive my tardiness, but I've been on the road," Hank began, sounding as cordial as he could while doing his best not to look too much like a sheep.

"Please, please, Mr. Henderson. No more Mr. Michelson. I prefer Walt."

"Very well. I prefer Hank."

Walt thanked Hank for coming, then launched into a review of what he knew about Hank—and what he knew was considerable. Hank found that fascinating, but also unnerving. *There's no way this man could know so much without an intelligence source.* He figured Walt and the power brokers within the First Floor Group were in cahoots with Ennui.

"You've gathered a great deal of information about me, Walt." Hank tried to sound casual, even flattered, but he had heard enough recitation from his resume. "What's on your mind?"

"I figure you're a man who can be trusted," Walt stated.

Hank smiled courteously, "I like to think so, provided the confidence isn't immoral or unethical."

Walt didn't expect Hank to be friendly toward him. "Well, whatever category you wish to assign my comments, I assure you they are neither of those things."

"Very well." Hank said flatly, again with only a hint of courteous smile.

Since before writing his note to Hank, Walt had determined that if given the chance, he would state his situation honestly and forthrightly.

From the moment he said he had been terminated from his role as senior leader, which he did right up front, Walt had Hank's attention. Hank only interrupted once to clarify a point regarding the Board's cause for dismissal. Walt told his story unabridged and without edit. It took a while, for which he was apologetic, but for which Hank was grateful. He needed all the pieces to this puzzle.

Walt was a fine communicator. So compelling was his verbal portrait of his termination that Hank felt as though he too had been fired. Walt described the days of disillusionment following as, "… the worst days of my life." He languished for a few moments in the darkness of his despondency. He revealed that his wife had spiraled into depression. Their children were trying to be brave and supportive, but with his dismissal, there had also been a breach of confidentiality. His name was slandered throughout the Round Tower, even into the castle, "And when my name was blackened, so were theirs," Walt said with genuine sadness. "It's disgusting—inflicting collateral suffering upon the innocents around me. They've done nothing. It's just meanness. But, I understand. I've done the same things, I'm ashamed to admit. It's the way the game is played." Walt was thoughtful for a second. "Nevertheless, I'm still irritated at the swath of destruction. I can't be certain I know who's responsible. And even if I could be, there's no paper trail. Of that, I'm certain!"

This last piece of information led Hank to believe his hunch was correct, that Ennui and her folks were behind this event. *But what did Walter Michelson do to get on her bad side?*

Walt recognized that he was ruined professionally, and Hank had to agree, although he didn't say as much. His reputation was wrecked, he stated, and if all he was saying was true, Hank had to concur about this too. His family was suffering mightily and there wasn't a thing he could do about it. On this point, Hank agreed as well. It looked bad for the entire Michelson family.

Walt told Hank he couldn't sleep. *No surprise there*, Hank thought.

But then Walt sat forward on the edge of his chair. He hadn't tasted his coffee, but he held it preciously in his hands as though a gift of the magi. "Hank, I eased from my side of the bed so as not to awaken Helen, crept through the house, and came here—to my study. In the quiet, in the deep of darkest night, at my lowest point, and in near despair, I cried out in my soul. That night..." he paused—perhaps for affect, or truly in consideration—"I discovered the light of the King. He met me here, Hank, in this room."

Hank smiled a sad smile. "The leader of the First Floor Group didn't know the light of the King?"

"Was the leader," Walt corrected, then smiled politely. "It's true, despite my affluence, position, and power I missed the true King. I talked about him, but I didn't see him until that night. As a result, I misrepresented him, got in his way, impeded his work, even abused his people. I couldn't see what I was doing for all the glare of success around me. It was like living in a house of mirrors. Once the glare was gone, I realized all that I valued was running through my fingers like so much sand, and what wasn't, was tarnishing."

Hank shook his head. "Mind if I refill my coffee?"

"No. Please, help yourself. I'm sorry. I'm not being a very good host. You can have anything you like. Have you eaten?"

"Oh, yeah. I'm fine. So, you realized you missed the true King. What'd you do?"

Walt pointed to his desk. "I cried out, in my agony and loss, for revelation. I pulled the King's teaching from my shelf, lit a candle, and began reading."

"Why that book?" Hank interrupted. "Why not something else?"

"I don't mean to sound arrogant, but I've read everything else, Hank. I've built my life and profession upon everything else only to realize the foundation was insufficient for the weight of my life's concerns. There was only one place to turn."

Hank nodded—once to the side.

"I have discovered the High King!" Walt said again, declarative. "Or, perhaps he located me. I'm not certain. Heretofore, I thought he was a good idea. But sitting in my chair, in the wee hours of countless night passages, I've discovered he alone is everything—and everything includes me. In the dark night of my soul, I saw the sunrise of the King."

"I see," Hank said. "And what have you done about what you've seen?"

"I've declared him my lord and King, the singular ruler of my life. His light has filled my heart."

"Hmm," Hank acknowledged, a touch indifferent. "I appreciate your story, Walt. Why are you telling it to me? I mean, I'm honored, and I celebrate with you, but why me?"

"I was hoping you could explain why the King would do this for me when I've done nothing for him."

What do I do now? Hank thought.

This man wounded Jack, or at least, his organization did so with his approval. This man has colluded with Ennui, maybe Zophos himself, to the offense of many who follow the King. This man plunged the bayonet into Jake Ingram when he was a casualty on the field of a noble cause. This man spoke against the King's reformation, and in the process, extinguished the flame in many young people's hearts, leaving them disillusioned and without hope. This very man! And this man wants me to draw alongside him and explain Father's heart to him.

Hank studied Walt, the epitome of poise and professionalism, organized and together even at this early and unexpected hour. To think, *Father came to Walt Michelson in the deep darkness and shone his light.*

Hank knew about being rescued from darkness. *I once dwelt in a pit, and felt myself defiled beyond remedy—as though I was Humpty Dumpty. Fallen. But the King—my Father and Brother—shined his light. Rescued me!*

He also recalled, his memories racing at light speed, Magician telling him shortly after he exited his dark pit of despair, *One day the King will commission you to return to that dark place.* Whatever else he knew, Hank Henderson knew the battle for the Round Tower was his return to the dark place. *As I was led to freedom, so the King has sent me to lead other captives from their prisons of darkness.* It was a remarkable thought! *I get it,* Hank said to Magician. *I get it! Live through me now, please.*

As he had done for Letizia, and Jake before her; as he had shared with Jack, sitting on broken walls, trash cans, and the other detritus of La Faim; as he had done for Ronan, and Audie, and Maria he did with the disgraced senior leader of the First Floor Group, Walter F. Michelson, the newest member of the King's Kingdom. Beginning with his own story of redemption and walking in the King's light, Hank explained his Father's heart to Walt. He taught him from the King's teaching, lacing together what he had written from his heart with Walt's conduct. And through Hank's advocacy on behalf of his Father, Walt grasped that he was the recipient of the King's unmerited favor, through no entitlement or virtue of his own, but for the sole reason of the King's mercy and Vassar's advocacy.

Although the wealth of information about the King deposited in Walt's head had been used over the years to counter the initiatives of the Kingdom, as Walt walked in the light, the Wizard of the Kingdom reframed the information. In rapid succession, information about the King became deep-seated knowledge that rooted their relationship. Inside Walt's heart, a stunning likeness of the King blossomed. Hank had never witnessed such a flurry of revelation, adoption, and transformation resulting in change. Cycle after cycle of Magician's sorcery hewed a haven of strength in Walter Michelson. Before Hank's eyes Walt transformed from one who knew to one known, from one possessing information about the King, to one acquainted with the King, from one discussing the King to one possessed by him.

Two days later, at Walt's invitation, Hank returned to the Michelson home. Walt had assembled his entire family.

It was a night of redemption. Knowing something of the heartaches around the table, Hank spoke specifically to the King's healing, restorative care, and everlasting love. The family heard from their patriarch. His story of life-change was evident to those who knew him best.

To the person, the Michelson family declared their allegiance to the High King. They sat down in darkness and rose up to walk in the light.

Over lunch a few days later, Walt and Jake met to discuss their past. There was forgiveness. There was mercy. Walt confessed his egregious failure of leadership when Jake was in his employment. He acknowledged his deeds in the dark that were an offense to Jake and a derailment of the King's reformation in the young people Jake served. There were tears. There was redemption.

Together, they walked in the sunrise from on high and the darkness was dispelled.

News of Walter F. Michelson's change of heart and passionate devotion to the High King spread within the First Floor Group. But its spread was irregular. Many wondered what happened. *Hadn't Walt always been devoted to the High King? Isn't that who we are and what we are about in the Round Tower? What changed?*

These were interesting questions—but few voiced them outside their own thinking. *Clearly, if the Board saw fit to dismiss Walt, it must have been for good cause. I should go along—keep quiet. Who am I to question the Board?*

Walt's dismissal and devotion troubled the waters of people's thinking. Since Walt's dismissal was the easier concept of the two to grasp—*He must have done something wrong!*—the majority quit thinking about Walt after they accepted his attributed culpability. Thus, neither Walt's devotion nor their own were considered any further.

To say the news of Walt's firing spread like wildfire would not be accurate. Wildfires move astonishingly fast and indiscriminately burn everything in their paths.

Those tending the status quo of the First Floor Group were unaffected—because the status quo was unaffected. Because the status quo was intact, others quickly affirmed that the Board acted correctly.

That Walt had compromised the status quo was sufficient to make him unfit. They had done their duty. It was for the good of the First Floor Group.

Some expressed displeasure at Walt's absence. They were told, without apology, "Not every day can be a good day and not everyone is qualified to be a member of the Tower."

Those in charge, those comfortable, those who valued the benefits of membership, and those interested in holding up their end, never missed Walt. If one cow is slaughtered does the herd suffer? It is what it is. They never grieved their offense of Walt for the same reason they never grieved their offense of Jack: they never saw their behavior as offensive.

The placid waters of the First Floor Group endured not the slightest ripple upon Walt's departure. The transformative light evident in their cast-aside leader reflected off the surface of their stoic comfort and the leadership took comfort in their noble action.

But underneath the still waters of the First Floor Group there was a current that carried the truth of Walt's change, his alteration, his transformation. It followed the course of hearts longing for their own story of change, channeled through dissatisfaction, and it soaked into those considering truth but not knowing how to appropriate it for themselves.

As news of Walt's change coursed in quiet contemplation among the First Floor Group it was carried into the Round Tower at large. It flowed around the dams and levees of exclusivity designed to distinguish one group from another. On every floor, in every sector, and in each group, people's hearts began to absorb the true life and light of the King. There was a resurgence of devotion to the King. Stories like Walt's increased, spreading through the channels, cuts, and courses of life in the Round Tower, flooding the moat and beyond into the castle.

Small groups—couples, young people, the old, infirmed, professional, working, and unemployed—of all stripes, color, ethnicity, and shapes formed around their common denominator of relation in the Kingdom of Light. Collections, assemblages, families, brotherhoods, sisterhoods, guilds, and tribes formed formally and informally for the purpose of personal identification fueled by vibrant relationship with the King of kings. They met over coffee cups, decanters, plates, and patios. Rich and poor, privileged and disenfranchised, cultured and crass they gathered, collected their courage, resolved their focus, and walked in the light.

What the leaders of the Round Tower meant to suppress, spread like a virus. Walt's story spread because he told it—humbly declaring who he missed in his grandeur and discovered in his grief. His story spread as it was repeated. His story spread as his life replicated in other's lives and they shared their stories.

Walt sensed the King capitalizing on their relationship. But unlike his days as senior leader, he didn't give a passing thought to measuring the King's activity. It was enough to know the King was insurgent and that they were allied.

While the surface waters of the Round Tower were unmoved, the level was dropping. Ennui and her team had manipulated the numbers for many years in a shell game designed to shroud losses from leaders and lull them into deeper and further complacency.

But Ennui wasn't manipulating these numbers.

Something is amiss, she brooded. *Every indicator shows no cause for alarm. My agents report nothing extraordinary. The Tower's leaders have not gone awry, except for Michelson. But he is gone. Historically, my numbers are good and the projections—even worst case—indicate success. Something is not right though.*

To anyone but Ennui the dimming of the light in the Round Tower would have been cause for celebration, indicative of victory, and portending Zophos' ascension to the King's throne. Her job was to diminish the light, and the plan seemed to be working.

But this darkening is not my doing, she knew.

An arrogant mind would attribute the dulling to ingenuity that achieved critical mass and a cascade of disillusionment as the Kingdom imploded. But Ennui was not "anyone" and she wasn't silly enough to delude herself with arrogance.

The light was not being repressed. It was escaping the confines of the Round Tower, the systems and structures, the committees and corporate mind that she had installed. *All my controls are in place,* she thought. *All my systems running normal. But the light is not contained.*

She tightened her demands. Required more reports. Increased programs. Poured resources into capital campaigns. She punished even hints of laziness or dilatory behavior. In her devotion to the dream of Zophos' reign she dared to consider that her organization had been compromised by the King. *It is unthinkable,* she knew. *But something has changed.*

Letizia continued sitting daily with Caroline, training her, guiding her thinking; instilling in her the propensities she had within herself to achieve the stated goals, but she was careful not to impose herself upon Caroline. She had no intention of remaking her in her own image.

Daily—no, hourly—Letizia's confidence in Caroline grew. She turned increasing levels of responsibility over to her protégé and was not disappointed. Of course Caroline made mistakes, and she asked questions, but they were mistakes she wouldn't make again and questions revealing a sharp mind peeling away layers of assumption, presumption, and inefficiency to discover the better, more-excellent, finer way.

The thing that gave Letizia the greatest comfort was that Caroline and Bernie bonded professionally. They were a team—perhaps a stronger team than she and Bernie. After all, Caroline wasn't burdened by the "other" business.

Caroline sensed where the trip wires were, the warnings that she inevitably would encounter following in Letizia's footsteps. And, she knew who was who, not by what they did professionally, but by Letizia's endorsement or lack thereof.

But when someone surfaced who knew Ms. Pintaro, and had not been endorsed otherwise by Letizia, the implication was clear: *This person is either unimportant to the office and my professional pursuits or works in the other business.* Caroline grew adept at stating, "I'm sorry. I'm not familiar with your work."

Letizia protected Caroline, Bernard, and her legitimate business. But she was under no delusions. Loosening her grip on the cash business was dangerous. To her credit, Letizia let go of the cash business very shrewdly. She never dealt directly with the low-level players, so they wouldn't notice any change in her. She met with the high-level players discreetly. She didn't name any names. She made no threats. Her message to each was the same: "I'm stepping away from our work together. Our professional relationship is in writing—sealed, duplicated, and secured in multiple locations. No one knows what your file contains except me. But, select others know where the files are located. If anything happens to me, your file will become public information."

They understood Letizia's message: As long as she was safe, they were safe. They each said the same thing, "Certainly, Ms. Pintaro. I understand." And, each thanked her.

But the mid-level people—the workers, the laborers, the executioners, the day-to-day working thugs? These were the question mark in Letizia's mind. A vendetta with life motivated them. Anger over these lifetime slights coursed like acid in their veins. They knew who was above them and who was below them. Yes. In this high-stakes game, these individuals were like Jokers, Joker's wild.

Jack was a leader with a platform. When he stepped up, La Faim listened. There was nothing subtle about Jack or his message. And, there was nothing subtle about La Faim. Fail today, the dump was close enough to smell. Succeed today, you survive to scratch and claw an existence tomorrow. In La Faim, satisfaction was avoidance of the dump, reward was living in La Faim.

Hank and Jack met often. Usually, they took seats along the main street of La Faim, opened the copy of Vassar's letter Hank had given to Jack—from which he was also teaching Jack how to read—and parsed and assessed every word and white space while La Faim listened and looked over their shoulders.

Hank fielded lots of questions, and not just from Jack. "What's that word say, Hank?" "Your brother really wrote you a letter?" "Why'd he say that?" "What's that mean?" "Why are you showing this to us?" "Why does the Crown Prince care?"

Unlike the educated and cultured, La Faim didn't hesitate to ask when they didn't understand. Explaining what Vassar meant drew the most frequent scoffs. Not because they didn't believe what Hank said about Vassar, but because they found it difficult to believe Vassar included them in his promises. But many believed. They believed because they knew Hank and trusted him. If he said his Brother included them in the promises spoken in his letter, that was good enough for them.

Jack declared—early on, after he had become a follower of the King—that everyone in La Faim had to follow his example. It took several days for Hank to realize that many of the newest members in the Kingdom were ushered in by the duress of Jack's knife, knuckles, and name. It took some serious explaining to Jack why this customary method of persuasion in La Faim was inappropriate for the Kingdom.

The day Hank's message of limited persuasion dawned on Jack was memorable. He was incredulous. "Why, Hank? It's for their own damn good. Said so yourself! These are my friends. Why wouldn't I tell him what to do once I know? Hell! They're looking to me. What kind of leader you think I am?"

Jack moderated the pressure he put on La Faim, and Hank was grateful. But he still suspected that when he returned to the castle, Jack reverted to the La Faim method of evangelism.

Hank thought about it, in conversation with Magician, as he walked back and forth between La Faim and the castle. *Why should I moderate Jack? Magician, you've met me under duress. Do you have any qualms about doing so in La Faim?*

It's a different place, La Faim, the reply began in Hank's mind. *Different from what you're comfortable with. But it's just different, not wrong. One reason we commissioned you to La Faim—we being your Father, Vassar, and me—is your ability to engage people in a variety of places, gain your bearings in the confusion of their lives, and lead them to the Kingdom. Don't forget! Your Father calls you, Polaris, the steady one, suitable for navigation.*

Hank responded thoughtfully, *Thank you. I appreciate your affirmation—and your reminder. I think I'd forgotten that.*

No kidding?

Here's the deal, Magician continued. *I'll meet you, Jack—anyone— and I'll meet anywhere, anytime, anyplace. I will never waste a particle of light that shines in the darkness.*

So what you're saying, Hank thought, *is that no matter how a person becomes aware of the Kingdom, we leverage the light to their advantage and Father's intention. That right?*

That's right. You've got it. Don't worry too much about Jack's style. The light is true. I'm not going to take advantage and abuse the light, and you aren't going to either. So, we work with the light given. Never mind the angle of the rays. We guide. We love. We help these wonderful souls navigate. That's what we do, Polaris.

Seize the ray of light! Be their guide, Polaris! Hank reflected often on Magician's strategy as he thought of Jack and La Faim. *When I see the light, step!*

And when you step, take La Faim with you. Magician's counsel was encouraging—free and open-handed.

Mentoring Jack was like hitching a Mustang to a buggy! Being an Oklahoma-Texas boy though, Hank held on. No conversation lacked fire, passion, fist pounding, curses, and strong words. No exchange between them traversed start-to-finish without Jack standing up at least once, then sitting again—closer—to engage Hank's mind and heart with his own.

Like a rodeo cowboy, Hank figured if he could manage Jack for "eight seconds," it was time to jump free. *Let him buck and run.* And that he did—and all those listening as well! In Jack, Hank and Magician loosed a wild stallion. In La Faim, a herd of wild horses.

Most evenings, when Jack bucked loose and climbed to a prominence to speak, Hank casually drifted toward the back of the assembled crowd. He listened with satisfaction to his mentee proclaim, in words that sometimes made Hank wince, all that Vassar's words and the light of the King had revealed in his heart.

Hank never knew when Jack's declarations concluded. When the hour grew late, so as not to distract, Hank backpedaled behind some shack or hovel or wall, avoided any unfamiliar cur that might bark, and meandered out of La Faim. Once out of sight, his face pointed toward the castle, Hank's eyes often filled with tears as he walked to Hoi Polloi with the sound of Jack's exhortations carrying on the wind and alighting in his heart, the mentor mentored by the mentee.

Hank thought he understood humility, but learning from Jack taught him to walk in that great gift of the mind.

Jake continued to do a stellar job of leading and caring for the men and women facilitating the small groups in and around the castle. He kept them focused, encouraged and guided their thinking about the Kingdom, and counseled them on difficult issues within their groups.

As groups within the Round Tower surfaced, Jake helped them select facilitators to coordinate their focus and function. As the number of groups increased, Jake introduced a friend, and now a colleague, to assist specifically in caring for leaders. "Walt Michelson is the perfect choice," he stated without doubt.

Most Wednesday evenings, unless he was at the Levine's, Hank spent the late afternoon and evening with the Ingrams. The children called him, Uncle H, and he was treated like family.

Since most mornings started early for Hank, it wore him down considerably to stay up late with Jake, a consummate night owl. Caroline and the kids would retire, and as the hour grew late and Jake's mind began churning out his best thinking, Hank would say to Magician, *Okay. You know what I need. Everybody who is anybody says I need to sleep—everybody except you, that is. I'm depending on you.* No matter his fatigue, Hank wouldn't trade his late-night discussions with Jake.

Long after the sorts of people Hank was used to seeing—the daytime folks—had gone to bed, Hank would hug Jake good-bye, pat him on the shoulder, and head home.

At first, Hank was repulsed by the whores who called to him as he walked toward home. The ladies and their customers in and around the brothels disgusted him. The stumblers, the drinkers, the revelers, the shadowy characters; the pimps pimping the bodies in their inventories; the stalkers, walkers, destitute, and deranged in the dark—all these bothered him when he first started walking home late.

At first.

In time, the prostitutes realized he wasn't a customer. The pimps acknowledged and the strippers returned his greeting. Those struggling through the night assumed he was one of them, hunched over under his own weight of disconsolation and too ashamed to carry it in the daylight.

He stopped one night to visit with a pimp. When asked what he was doing out so late, Hank told him. "I meet most Wednesdays with a friend. We discuss the light and the life of the High King."

After that visit, word spread, and most Wednesday evenings the creatures of the night waited for him. He didn't know the extent of grit in their worlds, but he understood the longing in each heart, the desire to matter, to be significant.

Unlike the sophisticated whose lives appeared in order, the people of the night approached him without façade, pretense, or charade. So, he spoke to them unfiltered about hope, fulfillment, faith, redemption, and true love. These things he knew personally. He told them his story, told them how he found significance, told them how he discovered security, acceptance, and personal worth. He didn't shy from revealing the nakedness of his pit and the faces of expectation.

They trusted him because of his honesty and truth. Nakedness they understood, cover up and rationalization they didn't tolerate.

They didn't stop whoring, pimping, or stripping. But they stopped him on Wednesday nights, inquired of the King, and looked into the light. In time, the light shined bright enough that they grasped hope, embraced faith, and were fulfilled by true love. Their lives were transformed, their professions were another matter.

Magician's counsel was priceless. *Hank, their professions aren't the problem—not their problem, not the King's problem with them. Darkness in their heart's the problem. Once they see the light, in time—not your time, mind you, but your Father's time—they will re-train their professional lives based upon walking in the light. I'll see to that myself.* Hank believed Magician would do what he said.

The light dawned in the darkness, like a sunrise at midnight. Whores, pimps, strippers, and customers declared allegiance to the King and welcomed Vassar into their hearts. And not only that, they followed the King's teaching, and engaged relationship with him fervently as Magician nurtured their understanding.

Hank capitalized upon the small group that informally met on the streets each Wednesday night. Their numbers grew as hope spread. Each Wednesday night after he left Jake's, having met with Magician in advance, Hank delivered a single thought from Vassar's letter to his nighttime friends.

Standing on a notorious corner under an oil-fueled lamp, a clutch of prostitutes, pimps, addicts, and customers huddled close to hear Hank's thoughts on them and the King. Quoting from Vassar's letter, Hank said, "While you live and work and fight in Gnarled Wood, Gnarled Wood is not your home. You are people of the light. You live and move and have significance because you are the sons and daughters of the High King of Glory! He loves you! Desperately loves you. Not for your service," he said, looking into the intent eyes of women dressed for work. "Not for your body," he said, looking at the child prostitutes and beggars. "Not for what you have to offer," he said, looking at the pimps, "and not because he knows you want something—need something," he said, looking at the customers and addicts. "No. Your Father in the Kingdom loves you because you are his, because you are the redeemed."

"Tell me again," a woman said, "about that word you used,

redeemed. What's that mean?"

There was no mystery to this woman. No question what she did for a living. She sold her body at the going rate—and did anything else her customers wanted if I might earn her a tip.

"To be redeemed," he began, "means that the King purchased eternal rights to you who were irretrievably worthless to him. He did this through the sacrificial effort of Vassar, his firstborn son of inestimable worth. In so doing, he determined that your value is forever established by Vassar, not by what men pay to fondle you. To be redeemed means that you who were once far away from the Kingdom have been brought near—even into the King's family. To be redeemed means that there is nothing you can do to be more accepted or less accepted than you are as the King's daughter."

Tears had formed in the woman's eyes—and in many other eyes in the group standing under the oil lamp. She reached for the hand of the woman next to her seeking reassurance—or maybe to share the glorious affirmation being spoken—and that woman reached for the hand next to her, who reached behind, and that one reached across for the hand of another, and the grasping-clasping continued until everyone standing in the night on the soiled street held onto someone daring to believe their redemption a reality.

Intensity burned in Hank as his Father's words, etched on the walls of his heart, found voice to exhort these once degraded—himself included. "To be the redeemed of the King means that he has called you who were degraded, holy, you who were lost, found, you who were destitute, rich, you who were rejected, claimed, and you who were defeated, victorious. To be redeemed means that when the King thinks of you, he shouts over you with the joy of a Father. To be redeemed means that he has come to you who were far off—even to this street— found you, opened his arms, pulled you close to his chest, kissed you on the head, and whispered in your ear, 'You are mine. Mine. You are my child. I love you. I will never leave you, never lose you. No, I could never ever in years numbered by ten thousands of years, never ever be separated from you. You are my redeemed."

Hank stopped talking. There was stunned, sacred silence in the small gathering. They tightened their grips on each other, pulled in closer. Their tears became sobs of astonishment. No one had ever spoken such things to them. To be wanted! None of them had any experience with want beyond being used.

Hank wasn't certain what to do next. He didn't feel any pressure or expectation...but he felt? *What?* he asked himself. *I feel alone—standing here with neither hand held. I feel isolated, and apart, from the group.*

He stepped closer. The group took him in among them, held his hand. And they shared light, and life, and tears of joy celebrating their redemption.

In time, as the group increased in numbers, Hank recommended they divide into small groups based upon their work. The street prostitutes met under lamps and on corners as they waited to turn tricks. The whorehouse prostitutes met in their rooms and behind their brothel. The pimps met with their ladies, and the gangs met in their hangouts. The strippers met in their dressing rooms—in varying states of dress and undress—before and after shows. Each Wednesday, after speaking from Vassar's letter, Hank left them with a relevant question to discuss, and they did so without the filters, apathy, and familiarity those in the Round Tower had to overcome.

Seeing the King's light transform hearts was rewarding to Hank. But when he thought of his Wednesday, late-night friends, he struggled with their lives. More pointedly, their lifestyles troubled him. They on the other hand, didn't seem bothered by skin, nakedness, revealing, sensuality, flaunting, and taunting. While he monitored and moderated his language, they had no verbal filters. He was careful to guard his reputation, but they couldn't have cared less. The more he was with them, the more he scrutinized his propriety—to subject it to his Father's perspective rather than his own.

When others in the Kingdom found out he was meeting with the debauched of the night, they questioned him hard—and with wisdom they claimed originated with the King. He was, after all, tampering with his reputation, not to mention subjecting himself to temptation.

Hank dismissed the temptation criticism. He had as strong a sex drive as anybody, but Wednesday late-night wasn't about sex, not even for the people working the late shift. He associated sex with love, affection, intimacy, and bonding. Sex for his nighttime friends was a professional tool—not much different from a carpenter's hands, a singer's voice, or a laborer's back. Hank visited with Magician about these conflicts many nights as he walked home after his Wednesday meetings. He heard nothing from the great Wizard but affirmation and, *I'm working on it. Trust me.*

What Hank did know—without a shadow of doubt—was that like him, the sunrise from on high had shined in the dead of night upon these squatting, lying, and walking in darkness. Until further notice, he would speak to them of the light. If his Father determined they should have another profession, Hank believed Magician would guide that process.

In another turn of events that Hank didn't see coming, Audie Vandermeer began visiting with the Wednesday-night ladies. To his surprise, they were all about the same age. *It's not the number of miles, it's the kind of miles*, he figured. As he observed, Audie and the Wednesday folks connected and their common bond with the King overcame their dissimilar backgrounds.

They met late afternoon, before work, and discussed the King and his teaching and how it applied to life. It was one of those things Hank kidded Magician about, teasing him about blending wholesome Audie with ladies of the night. *It's like oil and water. Just because they're both liquids, Wizard, doesn't mean they belong together.*

Magician pointed out that the proof of his work was in the pudding. *And yes, Hank. Pudding is a liquid.*

CHAPTER 26

Levine's Livery and Pub

Hank and Letizia met first one place, then another, and they met frequently. Since life was so much simpler at the Levine's than it was in the castle or the Tower, they often rendezvoused there to walk with Celia, linger over meals, and enjoy respites from the constraints on their lives. They read Vassar's letter together, discussed their thoughts and insights, and expressed shared confidence in their Father. They talked of Vassar—and Hank told her of Vassar's campaigns, his heart, his warrior-spirit, and of his integrity. She told Hank about her conversations with Magician, of how she and Caroline visited with him, consulting him on issues large and small.

Letizia sat near Hank at the fire pit outside the Levines' and quizzed him about his self-maintenance. He talked about rising early each morning to read Vassar's letter, consider his focus for the day, and discuss the issues ahead with Magician. She knew about him being wounded during battle in the pit and his struggle with pain, but he told her more about his morning stretches. "Initially I resented having to stretch rather than jump out of bed and get started on my day. But now, that twenty or thirty minutes is when I talk with Magician about all that's on my mind."

"Everything?" she asked.

"It's like making stew," he said. "I throw everything I've got into the mix. He told me he wanted to carry my burdens, and I've learned he's serious. Most of my burdens are in my head," Hank said, which resulted in a knowing smile from Lettie, "so I tell him all my thoughts—the good, the bad, and the ugly, the organized and the disorganized."

Hank reviewed his evening walks. "This is my time to be quiet.

Within a quarter of a block, I ask, 'Papa, what's on your mind tonight?' And I listen to hear what Magician says to me."

That led to a discussion about the different roles played by the King, Vassar, and Magician. Understandably, Letizia was having a hard time categorizing this representative propensity of her Father.

"I think Father knew it would be supremely difficult for us to understand him," Hank said in a quiet voice. "I think he knew we would struggle to comprehend what he does, how he does it, what he knows, and what he's capable of doing. So in his wonderful way, he gives us jumping-off points for how to think about him."

Letizia said, "When he tells us he is our Father, he's giving us a framework to think about his care, his protection, his provision, his unfailing love, power, and our security in the family."

"I think you're right, Lettie. The King promises to be everything we need, so when I find myself needing a father, I speak to Father."

She continued, "And when we need explanation, comfort, insight, companionship, we call upon Magician."

"I agree," Hank said.

"So I think I understand enough of the King as my Father to embrace him, to believe him, and to trust him," Letizia said. "And I think I understand enough of the King as Magician, residing within my heart, reigning there, speaking to me about his truth and my desires to trust him."

They sat close, staring into the fire. "I think I hear a 'but' coming," Hank noted, leaning against her shoulder. It was the first cold snap, signaling that fall would soon hand off its duties to winter.

"Yeah, you do," she said. "But the King as Vassar escapes me. I know what Father does, or at least I know enough to think about what he does for a while; then I get stuck. And the same with Magician. But what does Vassar do?"

She leaned closer—almost a snuggle. They looked into the fire. A moment passed and with it a sacred silence.

"Vassar is the one who understands, Lettie. He knows—knows all the hardship, the heartache, the loss. He knows all the wounds we suffer, the grief we bear, and the brokenness we feel. He knows what it is to be afraid, to be alone, to be betrayed—and, he knows what it is to be rescued, retrieved, and restored. He understands redemption, advocacy, and intercession. He knows about disappointment and understands victory. In short, he's the older brother running to our defense, kidding us, but taking on anybody who threatens us. Vassar accepts us, carries us, justifies us, heals us, and redeems us into the family. He shouts—to anyone who'll listen—that we are his kid brother and sister."

Letizia considered for a long moment what Hank said about Vassar. "There are times when a girl needs a brother, Hank."

He made certain Letizia made it safely to her room at the Levine's. Her new security man, William Stephenson, *nom de guerre*, "Bull," had been the perfect choice. Discreet, careful, nearly invisible, and formidable. Bull observed from the shadows.

After she was safely in her room, Hank went back outside. He stood by the dying embers, staring, thinking, letting his heart soak in the night air, his friendship with Lettie, and the affirmations they shared about the King's persona.

Before he went inside, Hank went to the stable. Celia greeted him as though she hadn't seen him in a month of Sundays. In actuality, it had only been a few hours. He enjoyed her warmth and closeness, her hot breath rhythmic on the side of his neck. He rubbed her ears and patted her shoulder.

The next morning over breakfast, Hank told Letizia about the dinner idea he had. "It will be a dinner to remember all that Vassar and the High King have accomplished for us. There's a suitable room in the back of Hoi Polloi," he told her. He went over the guest list he had in mind and asked her thoughts.

"It's a wonderful idea, Hank."

"You know, Lettie. Throughout history it has been common practice for people to give their lives so their king can live. But in the case of the High King, he gave his life so we, his people, can live."

Hank reserved the back room at Hoi Polloi. He arranged the menu with the manager, who had become a good friend, and explained that the meal and order of service were to be a surprise for the guests. He paid a cash deposit, even though the manager insisted that wasn't necessary, and waited an eternity for the anticipated evening.

Nine days later, as planned, Hank's guests arrived at Hoi Polloi. He had issued each a different time for arrival to avoid any probability of them arriving all at once.

Jack arrived first, swaggering per usual, dressed in a garish shirt indicative of his personality, and probably his only piece of clothing remotely appropriate for a nice dinner. At his side was Ronan Chandler. Hank had taken Ronan with him to La Faim, thinking he might find it interesting. He found it more than interesting. The King's initiative there was compelling, and not only that, he and Jack connected and friendship flourished.

Hank greeted them. Jack's ready laugh and strong voice filled the room with excitement and energy. He was elated to be included and made no effort whatsoever to edit his inquisition regarding what was in store for the evening. But Hank wasn't about to tip his hand. Hank had briefed Jack, as much as one can brief a stampede, regarding dinner etiquette. Not that it mattered to Hank—he had eaten plenty of meals with Jack—but he didn't want him to be embarrassed for lack of knowledge. So far, so good. Never mind all that had been served was drinks.

Walter and Helen Michelson arrived next. As expected, they carried themselves with professional aplomb and good grace. Jack could engage a post, but then, so could Mrs. Michelson.

Jake, Caroline, and Audie arrived having traveled together. Ronan and Audie greeted each other with a smile and polite hug, evidence of their redeemed, if casual friendship.

In Hank's mind, and he had discussed it with Letizia to gain her feminine wisdom, Audie and Ronan were both fine folks, but probably not a great match. "Ronan's a good man, a steady man. Audie is a brilliant woman," he told Letizia during one of their walks.

"In the long run," Lettie had stated, "she will be happier with a more high-powered counterpart. As a friend, Ronan can be a wonderful contributor to her life. As a romantic friend, Ronan will get run over— as they have already demonstrated, and that will not be a good plan for either of them."

It was wise counsel.

Hank had also invited two small group facilitators and their spouses, one couple from the castle, and one from the Round Tower. They arrived Hoi Polloi one after the other. Neither couple had met the other.

The logic of inviting the small group facilitators—at least it seemed logical to Hank—was to provide backup for Jake and Walt when they spoke later about the dinner. If he was hearing correctly from Magician, the wizard was planning to utilize the dinner at Hoi Polloi to capitalize upon the veracity of the King's covenant. Thus, a representative cross section was important.

Hank made his way across the room and greeted the facilitators, "Thank you for coming. I'm glad you could make it. Any difficulty finding Hoi Polloi?"

He hadn't met either spouse.

Hank purposefully gave Letizia a later arrival time. A couple of days before the event, he stole a secret moment with Bull, explaining his concern about having this group assembled in one place. He told

Bull he didn't expect trouble, but that he had deliberately given Letizia the later arrival time so that he—Bull—might notice if anything was amiss as they approached. He instructed Bull that if he had any apprehension, for any reason, to take Letizia home. He needed no further explanation.

Letizia entered the back room radiant, confident, and lovely. Hank greeted her, introduced her, and enjoyed listening as she carried on conversation with the others.

Now that all twelve guests had arrived and mingled, Hank encouraged them to take their seats. Since he was the host, and the thirteenth person, Hank assumed his place at the head of the table. Before sitting, he picked up his glass, "Thank you for coming this evening. It's wonderful to be among friends, isn't it?"

Affirmations passed across the table and around the room.

"Speaking of friendship, I toast ours this evening, but in a deeper, more profound, and fundamental relationship, I propose a toast this evening to our family: to each of you, to our Father, the High King of Glory, but specifically this evening, I toast our Older Brother, Vassar." Hank lifted his glass.

"Hear, hear!"

"Cheers!"

Glasses clinked. There was joy. Anticipation was in the air, but comfort even more so.

Drawing upon his memory of the meal his Father served at his refuge in the mountains, as well as the Seder of Jewish Passover, Hank asked the staff of Hoi Polloi to serve a bitter salad for openers. Since everyone waited to eat until all were served, no one warned anyone else that the salad was potently bad. With the first mouthful of romaine root and grated horseradish, faces twisted with the bitter taste. One and all looked to the head of the table. They could tell Hank's salad was just as bad as theirs. But he chewed, and motioned with his hand for them to chew as well.

After the first bite of salad was swallowed, Hank said, "This bitter salad is a symbol," he began, but paused, struggling to manage his emotion. "As its taste lingers, we must never forget the bitter bondage of our lives dominated by Zophos' deception. He promised that if we believed in ourselves—believed that if we could endure, and would persist, then we could overcome the disappointments and shortfalls of life. He promised satisfaction in life. He implied that we could realize self-fulfillment.

"We each bring formidable and diverse abilities to the quest of achieving self-actualization. Our individual circumstances in this crusade are unique." Hank paused, looking at Jack, then to Walt—men whose paths were as divergent as any. "But the outcome of our days, reigning as absolute monarchs over our domains, rendered to each of us the same outcome: a dry and bitter taste that seized our throats; a thirst that wouldn't be quenched; a dark vacuum that absorbed all we invested and left us wanting, our souls destitute. We lusted but were not satisfied, hungered but were not sated, longed but were unfulfilled. Our hearts desired light, but dwelt in darkness. We missed out! Originally designed to reign in the Kingdom, we were instead enslaved in Gnarled Wood "

Hank scooted his chair from the table and stood to receive the prepared plate carried by a wait-staff. The contents were wrapped in a piece of linen.

He asked Jake, seated to his right, to hold the plate while he lifted and set the package on the table. Carefully unfolding the four corners of the linen and spreading it smoothly in front of him, Hank revealed three pieces of flatbread stacked one on top of the other. The middle piece was wrapped in its own piece of linen.

Taking the middle piece of unleavened bread, Hank unwrapped it and held it up for all to see. It had dark scars burned across it from the grill.

Letizia noted tears in Hank's eyes as he broke the scarred bread into two parts. She brushed her own away with her index finger. Her mind didn't fully understand the symbolism, but her heart did.

Hank laid the larger piece of bread back on the linen, wrapped it up, and as his Father had done when they shared this meal, Hank took the broken bread and placed it inside his shirt against his heart. There it rested, close to the satchel containing Vassar's letter.

Picking up the torn section of the middle piece of bread, Hank broke a piece for himself and passed the remainder. Each of his friends followed his lead as the wait staff refilled each wine glass with red wine and strategically placed bowels of finely chopped fruit and nuts, mixed in a brown-sugar paste, on the table.

Before he spoke, Hank composed himself while calling out in his heart to his colleague and comfort, the mighty Wizard-warrior, Magician. *Live through me! Speak through me! Help me remember—please, remind me! The stakes are great and the story is profound. Fight through me now for the hearts at this table. And whatever else may transpire, help me do my Brother justice.*

"I want to speak of history and reality—the historical present that is true for each of us," Hank began. "I've asked you to share a meal with me, and as we do, to enter into this history that encompasses us this moment, and the next, and the next even to our dying day and beyond.

"We are gathered here this evening, a collection of lost prodigals now found, forgiven, and made new. Our hearts are filled with the light of life who has drawn us close. Exactly how this transformation has occurred is a mystery that escapes logic, but that it has transpired is undeniable! At the intersection of what our minds comprehend and our hearts declare is faith in the King, an abiding belief that he has made us new and destined our lives together.

"By what sacrifice was our adoption into nobility made? What possible provision could be made to endow worth upon our souls— souls so irretrievably worthless to the King? And by what magnitude of light could dark hearts, hard as stone, be made new and malleable—and have etched upon their walls the thoughts, desires, and dreams of the High King?

"Tonight we gather to recall, to remember, and to vicariously relive the divine initiative that secured our redemption. Each of us are recipients of the King's mercy, but let's be clear about this mercy. He has not extended to us his helping hand nor written to us with wise counsel. Neither has he called to us from his throne and invited us to come, to make our way independently by whatever ingenious but pitiful means, to join him for this dinner. No! A thousand times, no! We are here this evening because he is here and in mercy we are in him, and where he is we must be because he has pledged upon his honor that nothing will ever separate us. He pursued us by the agency of his mercy when we were running. By his mercy he sought us out when we were indifferent. In mercy he has not been kind! Rather, by his mercy he has included us in his life, lives through us in light, and has with mercy made us joint heirs with his son, Vassar, our Older Brother."

Hank undid the scarlet sash given him by Vassar and intended as a reminder of redemption, and wiped the tears from his cheeks and chin. "Vassar! Our Brother. The mighty warrior! He is the one who is the mercy of the High King. He has brought us together in this place!

"In the wisdom of the King, Vassar, and Magician it seemed best to them to justify our lives through the sacrifice of Vassar's life. You know this story! We have discussed it many times. Tonight, in this meal, we remember his sacrifice by reliving it in these symbols of bread and wine.

"Counseling together before the foundations of Gnarled Wood were laid, this trinity from whom we now derive our identities, covenanted together. Through the breaking of his body, Vassar bore the wounds and scars of our transgressions. He took upon himself the full weight of our servitude to Zophos and under such weight and duress, plummeted to hell. And there, as us and for us, took our brokenness and made it his.

"But in the pouring out of his blood, as guarantor, Vassar captured forever the breadth, and depth, and complete provision contained in the covenant between the King and him. Because Vassar is one of us, as mercy and in mercy, he carried us with him. In him, our rebellion was dealt a fatal blow. In him, that which separated us from the King was buried. And when the King invaded hell to rescue Vassar from Zophos and raise him to his rightful prominence in the Kingdom, because of Vassar's kind mercy, we were raised in him."

Hank held up his piece of the broken, scarred, unleavened bread. "Because of Vassar's stripes, we are healed.

"As their pledge of faithfulness to us, the King and Vassar agreed that Magician should live in each of us. In him we live, and move, and have our existence."

Hank again held up his broken piece of flatbread. "Repeat after me, please: Magician, I call upon you to achieve this remembrance in me."

Twelve voices stated—some declarative, some whispering, all sincere. "Magician, I call upon you to achieve this remembrance in me."

"Now, follow my lead," Hank stated. He took some of the bitter salad, placed it on his torn piece of bread and then added a portion of the brown-sugar mix to it.

After everyone followed suit, Hank held his bread and said, "When you eat this, remember Vassar's sacrifice for you—for us all." The bread and salad and spread were sweet on their tongues.

Taking up his goblet filled with red wine, Hank held it to indicate a toast. "When you drink this wine—what Vassar called, 'The blood of the new covenant'—remember his sacrifice." Hank lifted his cup, and just before drinking, remembered, and whispered into the wine, "Here's to you, Brother."

Hank sat down and dinner was served. Pork tenderloin, smoked on an open fire. The cook had sliced the meat lengthways, inserted fruits and caramelized nuts, tied the loin back together, and basted it while over the fire. Potatoes, carrots, and onions were baked in a cast iron pot seasoned by years of cuisine.

There was joy. The room filled with laughter. Friendship. Family. Acceptance.

Plates were cleared, glasses refilled, and the expectation was that desert would come next. Once again, Hank rose to speak. "Friends, our Older Brother has worked miracles in our lives." As he was speaking, he withdrew the linen-wrapped remnant from against his heart. He unwrapped it, broke a piece, and passed it. After the bread had gone around the table, the wait staff brought an apple cobbler. "Let's enjoy this bite of bread with this desert," Hank said, "and celebrate our stories and friendships—the sweet redemption that is ours through Vassar."

"Hear! Hear!" Walt spoke out, lifting his glass. "Damn straight!" Jack barked in support of Walt's toast.

Shoulder-to-shoulder, elbow-to-elbow, the members of the forever family honored and celebrated the courage, sacrifice, and love of their patriarchs, the High King and Vassar. As Hank observed, he said in his heart, *Nicely done, Magician. Nicely done.*

No one wanted the night to conclude, but tomorrow and its demands wouldn't wait. There were hugs and handshakes, kisses and tears; arms were slung over shoulders, hands were held, and the family promised to gather again soon.

In fall's fainting grip, the night was misty and cold. Jack marched euphorically through the fog toward La Faim, stopping occasionally to dance in the road, singing the only songs he knew: drinking songs from the pub in La Faim. The words weren't important to him, rather that he was making melody in his heart. He was his own band, drum corps, and director. The King was resplendent as his appreciative audience.

Jake, Caroline, and Audie left together. They took their time, strolling, enjoying their memories, while allowing for the weather's effect on Jake's joints. He was fine with the pain; it kept him focused. Caroline on his right arm, Audie on his left, *A magical night*, he thought. *What more could a man desire?*

The two couples who were small group facilitators had arrived in personal carriages. Their conversations kept pace with the clip-clop of their horses' hooves on the cobblestones. Each had granted Jake and Walt *carte blanche* to tap their ready-service. They were excited about hosting their small groups and ready to encourage other facilitators. "Call upon me! For whatever," each said.

The Michelson's, Letizia, and Bull left together.

Ronan remained with Hank, helping, watching, admiring—soaking up what he could of the aura remaining in the back room of Hoi Polloi.

Hank settled the bill with the manager, tipped the wait staff, and complimented the cooks. With their help and hosting, the evening came off better than he even imagined. When he and Ronan stepped into the mist, it was almost midnight.

Hank loved nights like this—always had. Inclement weather energized his soul. He loved the wind in his face, the bite of frost; the pelting of rain, crunching snow, and squishing mud. Feeling the mist against his cheeks was refreshing.

He carried on a vibrant, energetic, and animated conversation with Ronan. He was a fine, fine man already doing good work and possessing significant promise. It was Hank's observation that walks like this, in weather like this, provided ample opportunity to leverage a young man up to the next level.

Ronan lapped up every moment. The evening catapulted him forward, galvanizing his convictions and confidence. Walking beside his mentor filled his heart.

The two arrows, fired simultaneously from crossbows at close range, found their marks. The first struck just below Bull's left shoulder blade, piercing through to his heart, lodging against a rib. The second entered at the base of his skull. After splintering the apex of his spine, the arrow's momentum wasn't spent until the broad-head protruded from Bull's throat.

William "Bull" Stephenson passed from this life almost instantly. He did so without struggle and without noise beyond the collapse of his earthly shell.

The timing was perfect, the work of assassins operating at the top of their profession. The dark-topped carriage stopped alongside Letizia exactly as Bull dropped lifeless. While there were other people traveling the thoroughfare, none saw the corpse or the abduction.

No one heard Letizia. She didn't scream or cry when thrown onto the carriage floor. Beyond her gasp of surprise when Bull was struck, there was no point in wasting her breath. She knew what was transpiring.

The driver followed the road beside the moat separating the Round Tower from the castle. On the back side of the Tower, the assassins flung their crossbows into the moat's inky waters. With the splash, the driver accelerated the team.

After a few more turns, the carriage slowed. The assassins leaped to the ground, glanced, and disappeared into the night. Letizia heard the slap of the reins on the horses' backs and felt the carriage lunge toward Gnarled Wood. She heard the whip snap. The horses responded in gallop. Branches scraped the sides of the coach. Twigs and leaves joined her on the floor. The carriage rocked and slipped against rocks and in ruts. They drove on, farther into the musky smell of deep timber that Letizia recognized as Zophos' lair.

The driver stopped his team, their bodies steaming in the damp cold. The boots resting on her body scraped her, stepped on her, as her captors climbed from the carriage. Rough hands grabbed her ankles and dragged her across the carriage floor. They didn't wait for her to find her footing. Her shoes were gone. The same hands that dragged her now held her biceps and towed her stumbling toward a cottage. She tried to get her feet under her, felt sharp pokes into her arches, felt her toes stub. Dim light shone under the door. Otherwise, the windows were shuttered.

As usual Ennui's dress was immaculate, her black hair down, hanging straight, separating over her shoulders, framing her expressionless face. "Good evening, Letizia."

The room was empty except for a dining table and chairs. A candle burned on the table, another on the mantle. A small fire flickered in the fireplace but was no match for the chill.

Two men stood on opposite sides of the small room. Letizia recognized both and liked neither. They made her blood run cold. They didn't move, even as she was dragged before Ennui. They stood with their hands clasped in front of them, staring at her with unblinking eyes pitted in hard faces atop thick necks. The two men who dragged her from the carriage, gripped her arms. A fifth followed, *The driver of the coach*, she assumed.

"You have been busy," Ennui stated, "pursuing other interests—interests that are not, shall I say, advantageous to you, to Zophos, and certainly not to me. Your activities are troubling. You have compromised. I do not like to be disappointed, Letizia. Surely you know this."

Letizia didn't answer.

"You have declared allegiance to the High King. Have you not?"

Letizia looked into Ennui's black eyes, languidly blinking under the weight of her long lashes, "Yes, ma'am. I have." There was no point justifying herself, no point offering explanation. She had been indicted, tried, and declared guilty. She was not brought to Gnarled Wood to reason with Ennui.

"Neither do I like disloyalty," Ennui replied. "This, you know about me as well, do you not?"

Letizia didn't reply.

"Yes. You know. You are too smart to feign ignorance, Letizia."

Uncharacteristically, the pitch and volume of Ennui's voice rose dramatically. Although coiffed in perfection, beauty, intelligence, and tranquility Ennui was a cauldron of hostility toward anything and anyone allied with the Kingdom of Light. Her eyes burned at her subordinate as she unleashed her tongue upon Letizia with invective, cursing, threat, and hatred for her and everything she stood for now.

Letizia had never heard Ennui raise her voice. But she railed now in fury, screeching, and yelling until the veins in her neck bulged and her eyes turned red with ruptured blood vessels. Ennui's teeth flashed as she screamed at the King's daughter.

She stepped up to Letizia and ripped her clothes and undergarments from her body with demonic strength. Her nails lacerated Letizia's skin. Grabbing her by the hair, Ennui yanked Letizia's head forward, backward, side-to-side.

Letizia was terrified with Ennui's brutality. Fear harnessed her hope and dragged it away from her like a petulant child. A thought clambered to the surface of her mind midst the tumult, *I will not leave you destitute. I'm here.*

Seizing a guard's knife, Ennui sawed away great hunks of Letizia's hair, cutting her scalp. The more she vented her rage, the more control evaded Ennui. She scratched, and slapped, and kicked Letizia's shins expending her anger.

The men on either side of Letizia, held her steady, unflinching. Letizia cried and absorbed Ennui's abuse with grunts and groans, but she never lashed out, did not plead for mercy. She fixed her mind on the King and stated to Magician in her thoughts, *The King is my light and my salvation; whom shall I fear? The King is the refuge of my life; whom shall I dread?* She fixed her mind—but doubt rose severe that she had staked her hope in spongy ground.

Letizia anticipated this might be her fate and believed she could endure. She had vowed a courageous withstanding of whatever Ennui and Zophos might do to her. It was the naiveté of those who are bold before torture, disillusioned with its commencement, demoralized by its severity, and haunted by their failure to withstand.

Her energy spent, Ennui stumbled toward the mantle for support. Holding herself up, she cast her arm in a sweep.

The men pinned Letizia to the floor, forced her, spread her, raped her, abused her; their gang violence propelling lust into perverse brutality. She felt herself fail, felt her viability disappear, felt her courage flee. Shame and self-loathing filled the vacancy.

Where is my savior? My rescuer? My King? Jester screamed at her conscience while the perversion escalated. *He's not here, he's not coming.* Jester turned the knife with his invective, *I am lost. Abandoned. Worthless. I have no value, no value beyond this abuse.*

Despair rose up and consumed her. Her soul that felt desired by the King—sought by the King—fled anguished as she was dehumanized. Ruined.

Seizing his momentum, Jester ridiculed her, *If only I was stronger, I could endure, and he would rescue me...but I can't. I am nothing. I am thrown away.*

Ennui hated the men. She despised their masculine anger thrust out in wonton, degraded abuse.

As their violence against Letizia escalated, Ennui became afraid. She kicked at the men, screaming for them to stop. Scratched them, hit them until one-by-one they receded, beaten back, and concluded their ravaging of Letizia.

"Put her on the table," she ordered.

Letizia looked at Ennui—a terrified, assaulted, absent stare.

Ennui nodded to the carriage driver.

A thought came to Letizia, *In the day of trouble he will conceal me in his heart. In that secret place he will hide me. He will lift me up in the arms of Vassar.* She heard a familiar voice, breaking with emotion, *"I am here. I will not leave you."* But Letizia turned away in her shame from the pledged strength and redemption.

The driver drew his knife and cut Letizia's abdomen. She screamed into the consuming evil.

Ennui glared with disgust at the driver for vomiting, retching in weakness. She berated the men as weak. Threatened them. Demeaned their performance. With her shaming and wickedness against Letizia, she regained her dominance. She demanded! A shamed man followed his orders, lifted the contents of Letizia's abdomen, and placed them between her breasts.

Ennui leaned over her eviscerated subject, "I do not tolerate disloyalty. Good-bye, Letizia."

The men set fire to Letizia's clothing, breaking the chairs and shutters to feed the growing flames. Ennui supervised until satisfied the cottage would be engulfed. Turning away, she entered her carriage alone, telling the men to ride outside. Ennui wrapped herself in a down comforter to ward off the cold, amused that she could smell Letizia's perfume inside the coach. The sun was rising as she rode toward the Round Tower. Ennui turned her thoughts to the tasks of the day, irritated that she had missed a night of sleep.

Feeling the flames singe her skin, smelling the assault of her burning flesh, feeling the acrid smoke engulf her lungs, Letizia turned to the light coming through the door. She felt he might come—hoped—but she cast her eyes down at her broken self, disemboweled, naked, soiled, and ravaged. She turned away, too ashamed to look.

He took her hand in his.

"Hank, thank you for coming," she managed to gasp, looking away.

"You're welcome, Lettie."

She felt his tears dripping on her flesh, soothing the hot blisters and contusions.

"I've been here all along, defending your heart before you ever asked—just as you trusted. But I'm not Hank. I'm his Brother, Vassar."

Vassar scooped Letizia into his arms, holding her close. Comfort. Healing. He kissed her on the head, and whispered in her ear, "Let's go home, Lettie."

CHAPTER 27

Letizia Pintaro's Office in the Round Tower

Caroline sensed Letizia's absence when she arrived at the office. She tried to reassure herself that her premonition was nothing. While not unprecedented for her not to show up all day, it was abnormal for her to do so without notice.

Caroline told Jake that evening of her foreboding. He was reassuring and she tried to take his comfort to heart. She slept fitfully though. Her mind wouldn't shut down and staring at the ceiling wasn't helpful for the plague of anxiety. She got out of bed in the early hours, made coffee, and attempted to read. But focus was evasive, comfort elusive. Her intuition wouldn't be quiet.

At the earliest hour she dared, Caroline jotted a note for Jake, left breakfast prepared, and departed for the office. Perhaps the demands of work would silence the haunting premonition.

Bernie was sitting in her office when she arrived. He stood when he heard her, turned. His eyes red, his face ashen. "She's dead, Caroline." Bernie blurted out, coming toward her. "They killed her!" He put his arms around Caroline, sobbing. "They killed her. They killed her."

They held each other for support, encumbered as they were under the significant load. Her tears soaked into his shirt, his into her hair. Their eyes burned and swelled with the acidic purge of sorrow. Haphazardly, under duress, and without due ceremony the living Letizia was replaced by memories of her.

"What happened?" Caroline asked, backing from Bernie's arms, wiping her eyes.

Bernie didn't know the full extent of Letizia's ordeal, but what he did know, he pledged never to tell Caroline. It was too horrific. "She was kidnapped, night-before-last, apparently on her way home from dinner at Hoi Polloi."

"I see," Caroline stated. "And Bull?"

"Bull is dead, too. Shot twice. The arrows came from crossbows. He died instantly. Passersby found his body and alerted the authorities."

Caroline knew Letizia's concerns about quitting her other business had come to pass. *Bull was assassinated.* Caroline's logic was sound, but she didn't suspect Ennui. Letizia had protected her from too much information, certainly she hadn't named names. Caroline knew Letizia worked for Ennui, but she had no reason to suspect her. On the contrary. Caroline made a mental note, *I must visit Ennui—make certain she is informed of Ms. Pintaro's passing.*

"The details are sketchy from here, Caroline," Bernie said.

Caroline sensed he was withholding information, but was appreciative of his protection.

"Whoever murdered Bull, kidnapped Ms. Pintaro and carried her into Gnarled Wood—to a cottage, deep in the forest. From what I'm told…" Bernie's eyes filled again, and through sobs, said, "…they burned the cottage with her in it."

Caroline considered this news. *It's bad enough to be burned alive,* she thought—hating the thought that followed. *I wonder if they burned the cabin to cover up what else they did to her?* Her mind ran rampant—until she reeled it back from imagined horrors.

Caroline was sobered. She had tears, but they came from anger, not grief.

Letizia's loss would circle her, stalk her like wolves waiting for opportunity, and close in soon enough. In time, she knew she would descend into the turbid waters of sorrow's depths, but for now the analytical aspect of her soul directed her. "How did you find this out, Bernie?"

Wiping his eyes with his sleeve, trying mightily to compose himself, he said, "I stopped by the pub after work—yesterday evening.

It was later than normal. One of our subcontractors approached me. We visited, exchanged casual information—nothing much. But as I finished my drink, he asked if we could step outside. Once it was private, he informed me of Letizia's demise."

Caroline nodded once. "How do you know he was telling you the truth?"

Bernie gathered his composure. "He told me where the cottage is."

Caroline walked to the door. Her assistant was just arriving. She asked that she call immediately for a carriage.

Bernie directed the driver toward the cottage. As they neared, smoke from the smoldering fire guided them to the remains. Only the chimney stood, and had it not been for the wet weather, the surrounding forest would not be standing.

Neither Caroline nor Bernie got down from the carriage.

Caroline instructed the driver to take her to Levine's Livery. "And please, let's not waste any time."

Larry Levine heard the carriage approaching fast, the horse pacing, lathered. The driver pulled hard on the reins. Larry nodded, aborted a customary greeting, and looked at the driver whose eyes motioned toward the carriage. Caroline inquired about Hank and was relieved to hear he was on the premises.

Following his morning routine, Hank sat at the table in his room reading from Vassar's letter. The last paragraph had captured his attention—for the last two mornings.

Hank, as your Older Brother, I've written to put your heart at peace. What lies ahead will be tremendously difficult. But don't fear. Have courage! You and I are victorious warriors!

I love you. See you soon,

Vassar

He loved his Brother's signature, but was considering the words, "don't fear," when Larry knocked on his door. After looking through his peep hole, Hank opened the door and greeted him, "Good morning, Larry."

"Good morning, Mr. Henderson. I'm sorry to bother you, but there is a woman here to see you by the name of, Caroline Ingram."

It was odd for Caroline to search him out at Levine's, especially given that it was a work day.

He put away Vassar's letter, carefully, just as he always did, and hurried to the lobby. As soon as he saw Caroline's face, he knew something was terribly wrong. "Caroline, what's the matter? Is it one of the children? Is Jake okay?"

She had managed her emotions with Bernie, but Hank was not her employee. He was Uncle H to her children. He was a father-figure to her. With Hank, she was safe. With him, she could be herself—and right now, her heart was a shambles.

All Caroline managed was, "It's Letizia! I'm sorry. I'm so sorry," she wailed, burying her face in his chest, wrapping her arms around his waist.

He didn't need any detail. Lettie was gone. He held Caroline—held onto her. But as her news found purchase in his soul, Hank couldn't stand. With her still in his arms, and he in hers, they collapsed under the weight.

Edging close, having been called into action by Larry, Maria handed clean dishtowels to Hank and Caroline. They cried and sobbed and wiped their faces. As their emotions ebbed, Caroline told Hank what she knew of Letizia's passing.

They moved to a table and sat. Maria brought water and fresh towels.

Bernie sat with Larry out front and waited. Few words passed between them as none were suitable.

Caroline and Hank cared for each another's questions and doubts.

But the magnitude of their loss was beyond immediate remedy. Only time and Magician could assuage the tumult, pacify the rage, and comfort the vacancy left with Letizia's departure.

Bernie suggested that Caroline and Hank take the carriage back to the cottage in Gnarled Wood while he waited at the Levine's.

Nothing had changed. Even though there were no flames, the heat was unapproachable. Still, Hank helped Caroline from the carriage and instructed the driver to wait a block or so away.

They stood still for a long, sad moment. Staring. Holding onto each other.

They returned to the Levine's, collected Bernie, and rode to the castle. While Caroline and Bernie informed the horrified office staff of Ms. Pintaro's murder, Hank went to Letizia's home.

Incessantly, Jester indicted the King for this tragedy. *If only he had been there, then I...,* he intoned in Hank's consciousness. *If he really loved her—and me, for that matter...,* implying she and he were both deceived. *If he's as powerful as he asserts, and truly has everything under control, how could this occur to her? To me?* On and on Jester harped. *Why have you taken away the most important person to me?* he questioned. Hank's thoughts built, tossed, and broke—waves in a hurricane sea.

Jester's questions, doubts, insinuation, and distrust accosted Hank's raw vulnerability. He didn't counter or combat; he was too tired, too shocked. But Jester's accusations and temptations added up, taking a toll upon him, and wearing down his resolve. Patiently. Carefully. Shrewdly, Jester worked the angles afforded him. In due course, he felt, he could seize upon Hank and gleefully watch him tumble into his pit of pity.

One would like to believe that even Jester respects loss. Hank knew better! Knew there was no honor or mercy in Jester. But he was overwhelmed, and in his susceptibility believed the best about Jester, believed he wouldn't be so callous as to disrespect the dead or prey upon the living in their grief. In his deception, he listened to Jester.

The constant in this assault—the immovable object upon which the waves of Jester's ranting continually crashed—was a singular conviction. While the tumult of Jester's questions and accusations piled higher and beat harder, like a lighthouse on a desolate, and forsaken coast, only this declaration stood and cast its light in answer to Jester's lashing. Hank could envision Vassar's script:

I've written to put your heart at peace. What lies ahead will be tremendously difficult. But don't fear. Have courage! You and I are victorious warriors!

Vassar's words were indelible, and Magician didn't back down. He defended his compromised *compadre*, Hank.

There was nothing flashy about Magician. No fancy swordplay. No boasts. No posturing, threatening, or posing. Just sound, classical defense. No matter Jester's approach, Magician countered with, *"I've written to put your heart at peace. What lies ahead will be tremendously difficult. But don't fear. Have courage! You and I are victorious warriors!"*

Initially it appeared Jester's ferocious and brazen assault was effective, but as his accusations reached critical mass, his storming garnered Hank's attention from Letizia's loss. He was drawn to Magician's simple encouragement—the fundamentals of his conviction—and he returned to what he knew to be true: "I've written to put your heart at peace. What lies ahead will be tremendously difficult. But don't fear. Have courage! You and I are victorious warriors!"

Momentarily, but longer than he wished, Hank had forgotten that Jester shows no mercy.

Vassar's tide rose in Hank.

Hank marched forward in step with Magician while Jester's accusations crashed against them. Why should a victorious warrior shy from difficulty or fear a defeated foe?

As Hank got close to Letizia's home, he slowed. Based on nothing more than a hunch, Hank selected a spot for surveillance where he could observe if anyone came and went. It was late in the afternoon, the weather again a heavy overcast, and it was time for dinner. *If someone is sorting through her things, there will be little point of continuing by candlelight on an empty stomach,* Hank thought.

His hunch paid off. As darkness encroached on daylight, two men exited Letizia's home. Hank recognized one of them from the ambush on the river bank. He knew from talking with Letizia that she had no lieutenant to step up and take her place and no intermediary between her and her boss. His suspicions were confirmed: *Ennui has to be complicit in Letizia's murder.*

After allowing time for the two men to disappear into the distance, Hank slipped from his surveillance. He had agreed to join Caroline and Jake for dinner.

Jake answered his knock. Rather than lose his composure in front of the children, Jake stepped outside to console Hank and comfort himself over their loss.

Hank and the Ingrams made small talk over dinner and while the kids were awake, but then huddled at the end of the dining table to talk. Hank inquired about Ennui. To his surprise, Caroline reported that she met with Ennui that afternoon and informed her of Letizia's death. Hank asked how she took the news. "Typical Ennui," Caroline reported. "If I didn't know better, I would say she couldn't have cared less. But, her brow did furrow," Caroline noted, granting Ennui the benefit of the doubt. "She asked if I had everything under control and offered assistance for anything I might need. Interesting lady," Caroline observed. "Very precise. Glad I don't have to work in the same office with her."

They reminisced about Lettie. They laughed and cried, dabbing at their eyes, and wondered what they were going to do about the absence.

It was later than normal when Hank quietly departed the Ingram's.

Hank spent the next weeks caring for his friends while largely deferring his own loss. He tended his essential needs, but stabilized those in his care first, living from his repository of strength. He spent more time with the Ingrams than anyone else. Of course, he wanted to make sure Caroline was keeping her head above water, but he also combated his loneliness with their closeness.

His deferral wasn't denial, nor was it survival. He acknowledged his loss. Oh! How he acknowledged Letizia's departure. But until the cyclone of others' bereavement subsided, the people in his charge needed the confidence of knowing his hand was on the tiller while in the midst of the storm. He knew the time would come when he could tend his own heart's grief.

Caroline regained her footing with remarkable speed. Her leadership cemented her place as the head of the office. But lest her recovery be attributed to being busy, Caroline grew personally in her reliance upon, and confidence in, the indwelling Magician. In addition, she and Jake remarked to Hank more than once that their personal relationship strengthened as they rebounded.

Jake and Walt had a problem. With word of Letizia's conversion and testimony, the number of those declaring allegiance to the King exploded in both the castle and the Tower. The demand for small groups increased dramatically, and to Hank's delight, Jake and Walt managed the growth with exemplary skill and resolute dependence upon Magician's leadership. After all, both had experience managing a revival.

Jack and Ronan were taking La Faim by storm while sharpening each other like iron against iron. Audie, bless her dear heart, was courageously loving and engaging the people of the night. It was outside her comfort zone, but she resolutely contended that she was where the

King wanted her to be. She consulted regularly with Jake on leadership development for burgeoning and unconventional small groups.

Once again, Hank noted that when pain presents itself, not only does the King provide grace and mercy in copious amounts, but he turns the unwelcome intruder's offense to the benefit of those he loves. In turn, his place in their lives is solidified and their identification in the family yields confidence. *It's uncanny! He takes any action by Zophos, any reversal or loss, and makes it redemptive.*

Still, that conviction and realization didn't erase Letizia's absence.

Hank moved to the Levine's full time and only returned to the castle as necessary. Some Wednesday nights he stayed over with the Ingrams, but only if he had an appointment Thursday morning. Otherwise, he didn't mind the nighttime walk back to his room at the livery.

He paid attention to his safety. Only a fool would drop his guard knowing Zophos was seeking the advantage. *He's like a big cat,* Hank thought, *always looking for a kill—just for the hell of it.*

That he had gotten the attention of someone higher up in the food chain was apparent. There were too many coincidences, too many familiar faces in a crowd, and too many close calls, not to mention the gut sense he couldn't escape. Still. There was nothing to fear, but everything to respect.

Hank knew he was safer at the Levine's. Anyone poking around was apt to run across a wary Levine. He also felt at home. It was quieter, affording him more solitude, more time for reflection, and more time for the disciplines that nourished his heart. Maria and her staff made fantastic meals, cleaned, did laundry, and made certain the wood was chopped and a fire going. His room was simple and his personal affects few, but this aided his focus, keeping him light and ready. But maybe most of all, he was close to Celia.

He felt silly finding comfort in a donkey. But with Celia he felt the freedom to be his unedited self. On more occasions than he cared to recall, he buried his face in Celia's hair coat and grieved. But her eccentricities, temperament, and personality caused him to smile

She expected him to take her walking, and that was good accountability for Hank. He needed to be out trekking the simple trails and picking his way through the woods—as part of his recovery. He needed to sit by the creek, lean against trees, and follow the tracks of bears hunting for dens. He needed to let the wind blow through his ears and clear his head.

As he roamed the woods and let time and Magician's touch comfort his heart, an idea had formed in his mind. And now, four days after he began, Hank studied the hewn cross he had constructed. It was straight and true, but rough, like he envisioned it would be when he began. The foot of the upright timber sat on the cross member of an "H"-shaped steel frame. Jackson Gutmann, Celia's former owner, constructed it for him. Like the horizontal piece of wood, the steel frame was secured to the cross with pegs Hank formed with a hand axe and whittled to size with his knife.

He returned to the task at hand: touching up the edge on the broad axe before putting it back in the Levine's tool shed. The stone irritated his blistered hands, which annoyed him, but he knew blisters were to be expected on hands unaccustomed to an axe handle.

Hank dragged his fingers across the edge. Satisfied, he carried the tool to the shed, replaced it, and fastened the door.

When he returned to the barn, Jay was examining the finished cross. "You've done a fine job on this, son. Never would have thought about a foundation like you devised."

"Well, I wanted it to be just right."

"I know, and I think you got that done."

The two men stood together, each with his thoughts.

"Shall I help you load it, son?"

Jay and Hank lifted the cross and laid it in the back of the wagon. As Hank tied it down, Jay went to get the mule. When he returned, he and Hank hitched the mule to the wagon and led her out into the yard. It was still early, so they went to the kitchen to drink coffee with Maria.

Caroline, Jake, and their kids arrived late morning. Natalie was with them, nestled with the kids under a blanket. Jake and Caroline sat together on the front seat of their rented carriage.

Maria had lunch prepared and packed in baskets. She and Jay put them in the back of the wagon and wedged each in place against the cross and the front of the wagon bed. Jay made certain the baskets were protected from the tools: two shovels, a pick, a sledge, a pry bar, and a rake.

Because of Jake's infirmity and his bad back, Hank asked Jack and Ronan to help them with the task ahead. They arrived from La Faim shortly after Natalie and the Ingrams.

Ronan drove the mule. The Ingrams fell in behind. Jack walked beside Hank in front of the procession and Celia followed Hank who held her lead in one hand and his staff in the other.

They walked for an hour and stopped in a meadow to eat lunch and let the kids play. The adults chatted, the mule slept in a sunbeam, and Celia munched meadow grass.

Hank excused himself and walked into the trees a short distance. He wanted one, final check to be certain his heart was satisfied. On his return, he moved a few branches out of his path. Less than an hour after they stopped, they were on the road again. It wasn't far now.

Hank's mind was a jumble of miscellaneous phrases, images, and words. None formed anything complete. Then out of the mistiness came, *Father knows what he's doing—and I am near you, as near as your thoughts and the desires of your heart.* He recognized the first words of Vassar's letter—could see them on the page and hear them so clearly he nearly turned to look for his Brother. Immediately, another line came, *I've written to put your heart at peace.* He didn't acknowledge Magician's contribution to his thoughts, but Hank knew in his heart where the focus came from, and not a moment early or late.

It was thirty minutes since they had eaten lunch. Hank and Jack had walked in silence for most of that time. Hank knew it was coming, but seeing their destination still took his breath away. Without preamble, Hank said, "Jack, Father knows what he's doing. Vassar is not absent and we are not alone. My heart's at peace."

The group assembled on the remains of the cabin where Letizia was murdered. They watched as Hank filled an urn with ashes from the residual in front of the hearth. There was no way to know if the ashes were hers or not, but that wasn't the point. They needed closure on their loss, a memorial for their grief, and a tribute in her honor.

Knowing how much Letizia loved Celia, Hank placed the urn on Celia's saddle and secured it. They retraced their path to the meadow where they had eaten lunch, collected the cross and tools from the wagon, and made their way into the woods.

Hank thought at first he would bury Letizia's ashes in the high places, perhaps even the King's refuge. But he realized later that doing so would make it impossible for Jake to participate in the burial or visit her memorial. Grasping his desire to include Jake focused him on the type location he desired to find, and these woods seemed appropriate. Jake made it to the granite outcropping Hank had selected without even a stumble.

Once Jack and Ronan had chipped and shaped the rock to receive the steel bracket on the bottom of the cross, the four men set the memorial in place and secured it with stones. Just as Hank intended, the cross itself didn't come in contact with the ground. He knew the wood would decay, but keeping it off the ground meant it wouldn't happen in his lifetime.

Jack opened the hole to receive the urn. When it was three-feet deep, he stepped back and laid the shovel aside. The Ingram children helped Hank carry the urn and place it in the ground.

Standing around the open hole, they reminisced about Letizia. Her physical absence was awful, but her presence in their minds and hearts was palpable. When it was quiet around the circle, they each dropped a mum on top of the urn. Jack replaced the dirt and closed the hole.

Back at the Levine's, Hank thanked each for joining him. He hugged them all, reassured Natalie, and kissed each Ingram child on the head as he helped them into their carriage. He watched until Jack and Ronan were about to disappear over the hill. They waved from the crest, knowing he would be looking.

After currying Celia and eating dinner, Hank retreated into a cold evening to sit by the fire pit in back of the house. He fed his fire until it blazed high and hot. Standing beside it with the poker in his hand, he said into the flames, "Vassar, I know you are here, in my heart. You promised you wouldn't ever leave me, and you haven't. I can't see you and I'd lie if I said I understand. But I trust you, Brother." His voice withdrew into thoughts, *It's been a good day, but a hard day. The next hard day in a series of hard days, in fact.*

He thought about Lettie, about sitting with her by the fire, discussing their Brother. *"Vassar's the one who understands. He knows— knows all the hardship, the heartache, the loss. He knows all the wounds we suffer, the grief we bear, and the brokenness we feel."*

Hank listened. He could almost hear Lettie say from the flames, *"There are times when a girl needs a brother, Hank."*

He took a deep breath and eased from his reminiscence. He poked at the fire. *It's been a brutal battle, Magician. My heart is hurting. Brother, you know. Would you heal me?*

Hank heard, *There's no healing for this, not from Vassar, not from anyone. I'm just nostalgic. No help's coming, not tonight anyway. If I'm going to get over Lettie, I'm going to have to put my time in. Just hunker down, stay busy. And, take care of it myself.*

Jester's condemnation was demoralizing. His accusation stung. But taking advantage of Lettie's absence was out of bounds—a step too far.

Hank looked into the darkness, "Jester, you lie. My heart is at peace, no matter what transpires. I refuse to own what you say. I refuse to embrace your fear, and I refuse to believe I'm alone. I renounce you."

He placed three more logs into the fire and retrieved his dram of whiskey from the stump where he set it. After shooing Jester away, he returned to thinking about his friends and the events of the day. He noticed his heart surface again after Jester's intrusive thoughts interrupted. Sacred images of Lettie and the miracle of her life came to him. He thought about the transformation of her heart from darkness to light. He remembered how their hearts connected and bonded to the King's. He thought, *I'm a better man because of her.*

Pressure pushed against his sternum. He touched his chest. *I wonder if that's Lettie's absence or presence? Maybe it's both. Maybe it's her way—and Father's way—of letting me know there's more to come, more to life and light than Gnarled Wood.*

He thought of what was at stake throughout Gnarled Wood, and for that matter, in the other world—in Montana and Fort Worth. *The conflict here, between Zophos and the King, is the same conflict that's there. Whether real or metaphor, the battle for the Round Tower is also my battle—to trust, to believe, to live true to myself, not as if my heart is torn between two loves.*

He stared into the fire. Sipped. *Like I said, Vassar, I trust you. I believe in you. Even against the loss of Lettie, I know you are good.*

A rebounding thought came, clear and sharp. *I trust you as well, Brother. And I believe in you. I believe in you enough to take you into my life.*

Hank smiled. Sipped. Stared into the flames, listening.

Winter came suddenly, invading like the Mongols. Cold rain fell the better part of a week as temperatures descended—then plunged.

Sleet replaced rain, then was usurped by wind-driven snow. Gnarled Wood, the castle, and its Tower were engulfed in blowing white upon frozen turf.

Jay Levine, his sons, and their staff were prepared. Wood was cut, gathered, and stacked for the fires. Hay and feed were stored for the livery. Provisions for the guests were in the cellar and the meat house was full of venison, bear fat, pork, and small game.

With the severity of the weather, there weren't many travelers. That meant the pub, and more specifically, the table by the fireplace was usually vacant and the dining hall quiet. Hank moved his morning solitude and contemplation from his cold room upstairs to the table by the fire downstairs.

He greeted Maria with a hug around her shoulders and retreated to the fire with coffee in hand. Opening Vassar's letter, he scanned it for encouragement. From the worn lines and frayed edges, Hank collected his Brother's counsel, letting his mind dwell on each phrase and sentence that captured his attention.

We are family, and as such, we are bonded and can never be separated. In spirit, I am in Father and Father is in me— just as I am in you and you are in me. We are in Father. He is in us. Magician is evidence of this. Father said so! We are a unit, a family. We are cut from the same bolt of genetic cloth and our lives are interwoven. We are inseparable!

Hank focused on a recurring theme: We are family. We are a unit. We are inseparable.

He heard Jester take issue. *If only Lettie wasn't dead.* The clear implication being, *I'm alone.*

Hank continued noting Vassar's words, but the mention of Lettie's name drew his heart up short. It wasn't that he didn't think about her.

He thought about her constantly. But he didn't think of her loss as a failure by Vassar or the King.

I know you've been pushed hard at times,

Hank didn't think he was pushed harder than anyone else. To do so would be flirting with Pity.

As he considered Vassar's line, on cue Jester reproduced Hank's tryst with Pity. He intoned she was a goddess, and as he had done before, he magnanimously offered her again as a viable consolation.

Hank's finger discovered a sticky spot on the table, a tackiness left from last night's desert. It reminded him that Pity's skin was sallow and sticky, her odor rancid. Pity was hardly the goddess Jester recreated. *Advantage, Magician,* he thought.

Still, Hank lingered over the line: "I know you've been pushed hard." In his mind's ear—that is, his heart—Hank heard, *And you have risen to the occasion.*

It had been a hard run, but Magician never wavered with his supply of grace. As he thought about it, Hank knew, *Grace is a training ground, run with tear-blurred eyes, that in the end leaves my heart strong, my muscles toned. I wouldn't wish my challenges on my worst enemy, but neither would I trade them for any treasure.*

Hank sipped his coffee and returned to Vassar's words.

Things are not going to be easy, Brother! The stakes have risen since we were last in Gnarled Wood,

If the stress of the last months is indicative of increased risk in Gnarled Wood, then the stakes have indeed risen, he considered. *Zophos is more desperate, thereby more dangerous. The King, more persistent, thereby more demonstrative with his love.*

That reminded Hank of another line from Vassar's letter. He scanned until he located the paragraph.

In everything you do, Brother, let your motive be love. Nothing is more powerful because love is the essence of who Father is. When you love, you portray Father, and the only way you can love as he loves is to live from your heart and let Magician's strength bolster you.

He knew this was true, knew that Love had taken up residency in his heart in alliance with Magician and Hope. *I know that I have loved,* he thought. *And I have loved deeply, otherwise my heart wouldn't hurt so badly.*

Jester chided him—accused him. *I could have loved more, though. I have it in me. That I might have loved a little is a poor excuse for not loving more.*

Just who the "I" was that expected him to do better, Hank wasn't certain. But whether Jester meant the unfulfilled expectation was the King's or his, either way Hank resented Jester for intruding on his solitude. He had been patient, but taking Letizia's death in vain and resurrecting images of the faces in his pit pushed Hank beyond his limit. "Go to hell!" Hank hissed.

"Strong words so early on such a fine morning."

Hank jerked. His face turned crimson with embarrassment. "Jay! You scared me. I'm so sorry. I wasn't talking to you. I didn't know you were there." Hank scooted his chair back, flustered.

Jay was no fool. Just who Hank was talking to, he didn't know; the room was empty except for the two of them. He didn't know the content of Hank's letter, but knew it was important. Powerful messages make for powerful responses, seen and unseen. He chuckled and put his hand on Hank's shoulder.

But Hank spilled his coffee when he bumped the table getting up to reassure Jay...who didn't need reassurance, but hugged Hank nevertheless. Maria heard the cup fall, appeared with a rag, and never gave a second thought to her husband in the arms of another man.

To Jay and Maria, Hank was their additional son. They were short on the details of his life, but they didn't need those to love him as their own. Maria sneaked in under Hank's arm and joined Jay's hug.

Jay held Hank by both shoulders. "Hank, everything's fine. I know you weren't talking to me. You've been doing some heavy lifting in your soul, son. Maria and the boys and I believe in you. No worries, now. You hear?"

Hank nodded. He thought about expending more energy explaining, but the words wouldn't form in his head.

"See here now," Jay said. "There's a fellow who's arrived to see you. He's waiting in the stable with Celia."

Hank's eyes narrowed. *Who in the name of time would be traveling in this nastiness?*

"It's alright," Jay reassured. "Go on. Don't keep the man waiting. We'll take care of things here."

Hank hurried across the yard separating the house from the stable and tugged the barn door open. While it was warmer in the barn—much warmer—it was still doggone cold. He walked past a row of stalls, the musky scent filling his head, and turned toward Celia's place.

A man wearing a bearskin coat and fur hat, with a light pack and snowshoes strapped to his back, stood in the aisle petting Celia. She turned toward her master. Her ridiculous ears waggled atop her wedge-shaped head.

Turning to face Hank, a giant smile covered Faith's face.

Even though it had been a few weeks since Hank had seen Faith, he was keenly aware of Faith's presence whether seen or not. He came and went, and when he was "away," his substance remained—similar to Love's and Hope's. Seeing the great man now, Hank rededicated himself to the peculiarity of him.

"What are you doing here?" Hank exclaimed. "It's early and the weather's awful."

Faith was dismissive with his explanation while shedding his pack, hat, and greatcoat. He unbuttoned his boiled-wool vest and unstrapped his belt and sheath knife, handed them to Hank, and said, "Follow the creek toward the High King's refuge. Take care of yourself. You'll know what to do once you're on the way."

Hank strapped on the belt and was buttoning the vest. "But Faith, it's winter! Miserable winter. Jay says it's the worst winter anyone can remember."

Faith stopped, tilted his head—considering. "I realize that, but you've made the trip before in the winter."

It was hard to argue with that fact.

"You'll do fine," Faith stated, deeming the weather inconsequential. "You've got Magician, haven't you?"

Hank couldn't resist gouging the Wizard. "Well, I suppose. I haven't heard from him in a while. You know how he is about difficult situations? I'm just glad you brought me this knife." Hank bent to strap on his snowshoes.

Before he put on Faith's hat, Hank stepped close to Celia. She pressed her face against his chest—more forcefully than usual. Hank braced himself, leaning into her. He buried his fingers into her coat and put his face alongside her neck. Her ear twitched with the tickle of his hair. "If it wasn't for the currying I give you every day, you would have dreadlocks, you know." He pressed against her neck until he memorized the feel of Celia against his face.

Hank patted her jaw. Turned.

He wrapped his scarlet sash twice around his face and tucked the ends into the bearskin coat. He pulled the fur hat down hard on his head, below his eyebrows and over his ears.

Looking out through the slit formed by the hat and the sash,

Hank grasped Faith's hand. He said nothing, just nodded once to his companion.

Taking a deep breath, Hank opened the back door of the barn. He put his hand into his mitten, and stepped into the blowing, swirling snow.

READING GROUP GUIDE
AND
QUESTIONS FOR CONSIDERATION

1. Who was your favorite character in the book and why did you like them in particular?

2. What scene was your favorite—or perhaps, with which scene did you most identify—and why?

3. Summarize how Hank took to heart the exhortation of Paul in the book's Encomium: "So then let us cast off the works of darkness and put on the armor of light."

4. Now that you have read this portion of Hank's continuing journey, how do you plan to "cast off the works of darkness and put on the armor of light" in your journey of faith?

5. What are Hank's two or three greatest strengths? His two or three greatest weaknesses? In which of these is he most vulnerable to Jester do you feel? (Don't forget that an unguarded strength is often your greatest weakness.)

6. Both Jester and Magician have taken note of Hank's strengths and weaknesses. Thinking about your answer to Question 5, what does Jester's input, i.e. temptation, sound like to Hank? What does Magician's counsel sound like to Hank? And finally, why are these powerful messages to Hank?

7. Early in the book, before Vassar and Hank have returned to Gnarled Wood, Vassar is lost in a snow storm. He finds his way back to Hank and their snow cave, but the whole experience undoes Hank's fragile conviction that God is good. Why do you think this undoing occurs in Hank's soul?

8. Throughout *Battle for the Round Tower* there is a secondary story that explores the King's goodness—or lack of goodness. The crux

of the conflict is that the King has the power to change bad things. But not only does the King not intervene when bad things happen, he allows them to occur, even baits Zophos into initiating bad circumstances. Yet, he claims to be a good individual. How do you reconcile the King's conduct with his claim of absolute goodness?

9. Ronan, Jack, and Letizia all become followers of the King over the course of the book, but each experiences a different process by which this occurs. What aspects of each person's conversion are you comfortable with and which aspects are you not? Do you believe each had a valid conversion into the King's family?

10. Do you believe Audie and Walt (the senior leader) had conversion experiences or were their eyes were just opened to the King? And why do you believe this?

11. One of the King's Ten Tenets is, "Inclusion in the King's family is available exclusively through Vassar's provision and life." Agree? Disagree? Provisionally agree? Partially agree? And, why?

12. How do you think Vassar feels about the Round Tower?

13. Why does the King allow Jester to operate? Why doesn't he simply have Magician dispatch Jester and be done with him once and for all?

14. Why did Hank read and consider Vassar's letter to him each morning? Observing this practice in Hank, what aspects of his daily discipline can you personally employ in reading Scripture?

15. Customarily, the practices of solitude, contemplation, and prayer are included in the short list of spiritual disciplines, or spiritual practices. You see Hank practice these disciplines in the book. He visits with his Father, Vassar, and Magician formally and informally and periodically he creates experiences of solitude, some short, but others last several days. Hank engages these disciplines in order to keep his soul healthy. How might you follow his example? How important do you feel the spiritual practices of contemplation, prayer, and solitude are? Attach a numeric value to quantify your

conviction. Let, 1 be low and 10 be high. If you feel these practices are important—you attached an 8, 9, or 10 to them—what adjustments will be necessary to properly institute them into the routines of your life?

16. The subtitle of *Battle for the Round Tower* is, "A Tale of Two Loves." After Ronan's sexual liaison with Sonja, Hank uses this phrase in his discussion with Ronan. Revisit this aspect of the story and consider who plays "Ronan" in your life and who plays the part of "Sonja." Hank also uses this phrase to position Ronan for the process of restoration in his life. What are the steps to restoration? If restoration is needed in your life, how might that process work? Who needs to be involved? Use the 1-10 scale introduced in the question above and attach a number to how hard this will be for you?

17. Although not described in these terms, throughout the book the Round Tower is portrayed as being composed of both an organization and an organism. One is dead, one is living. Both are inseparably intertwined. Review how you answered the question regarding how Vassar feels about the Round Tower (Question 12). Now consider how you feel about the Round Tower. If there is disparity between you and Vassar, how might you reconcile your differences? What posture/attitude/disposition do you believe Magician might lead you to adopt regarding the Tower?

18. Ennui is one of the more formidable characters in this book and its predecessor, *No Mercy*. Her very name means apathy or indifference; boredom, tedium, lack of interest. How pervasive is *ennui* in your life? Your marriage? Your family? Your church? Quantify your answers using the 1-10 scale. What can you do about this *ennui*—what will you do about this?

19. Letizia's murder is complex and immensely difficult. There are lots of questions—lots of directions to go in drawing upon her experience for your own benefit. Here are a few thoughts to keep

you focused: Where was Vassar? Should he have done something different? Something more? Vassar begins his intervention in Letizia's brokenness with comfort and blessing—holding her close, kissing her head, whispering in her ear. First, work your way through Letizia's experience, not only in the moment of her rescue by Vassar, but in the unwritten pages that follow. What do you envision happened? What else do you think Vassar whispered into Lettie's ear as he carried her home? How do you reconcile how Vassar feels about Lettie and how Lettie feels about herself? What is Lettie's value to Vassar? Second, after using Letizia's story as a case study, review your own life-story and consider the same questions for yourself. Do not be dismissive of your story if it does not include trauma like Letizia's. All evil and temptation and subterfuge are a violation.

20. At the conclusion of the book, Hank says good-bye to Celia and his friend, Faith, leaves the Levine's barn, and steps into a snow storm. Where is he going and for what purpose? Why do you think so? And, what's your best guess about what awaits in book 3?

THE TEN TENETS OF THE KING

1. The King is sovereign.
2. The King's book is inspired, infallible, and authoritative.
3. Vassar is the King's son, through whom are all things and by whom we exist. Out of him, and through him, and into him are all things.
4. Inclusion in the King's family is available exclusively through Vassar's provision and life.
5. Magician produces and exhibits his character qualities in and through the King's followers, guiding them, energizing them to walk in the light, and speaking with them about all that is true.
6. Those redeemed through Vassar's provision enjoy irrevocable inclusion in the King's family, affording them access to all the rights, identity, and privileges contained therein.
7. The King's family members are commissioned to be his representatives and advocates throughout Gnarled Wood, the castle, the Round Tower, and to each other.
8. The redeemed of Vassar have hearts of light that desire to honor the King, Vassar, and Magician with recognition, affirmation, and loyalty.
9. The redeemed of Vassar are co-heirs with him to all that belongs to the King. They freely and responsibly give to others from the life, time, and resources entrusted to them by him.
10. The redeemed of Vassar desire close connection with the King's family for this is essential to life, wellbeing, progress, and protection.

VASSAR'S LETTER

My dear Brother, Hank:

Don't worry! I know you didn't anticipate this, but Father knows what he's doing—and I am near you, as near as your thoughts and the desires of your heart, like Magician.

Know that I am working in advance, preparing the way. I'll meet with you frequently, but don't ever hesitate to draw upon the tremendous resource inside you.

Magician is not only a great friend and comfort, he will never leave you. Even though it will appear you are abandoned, don't ever forget that he lives in you and that you are never in the dark. In your heart, the sunrise from on high is always dawning, illuminating everything Father has written on your heart's walls. Magician is committed to explaining all you desire to know. If you need anything—anything at all—just ask. I'll see that you have everything you need.

I think you know, but for the umpteenth time—because I can never say it enough—I love you, Brother! I'm so thrilled you have Magician to help you and guide you—no matter what. Rely upon him for everything.

I anticipate Jester's plan of attack is most likely to suggest that you are isolated!

Hank, I have two thoughts about this: First, our Father lives and his light will not be extinguished. Second, he won't abandon us. No doubt Jester will suggest that you are orphaned. Don't believe him, not for a moment. You are not left behind.

We are family, and as such, we are bonded and can never be separated. In spirit, I am in Father and Father is in me—just as I am in you and you are in me. We are in Father. He is in us. Magician is evidence of this. Father said so! We are a unit, a family. We are cut from the same bolt of genetic cloth and our lives are interwoven. We are inseparable!

I don't need to remind you that Father has written his priorities and perspectives on the walls of your heart—for perpetual reference. You know as well that there is no one better than Magician to counsel, reinforce, and align you with your heart's desires regardless of life's circumstances.

Speaking of whom, let me remind you again to rely upon Magician for everything. He will teach and guide you; he will help you remember everything that you, and Father, and I have discussed. He will explain the intricacies of the Kingdom, provide legal insight on the family's covenant, and as you know, he is a formidable force to have on your side when conflict arises. Look to him. If you do so, there is no reason to be afraid of what's before you.

No matter if all hell is breaking loose, be at peace, Brother. Greater is he who lives in you than he who rules Gnarled Wood and beyond. That's not hyperbole! Magician is more powerful than Jester and Zophos put together, so don't be afraid if they assemble themselves against you.

You are such a magnificent person, Hank. I'm really

proud that you are my Brother, but I'm even prouder that you are my friend. I haven't pulled any punches with you. I've told you everything I know and I've shared everything with you that Father has shared with me. And, you've digested it. Amazing!

Thank you for believing—believing not only in Father, but also for believing in me. Thank you as well for your trust. I know you've been pushed hard at times, but you have risen to the challenge. You've done so consistently, and that is impressive. I trust you as well—as does Father, otherwise the current plan would be modified.

Father believes in you. After all, he created this plan and chose you to carry it out. He knows you will represent him well, and I have every confidence in you too. If I didn't, I would have advocated for a different plan, but here we are!

Things are not going to be easy, Brother! The stakes have risen since we were last in Gnarled Wood. While Zophos is utilizing his shock and awe capabilities in some parts of the castle, he has switched tactics in other areas; most of the shock and awe there is a diversion. Always the pragmatist—and opportunist—Zophos is operating in a more clandestine manner. He's pouring exorbitant amounts of money, effort, and personnel into subversion, espionage, and subterfuge. Always there is his illusion of light. He is a deceiver.

The inclination is to engage him at his level, but there is a more powerful weapon. In everything you do, Brother, let your motive be love. Nothing is more powerful because love is the essence of who Father is. When you love, you portray Father, and the only way you can love as he loves is to live from your heart and let Magician's strength bolster you. Read that line again. I'll bet you felt your heart jump, didn't you?

Make no mistake though: Love will earn you hate. It will associate you with Father, and you know as I do that those who belong to Zophos utterly despise the High King. But while there is no pleasure in being hated—Zophos' folks feel the same about me as they do about you—there is nothing to fear. Nothing! Just ask Magician. He knows the drill.

Rely on Magician. I make no apology for reiterating myself. You know how to do this! And as you rely on him for strength and perspective, he will guide you, protect you, and keep you from stumbling. Even if your life is compromised and death is imminent, no worries; Magician will guide you to victory—not only in this life, but the next as well.

Hank, let me remind you: Magician has permission and power to speak for the High King. I have given him authority to speak for me as well. He knows us perfectly, and he knows exactly what you need at any given moment. So, if you want to get Father's or my counsel with only a second's notice, Magician's your man!

If I were you, given the weight of this evening's meeting, I would go straight to Magician and ask him to bolster your sense of wellbeing. This is a heavy-duty project. I'd ask him to bring peace to your soul. Before I sat down to write you, this is what I did with Father and Magician.

Brother, every circumstance is going to scream that

you are overwhelmed, outnumbered, and that you will be assimilated into the castle, the routines of the Round Tower, and the lethargy of life in Gnarled Wood. Don't you believe it for a moment! While you live and work and fight in Gnarled Wood, Gnarled Wood is not your home. You live and move and have significance because you are a son of the High King!

I know Jester will try to tell you otherwise, but this is the absolute truth! It is true for me, it is true for you. Where Father lives, that is where you, and I, and Magician live as well. But right now, we are privileged to be on special assignment to Gnarled Wood as representatives of the King.

To state the obvious: If Father didn't trust you, and believe in you, he wouldn't have chosen you for this mission. He loves you, Hank, and he knows you love him too.

I'm back now where I started: with love. Love as he loves. Love like you are loved. Wow! You will be one powerful soul if you do so. Already are, now that I think about it!

Hank, as your Older Brother, I've written to put your heart at peace. What lies ahead will be tremendously difficult. But don't fear. Have courage! You and I are victorious warriors!

I love you. See you soon,
Vassar

Vassar's Letter Numbered
by Parra, for Mr. Henderson

1. My dear Brother, Hank:
2. Don't worry! I know you didn't anticipate this, but Father knows what he's doing—and I am near you, as near as your thoughts and the desires of your heart, like Magician.
3. Know that I am working in advance, preparing the way. I'll meet with you frequently, but don't ever hesitate to draw upon the tremendous resource inside you.
4. Magician is not only a great friend and comfort, he will never leave you. Even though it will appear you are abandoned, don't ever forget that he lives in you and that you are never in the dark.
5. In your heart, the sunrise from on high is always dawning, illuminating everything Father has written on your heart's walls.
6. Magician is committed to explaining all you desire to know.
7. If you need anything—anything at all—just ask. I'll see that you have everything you need.
8. I think you know, but for the umpteenth time—because I can never say it enough—I love you, Brother! I'm so thrilled you have Magician to help you and guide you—no matter what. Rely upon him for everything.
9. I anticipate Jester's plan of attack is most likely to suggest that you are isolated!
10. Hank, I have two thoughts about this: First, our Father lives and his light will not be extinguished. Second, he won't abandon us. No doubt Jester will suggest that you are orphaned. Don't believe him, not for a moment. You are not left behind.
11. We are family, and as such, we are bonded and can never be separated. In spirit, I am in Father and Father is in me—just as I am in you and you are in me. We are in Father. He is in us. Magician

is evidence of this. Father said so!

12. We are a unit, a family. We are cut from the same bolt of genetic cloth and our lives are interwoven. We are inseparable!

13. I don't need to remind you that Father has written his priorities and perspectives on the walls of your heart—for perpetual reference.

14. You know as well that there is no one better than Magician to counsel, reinforce, and align you with your heart's desires regardless of life's circumstances.

15. Speaking of whom, let me remind you again to rely upon Magician for everything. He will teach and guide you; he will help you remember everything that you, and Father, and I have discussed. He will explain the intricacies of the Kingdom, provide legal insight on the family's covenant, and as you know, he is a formidable force to have on your side when conflict arises. Look to him. If you do so, there is no reason to be afraid of what's before you.

16. No matter if all hell is breaking loose, be at peace, Brother.

17. Greater is he who lives in you than he who rules Gnarled Wood and beyond. That's not hyperbole!

18. Magician is more powerful than Jester and Zophos put together, so don't be afraid if they assemble themselves against you.

19. You are such a magnificent person, Hank. I'm really proud that you are my Brother, but I'm even prouder that you are my friend.

20. I haven't pulled any punches with you. I've told you everything I know and I've shared everything with you that Father has shared with me. And, you've digested it. Amazing!

21. Thank you for believing—believing not only in Father, but also for believing in me.

22. Thank you as well for your trust. I know you've been pushed hard at times, but you have risen to the challenge. You've done so consistently, and that is impressive. I trust you as well—as does Father, otherwise the current plan would be modified.

23. Father believes in you. After all, he created this plan and chose you

to carry it out. He knows you will represent him well, and I have every confidence in you too. If I didn't, I would have advocated for a different plan, but here we are!

24. Things are not going to be easy, Brother!

25. The stakes have risen since we were last in Gnarled Wood. While Zophos is utilizing his shock and awe capabilities in some parts of the castle, he has switched tactics in other areas; most of the shock and awe there is a diversion.

26. Always the pragmatist—and opportunist—Zophos is operating in a more clandestine manner. He's pouring exorbitant amounts of money, effort, and personnel into subversion, espionage, and subterfuge. Always there is his illusion of light.

27. He is a deceiver.

28. The inclination is to engage him at his level, but there is a more powerful weapon. In everything you do, Brother, let your motive be love. Nothing is more powerful because love is the essence of who Father is.

29. When you love, you portray Father, and the only way you can love as he loves is to live from your heart and let Magician's strength bolster you. Read that line again. I'll bet you felt your heart jump, didn't you?

30. Make no mistake though: Love will earn you hate. It will associate you with Father, and you know as I do that those who belong to Zophos utterly despise the High King.

31. But while there is no pleasure in being hated—Zophos' folks feel the same about me as they do about you—there is nothing to fear. Nothing! Just ask Magician. He knows the drill.

32. Rely on Magician. I make no apology for reiterating myself. You know how to do this!

33. And as you rely on him for strength and perspective, he will guide you, protect you, and keep you from stumbling.

34. Even if your life is compromised and death is imminent, no worries;

Magician will guide you to victory—not only in this life, but the next as well.

35. Hank, let me remind you: Magician has permission and power to speak for the High King. I have given him authority to speak for me as well. He knows us perfectly, and he knows exactly what you need at any given moment.

36. So, if you want to get Father's or my counsel with only a second's notice, Magician's your man!

37. If I were you, given the weight of this evening's meeting, I would go straight to Magician and ask him to bolster your sense of wellbeing. This is a heavy-duty project. I'd ask him to bring peace to your soul. Before I sat down to write you, this is what I did with Father and Magician.

38. Brother, every circumstance is going to scream that you are overwhelmed, outnumbered, and that you will be assimilated into the castle, the routines of the Round Tower, and the lethargy of life in Gnarled Wood. Don't you believe it for a moment!

39. While you live and work and fight in Gnarled Wood, Gnarled Wood is not your home.

40. You live and move and have significance because you are a son of the High King!

41. I know Jester will try to tell you otherwise, but this is the absolute truth! It is true for me, it is true for you. Where Father lives, that is where you, and I, and Magician live as well.

42. But right now, we are privileged to be on special assignment to Gnarled Wood as representatives of the King.

43. To state the obvious: If Father didn't trust you, and believe in you, he wouldn't have chosen you for this mission.

44. He loves you, Hank, and he knows you love him too.

45. I'm back now where I started: with love. Love as he loves. Love like you are loved. Wow! You will be one powerful soul if you do so. Already are, now that I think about it!

46. Hank, as your Older Brother, I've written to put your heart at peace.
47. What lies ahead will be tremendously difficult. But don't fear. Have courage! You and I are victorious warriors!
48. I love you. See you soon, Vassar

THE GOSPEL ACCORDING TO JOHN, CHAPTERS 14-16
the basis of Vassar's letter to Hank
English Standard Version (ESV)

14 "Let not your hearts be troubled. Believe in God; believe also in me. ²In my Father's house are many rooms. If it were not so, would I have told you that I go to prepare a place for you? ³And if I go and prepare a place for you, I will come again and will take you to myself, that where I am you may be also. ⁴And you know the way to where I am going." ⁵Thomas said to him, "Lord, we do not know where you are going. How can we know the way?" ⁶Jesus said to him, "I am the way, and the truth, and the life. No one comes to the Father except through me. ⁷If you had known me, you would have known my Father also. From now on you do know him and have seen him."

⁸Philip said to him, "Lord, show us the Father, and it is enough for us." ⁹Jesus said to him, "Have I been with you so long, and you still do not know me, Philip? Whoever has seen me has seen the Father. How can you say, 'Show us the Father'? ¹⁰Do you not believe that I am in the Father and the Father is in me? The words that I say to you I do not speak on my own authority, but the Father who dwells in me does his works. ¹¹Believe me that I am in the Father and the Father is in me, or else believe on account of the works themselves.

¹²"Truly, truly, I say to you, whoever believes in me will also do the works that I do; and greater works than these will he do, because I am going to the Father. ¹³Whatever you ask in my name, this I will do, that the Father may be glorified in the Son. ¹⁴If you ask anything in my name, I will do it.

¹⁵"If you love me, you will keep my commandments. ¹⁶And I will ask the Father, and he will give you another Helper, to be with you forever, ¹⁷even the Spirit of truth, whom the world cannot receive, because it neither sees him nor knows him. You know him, for he dwells with you

and will be in you.

¹⁸ "I will not leave you as orphans; I will come to you. ¹⁹ Yet a little while and the world will see me no more, but you will see me. Because I live, you also will live. ²⁰ In that day you will know that I am in my Father, and you in me, and I in you. ²¹ Whoever has my commandments and keeps them, he it is who loves me. And he who loves me will be loved by my Father, and I will love him and manifest myself to him." ²² Judas (not Iscariot) said to him, "Lord, how is it that you will manifest yourself to us, and not to the world?" ²³ Jesus answered him, "If anyone loves me, he will keep my word, and my Father will love him, and we will come to him and make our home with him. ²⁴ Whoever does not love me does not keep my words. And the word that you hear is not mine but the Father's who sent me.

²⁵ "These things I have spoken to you while I am still with you. ²⁶ But the Helper, the Holy Spirit, whom the Father will send in my name, he will teach you all things and bring to your remembrance all that I have said to you. ²⁷ Peace I leave with you; my peace I give to you. Not as the world gives do I give to you. Let not your hearts be troubled, neither let them be afraid. ²⁸ You heard me say to you, 'I am going away, and I will come to you.' If you loved me, you would have rejoiced, because I am going to the Father, for the Father is greater than I. ²⁹ And now I have told you before it takes place, so that when it does take place you may believe. ³⁰ I will no longer talk much with you, for the ruler of this world is coming. He has no claim on me, ³¹ but I do as the Father has commanded me, so that the world may know that I love the Father. Rise, let us go from here.

15 "I am the true vine, and my Father is the vinedresser. ² Every branch in me that does not bear fruit he takes away, and every branch that does bear fruit he prunes, that it may bear more fruit. ³ Already you are clean because of the word that I have spoken to you. ⁴ Abide in me, and I in you. As the branch cannot bear fruit by itself, unless it abides in the vine, neither can you, unless you abide in me. ⁵I am the vine; you are the branches. Whoever abides in me and I in him, he it is that bears much fruit, for apart from me you can do nothing. ⁶If anyone does not abide in me he is thrown away like a branch and withers; and the branches are gathered, thrown into the fire, and burned. ⁷If you abide in me, and my words abide in you, ask whatever you wish, and it will be done for you. ⁸By this my Father is glorified, that you bear much fruit and so prove to be my disciples. ⁹As the Father has loved me, so have I loved you. Abide in my love. ¹⁰If you keep my commandments, you will abide in my love, just as I have kept my Father's commandments and abide in his love. ¹¹These things I have spoken to you, that my joy may be in you, and that your joy may be full.

¹²"This is my commandment, that you love one another as I have loved you. ¹³Greater love has no one than this, that someone lay down his life for his friends. ¹⁴You are my friends if you do what I command you. ¹⁵No longer do I call you servants, for the servant does not know what his master is doing; but I have called you friends, for all that I have heard from my Father I have made known to you. ¹⁶You did not choose me, but I chose you and appointed you that you should go and bear fruit and that your fruit should abide, so that whatever you ask the Father in my name, he may give it to you. ¹⁷These things I command you, so that you will love one another.

¹⁸"If the world hates you, know that it has hated me before it hated you. ¹⁹If you were of the world, the world would love you as its own; but because you are not of the world, but I chose you out of the world, therefore the world hates you. ²⁰Remember the word that I said to you: 'A servant is not greater than his master.' If they persecuted me, they will also persecute you. If they kept my word, they will also keep yours. ²¹But all these things they will do to you on account of my name, because they do not know him who sent me. ²²If I had not come and spoken to them, they would not have been guilty of sin, but now they have no excuse for their sin. ²³Whoever hates me hates my Father also.

²⁴ If I had not done among them the works that no one else did, they would not be guilty of sin, but now they have seen and hated both me and my Father. ²⁵ But the word that is written in their Law must be fulfilled: 'They hated me without a cause.'

²⁶ "But when the Helper comes, whom I will send to you from the Father, the Spirit of truth, who proceeds from the Father, he will bear witness about me. ²⁷ And you also will bear witness, because you have been with me from the beginning.

16 "I have said all these things to you to keep you from falling away. ² They will put you out of the synagogues. Indeed, the hour is coming when whoever kills you will think he is offering service to God. ³ And they will do these things because they have not known the Father, nor me. ⁴ But I have said these things to you, that when their hour comes you may remember that I told them to you.

"I did not say these things to you from the beginning, because I was with you. ⁵ But now I am going to him who sent me, and none of you asks me, 'Where are you going?' ⁶ But because I have said these things to you, sorrow has filled your heart. ⁷ Nevertheless, I tell you the truth: it is to your advantage that I go away, for if I do not go away, the Helper will not come to you. But if I go, I will send him to you. ⁸ And when he comes, he will convict the world concerning sin and righteousness and judgment: ⁹ concerning sin, because they do not believe in me; ¹⁰ concerning righteousness, because I go to the Father, and you will see me no longer; ¹¹ concerning judgment, because the ruler of this world is judged.

¹² "I still have many things to say to you, but you cannot bear them now. ¹³ When the Spirit of truth comes, he will guide you into all the truth, for he will not speak on his own authority, but whatever he hears he will speak, and he will declare to you the things that are to come. ¹⁴ He will glorify me, for he will take what is mine and declare it to you. ¹⁵ All that the Father has is mine; therefore I said that he will take what

is mine and declare it to you.

[16] "A little while, and you will see me no longer; and again a little while, and you will see me." [17] So some of his disciples said to one another, "What is this that he says to us, 'A little while, and you will not see me, and again a little while, and you will see me'; and, 'because I am going to the Father'?" [18] So they were saying, "What does he mean by 'a little while'? We do not know what he is talking about." [19] Jesus knew that they wanted to ask him, so he said to them, "Is this what you are asking yourselves, what I meant by saying, 'A little while and you will not see me, and again a little while and you will see me'? [20] Truly, truly, I say to you, you will weep and lament, but the world will rejoice. You will be sorrowful, but your sorrow will turn into joy. [21] When a woman is giving birth, she has sorrow because her hour has come, but when she has delivered the baby, she no longer remembers the anguish, for joy that a human being has been born into the world. [22] So also you have sorrow now, but I will see you again, and your hearts will rejoice, and no one will take your joy from you. [23] In that day you will ask nothing of me. Truly, truly, I say to you, whatever you ask of the Father in my name, he will give it to you. [24] Until now you have asked nothing in my name. Ask, and you will receive, that your joy may be full.

[25] "I have said these things to you in figures of speech. The hour is coming when I will no longer speak to you in figures of speech but will tell you plainly about the Father. [26] In that day you will ask in my name, and I do not say to you that I will ask the Father on your behalf; [27] for the Father himself loves you, because you have loved me and have believed that I came from God. [28] I came from the Father and have come into the world, and now I am leaving the world and going to the Father."

[29] His disciples said, "Ah, now you are speaking plainly and not using figurative speech! [30] Now we know that you know all things and do not need anyone to question you; this is why we believe that you came from God." [31] Jesus answered them, "Do you now believe? [32] Behold, the hour

is coming, indeed it has come, when you will be scattered, each to his own home, and will leave me alone. Yet I am not alone, for the Father is with me. [33] I have said these things to you, that in me you may have peace. In the world you will have tribulation. But take heart; I have overcome the world."

Cast of Characters

Absaroka Range (ab-soar'-e-kah) A sub-range of the Rocky Mountains in the United States, stretching about 150 miles across the Montana-Wyoming border. There are 47 peaks over 12,000 ft (3,700 m).

Castle, the The castle represents countries, cities, towns, and collectives of mankind throughout the world.

Competence An allegorical colleague of Jester's.

Jester employs Competence to wound Hank in the hip and lower back with twin daggers.

Ennui (ahn'-wee) A woman employed by Zophos to undermine the Round Tower from within.

Her primary tactics are apathy, indifference, lack of action, and intolerance for any perceived lack of tolerance. In fact, this is the meaning of her name.

She is highly esteemed within the Round Tower because of her balance and dispassion. Many in the Tower look to her for counsel and hold her perspective in highest regard.

Erymos (eh-ray'-moss) Accessed through a slot canyon, Erymos is a property owned by the High King. It is a lodge-type facility built into a rock cliff. Vassar and Hank first meet their Father, the High King, at Erymos.

Faith An allegorical knight in the Kingdom of Light assigned to accompany Hank, Vassar, and Magician through *No Mercy*. Faith is sent to the Round Tower to prepare for Hank's eventual arrival. Also known as, Pistis and Pistos.

Flesh A concept—the habitual patterning of thought, emotion, and behavior with which Jester correlates his perspectives. It is rooted in an independent quest to secure life's necessities, i.e., love, acceptance, security, belonging, worth, competence, significance, etc.

Gnarled Wood Is the earth and all it contains, above and below, after the rebellion of Zophos. It is the world's systems and is home to people, Zophos, and the Dark Army. The castle and the Round Tower are located in Gnarled Wood.

Henderson, Henry H. "Hank" Commonly known as, Hank. He lives in Fort Worth, Texas, grew up in Oklahoma, and is Co-Founder and CEO of a marketing firm specializing in media, publishing, and the nonprofit sector of business. His hobby is fly fishing.

Henderson, Vassar X. The Crown Prince of the Kingdom of Light. Vassar is Hank's Older Brother and portrays the character of Jesus Christ.

High King of Glory, the The High King of Glory is King of the Kingdom of Light. He is Vassar and Hank's Father and often appears as light.

The King portrays the character of God.

Hope An allegorical knight in the Kingdom of Light assigned to accompany Hank, Vassar, and Magician through *No Mercy*. Hope is sent to the Round Tower to prepare for Hank's eventual arrival.

Jack (aka, Sjakal)   Gang leader and Hank's friend from La Faim. See entry for, Sjakal.

Jester   Accomplice of Zophos. Jester utilizes circumstance and happenstance to offer commentary—always disguised as thoughts—correlated with a person's habitual patterns of thinking, emotion, and behavior.

Jester portrays the character of sin, the law of sin, the power of sin, or the principle of sin. He is the counterpart to the Holy Spirit. In the King's book, he first appears in Genesis 4:7. The most complete commentary on him is found in the King's book, Romans 7:7ff.

The circumstance Jester seizes upon is the world system—portrayed in these books as Gnarled Word, the castle, and aspects of the Round Tower.

La Faim (la fah-eem')   A town outside the castle and just this side of the dump. Its name means, the hunger.

Love   An allegorical knight in the Kingdom of Light assigned to accompany Hank, Vassar, and Magician through *No Mercy*. Love is sent to the Round Tower to prepare for Hank's eventual arrival.

Magician   The Kingdom of Light's wizard and sorcerer. He advocates on behalf of the High King and Vassar, speaking as them and for them. He resides within, speaking with thoughts. His counterpart is Jester.

Magician portrays the character of the Holy Spirit.

Malden Creek   A fictional river in Southwestern Montana.

Mat, or Hank's Mat   Hank's mat is made of woven grass. He views and claims the mat as his self-provision.

Parra (pear'-uh)   Hank's valet while at the King's facility in the wilderness.

Pintaro, Letizia (le-teez'-i-uh)   Associate of Ennui.

Pit, the   The pit is the place into which Hank falls in *No Mercy*.

Pity   An allegorical character portraying the self-diminishment intended to elicit sympathy and validation from others. In Pity the diminished state of self is justified and confirmed, but without remedy or solution.

Pity divides the human soul irreconcilably between mind and emotion, seeming to paralyze the freedom of the will to act. Thus, Pity creates what appears to be an unsolvable problem with no recourse but to embrace her as the only consolation.

Round Tower, the   The Round Tower is the image of the church. It contains both the living organism that is the family of God as well as the bureaucratic organization.

Significance   Significance is an allegorical woman in cahoots with Jester. She is the physical image of the drive for importance, worth, and value.

Sin   See notes for Jester.

Sjakal (sha-kol')   Also known as, Jack. Gang leader and Hank's friend from La Faim.

Zophos (zoh'-foss) Leader of the Dark Army. Zophos rebelled against the High King and attempted a *coup d'état*. He failed, but not before enticing a third of the King's army to follow him.

In what some say was an error in judgment, the High King opted not to immediately destroy Zophos for his rebellion. Rather, he banished him and his sympathizers to Gnarled Wood—where people live—until he prepared a more fitting punishment for his rebellion.

Zophos is the prince of the air. He travels by this means and uses it to create confusion, especially for mortals whose primary forms of relaying information to each other are dependent upon air and air waves.

Zophos portrays the character of Lucifer or Satan.

ACKNOWLEDGMENTS

The unwavering, unflagging support of my wife, Dianne, goes beyond my ability to properly acknowledge. She simply never flinches when the subject of my writing comes up—not in private conversation, not in public conversation. I am a blessed man to have this woman in my life, but that she shares my heart gives me courage and confidence.

In alphabetical order, I am grateful to my advance readers. They looked at the manuscript when it wasn't worth reading, at great expenditures of personal time, and played key roles in bringing *Battle for the Round Tower* to a refined conclusion. I'm indebted to Laura Austin, Melinda Connell, Victor Erwin, Reny Greenleaf, Karla Hagan, Pat Hawkins, Cathy Hutchison, Nicole Mager, Tyson Martin, Anthony Meadows, Heather Meyer, Marshall Moore, Tricia Pitts, Sandy Raymer, Lamar Smith, Randy Spencer, and Tom and Elise Wilkes. And for the record, I fear I have left someone out and apologize for my unintentional slight.

The scene depicting Letizia Pintaro's death was immensely difficult to write. Given the circumstance of her passing, the reputation of God and His heart toward those who suffer in this manner, and those who would identify with her trauma, I knew my word selection and sentence structure had to be as close to perfect as humanly possible. I'm deeply grateful for the time, expertise, and multiple reviews of Catherine Darnell.

The design and layout of this book is representative of Lindsay Inman's creative abilities. For example, note in the cover design that while there are two "T's" in "Battle" and two "O's" in "Round" and "Tower" respectively, each is individually designed. This attention to detail is indicative of the heart and soul Lindsay brought to her work and to your reading pleasure. What is not readily evident is her tremendous devotion to serve you and me through her attitude, diligence, and courage to step into new arenas of endeavor. Thank you, Lindsay. I admire you.

I am grateful to MC2 Graphics for their care and expertise typesetting the book. They assembled the parts into this readable whole.

As I got closer to publication, Caleb Anthony offered wonderful suggestions, counsel, and perspective regarding how to inform readers that *Battle for the Round Tower* exists. He offered expertise and thoughtful advice on social media marketing and electronic communications.

Thank you to Steve Parolini for gracefully editing my work. Even though I know the editorial process is necessary and am committed to the critical oversight, it remains a vulnerable experience to have my worked critiqued. Steve did so professionally, adeptly, and with genuine care for my heart and work. I'm grateful.

Who remains? Those of you who visited with me, listened to my wandering and wondering and internal debate, and contributed to me with words and expressions and friendship. There are those who looked after my heart, making certain I kept my wits about me and my thoughts in line. While *Battle for the Round Tower* is a work of fiction, it is not a work of fantasy. To the people who have helped form my thinking, refine my outlook, and develop whatever skills I have as a writer and human being, I recognize you and I am thankful.

Finally, like Hank, I'm cognizant of the fact that the Holy Spirit—the Wizard of the Kingdom of Light—advocated on my behalf as I wrote. I am very aware of His defense, counsel, and encouragement. It is an interesting experience to delve into the mind and strategic initiative of Satan for the benefit of others. But as Hank returned to the pit of darkness in search of those who needed rescue and was supported and led by Magician, it was my experience to do this in writing *Battle for the Round Tower*. Thank you, Holy Spirit.

An Interview with Preston Gillham

Q: *Battle for the Round Tower* is a sequel to your first novel, *No Mercy*. How do the books fit together?

A: At face value, *Battle for the Round Tower* is a continuation of Hank Henderson's adventures in Gnarled Wood. But as in the first book, there are a couple of additional layers. In *No Mercy* there was the epic battle between flesh and spirit. Throughout those pages, we wanted to know if this is a winnable battle or not. In *Battle for the Round Tower*, we explore how a man empowered by Magician and confident with his place in the Kingdom manages himself across the spectrum of life. In addition, the book examines whether or not God is good. A lot of people don't wrestle with this doubt, but Hank does.

Q: You wrote in your blog that it took seven years to write *No Mercy*. How long did it take to write *Battle for the Round Tower*?

A: It did take a long time to write *No Mercy*. I think when I set my mind to writing, it actually took six or seven months. *Battle for the Round Tower* also took about seven months once I got started, another four months for editing.

Q: Do you write every day?

A: Pretty much. I'm sure there were a few days when I didn't write, but not over four or five.

Q: Do you write from an outline?

A: When I write nonfiction I do use an outline. In fact, I create an outline that makes sense to me and then keep expanding it until I have paragraphs. However, fiction is completely different for me. I said to someone the other day, writing fiction is like reading fiction, just slower. I have ideas about the story line, of course, and have a general sense of what is going to transpire. But in many ways, I'm just as surprised at the story's twists and turns as the reader is.

Q: Are your characters planned?

A: Yes and no. Some of the characters are well formed in my head before I begin, but there are others that I get to know when they appear in the manuscript.

Q: Once again, you have chosen fiction to convey real life. Why not write a nonfiction book and teach your readers in a more traditional manner?

A: There are several reasons for using fiction, not the least of which is that I enjoy that style of writing much more than I do nonfiction. But beyond my preference as a writer, I'm not satisfied that our nonfiction books are accomplishing what we need from them. We need life-change. We need to implement our theology. We don't really need to know more as badly as we need to apply what we know.

Q: So you use the literary tool of fiction to illustrate.

A: There you go. One of the greatest change agents is modeling, and in Hank I've tried to create a model for my readers. If Hank can interact with Magician like he does in the book, then maybe we can interact with the Holy Spirit in a similar fashion. In addition, I wanted the freedom of fiction. Neither *No Mercy* nor *Battle for the Round Tower* are nice books. Both are challenging stories, but neither is hard for the heck of it. Rather, it is next to impossible to value triumph if you have not known defeat.

Q: So you are hoping to use fiction to create change?

A: I am. I've been concerned for a number of years about the apathy— the *ennui*, there's that name and character from the books—that I encounter in Believers. After so many exposures to the same message, it is hard not to become anesthetized to what we are encountering. It has been a long time since I've been moved deeply by a sermon on salvation, not because I don't care, but because I'm overexposed to the subject. And I need to be moved, on that subject and others, like the war between the flesh and the spirit, the importance of solitude and prayer, the deceitfulness of Jester, and the reality of spiritual warfare. Given this, I felt fiction afforded me the candor I sought to speak about important subjects in a new way.

Q: You write powerfully about the Round Tower, the metaphorical church. And, you don't cut the church much slack. How do you view the church?

A: Jesus said, to whom much is given, much is required. I'm concerned because the church is entrusted with treasures of inestimable worth and we spend inordinate amounts of time hoarding these treasures and protecting our hoard. I'm concerned because Believers are tolerating this behavior from themselves and their leaders. Of course, this has been going on for many years, but a major shift is occurring in the church, especially the church in the West. There is an exodus of passionate followers of Christ into other venues where they hope to connect with other Believers interested in making their faith relevant every day. I care deeply about the church, so deeply that I am laboring to write something that will get our attention and begin the process of change that is needed. I am also writing to put practical ideas forward for consideration, ideas about how Believers can connect with each other and form meaningful bonds, support one another in trying times, grow in their faith, transform personally, and tap into vibrant relationship with Jesus Christ. In short, I'm writing about resurgence in the Body of Christ.

Q: And what are you doing about the criticism I'm certain you are receiving, especially from those who feel you are attacking the church?

A: I accept it and consider it. Of course, there are folks who rant just to hear themselves rant. There are others though who provide meaningful clues in their anger about valid concerns. When I see these, I have a better chance of engaging in a productive way. I don't claim to have the market cornered on what the future of the

Western church looks like, but I am confident something needs to change right away. It would be irresponsible of me to point out the problems without at least offering some proactive options for consideration.

Q: And here you are referencing the small groups?

A: Yes, the geographic-based small groups and the ten tenets of the King's teaching. Let me expand my rationale on this from what I put forward in *Battle for the Round Tower*. We know historically that God has consistently utilized small clutches of Believers to be the church. He is doing this again today in China, South America, Korea, Africa, and other places. Said another way, God isn't opposed to the organization of the institutional church, but neither is He dependent on it or committed to it. When two or three members of God's family are together, they are having church because God is there and they are there. Sometimes there is organizational structure to facilitate this, but not always. God is absolutely committed to His people. He makes no such promise to an organizational system. So as Believers, we need to gather, and we need to gather in profitable, meaningful ways. The closer we are to one another geographically, the greater the likelihood that we will not only connect with each other, but we will share life together—our joys, struggles, family, heartaches, and happiness. In turn, this helps us realize how relevant our faith and relationship with Christ are.

Q: And the ten tenets you reference?

A: Ah, yes. The ten tenets I suggest are fundamentals of the faith, essentials. I'm not trying to say this is a close, exhaustive, or conclusive list. What I am attempting to do is define ten, key elements of spiritual growth to help us refocus and regain traction. These ten tenets are essentials that we must have working in our lives at a fairly high level to be healthy members of the faith family. If I'm proficient in these ten tenets, then it is likely I will be able to self-maintain my spiritual life and guide others on their growth plane to do the same. Further, by defining spiritual growth in this manner, we stand a better chance of remediating struggles or impediments while evaluating progress. Again, I'm not proposing an absolute here, just a starting point that will help us return to relevance. Certainly we are to consider the whole counsel of God in Scripture, but the likelihood of being able to do that with everyone moving every 18 months, being distracted by insane lives, and a text containing 66 books is nil. The enormity of spiritual maturity is one thing that can cause us to run aground, so I offer these tenets as a beginning point. They are not an end all. However, I will say that in my coaching and strategic planning work with churches, we have implemented variations of what I have put in *Battle for the Round Tower* and it works.

Q: What are you hoping your readers gain from reading *Battle for the Round Tower*?

A: I'm hoping it is a fun read, for sure. Beyond this, I'm hopeful readers will identify with Hank and emulate the way he lives. Like all of us, Hank is a flawed man, but he walks with God, and he prays, and he interacts with the Holy Spirit—Magician. He fails and he rebounds, is wounded and hurts and recovers, and is disappointed and shows us how to manage that. He's a real-type guy. And then, I wanted to examine in these pages whether God is good. Of course, I was taught that He is, and I believe this is true. But during my challenging times and dark times, like Hank, I am susceptible to believe God may be good to others but He is not good to me. Finally, I hope that when readers get to the conclusion of the book they are excited about reading the third book.

Q: There is a third book?

A: There is a third book. That is the good news. The bad news is the third book exists principally in my head.

Q: I see. When will you begin writing?

A: For me, and my writing style, I've begun. I haven't sat down and begun creating at the keyboard yet, but I am aware that my heart is hard at work. I suspect that once I get past the end of the year, I will sense the nudge that draws me into my writer's heart.

Q: Do you have a working title for the next book?

A: Yes. It is, *Mercy*.

Q: So the first book in the trilogy examines the battle between flesh and spirit, the second explores self-care and the goodness of God. The third book will...?

A: *Mercy* will compare the rational and logical aspects of God's grace alongside the irrational and illogical aspects of His mercy. Of course, the reason I'm interested in this for Hank is that by grappling with and grasping God's mercy, he will dispel Jester's unrealistic expectations and portrayals of the King, specifically his goodness. And obviously, *Mercy* ties back to the first book.

Q: Thanks for visiting with us.

A: My pleasure. Thanks for reading and considering.

ABOUT THE AUTHOR

Preston lives with his wife, Dianne, and their barkless dog, Braxie, in Fort Worth, Texas. He and Dianne have twins who live in heaven, Alex and Anna. At the time of publication, they would be 11.

Battle for the Round Tower is his second novel and is a sequel to *No Mercy*, also published by Bonefish Publication in 2009. Preston is the author and contributing author of several books. He has written many articles and participated in the creation of numerous audio and video resources. He writes the blog, "Life and Leadership," at PrestonGillham. com.

Preston co-founded and guided the nonprofit organization, Lifetime Guarantee Inc., for over thirty years. In 2008 he transitioned himself, the Board of Directors, and the organization to the next generation of leaders. More information is available at, lifetime.org/author/preston.

This leadership experience led Preston into numerous churches, non-government organizations, nonprofits, and for-profit companies both at home and abroad. With the expertise he gained, Preston is an active advisor to executives, leaders, and Boards of Directors. He is skilled in crafting and guiding corporate transitions, managing change, facilitating human development, and mentoring tomorrow's leaders.

Preston enjoys his bicycle, fly fishing, and relishes any opportunity to be outside. More about Preston can be found at, PrestonGillham. com/about.

About the Book

Battle for the Round Tower is the second book in a planned, three-book series. The first book is, *No Mercy* and is available through BonefishPublication.com and wherever books are sold.

Steve Parolini served as principle editor. He can be contacted via, NovelDoctor.com.

Lindsay Inman designed the cover and internal features of both the print and electronic versions of the book. She can be contacted via, lrinman@yahoo.com.

MC2 Graphics typeset the book for print. You can contact them at, MC2Graphics.com.

Convertabook.com and BookBaby.com facilitated bringing *Battle for the Round Tower* into all the nooks and crannies of the e-book market.

About Bonefish Publication

www.BonefishPublication.com

Bonefish Publication
2020 Wilshire Blvd
Fort Worth, TX 76110

817-585-4185

info@BonefishPublication.com

GILLHAM CONSULTING
AND
ADDITIONAL RESOURCES

To find out more about Preston's *guiding and consulting* through Gillham Consulting, visit:

www.PrestonGillham.com/consulting

To contact Preston about *speaking, teaching, or facilitation engagements,* visit:

www.PrestonGillham.com

or email:

Preston@PrestonGillham.com

or phone:

817-585-4185

For additional *resources* by Preston, visit:

www.PrestonGillham.com

www.PrestonGillham.com

Made in the USA
Lexington, KY
08 August 2014